Patricia Smith's

DOLL VALUES

Antique to Modern

Twelfth Edition

COLLECTOR BOOKS

A Division of Schroeder Publishing Co., Inc.

Searching For A Publisher?

We are always looking for knowledgeable people considered experts within their fields. If you feel that there is a real need for a book on your collectible subject and have a large comprehensive collection, contact Collector Books.

Additional copies of this book may be ordered from:

Collector Books
P.O. Box 3009
Paducah, KY 42002-3009

@ $12.95. Add $2.00 for postage and handling.

Printed by IMAGE GRAPHICS, INC., Paducah, Kentucky

CREDITS

Gloria Anderson, Joan Aschbraner, Sandy Johnson-Barts, Sally Bethschieder, Kay Brandsky, Joanna Brunken, Sylvia Bryant, Ellie Bustos, Barbara Cain, Susan Caldwell, Susan Cap, Sandra Cummins, Renie Culp, Lynn Dowdy, Ellen Dodge, Marie Ernst, Frasher Doll Auctions (Rt. 1, Box 72, Oak Grove, MO 64075), Henrietta Fox, Maureen Fukushima, Pat Graff, Susan Giradot, Green Museum, Sharon Hamilton, Carmen Holshoe, Steve Humphries, Marcia Jarmush, Cris Johnson, Phyllis Kates, Jo Keelen, Shirley Knowles, Diane Kornhauser, Evelyn Krouse, Theo Lindley, Katie & Melissa Levitt, Kris Lundquist, Margaret Mandel, Marrianne's, Patty Martin, Jeannie Mauldin, Cynthia Matus, Helen McCorkel, Mary McGuire, Chris McWilliams, Marge Meisinger, Marla Mikesh, Peggy Millhouse, June Murkins, Jeannie Nespoli, Lani Petite, Marcia Piecwicz, Peggy Pergrande, Doris Richardson, Kathy Riddick, Dorothy Rigg, Arlene Shapiro (Meyer's Shop, 595 Highway 18, New Brunswick, NJ 08816), June Schultz, Shirley's Doll House (P.O. Box 99, Wheeling, IL 60090), Cindy Slater, Janet & Bob Slivka, Ricki Small, Jessie Smith, Virginia Smith, Virginia Sofie, Pat Sparks, Paul Spenser (1414 Cloverleaf, Waco, TX 76705), David Spurgeon, Bonnie Stewart, Turn of Century Antiques (1475 Broadway, Denver, CO 80210), Lois Thomas, Jean Truman, Kathy Tvrdik, Jeannie Venner, Ann Wencel, Jackie Whitemarsh, Mary Williams, Patricia Wood, Glorya Woods, Ciny Young

ON THE COVER

Back row (left to right): German pull toy on wooden platform with wheels, holds broom, ca. 1910 - $950.00. 22" marked Jumeau with closed mouth in factory dress - $4,600.00. 16" nursing Bru (Bébé Teteur), original - $9,000.00. 15" German Santa made of composition - $400.00.

Front row (left to right): Very rare 20" character Jumeau, 200 series, original - $53,000.00. 17" gold mohair bear - $350.00. Rare German doll marked "111" (may be missing K✿R) - $24,000.00. 8½" Armand Marseille googly, mold #200, original - $1,600.00.

Cover photography courtesy Frasher Doll Auctions
Cover design: Beth Summers
Book layout: Karen Geary

PRICES

This book is divided into "Antique" and "Modern" sections, with the older dolls in the first section and the newer dolls in the second section. To make a quick reference, each section alphabetically lists the dollmaker, type of material, or name of doll. (Example: Bye-Lo or Kewpie.) An index is provided for locating a specific doll.

In antique dolls, the uppermost concern is the condition of the head and body. It is also important for the body to be correct to the doll. An antique doll must be clean, nicely dressed, and ready to place into a collection. It must have no need of any repair for it to bring book price. An all original doll with original clothes, marked shoes, and original wig will bring a lot more than list price. Boxes are very rare and also will bring a higher price for the doll.

In modern dolls, the condition of the doll is the uppermost concern in pricing. An all original modern doll in excellent condition will bring a much higher price than listed in this price guide. A doll that is damaged, without original clothes, soiled and dirty, will bring far less than the top price listed. The cost of doll repairs and cleanup has soared, so it is wise to judge the damage and estimate the cost of repairs before you attempt to sell or buy a damaged doll. An excellent reference concerning storing and restoring is *Dolls – Preserve and Restore Your Collection* by Kathy Tvrdik (6415 S.W. 27th Street, Topeka, KS 66614).

For insurance reasons, it is very important to show the "retail" price of dolls in a price guide and to try to be as accurate as possible. The "retail" price can be referred to as "replacement cost" so that insurance companies or postal services can appraise a damaged or stolen doll for the insured, and the collectors can judge their own collections and purchase adequate amounts of insurance.

No one knows your collection better than yourself and in the end, when you consider a purchase, you must ask yourself if the doll is affordable to you and whether you want it enough to pay the price. You will buy the doll, or pass it up — it is as simple as that!

Prices shown are for dolls that are clean, undamaged, well-dressed, and in overall excellent condition. Many prices are also listed for soiled, dirty, and re-dressed dolls.

Antique and Older Dolls

Back row: 24" "Floradora" by Armand Marseille. Shown with doll marked "1912" with original wig and fully jointed body. Front row: 20" French doll with bisque head on shoulderplate and kid body. Marked "DEP." 20" Handwerck with sleep eyes on jointed body. Marked "DEP." "Floradora" - $445.00, "1912" - $385.00, DEP - $950.00, Handwerck - $575.00.
Courtesy Turn of Century Antiques.

Henri Alexandre dolls were made from 1889 to 1891 only. The dolls have closed mouths with a white space between the lips, fat cheeks, and early French bodies with straight wrists. (Also see under "Phénix" section.)

16" - $5,400.00; 19" - $6,250.00; 23" - $7,000.00.

Mark:

ALL BISQUE – FRENCH

French all bisque dolls are jointed at the necks, shoulders, and hips. They have slender arms and legs, glass eyes, and most have kid-lined joints. Most of the heads have sliced pates with tiny cork inserts. French all-bisque dolls have finely painted features with outlined lips, well-tinted bisque, and feathered eyebrows. They can have molded-on shoes, high-top boots with painted toes, high-top buttoned boots with four or more painted straps.

They can also be barefooted or just have stockings painted on the legs.

Any French bisque should be in very good condition, not have any chips, breaks, or hairline cracks to bring the following prices. *Allow much more for original clothes;* less for damage or repairs.

Bare Feet: 4" - $900.00; 6" - $1,350.00; 9" - $2,000.00.

Bru Type with glass eyes: Five-strap boots. Outlined lips. (See photo in

5½" French all bisque with slim body and limbs, painted-on long white stockings, and multi-strap boots. Has glass set eyes, closed mouth, and original clothes. Shown with old French enameled furniture. Doll - $2,100.00. Furniture - $1,000.00 up. *Courtesy Shirley's Doll House.*

Series 3, pg. 25.) 6" - $1,850.00. **Painted eyes:** 6" - $900.00 up.

Jointed Elbows: 5" - $2,200.00; 8" - $3,000.00.

Jointed Elbows and Knees: 6'' - $3,000.00; 8" - $3,800.00.

Marked E.D., F.G.: Or other French makers. Glass eyes, bare feet. Allow more

for original clothes. 6½" - $2,000.00; 8½" - $2,400.00.

S.F.B.J., UNIS: Or other late French all bisques. Painted eyes. 6" - $500.00; 8" - $700.00.

Swivel Neck: (Socket head) Molded shoes or boots. 6" - $1,200.00; 6" repaired - $600.00; 8" - $1,950.00; 8" repaired - $800.00.

ALL BISQUE – GERMAN

German-made all bisque dolls run from excellent to moderate quality. Prices are for excellent quality and condition with no chips, cracks, breaks, or hairlines. Dolls should be nicely dressed and can have molded hair or wig. They generally have painted-on shoes and socks. Allow much more for original clothes. Circa 1880s–1930s.

Bathing dolls: See that section.

Black or brown dolls: See that section.

French types: 1880s–1910. Slender dolls with one-piece body and head. Usually wire or peg-jointed shoulders and hips. Closed mouth. Allow much more for original clothes. (Many are in regional costumes.) **Add more for unusual color boots,** such as gold, yellow, or orange. All in good condition. **Glass eyes:** Open or closed mouth. 4" - $300.00; 5–6" - $475.00. **Swivel neck:** Closed mouth. 4" - $375.00; 5–6" - $500.00; 8½" - $900.00; 10" - $1,300.00. **Bent at knees:** 6" - $225.00 up. **Jointed knees and/or elbows:** 6" - $1,700.00; 8" - $2,200.00. **Jointed knees and/or elbows with swivel waist:** 6" - $2,850.00; 8" - $3,200.00. **Swivel waist only:** 6" - $2,000.00. **Painted eyes, swivel neck:** Open or closed mouth. Painted one-strap shoes. 4" - $175.00; 6" - $285.00; 8" - $400.00; 10" - $675.00.

Glass eyes, one-piece body and head: (Sometimes legs.) Ca. 1880–1913. Excellent bisque, open/closed mouth,

sleep or set eyes, good wig, and nicely dressed. Molded one-strap shoes. Allow more for unusual footwear such as yellow boots, multi-strap boots. 3" - $200.00; 5" - $250.00; 6" - $325.00; 7" - $375.00; 8" - $425.00; 9" - $550.00; 10" - $700.00; 12" - $800.00 up. **Bent at knees:** 6" - $225.00 up. **Mold #100, 125, 161, 225 (Alt, Beck, & Gottschalck):** 1911 on. Chubby body and limbs. 5" - $200.00; 6½" - $285.00; 8" - $400.00; 10" - $650.00. **Mold #130, 150, 168, 184, 257, 602, 790 (Bonn or Kestner):** Painted blue or pink stockings, one-strap black shoe: 4" - $285.00; 6" - $375.00. 7" - $400.00; 8" - $500.00; 9" - $550.00; 10" - $700.00; 11" - $900.00; 12" - $1,100.00 up. **Mold #155, 156 (smile):** 6" - $425.00. **Swivel neck:** 5½" - $575.00; 7" - $750.00. **Mold #160:** Molded hair. 5½" - $350.00. **Mold #168:** 9" - $400.00. **Mold #790:** 5½" - $450.00.

Painted eyes, one-piece body and head: (Sometimes legs.) Ca. 1880–1913., 1921–1932. Molded hair or wig, open or closed mouth, painted-on shoes and socks. Dressed or undressed. All in good condition. Allow more for unusual footwear such as yellow boots. 1½–2" - $75.00; 4–5" - $165.00; 6½" - $200.00; 8" - $285.00; 10" - $700.00. **Swivel neck:** 2" - $115.00; 4" - $165.00; 6½" - $225.00; 8" - $325.00. **Swivel neck with molded hat:** 4" - $800.00. **Black stockings, tan slippers:** 6" - $325.00. **Ribbed (shirred) hose:** 4½" - $185.00; 6" - $300.00; 8" - $425.00.

Molded hair: 4" - $175.00; 6½" - $300.00. **Early very round face:** 7" - $2,100.00. **Mold #130, 150, 160, 168, 184, 208, 602 (Kestner):** 5" - $200.00; 6" - $250.00; 7" - $300.00; 8" - $375.00; 9" - $525.00; 10½" - $800.00; 12" - $1,000.00.

Glass eyes, swivel neck: Pegged or wired joints, open or closed mouth, molded-on shoes or boots and stockings. All in good condition. Allow more for unusual footwear such as yellow boots, multi-strap boots. Very good quality. 3" - $250.00; 4" - $300.00; 5½" - $450.00; 7" - $625.00; 8" - $725.00; 9" - $825.00; 10" - $1,200.00. **Mold #130, 150, 160, 208, 602, 620 (Kestner):** 4" - $450.00; 6" - $550.00; 8" - $850.00; 10" - $1,200.00. **Simon & Halbig or Kestner types:** Closed mouth, excellent quality. 5" - $750.00; 6" - $1,100.00; 8" - $1,800.00;

4" all bisque with tiny open/closed mouth, glass eyes, swivel neck, ribbed socks with blue line on top, and molded shoes with two straps and black bows. Marked with "O" on head and "620" on body. $450.00.

10" - $2,200.00. **Jointed knees:** 5½–6½" - $2,900.00. **In original factory case or box with clothes and accessories:** 5" - $3,500.00. **Bare feet:** 5" - $1,600.00; 7½" - $2,400.00. **Early round face:** 6" - $850.00; 8" - $1,250.00. **#184 Kestner:** Sweet face, solid color boots. 4–5" - $700.00; 8" - $1,600.00. **Mold #881, 886, 890 (Simon & Halbig):** Painted high top boots with 4 or 5 straps. 4½" - $750.00; 7½" - $1,600.00; 9¼" - $2,000.00. **Long stockings:** Above knees. Can be black, blue, green, or yellow. Perfect condition. 5½" - $700.00; 7" - $975.00.

Flapper: One-piece body and head, thin limbs. Fired-in tine bisque. Wig, painted eyes, painted-on long stockings, one-strap painted shoes. 6" - $325.00; 8" - $450.00. **Molded hair:** 6" - $350.00; 8" - $450.00. **Later (1920s–1930s): Pink bisque:** Wire joints, molded hair, painted eyes. 4" - $90.00. **Molded hat:** 5" - $325.00 up. **Aviatrix:** 6" - $300.00. **Swivel waist:** 5" - $350.00. **Molded cap with rabbit ears:** 5" - $385.00. **Medium quality bisque/artist workmanship:** 5" - $125.00; 7–8" - $225.00.

Molded-on clothes or underwear: Ca. 1890s. Jointed at shoulders only or at shoulders and hips. (Molded-on hat or bonnet are listed below.) **Painted eyes:** Molded hair, molded shoes or bare feet. Excellent artist workmanship. No cracks, chips, or breaks. 5" - $165.00; 7" - $350.00. (See photo in Series 5, pg. 11.) **Glass eyes:** 5" - $385.00; 7" - $525.00. **Medium to poor quality:** 3" - $75.00; 4" - $90.00; 6" - $125.00.

Molded-on hat or bonnet: In perfect condition. 5–6½" - $365.00 up; 8–9" - $500.00 up. **Stone (porous) bisque:** 4–5" - $125.00; 6–7" - $150.00. **Glass eyes:** 5½" - $450.00; 8" - $600.00. **Swivel neck, early round face:** 7" - $2,100.00.

Marked with maker: (S&H, JDK, A.B.G., mold #369. See photo in Series 9, pg. 9.) Closed mouth, early fine quality face. 7" - $1,800.00; 9" - $2,200.00 up. **Same, with open mouth:** Later quality bisque. 6" - $450.00; 8" - $850.00; 10" - $1,000.00. **K✿R:** 8" - $1,300.00 up.

Hertel, Schwab: See that section.

Limbach Mold #573, 620, etc: Marked with three-leaf clover. 5" - $100.00. **Swivel neck:** 6" - $225.00. **One-piece body and head:** 6" - $125.00. **Glass eyes:** 5" - $175.00; 8" - $265.00. **Baby:** 5" - $95.00; 7" - $150.00; 12" - $375.00.

Schmidt, Bruno: Baby, mold #425. 7" - $275.00.

Mold 415: Aviator with molded-on goggles and cap. 4" - $250.00; 6" - $400.00; 8" - $525.00 up.

Pink bisque: 1920s and 1930s. Jointed shoulders and hips. Painted features. Can have molded hair or wig. Excellent condition. 2–3" - $40.00; 4–5½" - $60.00. **Bow loop in hair:** 3" - $60.00; 7" - $85.00.

Wrestler (so called), some mold #102: (See photo in Series 7, pg. 10.) Considered French. Fat thighs, arm bent at elbow, open mouth (can have two rows of teeth) or closed mouth. Stocky body, glass eyes, socket head, individual fingers or molded fists. All in good condition. **Painted boots:** 6" - $1,100.00; 8" - $1,400.00; 9" - $1,600.00. **Bare feet:** 5–6" - $1,800.00. **Long painted stockings to above knees:** 6½" - $1,800.00; 8" - $2,000.00. **Jointed elbows and knees:** (See photo in Series 7, pg. 6.) 6" - $1,750.00; 8" - $2,000.00. **Jointed shoulders only:** (See photo in Series 9, pg. 9.) Painted-on

two- or three-strap boots, painted eyes, round early face. 6" - $600.00.

Immobilies: Figures with no joints. **Child:** 3" - $40.00 up. **Adults:** 5" - $145.00 up. **Santa:** 4" - $125.00. **Child with animal on string:** 5" - $150.00 up.

Orientals: Unmarked and marked with maker. See Oriental section.

2½" all bisque that is jointed at neck, shoulders, and hips. Original Cossack style uniform. Fastened to mandolin-shaped candy container lined with gold embossed paper. Mint and complete - $365.00. *Courtesy Virginia Sofie.*

ALL BISQUE – BABIES

All bisque babies were made in both Germany and Japan, and dolls from either country can be excellent quality or poor quality. Prices are for excellent painting and quality of bisque. There should be no chips, cracks, or breaks. Dressed or nude - 1900; bent limbs - after 1906.

Germany (Jointed necks, shoulders, and hips): Wigs or painted hair.

Glass eyes: 4" - $185.00; 5" - $225.00; 7" - $325.00; 9" - $550.00. **Painted eyes:** 4" - $100.00; 5" - $165.00; 6½" - $225.00; 9" - $365.00.

Germany (Jointed at shoulders and hips only): Well-painted features, free-formed thumbs and many have molded bottle in hand. Some have molded-on clothes. 4" - $70.00; 6" - $145.00.

Germany (character baby): Jointed shoulders and hips, molded hair, painted eyes with character face. 4" - $185.00; 6" - $225.00. **Glass eyes:** 4" - $325.00; 6" - $425.00. **Mold #830, 833, and others:** 8" - $550.00 up; 11" - $1,200.00 up. **Swivel neck, glass eyes:** 6" - $575.00; 10" - $1,000.00 up. **Swivel neck, painted eyes:** 6" - $375.00; 8" - $500.00; 10" - $800.00.

Germany (toddler) #369, 372: Jointed neck, glass eyes, perfect condition. 7" - $700.00; 9" - $1,000.00; 11" - $1,300.00 up.

"Candy Babies": (Can be either German or Japanese.) Ca. 1920s. Generally poorly painted with high bisque color. Were given away at candy counter with purchase. 4" - $25.00; 6" - $40.00.

Pink bisque baby: Ca. 1920s. Jointed at shoulders and hips, painted features and hair, bent baby legs. 4" - $50.00; 8" - $95.00.

Mold #231: (A.M.) Toddler with open mouth, glass eyes. 9" - $1,400.00 up.

Little all bisque German child with painted hair and features in very unique Jules Vern style balloon with hand-blown glass insert and wicker basket. It may have been a hanging crib toy. Held by rare mold #601 Simon & Halbig. (See that section for description.) All bisque in balloon (1991 value) - $600.00.
Courtesy Lois Thomas.

Left: 6" all bisque baby with painted features and open/closed mouth. Has excellent detail to hair, legs, and feet. Right: 6" character baby with sleep eyes. Has muslin straight legged body with squeaker in torso and full papier maché arms that are wire jointed. Marked "3/0 Germany." Painted features - $200.00. Sleep eyes - $300.00.

ALL BISQUE – CHARACTERS

All bisque dolls with character faces or stances were made both in Germany and Japan. The German dolls have finer bisque and workmanship of the painted features. Most bisque character dolls have jointed shoulders only, with some having joints at the hips. A very few have swivel heads. They can have molded-on shoes or be barefooted. Prices are for dolls with no chips, cracks, hairlines, or breaks.

Baby Bo Kaye: Made by Alt, Beck & Gottschalck. Marked with mold **#1394.** 5" - $1,300.00; 7" - $1,600.00.

Baby Bud: Glass eyes, wig: 6–7" - $650.00 up.

Baby Darling, Mold #497, Kestner #178: (Allow more for toddler body.) **Swivel neck, glass eyes:** 5" - $500.00; 9" - $900.00. **One-piece body, painted eyes:** 7" - $450.00; 9" - $700.00; 11" - $900.00 up.

Baby Peggy Montgomery: Made by Louis Amberg. Marked with paper label. 4" - $400.00; 6" - $575.00.

Bonnie Babe: Made by Georgene Averill. Has paper label. 5" - $650.00; 7" - $825.00. **Molded-on clothes:** 6" - $1,000.00.

Bye-Lo: Made by J.D. Kestner. Has paper label. **Jointed neck, molded hair, glass eyes:** 4" - $475.00; 6" - $600.00. **Jointed neck, wig, glass eyes:** 5" -

$575.00; 8" - $1,000.00. **Painted eyes, molded hair, one-piece body and head:** 5" - $265.00; 7" - $475.00. **Immobilies:** "Salt" and "Pepper" on back or stomach. 3–3½" - $325.00. **One piece:** Various poses. 3" - $325.00.

Campbell Kids: Molded-on clothes, "Dutch" hairstyle. 5" - $225.00.

Chin-Chin: Made by Heubach. 4½" - $350.00. Poor quality: 4½" - $175.00.

Didi, Fefe (Fifi), Chi Chi, Mimi, Veve (Vivi): Made by Orsini. 5–6" - $1,300.00 up. **Painted eyes:** $600.00 up.

Googly: 1911 on. **Glass eyes:** 4" - $350.00, 6" - $550.00. **Painted eyes:** 4" - $265.00; 6" - $400.00. **Glass eyes, swivel neck:** 6" - $650.00; 8" - $1,000.00. **Jointed elbow and/or knees:** (See photo in Series 9, pg. 88.) 6" - $2,600.00; 7–7½" - $2,800.00. **Marked with maker:** Example K✿R. 6½" - $2,600.00 up. **#217, 501, and others:** 4" - $465.00; 6" - $625.00. **#182, 292:** Swivel neck. 5" - $585.00; 7" - $785.00.

Grumpy Boy: Marked "Germany." 4" - $135.00. Marked "Japan": 4" - $40.00.

Happifats: 5" boy or girl. Each - $325.00 up.

Hebee or Shebee: 5" - $475.00. (See photo in Series 5, pg. 11; Series 7, pg. 9.)

Heubach: Molded hair, side glance eyes. Molded ribbon or bows: 7" - $700.00; 9" - $900.00. Wigged: 7" - $950.00.

Bunny Boy or Girl figurine: By Heubach. 5" - $325.00; 8½" - $625.00.

Little Imp: Has hooved feet. 6½" - $475.00.

Kestner: Marked mold **#257, 262,** etc. **Baby:** Glass eyes, swivel head. 9–10" -

$1,000.00. **One piece body and head:** 5½–6½" - $325.00.

Max and Moritz: Kestner. See All Bisque – Comic Character. (See photo in Series 7, pg. 12.)

Medic: One piece, uniform molded-on, carries case. (See photo in Series 7, pg. 9.) 3½–4" - $200.00.

Mildred (Prize Baby) #880: 1913. 7" - $1,400.00; 8½" - $1,700.00.

Orsini: Head tilted to side, made in one piece and hands hold out dress. 4" - $550.00; 6" - $700.00.

Our Fairy: Molded hair and painted eyes. (See photo in Series 7, pg. 81.) 9–10" - $1,600.00. **Wig and glass eyes:** 9–10" - $1,850.00.

Our Mary: Has paper label. 5½" - $475.00.

Peek-a-boo: By Drayton. 5" - $300.00.

Peterkin: 5" - $250.00; 9" - $475.00.

Peterkin, Tommy: Horsman. 4" - $250.00.

Queue San Baby: Various poses. **Germany:** 6" - $235.00. **Japan:** 5" - $70.00–90.00.

Scootles: Made by Cameo. 7" - $750.00 up.

Sonny: One-piece body and head. Made by Averill. 5" - $500.00 up. **Glass eyes, swivel neck:** 7" - $1,300.00.

Tynie Baby: Made by Horsman. **Glass eyes:** 6" - $850.00; 9" - $1,350.00. **Painted eyes:** 6" - $485.00.

Wide Awake Doll: Germany: 7" - $350.00. Japan: 7" - $125.00.

"Knotters" are called "nodders" since when their heads are touched, they "nod." The reason they should correctly be called "knotters" is due to the method of stringing. The string was passed through a hole in the head and knotted. They can also be made with cutouts on the bodies to take a tiny rod that comes out of the side of the neck. Both styles were made in Germany and Japan, circa 1920s.

Santa Claus or Indian: 6" - $135.00–165.00.

Teddy Bear: 5" - $145.00.

Other Animals: Rabbit, dog, cat, etc. 3½–5" - $25.00–75.00. **Molded-on clothes:** 4" - $125.00 up.

Comic Characters: Uncle Walt, Skeezic, Rachel (black), Kayo, Moon Mullins, Orphan Annie, Andy Gumps, Chester, Ching Chow, Smitty, Herby, Sandy (dog). 3½–5" - $65.00– 235.00 up.

Children/Adults: Made in Germany. 4½–5½" - $35.00–145.00.

Japan/Nippon: 3½" - $20.00; 4½" - $40.00.

Sitting Position: 5" - $135.00 up; 9" - $250.00 up.

All bisque dolls from Japan vary a great deal in quality. They are jointed at shoulders and may have other joints. Good quality bisque is well painted with no chips or breaks. (Also see All Bisque – Characters and Nodder sections.)

Marked Nippon: The mark "Nippon" ceased in 1923. 4" - $30.00; 6" - $50.00.

"Betty Boop": Bobbed hair style, large painted eyes to side, and one-piece body and head. 4" - $40.00; 6–7" - $65.00.

Child: With molded clothes. 4½" - $20.00; 6" - $40.00.

Child: 1920s and 1930s. Pink or painted bisque with painted features. Jointed at shoulders and hips. Has molded hair or wig. Excellent condition. 3" - $18.00; 4–5" - $30.00; 7" - $50.00 up. **Bow loop in hair:** 4" - $40.00; 7" - $60.00.

Comic Characters: See All Bisque – Comic Characters or Nodders sections.

Occupied Japan: 3½" - $20.00; 5" - $30.00; 7" - $45.00.

Immobilies: Figurines with no joints. (Add 50% more if German.) **Bride & groom cake top:** 6–6½" - $110.00. **Children:** 3–4" - $15.00–25.00; 6–7" - $30.00–50.00. **Teddy Bears:** 3" - $45.00 up. **Indians, Dutch, etc:** 2½" - $18.00 up. **Santa Claus:** 3½" - $55.00 up. **Adults:** 5" - $65.00. **Child with animal on string:** 3½" - $45.00–80.00.

Bent leg baby: May or may not be jointed at hips and shoulders. Very nice quality. 3½–5" - $30.00–70.00.

Bye-Lo copy: (See photo in Series 6, pg. 12.) 3½" - $80.00, 5" - $125.00. **Medium to poor quality:** 3½–5" - $6.00–45.00.

Large 7" all bisque "Betty Boop" type doll that is jointed at shoulders only. Made in Japan. $45.00. *Courtesy Kathy Tvrdik.*

4½" girl and 4½" boy with dog tied to hole in hand. Both have molded-on clothes and painted features. She is marked "S541/Made in Japan," and he is marked "Japan/S1624." Both are above average quality. Girl (this quality) - $40.00; Boy - $50.00. *Courtesy Virigina Sofie.*

Cowboy and Indian immobilies made in Japan. Figures like these can be incised or stamped with country of origin. 3" with paint flakes - $18.00 up. (If in perfect condition - $22.50 up.) 3½" with paint flakes - $22.00. (If in perfect condition - $27.50 up.) *Courtesy Virgina Sofie.*

Annie Rooney, Little: Made in Germany. 4" - $225.00; 7" - $400.00.

Betty Boop: With musical instrument. Made in Japan. 5" - $60.00 up.

Betty Boop: Fleisher Studios. Made in Japan. 4" - $32.50 up.

Dick Tracy: Made in Germany. 5" - $175.00.

Made in Japan: Paint washes off easily. 3–4½" - $25.00 up.

Jackie Coogan: Japan. 6" - $135.00.

Katzenjammer Kids: 4" - $60.00 each ; 6" - $120.00 each. **Mama:** 4" - $65.00; 8" - $110.00. **Papa:** 4" - $65.00; 8" - $165.00. **Uncle Ben:** 4" - $60.00, 8" - $125.00.

Max or Moritz: K✿R. Ca. 1913. Designed by Wilhelm Busch. Swivel necks. 6–6½". Each - $1,850.00 up.

Mibs: See Amberg, Louis.

Mickey Mouse: Walt Disney. 5" - $200.00 up. **With musical instrument:** $250.00 up.

Minnie Mouse: Disney. $225.00 up.

Moon Mullins and Kayo: 4" Mushmouth (black), Uncle Willie, Aunt Mamie, Little Egypt, Emmy, and Lord Plushbottom. Each - $65.00 up.

Orphan Annie: 3½" - $50.00.

Mr. Peanut: Made in Japan. 4" - $30.00.

Our Gang: Boys: 4" - $40.00. Girls: 4" - $50.00.

Popeye: 3" - $125.00 up.

Seven Dwarfs: Walt Disney. 3½". Each - $85.00 up.

Skeezix: 4" - $65.00.

Skippy: (See photo in Series 6, pg. 13.) 5" - $90.00.

Snow White: Japan. 5½" - $100.00. **Boxed with Dwarfs:** $625.00 up. (See photo in Series 6, pg. 13.) Germany: $800.00.

Three Bears & Goldilocks: Japan: In boxed set. $275.00 up. Germany: $475.00 up.

Painted bisque has a layer of paint over the bisque which has not been fired. The color can be washed off or can come off with the glue of a wig. These dolls have molded hair, painted features, painted-on shoes and socks, and are jointed at shoulders and hips. All should be in good condition with no paint chips.

Boy or Girl: German: 3" - $25.00 up; 4½–5" - $55.00–60.00 up. Japan: 3" - $10.00 up; 5" - $20.00 up.

Baby: Germany: 3½" - $45.00 up; 5" - $55.00 up. Japan: 3" - $12.00 up; 5" - $20.00 up.

Alt, Beck & Gottschalck was located at Nauendorf, Germany, near Ohrdruf, as a porcelain factory from 1854. It is not known when they started making dolls. The firm was the maker of both the **"Bye-lo"** baby and **"Bonnie Babe"** for the distributor, George Borgfeldt. The leading authorities in Germany, and now the United States, have assigned nearly all the turned-head dolls as being made by Alt, Beck & Gottschalck, with the bodies being made by **Wagner & Zetzsche.** It is claimed that this firm produced dolls with tinted bisque and molded hair (see that section of this book), as well as wigged turned head and shoulder head dolls and also dolls made of china. There is a vast variation to the eyebrows among these dolls. (Also see All Bisque section.)

Marks:

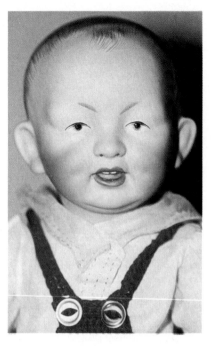

12" toddler with protruding ears, intaglio painted eyes, and deep cheek dimples. Open/closed mouth with two modeled teeth that rest on tongue. On fully jointed toddler body. $1,300.00. *Courtesy Jean Truman.*

Babies: After 1909. Open mouth, some have pierced nostrils, bent leg baby body, and are wigged. Prices will be higher if on toddler body or has flirty eyes. Clean, nicely dressed, and with no cracks, chips, or hairlines. 12" - $375.00; 16" - $500.00; 21" - $800.00; 26" - $1,600.00.

Child #1361, 1362, 1367, etc.: Socket head on jointed composition body, sleep or set eyes. No crack, chips, or hairlines. Clean and nicely dressed. 12" - $400.00; 16" - $500.00; 22" - $675.00; 24" - $800.00; 27" - $1,000.00; 32" - $1,200.00; 36" - $1,700.00.

Character child or baby: Ca. 1910 on. Socket head on jointed composition body, glass or painted eyes, open mouth. Nicely dressed with good wig or molded hair with no hairlines, cracks, or chips.

#630: 21" - $2,200.00. **#911, 916:** Closed mouth. 22" - $2,600.00. **#1322:** Two teeth rest on tongue in closed mouth. 12" - $800.00; 15" - $1,800.00. **#1352, 1361:** 12" - $400.00; 15" - $525.00, 18" - $625.00, 22" - $850.00. **#1357, 1358, 1359:** Molded center part hair, bun, and molded ribbon. Deep dimples. Wide open/closed mouth. **Painted eyes:** 14" - $650.00; 19" - $1,600.00. **Glass eyes:** 16" - $1,000.00; 21" - $2,400.00. **#1362 "Sweet Nell":** (See photo in Series 9, pg. 166; Series 11, pg. 14.) 16" - $675.00; 20" - $975.00; 30" - $1,250.00 up. **#1367:** 15" - $475.00; 19" - $725.00. **#1394 "Baby Bo-Kaye":** 5" - $1,300.00; 7" - $1,600.00.

Turned shoulder head: 1880s. Bald head or plaster pate. Kid body with bisque lower arms. All in good condition with no chips, hairline and nicely dressed. Dolls marked "DEP" or "Germany" date after 1888. Some have the Wagner & Zetzsche mark on head or paper label inside top of body. Some mold numbers include: **639, 698, 784, 870, 890, 911, 912, 916, 990, 1000, 1008, 1028, 1032, 1044, 1046, 1064, 1123, 1127, 1142, 1210, 1234, 1235, 1254, 1288, 1304. Glass eyes, closed mouth:** (Allow more for molded bonnet or elaborate hairdo.) 12–13" - $575.00; 16" - $1,000.00; 18" - $1,500.00; 22" - $1,800.00; 26" - $2,350.00. **Glass eyes, open mouth.** 16–17" - $500.00; 21" - $625.00; 25" - $700.00. **Painted eyes, open mouth:** 14" - $275.00; 20" - $500.00. **Painted eyes, closed mouth:** 14" - $385.00; 20" - $700.00.

Bisque shoulder head: 1880s. Molded hair, cloth or kid body, bisque lower limbs. No damage and nicely dressed. Same mold numbers as turned shoulder head dolls above. (Allow much more for molded bonnet or hat.) **Painted eyes, closed mouth:** 15" - $400.00; 18" - $500.00; 22" - $650.00. **Glass eyes, closed mouth:** 15" - $800.00; 18" - $1,000.00; 22" - $1,200.00. **Painted eyes, open mouth:** 15" - $250.00; 21" - $450.00. **Glass eyes, open mouth:** 15" - $450.00; 21" - $625.00.

Glazed china shoulder head: 1880s. Blonde or black hair, china limbs (or leather), cloth body, and nicely dressed with no damage. **Mold #784,**

786, 1000, 1003, 1008, 1028, 1032, 1046, 1142, 1144, 1210. May also have mark ⚒ or ✗.. 15" - $365.00; 19" - $500.00; 23" - $825.00.

19" turned head doll made by Alt, Beck & Gottschalk. Has closed mouth, leather boots, bisque lower arms, and very early outlined, cobalt blue glass eyes with molded lids. Marked with four numbers plus number 8. This doll was most likely made by Simon & Halbig, but marked dolls made in this style have been dumped into A.B.G. or Hertal & Schwab categories. $1,650.00. *Courtesy Jean Truman.*

AMBERG, LOUIS & SONS

Louis Amberg & Sons were in business from 1878 to 1930 in New York City and Cincinnati, Ohio.

Prices are for dolls in perfect condition, with no cracks, chips, or breaks, clean and nicely dressed. (Allow more for original clothes and wig.)

Marks:

L.A. & S. 1926

AMBERG

L.A. & S. 1928

Baby Peggy (Montgomery): 1923 and 1924. Closed mouth, socket head. (See photo in Series 11, pg. 15.) **Mold #973 (smiling) or 972 (solemn):** 17" - $2,300.00; 22" - $2,650.00.

Baby Peggy mold #983 or 982: Shoulder head. 17" - $2,300.00; 23" - $2,750.00.

Baby Peggy: All bisque. 4" - $400.00; 6" - $575.00.

Baby Peggy: 1923. Composition head and limbs with cloth body. Painted eyes with molded lower eyelids. Closed mouth with visible teeth or painted teeth. Molded brown short bobbed hairdo or mohair wig. 15" - $365.00; 18" - $500.00; 23" - $750.00.

Baby, mold #88678: Cloth body. 16" - $1,300.00; 23" - $1,500.00.

Left: 14" "Sue" or "Edwina" made of all composition with large round ball joint at waist and painted features. Has molded bangs swept to side with side part. Marked "Amberg. Pat. Pend. L.A. & S. 1928." Right: 13" fully jointed "Scootles" made of all composition. Made by Cameo in 1940s. 14" - $450.00. 13" - $500.00. *Courtesy Frasher Doll Auctions.*

Charlie Chaplin: 1915–1920s. Portrait head of composition with painted features, composition hands, cloth body and legs. Black suit and white shirt. Cloth tag on sleeve or inside seam of coat. Marked "Amberg. Essamay Film Co." (See photo in Series 1, pg. 79.) 13" - $450.00; 17" - $675.00.

Newborn Babe: Bisque head with cloth body and can have celluloid, composition or rubber hands. Lightly painted hair, sleep eyes, closed mouth with protruding upper lip. 1914 and reissued in 1924. Marks: "L.A.&S. 1914/**G45520** Germany." Some will be marked "L. Amberg and Son/**886**" and some will be marked "Copyright by Louis Amberg." (See photo in Series 7, pg. 15.) 8" - $365.00; 11" - $425.00; 14" - $500.00; 18" - $825.00.

Newborn Babe: Open mouth version. Marked "L.A.&S. **371**." 9" - $375.00; 16" - $600.00.

Mibs: Marked "L.A.& S. 1921/ Germany" and can have two different paper labels with one "Amberg Dolls/ Please Love Me/I'm Mibs," and some with the same label, but does not carry the name of Amberg. Molded hair with long strand down center of forehead. Composition head and limbs with cloth body, painted eyes. All in good condition. (See photo in Series 6, pg. 17.) 12" - $550.00; 16–17" - $850.00.

Mibs: All bisque. May be marked "1921" on back and have paper label with name. 3½" - $225.00; 5" - $400.00.

Sue (Edwina, Peggy, or "It"): 1928. All composition with painted features, molded hair and with a waist that swivels on a large ball attached to the torso. Jointed shoulders, neck and hips. Molded hair has side part and swirl bangs across forehead. Marked "Amberg/Pat. Pen./L.A.&S." (See photo in Series 6, pg. 17.) 14" - $450.00.

Twist bodies (Tiny Tots, Teenie Weenies): 1926, 1928. All composition with swivel waist made from large ball attached to torso. Boy or girl with molded hair and painted features. Tag attached to clothes: "An Amberg Doll/Body Twist/ Pat. Pend. #32018." 7½–8½" - $200.00.

Vanta Baby: 1927. Composition head and limbs with fat legs. Cloth body, spring strung, sleep eyes, open/closed mouth with two teeth. Made to advertise Vanta baby garments. Marked "Vanta Baby-Amberg (or L.A.&S.)" 18" - $265.00; 23" - $375.00. **Same but with bisque head, glass eyes, open mouth:** (See photo in Series 6, pg. 17.) 18" - $1,100.00; 24" - $1,700.00. **Glass eyes, closed mouth:** 18" - $1,400.00; 24" - $2,000.00.

Amfelt Art Dolls: Cloth bodies with cloth or felt limbs and metal disk joints. Fingers are stitched with free standing thumb. Various materials, such as composition and papier maché, were used for the heads. Doll clothes and bonnets were made of felt. 15" - $365.00; 18" - $485.00; 22" - $600.00.

ARMAND MARSEILLE

Armand Marseille made the majority of their dolls after the 1880s and into the 1920s, so they are some of the most often found dolls today. The factory was at Koppelsdorf, Germany. Although "Armand Marseille" has been glamourized by German authors, the facts are Herman "Marseille" Schultz died in 1925 after his son, Herman II, took over in 1917 and his sister, Beatrice, married the son of Ernst Heubach. Herman Schultz II was born in 1885 and was forced to leave East Germany when he was 65. His son was forced to leave in 1979. He found molds remaining in the basement of his grandfather's old factory and attempted to re-enter the doll market using the mold #390. He was not successful.

A.M. marked dolls can be of excellent to very poor quality. The finer the bisque and artist workmanship, the higher the price. This company also made a great many heads for other companies, such as George Borgfeldt, Amberg (Baby Peggy), Hitz, Jacobs & Kassler, Otto Gans, Cuno & Otto Dressel, etc. They were marked with "A.M." or full name "Armand Marseille."

Prices are for perfect dolls with no chips, cracks, breaks, or hairline cracks. Dolls need to be clean and nicely dressed.

Mold #370, 326, 309, 273, 270, 375, 376, 920, 957: Kid or kidaleen bodies, open mouths. 10" - $195.00; 15" - $165.00; 18" - $225.00; 24" - $350.00; 28" - $475.00.

Mold #390, 266, 300, 310 (not "Googly"), 384, 390N, 391, 395: Socket head, jointed body and open mouth. 15" - $175.00; 18" - $275.00; 21" - $325.00; 24" -

25" mold #390N with open mouth and sleep eyes. On fully jointed body. Very pretty. $600.00. *Courtesy Turn of Century Antiques.*

$450.00; 28" - $575.00; 30" - $700.00; 32" - $850.00; 36" - $1,100.00; 42" - $1,950.00.
Closed mouth: 6" - $200.00; 8" - $300.00.
Crude body: 8" - $150.00; 10" - $245.00.
Jointed body: 8" - $245.00; 10" - $300.00.
Flapper: 5-piece body with long painted stockings. 9" - $285.00.

Large Sizes Marked Just A.M.: Jointed bodies, socket head and open mouths. (Also see Closed Mouth under Character Child.) 32"- $1,400.00; 35" - $1,600.00; 40" - $2,000.00 up.

Mold #1776, 1890, 1892, 1893, 1894, 1896, 1897 (which can be a shoulder head or have a socket head);

20" "Queen Lousie" with very excellent quality bisque and in mint condition. All original from head to toe. Original - $550.00 up. Re-dressed - $450.00. *Courtesy Jeannie Nespoli.*

1898, 1899, 1901, 1902, 1903, 1908, 1909, 3200: Kid or kidaleen body, open mouth. (See below for prices if on composition bodies.) 9" - $145.00; 15" - $175.00; 18" - $265.00; 21" - $325.00; 25" - $425.00; 27" - $550.00. **On composition jointed body:** 10" - $225.00; 13" - $275.00; 18" - $465.00; 22" - $525.00; 25" - $645.00; 28" - $745.00; 32" - $900.00; 36" - $1,200.00.

Alma, Floradora, Mabel, Lilly, Lissy, Darling, My Dearie, My Girlie, My Playmate, Sunshine, Dollar Princess, Duchess, 3700, 14008: 1890s. Kid or kidaleen body. 12" - $165.00; 15" - $250.00; 18" - $325.00; 22" - $400.00; 26" - $485.00; 30" - $900.00. **On composition body:** 15" - $365.00; 19" - $500.00; 24" - $575.00; 27" - $750.00; 32" - $950.00.

Queen Louise, Beauty, Columbia, Jubilee, Majestic, My Companion, Pansy, Princess, Rosebud, Sadie: Kid or kidaleen body. 14" - $250.00; 16" - $365.00; 19" - $450.00; 24" - $545.00; 28" - $675.00; 32" - $950.00 up. **On composition body:** 12" - $250.00; 16" - $345.00; 19" - $525.00; 22" - $550.00; 28" - $650.00; 30" - $975.00; 34" - $1,200.00.

#2000: Kid or kidaleen body, glass eyes. 14" - $725.00; 17" - $900.00. **Jointed body:** 14" - $900.00; 17" - $1,100.00.

Babies (infant style): Some from 1910; others from 1924. Can be on composition bodies, or have cloth bodies with curved or straight cloth legs. (Add $100.00–200.00 more for toddler babies.)

Mold #340, 341, 345: With closed mouth. **My Dream Baby**, also called **Rock-A-Bye Baby**. Made for the Arranbee Doll Co. **Composition body:** 6–7" - $175.00; 9" - $225.00; 12" - $300.00; 14" - $375.00; 16" - $475.00; 20" - $600.00; 24" - $875.00; 28" - $1,100.00. **Toddler:** 20" - $700.00; 25" - $1,000.00.

Mold #345, 351: With open mouth. Same as above, but some will also be marked **"Kiddiejoy"** or **"Our Pet."** 7–8" - $185.00; 10" - $250.00; 14" - $475.00; 20" - $685.00; 28" - $1,200.00.

Mold #340, 341 or 345, 347, 351: Twin puppets in basket - $600.00 up. Hand puppet, single doll - $325.00 up.

Mold #341, 345, 351 ("Kiddiejoy" or "Our Pet"): With fired-on black or brown color. See Black section. (See photo of #345 in Series 5, pg. 17.)

Babies, mold #256, 259, 326, 327, 328, 329, 360, 750, 790, 900, 927, 970, 971, 975, 980, 984, 985, 990, 991, 992, 995, 996, 1321, 1330, 1330A, 1333: 1910 on. (Add $100.00–200.00 for toddler bodies or flirty eyes.) 9" - $225.00; 12" - $300.00; 15" - $450.00; 17" - $575.00; 20" - $650.00; 23" - $785.00. **Same mold numbers, but painted bisque:** 13" - $185.00; 17" - $300.00; 20" - $400.00; 23" - $525.00.

Character Babies: 1910 on. (Add $100.00–150.00 for toddler body.) Composition jointed body. Can have open mouth or open/closed mouth.

Mold # 225: 1916. Baby, toddler. (Also see child.) Glass eyes, upper and lower teeth. 17" - $3,000.00; 20" - $3,900.00.

Mold #233: 9" - $265.00; 13" - $550.00; 16" - $650.00; 19" - $875.00.

Mold #248, 251 with open/closed mouth: 14" - $1,600.00; 16" - $1,750.00. **Open mouth:** 14" - $800.00.

Mold #327, 328: 8" - $225.00; 12" - $325.00; 16" - $550.00; 20" - $625.00.

Mold #346: 18" - $700.00; 20" - $765.00; 25" - $875.00.

Mold #347: 16" - $550.00; 19" - $700.00.

Mold #352: (See photo in Series 7, pg. 18.) 10" - $250.00; 15" - $450.00; 18" - $600.00; 25" - $1,100.00.

Mold #355: A. Eller/3K. Closed mouth, sweet face. 13" - $600.00; 18" - $825.00.

Mold #362: 9" - $245.00; 17" - $625.00; 22" - $850.00.

Mold #410: Two rows of teeth, some are retractable. 16" - $1,150.00; 18" - $1,400.00; 23" - $1,700.00.

Mold #518: 16" - $575.00; 22" - $675.00.

14" Armand Marseille "Kiddiejoy" using mold #351 "Dream Baby." Has sleep eyes and open mouth. On five-piece bent limb baby body. $475.00. *Courtesy Cris Johnson.*

20" doll with open/closed mouth, sleep eyes, and fully jointed body. Has very character face. Marked "590 A 5 M Germany DGRM." $2,300.00. *Courtesy Turn of Century Antiques.*

Mold #506A, 560A: 13" - $450.00; 15" - $575.00; 20" - $850.00.

Mold #560, 570: Open/closed mouth. 7" - $250.00; 12" - $475.00; 16" - $1,400.00; 20" - $1,800.00.

Mold #550, 580, 590: (See photos in Series 1, pg. 48; Series 4, pg. 18; Series 7, pg. 19.) **Open/closed mouth:** 14" - $1,250.00; 17" - $1,650.00; 21" - $2,100.00. **Open mouth:** 12" - $625.00; 18" - $950.00.

Mold #750: Character face. Rare. 14" - $1,350.00 up; 17" - $2,000.00 up.

Mold #920: Cloth body, shoulder head. 20" - $850.00 up.

Mold #970: 16" - $475.00; 20" - $685.00; 24" - $965.00.

Baby Gloria (Mold #240): (See photo in Series 5, pg. 18; Series 11, pg. 20.) 10" - $375.00; 16" - $675.00; 19" - $975.00; 22" - $1,450.00.

Baby Phyllis: Heads by Armand Marseille. Painted hair, closed mouth. 10" - $350.00; 16" - $600.00; 20" - $1,100.00. **Composition head:** Dimples, open mouth. 20" - $365.00.

Baby Florence: 12" - $475.00; 16" - $750.00; 19" - $1,250.00.

Baby Betty: 1890s. Jointed composition child body, but few heads found on bent limb baby body. (See photo in Series 8, pg. 20; Series 11, pg. 17.) 14" - $400.00; 18" - $575.00; 22" - $650.00. **Kid body:** 16" - $265.00; 19" - $450.00.

Fany Baby: Mold #231 along with incised "Fany." Can be baby, toddler or child. With wig: 15" - $4,300.00; 18" - $5,850.00.

Fany Baby: Mold #230 along with incised "Fany." Molded hair. 15" - $4,500.00; 18" - $6,000.00; 22" - $7,300.00.

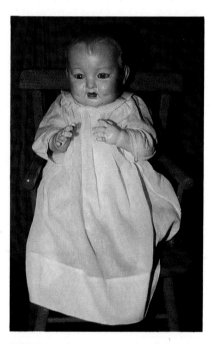

20" baby with composition head and arms and cloth body and legs. Has molded hair and tongue, dimples, and two upper teeth. Most likely made in late 1920s by Armand Marseille. Marked "Baby Gloria - Germany." $365.00. *Courtesy Jeannie Mauldin.*

16" very rare character doll with rare mold number by Armand Marseille. She has a very character face with wide open mouth and *two rows of teeth* — six upper and lower. Has sleep eyes and outlined lips. On a straight wrist jointed body. Marked "225/Armand Marseille/A 2 M/Made in Germany/DRGM." $4,000.00. *Courtesy Mary McGuire.*

Just Me: Mold #310. See Googly section.

Melitta: (See photo in Series 8, pg. 20.) **Baby:** 16" - $550.00; 19" - $750.00. **Toddler:** 20" - $1,000.00; 25" - $1,500.00.

Character Child: 1910 on. May have wig, molded hair, glass or intaglio painted eyes, and some will have fully closed mouths while others have open/ closed mouth. For these prices, doll must be in excellent condition and have no damage.

Mold #225 (Little Mary): Open mouth with two rows of teeth. Glass eyes. (See photo in Pat Smith's *Armand Marseille 1865–1925* book, pg. 133.) 14" - $3,600.00; 17" - $4,200.00.

Mold #250: 11" - $585.00; 15" - $795.00; 18" - $1,000.00.

Mold #251 with open/closed mouth: (See photo in Series 11, pg. 19.) 16" - $1,800.00; 19" - $2,100.00. **Open mouth:** 16" - $950.00.

Mold #340: 14" - $2,650.00.

Mold #345: Closed mouth, intaglio eyes. (See photo in Series 5, pg. 17.) 12" - $1,100.00; 16" - $1,900.00.

Mold #350: Socket head, glass eyes, closed mouth. 10" - $1,100.00; 17" - $2,400.00; 21" - $3,000.00, 26" - $3,700.00.

Mold #360: 13" - $450.00; 17" - $785.00.

Mold #372 "Kiddiejoy": Ca. 1924. Kid body, molded hair, glass eyes. (See photo in Series 5, pg. 18.) 13" - $450.00; 17" - $625.00; 20" - $985.00.

Mold #400: Glass eyes, socket head and closed mouth. (See photo in Series 8, pg. 21; Series 9, pg. 22.) 12" - $1,800.00; 15" - $2,200.00; 18" - $3,000.00; 22" - $3,500.00.

Mold #401, 449: Painted eyes, socket head and closed mouth. (See photo for #401 in Series 3, pg. 39.) 10" - $485.00; 17" - $1,150.00; 20" - $1,450.00. **Painted bisque:** (See photo in Series 11, pg. 21.) 9" - $285.00; 16" - $725.00; 19" - $1,000.00 up.

Left: 13" character with sleep eyes, hair lashes, closed mouth, and mohair wig. On jointed body with straight wrists. Dressed in old outfit. Marked "Armand Marseille 400 Germany 4/0." Right: 23" doll with all kid fashion body. Marked "F.G. 7" (Gauthier). 13" - $1,900.00. 23" - $3,500.00. *Courtesy Frasher Doll Auctions.*

Mold #450: Socket head, glass eyes and closed mouth. 14" - $725.00; 17" - $1,300.00; 21" - $1,800.00.

Mold #500, 520: Molded hair, intaglio eyes, open/closed mouth. (See photo for #500 in Series 3, pg. 39.) 10" - $565.00; 16" - $1,000.00; 20" - $1,500.00.

Mold #500, 520, 620, 630, 640: Wigged, glass eyes and open/closed mouth. **Composition, jointed body:** 10" - $650.00; 15" - $1,200.00; 18" - $2,100.00. **Same, with kid body:** 15" - $685.00; 18" - $1,200.00.

Mold #550, 600, 640: (See photo in Series 7, pg. 19; Series 8, pg. 21.) **Molded hair, painted eyes:** 12" - $1,000.00; 15" - $1,600.00. **Glass eyes:** 12" - $1,600.00; 15" - $2,500.00; 18" - $3,200.00. **Closed mouth, dimples:** 15" - $1,800.00.

Mold #570, 590 with open mouth: (See photos in Series 4, pg. 18; Series 7, pg. 19.) 10" - $485.00; 16" - $900.00. **Open/ closed mouth:** 17" - $2,000.00.

Mold #700: (See photo in Series 8, pg. 21; Series 9, pg. 23.) **Glass eyes:** 13" - $1,700.00; 16" - $2,700.00; 19" - $3,300.00. **Painted eyes:** 16" - $2,100.00.

Mold #701, 709, 711: Glass eyes, closed mouth, sweet expression. 10" - $1,200.00; 17" - $2,600.00.

Mold #800, 820: Child. Glass eyes, open/closed mouth. (See photos in Series 6, pg. 21; Series 8, pg. 21; Series 10, pg. 23.) 14" - $1,500.00; 17" - $2,300.00; 21" - $2,750.00.

Mold #950: Painted hair and eyes, open mouth. 12" - $675.00; 16" - $1,000.00.

Character marked only "A.M.": Closed mouth. (See photo in Series 4, pg. 17.) **Intaglio eyes:** 17" - $4,600.00. **Glass eyes:** 18" - $5,200.00.

Googly: See Googly section.

Black/Brown Dolls: See that section.

Adult Lady Dolls: 1910–1920s. Adult face with long, thin jointed limbs. Knee joint is above knee area. Painted-on shoes.

Mold #300: 10" - $1,300.00; 14" - $1,650.00.

Mold #400, 401 with closed mouth: 10" - $1,400.00; 15" - $2,300.00; 18" - $2,600.00. **Open mouth:** 10" - $800.00; 15" - $1,200.00; 18" - $1,500.00.

Mold #800: Lady with thin face, closed mouth, and glass eyes. High heel feet. (See photo in Doll Values 10, pg. 23.) 10" - $1,000.00; 14" - $1,450.00.

Painted bisque, mold #400, 401, 449: 14" - $725.00; 17" - $950.00.

Painted bisque, mold #242, 244, 246, etc.: 14" - $425.00; 18" - $675.00; 25" - $975.00.

Biscoloid, mold #378, 966, etc.: Like painted bisque but material under paint more plastic type. 15" - $525.00; 17" - $700.00.

19½" doll with sleep eyes with hair lashes. On fully jointed body. All original wig and clothes. Marked "Armand Marseille/Germany/A 3 M." $325.00. *Courtesy Carmen Holshoe.*

ARNOLD, MAX

Max Arnold made dolls from 1876 into the 1920s in Germany.

Mark:

M.O.A.

(for Max Oscar Arnold)

Child: Marked **150, 200,** or just M.O.A. (See photo in Series 11, pg. 22.) **Excellent bisque:** 10" - $200.00; 14" - $300.00; 19" - $500.00; 22" - $700.00; 30" - $1,000.00. **Poor to medium bisque:** 15" - $165.00; 20" - $300.00; 24" - $450.00. **Baby:** 12" - $165.00; 16" - $285.00; 19" - $500.00.

A. Thuillier made dolls in Paris from 1875 to 1893 and may be the maker of the dolls marked with "A.T." A.T. marked dolls can be found on wooden, jointed composition, or kid bodies and can range in sizes from 14" to 30". The dolls can have closed mouths or open mouths with two rows of teeth. The following prices are for marked A.T. dolls on correct body, clean, beautiful face, dressed nicely, and with no damage, such as a hairline cracks, chips, or breaks. (See photos in Series 7, pgs. 21–22.)

Marks:

A.T. N°3
A N°6 T
A. 8 T.

Closed mouth: Jointed composition body. (See photos in Series 7, pg. 21–22; Series 8, pg. 23.) 15" - $38,000.00; 17" - $42,000.00; 21" - $48,000.00; 25" - $54,000.00.
Kid body, closed mouth: Bisque lower arms. 15" - $40,000.00; 18" - $46,000.00; 24" - $52,000.00.

Open mouth: Jointed composition body. (See photos in Series 9, pg. 24; Series 10, pg. 25.) 16" - $13,000.00; 19" - $15,500.00; 23" - $20,000.00; 28" - $26,500.00.

19" with closed mouth and large paper-weight eyes. On jointed A.T. body with straight wrists. Marked "A. 8 T." on head. $45,500.00. *Courtesy Ellen Dodge.*

AVERILL, GEORGENE (MADAME HENDREN)

Georgene Averill used the business names of Madame Georgene Dolls, Averill Mfg. Co., Georgene Novelties, and Madame Hendren. Averill began making dolls in 1913 and designed several for George Borgfeldt.

First prices are for extra clean dolls. Second prices for dolls with chips, craze lines, dirt, or missing some or all of the original clothes.
Baby Georgene or Baby Hendren: 1918 on. Composition/cloth and marked with name on head. (Add more if tagged and mint in box.) Original. (See photo in Series 4, pg. 23.) 15" - $225.00, $70.00; 20" - $325.00, $95.00; 25" - $400.00 up, $100.00.
Baby Yawn: Composition with closed eyes and yawn mouth. 16" - $475.00, $150.00; 19" - $575.00, $200.00.
Body Twist Dolls: 1927. Composition with large ball joint at waist, painted hair and features. 14" - $400.00, $85.00.
Bonnie Babe, mold #1368-140 or 1402: 1926. Bisque head, cloth body,

open mouth/two lower teeth, molded hair and composition arms/or hands. 14" - $950.00; 17" - $1,200.00; 25" - $1,850.00 up. **Celluloid head:** 16" - $675.00 up. **Composition body, bisque head:** (See photo in Series 8, pg. 11.) 10" - $985.00; 15" - $1,300.00.

Bonnie Babe: All bisque. See All Bisque section.

CLOTH DOLLS

Made in 1930s. Mask face with painted features, yarn hair, cloth body. First price for clean dolls; second for soiled dolls.

Characters: Such as **Becassine,** etc. 1950s. Must be mint. (See photo in Series 7, pg. 24; Series 8, pg. 24.) 14" - $425.00 up.

International: (See photos in Series 5, pg. 22; Series 9, pg. 27.) 13" - $125.00,

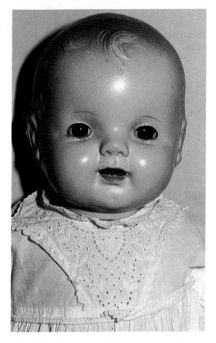

27" doll with composition head and limbs, cloth body, and molded hair. Has open mouth with two lower teeth and sleep eyes. Marked "Baby Hendren." $475.00.
Courtesy Frasher Doll Auctions.

$35.00; 16" - $185.00, $60.00; 21" - $300.00, $95.00.

Children: (Add more if mint in box.) 13" - $125.00; $45.00; 16" - $200.00, $70.00; 22" - $300.00, $90.00; 24" - $350.00, $125.00. (See photo in Series 9, pg. 27.) **Musical:** 15" - $275.00, $85.00. **Brownies:** 15" - $250.00, $80.00. **Scout:** (See photo in Series 7, pg. 23.) 14" - $265.00, $85.00.

Tear Drop Baby: One tear painted on cheek. 16" - $325.00, $60.00.

Animals: 1930s on. Must be mint. **B'rer Rabbit, Fuzzy Wuzzy, Nurse Jane, Uncle Wiggily, etc.:** (See photos in Series 7, pg. 25; Series 8, pg. 25; Series 9, pg. 27.) 18" - $600.00 up. **All bisque cat (mold #891) and dog (mold #890):** Jointed shoulder, neck, and hips. Glass eyes, modeled-on booties. 5–6" - $1,800.00 up; 10–11" - $2,800.00 up.

Comic Characters (Alvin, Little Lulu with round face, fat cheeks, **Nancy, Sluggo, Tubby Tom):** 1944–1951. All cloth with mask faces and painted features. 15" - $500.00. **Little Lulu:** In rare cowgirl outfit. 15" - $585.00. **Dolly Dingle:** 14" - $550.00.

COMPOSITION DOLLS

Children: Composition with cloth body. Perfect and original. 16" - $275.00, 19" - $450.00; less than mint - $95.00 up. **Scout, Pirate, Brownie, Storybook (Little Boy Blue, Mother Goose, Captain Kidd, etc.):** 15" - $365.00, $100.00; 19" - $600.00, $200.00. **"Patsy" type:** 14" - $285.00, $100.00.

Dolly Dingle: (For Grace Drayton) Composition. 14" - $450.00 up, $100.00.

Dolly Record: 1922. Composition with record player in back. Near mint condition. (See photo in Series 10, pg. 26.) 26" - $550.00, $250.00.

Googly: Composition/cloth. 12" - $250.00, $70.00; 14" - $325.00, $100.00; 16" - $465.00, $150.00.

Indian, Cowboy, Sailor, Soldier, Scout, Pirate: Composition/cloth, molded hair or wig, sometimes yarn hair, painted features. (See Indian photo in Series 1, pg. 57.) 9" - $145.00, $35.00; 15" - $400.00, $100.00.

Krazy Kat: 1916. Felt, unjointed. (See photo in Series 6, pg. 27.) 14" - $350.00, $85.00. 18" - $500.00, $125.00.

Snookums: 1927. Composition/cloth. Smile face, character from George McManus's "The Newlyweds." 14" - $400.00, $100.00.

Vinyl Head, Laughing Child: With oil cloth body. Must have good color vinyl. 26" - $225.00, $80.00.

Whistling Dan: 1925–1929. Sailor, cowboy, policeman, child, etc. (See photo in Series 6, pg. 26.) 14" - $250.00, $85.00; 16" - $300.00, $100.00.

Whistling Rufus/Nell: Black doll. Whistles well. (See photo in Series 10, pg. 27.) 14" - $425.00, $125.00.

Whistling Dolly Dingle: 14" - $425.00, $125.00.

Babies, Infant Types: 1920s. Composition/cloth, painted hair, sleep eyes. 13" - $165.00, $65.00; 17" - $245.00, $90.00; 20" - $300.00, $125.00.

Lenci types: Circa late 1920s. Flocked type faces, cloth body, rest composition. Felt and organdy costumes. Stamped on back "Genuine Madame Hendren Doll/Made in U.S.A." Dress tagged. 14" - $300.00; 18" - $500.00.

"Little Sister" was designed by Grace Corey Rockwell and made by Madame Hendren. Made of all composition with painted hair and features. Has I.D. in coin holder for good luck. The dress looks like the one for the early "Little Orphan Annie" doll, but it is apparently original to this doll. $365.00. *Courtesy Ellen Dodge.*

BABY BO-KAYE

Bisque heads for Baby Bo-Kaye were made by Alt, Beck & Gottschalck in 1925. Celluloid heads were made in Germany, and composition heads were made in the U.S. by Cameo Doll Company. Designer of the doll was Joseph L. Kallus, owner of Cameo Doll Co. (See photo in Series 8, pg. 26; Series 9, pg. 28.)

Bisque head, mold #1307-124, 1394-30, 1407: Molded hair, open mouth, glass eyes, cloth body, composition limbs. In overall good condition with no damage. 15" - $2,300.00; 18" - $2,700.00.

Celluloid head: Same as bisque head description. 14" - $425.00; 17" - $775.00.

Composition head: Same as above description. 13" - $450.00. Light craze: 15" - $375.00. Cracks and/or chips: 15" - $110.00.

All bisque: 5" - $1,300.00; 7" - $1,600.00.

BAHR & PROSCHILD

Bahr & Proschild operated at Ohrdruf, Germany from 1871 into the late 1920s. They also made celluloid dolls (1910). Also see Swaine & Co. (S&C) for B.P. mark.

Marks:

Character Baby: 1909 on. Bent limbs, sleep eyes, wigged and open mouths. Allow $100.00–150.00 more for toddler body. Clean, nicely dressed and no damage.

Baby, mold #592: 10" - $575.00. **Toddler:** 12" - $825.00.

Mold #585, 586, 587, 604, 620, 624, 630, 678, 619, 641: 13" - $450.00; 16" - $575.00; 19" - $650.00; 23" - $900.00. **Toddler:** 10" - $500.00; 15" - $750.00; 18" - $1,000.00.

Mold #169: 13" - $450.00; 19" - $750.00; 24" - $925.00.

Character Child: (Also see Swaine & Co.) Can be on fully jointed composition body or toddler body. Ca 1910. Nicely dressed, clean, no damage. Can have molded hair or be wigged.

Mold #526 and other 500s, 2072, or marked B.P. baby body: 1910. Open/closed mouth. 15" - $2,900.00; 19" - $3,900.00.

Mold # in 200 and 300 series: Now attributed to Bahr & Proschild. **Child, open mouth:** Circa 1880s. Full cheeks, jointed composition body. Can be on French body. Prior to recent findings, these dolls were attributed to Kestner.

18" made by Bahr & Proschild. Has open/closed mouth with two molded teeth. Clothes maybe all original. Marked "BP" in heart. $695.00. *Courtesy Barbara Earnshaw-Cain.*

Mold #204, 224, 239, 246, 273, 274, 275, 277, 281, 286, 289, 293, 297, 309, 325, 332, 340, 379, 394, etc.: 1880s. Same as previous listing. **Five-piece body:** 8" - $350.00. **Fully jointed body:** 8" - $350.00. 10" - $500.00; 14" - $675.00; 17" - $750.00; 20" - $850.00; 23" - $1,000.00. **Kid bodies, open mouth:** 16" - $400.00; 18" - $550.00; 24" - $675.00.

Mold # in 200 or 300 series, closed mouth: Circa 1880. Same as above. **Dome head** or **"Belton type,"** socket head on composition or kid body with bisque shoulder plate. 13" - $1,500.00; 17" - $1,900.00; 22" - $2,450.00; 25" - $2,900.00.

Mold #224: Light cheek dimples. Open mouth, large glass eyes. Looks very much like Simon & Halbig. 15" - $850.00; 21" - $1,150.00.

Mold #360: Character face with "long" look, glass eyes, full cheeks. 21" - $1,200.00. **Open mouth:** 24" - $1,500.00.

Mold #2025: Painted eyes, closed mouth: 15" - $1,400.00. **Glass eyes:** 20" - $4,100.00.

Mold #2072, child: Closed mouth, glass eyes. (See photo in Series 10, pg. 29.) 16" - $2,600.00. **Toddler:** 20" - $4,100.00.

11½" "The Spearmint Kid with the Wrigley Eyes" has celluloid face mask and painted features. It is all felt except the lower torso which is a muslin type material on a piece of wood with a hole in the center. The legs and feet are also wooden. There is a coil spring in the body, and when pushed down, the doll whistled. Hands are sewn together and holding round name tag. In 1912, "The Spearmint Kid" appeared in *Playthings* magazine. In the same year, the figure was offered for 50¢ and three chewing gum pack wrappers. Baker & Bennett held the license and was the distributor. Doll was made by National Toy Mfg. Co. Only known price - $475.00. *Courtesy Carmen Holshoe.*

The wedding of Tom Thumb and Lavina Warren, promoted by P.T. Barnum in 1863, pushed the Civil War off the front pages by its uniqueness. Tom Thumb's real name was Charles Sherwood Stratton and he was known as the "General." Being the most famous midget in history, he made himself and P.T. Barnum rich. Barnum was only 32 years old when he discovered Tom Thumb, who in turn, was only five years old and weighed less than 16 pounds. Tom was born in Bridgeport, Connecticut, in January 1838, and weighed nine pounds, two ounces at birth. For awhile he continued to develop at a normal pace, weighing 15 pounds at five months, and measuring two feet, one inch tall. At this point, he apparently just stopped growing, but apart from his small size and weight, he was a normal child.

Tom Thumb, the two-foot midget, with bride

4½" "Lavina" and "Tom Thumb" French all bisque dolls with large early cobalt blue glass eyes, closed mouths, and swivel necks. Both have mohair wigs. Her hair goes to waist in back. Each hold a wedding candle wrapped in gold at hand level. They are all original and marked "4" on their backs. Each - $1,300.00. *Courtesy Carmen Holshoe.*

P.T. Barnum took the child and mother to New York, added six years to the child's age, and advertised him as being 11 years old. He feared some might take offense to a five-year old being shown to the public. "Little General Tom Thumb" was an instant hit with his charm, wit, and natural talent as a performer.

In 1862, Tom Thumb was 24 years old and had grown 10 inches and weighed 52 pounds. He had grown a mustache and obtained a mature look. It was then he met Lavina Warren, who was also working for Barnum. They were married February 10, 1863, in New York. By 1869, the couple had toured China, Egypt, Japan, Australia, as well as Europe. When they came home in 1872, they had traveled 56,000 miles and had given 1,471 performances. Memento dolls were sold for many years after the actual wedding.

BATHING DOLLS

Bathing dolls of the 1920s can be in any position, including standing on a base. They are all bisque and will have painted-on bathing costumes or be nude. They were made in Germany and some in the United States. Prices are for dolls with no damage, chips, or breaks. Must be clean.

Excellent quality bisque and artist workmanship, painted eyes: 3" - $250.00; 6" - $400.00; 9" - $525.00 up. **Glass eyes:** 5" - $400.00; 6" - $650.00. **Swivel neck:** 5" - $675.00; 6" - $725.00. **With animal:** 5½" - $1,500.00 up. **Two modeled together:** 4½–5½" - $1,600.00 up. **Holding one leg up:** 5" - $450.00 up. **Both arms raised in air:** 5" - $600.00 up. **Molded ballet slippers:** 7½" - $450.00 up. **Molded-on Grecian beaded swimsuit:** 6" - $900.00 up. **Mohair wig, knees crossed:** 7" - $600.00 up. **Sitting on boat:** 7½" - $950.00 up.

Marked Japan: Fair quality of bisque and workmanship. Some pebbling worn off. 3" - $75.00; 5–6" - $100.00; 9" - $175.00. **Unusual or with animal:** 4" - $250.00; 6" - $350.00.

Ederle, Gertrude: In diving pose. (See photo in Series 7, pg. 26.) 8" - $700.00; 13" - $1,450.00; 18" - $1,850.00.

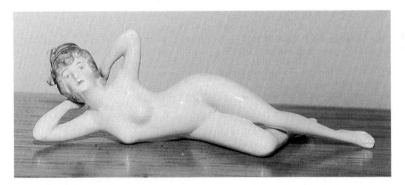

7" bathing beauty that was made in Germany. Her hands are behind her head but not touching the head. Molded hair with ribbon. An especially top quality bather. $475.00. *Courtesy Susan Girardot.*

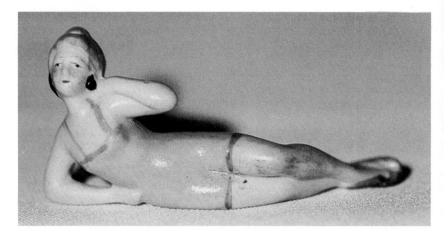

3½" bather dressed in matching swimsuit, slippers, and cap. Marked "Germany." $65.00.

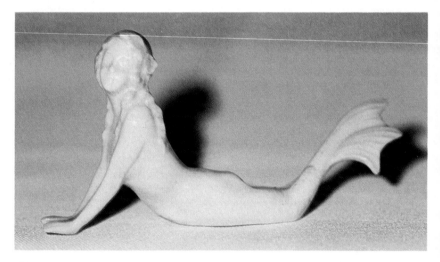

4¼" mermaid with pearl luster finish and a touch of paint on curly hair that is to the waist in back. Incised mark: Foreign. $125.00.

BELTON-TYPE

"Belton-type" dolls are not marked or will just have a number on the head. They have a concave top to a solid uncut head with one to three holes for stringing and/or plugging in wig. The German dome heads have a full round solid uncut head, but some of these may even have one or two holes in them. (See photo in Series 7, pg. 28.) This style doll was made from 1875 on, and most likely a vast amount of these dolls were actually German made, although they must be on a

14½" Belton-type with closed mouth and beautiful glass set eyes. On French jointed body. $1,900.00. *Courtesy Kathy Riddick.*

French body to qualify as a "Belton-type." Since these dolls are found on French bodies, it can be assumed the German heads were made for French firms.

Prices are for nicely dressed dolls with excellent quality bisque with **closed or open/closed mouths.** Bodies are French with straight wrists and no damage.

French style face, #124, 125, 136, 137, 191, etc.: Five-piece body: 8" - $750.00. **Jointed body:** 9" - $1,100.00; 13" - $1,850.00; 16" - $2,000.00; 18" - $2,700.00; 21" - $3,000.00; 24" - $3,400.00; 27" - $3,900.00 up.

Bru look: 17" - $2,700.00; 20" - $3,100.00.

German style face: 10" - $1,100.00; 12" - $1,250.00; 14" - $1,400.00; 16" - $1,600.00; 21" - $2,100.00; 25" - $2,500.00. **Five-piece body:** 8" - $800.00.

#200 and #300 series: See Bahr & Proschild section.

18" Belton-type with open/closed mouth and white space between. Has set glass eyes. On jointed French body with straight wrists. $2,700.00. *Courtesy Barbara Earnshaw-Cain.*

Charles M. Bergmann made dolls from 1889 at both Waltershausen and Friedrichroda, Germany. Many of the Bergmann heads were made for him by other companies, such as Simon & Halbig, Kestner, Armand Marseille, and others.

Marks:

C.M. BERGMANN

S. & H
C.M. BERGMANN
*Waltershausen
Germany*

Child: 1880s into early 1900s. On fully jointed composition bodies and open mouth. (Add $100.00 more for heads also marked S&H.) 9" - $300.00; 14" - $365.00; 18" - $445.00; 22" - $575.00; 28" - $800.00; 34" - $1,200.00; 42" - $1,950.00.
Elenore: Open mouth. Marked "CMB/SH." 18" - $700.00.
Character Baby: 1909 and after. Socket head on five-piece bent limb baby body. **Open mouth:** 10" - $325.00; 14" - $425.00; 18" - $575.00; 21" - $700.00.
Baby, mold #612: Open/closed mouth. 14" - $1,500.00; 18" - $2,100.00.
Lady doll: Adult-style body with long thin arms and legs. "Flapper-style" doll. 12" - $625.00; 16" - $850.00; 20"- $1,500.00.

23" C.M. Bergmann doll with open mouth, sleep eyes, and excellent bisque. On fully jointed body. Marked "S&H/C.M.B./9½." $575.00. *Courtesy Virginia Sofie.*

B.F.

The French dolls marked "B.F." were made by Ferte (Bébé Ferte.) Some collectors refer to them as Bébé Française by Jumeau. They are now being attributed to Danel & Cie who also used the Bébé Française trademark. They have closed mouths and jointed French bodies with most having straight wrists. (See photos in Series 4, pg. 28 and Series 10, pg. 32.)

Marks:

B 6 F

Child: 13" - $2,600.00; 16" - $3,000.00; 20" - $4,000.00; 24" - $4,800.00; 27" - $5,800.00.

Dolls marked "B.L." are referred to as "Bébé Louvre," but they most likely were made by Alexandre Lefebvre, who made dolls from 1890 and by 1922 was part of S.F.B.J. (See photo in Series 7, pg. 30; Series 8, pg. 31; Series 9, pg. 34; Series 10, pg. 33.) Allow more if all original. 12" - $2,400.00; 17" - $3,900.00; 20" - $4,300.00; 24" - $5,000.00; 26" - $5,400.00.

Very exceptional 18½" "Bébé Louve" with open/closed mouth with white space between lips. Has jointed body with Bebe Jumeau label. Original wig and clothes may be original. Marked "B. 7 L." Original and this quality - $4,600.00. *Courtesy Frasher Doll Auctions.*

BLACK OR BROWN DOLLS

Black or brown dolls can have fired-in color or be painted bisque, composition, cloth, papier maché, and other materials. They can range from very black to a light tan and also be a "dolly" face or have Black features.

The quality of these dolls varies greatly and prices are based on this quality. Both the French and Germans made these dolls. Prices are for undamaged, nicely dressed, and clean dolls.

Alabama: See Cloth Doll section.

All bisque: Glass eyes, one-piece body and head. 4–5" - $200.00–400.00 up.

All bisque: Glass eyes, swivel head. 5–6" - $300.00–500.00 up.

All bisque: Painted eyes, one-piece body and head. 5" - $200.00. **Swivel head:** 5" - $475.00. **French type:** 4" - $475.00 up.

All bisque marked with maker (S&H, JDK, etc.): 6½–7" - $1,200.00 up.

Armand Marseille (A.M.) #341 or 351: (See photo in Series 8, pg. 32.) 9" - $350.00; 14" - $575.00; 18" - $875.00; 21" - $1,200.00. **#362, 396, 513, 518:** 15" - $725.00; 20" - $925.00. **#390, 390n:** (See photo in Series 6, pg. 39.) 15" - $525.00; 18" - $750.00; 22" - $875.00; 29" - $1,200.00. **#451, 458 (Indians):** 9" - $325.00; 12" - $485.00. **#970, 971, 992, 995 (Baby or Toddler):** 10" - $275.00; 15" - $550.00; 19" - $900.00. **#1894, 1897, 1912, 1914:** 10" - $300.00; 15" - $575.00.

Baby Grumpy: Made by Effanbee. 10" - $265.00; 16" - $450.00. Craze, dirty: 10" - $95.00; 16" - $125.00.

Bahr & Proschild #277: Open mouth. 10" - $600.00; 15" - $1,500.00.

Bruckner: See Cloth section.

Belton-type: Closed mouth. 12" - $1,800.00; 15" - $2,700.00.

Bru Jne: 18" - $24,000.00 up; 22" - $33,000.00 up.

Bru (circle dot or Brevette): 15" - $23,000.00 up; 18" - $28,000.00 up.
Bubbles: Made by Effanbee. 17" - $425.00; 22" - $650.00. Craze, dirty: 17" - $100.00; 22" - $200.00.
Bye-Lo: 16" - $2,800.00 up.
Candy Kid: 12" - $285.00 up. Craze, dirty: 12" - $125.00.
Celluloid: All celluloid. (Add more for glass eyes.) 10" - $185.00 up; 16" - $365.00; 19" - $625.00. **Celluloid shoulder head, kid body:** (Add more for glass eyes.) 17" - $325.00; 21" - $450.00.

14" with ethnic features, open mouth, and original wig. On composition jointed body with straight wrists. Marked "Made in Germany 2." Shown with early Steiff Scottie made of black mohair. Has paper tag and ear button. Doll - $2,900.00 up. Dog - $1,200.00. *Courtesy Frasher Doll Auctions.*

Chase, Martha: 22" - $7,200.00; 26" - $9,000.00.
Cloth: See Cloth Doll section.
Composition: Made in Germany. Glass eyes, sometimes flirty. 12" - $325.00; 14" - $475.00; 18" - $700.00; 23" - $900.00 up.
E.D.: Open mouth: 15" - $2,100.00; 23" - $2,700.00.
F.G.: Open/closed mouth. 18" - $4,000.00. **Fashion:** Kid body, swivel neck. 13" - $2,200.00; 18" - $4,000.00 up.
Fashion: Swivel neck, articulated body, original. 15" - $12,500.00. **Shoulder head:** Original. 15" - $5,800.00. **Redressed:** 15" - $3,200.00.
French, unmarked or marked "DEP": (See photo in Series 7, pg. 33.) **Closed mouth, bisque head:** 13" - $1,900.00 up; 16" - $3,200.00; 21" - $4,400.00. **Closed mouth, painted bisque:** 15" - $975.00; 20" - $1,200.00. **Open mouth, bisque head:** (See photo in Series 7, pg. 33.) 10" - $600.00; 16" - $1,200.00; 21" - $2,100.00. **Open mouth, painted bisque:** 14" - $600.00; 19" - $900.00. **With Black features:** 18" - $4,600.00 up.
French marked "SNF": Celluloid. 15" - $325.00; 19" - $575.00.
Frozen Charlotte/Charlie: 3" - $125.00; 6" - $200.00; 9" - $325.00. **Jointed shoulder:** 3" - $185.00; 6" - $300.00.
German, unmarked: Open mouth, bisque head: 10" - $500.00; 13" - $650.00; 15" - $850.00. **Open mouth, painted bisque:** 14" - $300.00; 18" - $500.00. **Closed mouth, bisque head:** 10–11" - $300.00; 14" - $400.00; 17" - $525.00; 21" - $800.00. **Closed mouth, painted bisque:** 16" - $350.00; 19" - $500.00. **Black features:** 15" - $3,000.00; 18" - $3,800.00.
Hanna: Made by Schoenau & Hoffmeister. 10" - $275.00; 13" - $375.00; 16" - $585.00; 19" - $785.00.
Heinrich Handwerck: Open mouth. 17" - $825.00; 21" - $950.00; 24" - $1,350.00.
Heubach, Gebruder: Sunburst mark. **Boy:** Eyes to side, open/closed mouth. 13" - $2,700.00 up. **#7657, 7658,**

7668, 7671: 10" - $1,350.00; 12" - $1,900.00. **#7661, 7686:** 12" - $1,400.00; 15" - $2,700.00; 18" - $3,900.00.

Heubach Koppelsdorf, #320, 339 350: 9" - $385.00; 14" - $565.00; 19" - $725.00; 22" - $950.00 up. **#399:** Allow more for toddler. (See photo in Series 2, pg. 32; Series 5, pg. 28; Series 8, pg. 32.) 10" - $425.00; 15" - $600.00; 19" - $825.00. **Celluloid:** 14" - $300.00; 17" - $600.00. **#414:** 10" - $325.00; 15" - $650.00; 18" - $1,100.00. **#418 (grin):** 10" - $700.00; 15" - $950.00. **#444, 451:** 10" - $425.00; 15" - $725.00. **#452:** Brown. Can be Spanish, Gypsy, Moor, etc. 7½" - $375.00; 10" - $475.00; 15" - $675.00. **#458:** 10" - $465.00; 15" - $700.00. **#463:** 12" - $600.00; 16" - $950.00. **#1900:** 14" - $500.00; 17" - $600.00.

Kestner, J.D.: #134: 12" - $575.00; 16" - $875.00. **#237, 245 Hilda:** 14" - $3,400.00; 17" - $5,200.00; 20" - $6,200.00; 24" - $7,100.00.

Kestner, J.D.: Child, no mold number. **Open mouth:** 12" - $450.00; 16" - $650.00. **Closed mouth:** 14" - $625.00; 17" - $950.00. **Five-piece body:** 9" - $285.00; 12" - $350.00.

Jumeau: Tete Jumeau, open mouth: 10" - $2,200.00; 16" - $2,800.00; 19" - $3,100.00; 24" - $3,600.00. **Tete Jumeau, closed mouth:** (See photo in Series 10, pg. 37.) 16" - $4,800.00; 19" - $5,400.00; 24" - $6,300.00. **E.J:** Closed mouth. 15" - $7,200.00; 18" - $8,600.00; 21" - $9,000.00. **Character:** Very character face. All very rare. 20" - $90,000.00. **Jumeau type, open mouth:** (See photo in Series 2, pg. 48; Series 7, pg. 33.) 13" - $1,200.00; 16" - $2,200.00; 18" - $3,000.00. **Jumeau type, closed mouth:** 12" - $2,400.00; 16" - $3,600.00; 19" - $4,800.00.

Kammer & Reinhardt (K✿R): Child, no mold number. 8" - $465.00; 15" - $725.00; 18" - $900.00. **#100:** (See photo in Series 6, pg. 38.) 10" - $700.00; 14" - $1,100.00; 17" - $1,600.00; 19" - $1,900.00. **#101, painted eyes:** 16" - $2,400.00.

Left: 11" baby with sleep eyes, closed mouth, pierced ears. On five-piece maché body. Has original costume. Right: 7½" Swiss metal rabbit by Bucherer. Metal ball-jointed body with composition hands and feet. All original. Doll - $500.00. Rabbit - $345.00. *Courtesy Frasher Doll Auctions.*

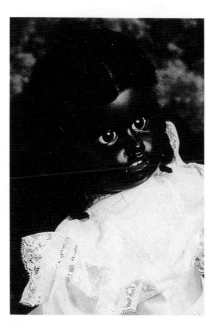

20" Gebruder Kuhnlenz doll with ethnic features and sleep eyes. Has open mouth with full lips and four teeth. On French jointed body with original wig. Marked "34-28." $6,500.00. *Courtesy Frasher Doll Auctions.*

#101, glass eyes: 18" - $5,200.00. **#114:** (See photo in Series 7, pg. 35.) 14" - $4,500.00. **#116, 116a:** 16" - $3,300.00; 20" - $3,900.00. **#126 baby:** (See photo in Series 5, pg. 28.) 9" - $525.00, 16" - $1,000.00. **#126 toddler:** 18" - $1,600.00.

Kewpie ("Hottentot"), bisque: 4" - $400.00; 5" - $565.00; 9" - $985.00. **Papier maché:** 8" - $265.00. **Composition:** 12" - $400.00; 15" - $725.00.

Konig & Wernicke (KW/G): 17" - $700.00. **Black features:** 17" - $1,000.00.

Kühnlenz, Gebruder, mold #34-17, 34-28, 44-16, etc.: Dolly face. (See photo in Series 10, pg. 38.) **Open mouth:** 12" - $550.00; 16" - $675.00. **Closed mouth:** 15" - $900.00; 18" - $1,800.00. **Black features:** 16" - $4,000.00 up; 20" - $6,500.00 up.

19" with painted bisque head and papier maché/composition body. Has flirty sleep eyes and open mouth. Marked "K&W" on head. $425.00. *Courtesy Frasher Doll Auctions.*

Moss, Leo: Papier maché head and lower limbs. Molded hair or wig. Inset glass eyes. Closed mouth, full lips, brown twill body. Excelsior filled. With or without tear on cheek. 1920s. 21" - $7,000.00; 26" - $7,900.00.

Papier maché: Black features. (See photo in Series 9, pg. 39.) 8" - $275.00; 13" - $525.00; 17" - $825.00. **Others:** 15" - $325.00; 22" - $685.00.

Paris Bébé: (See photo in Series 10, pg. 36.) 15" - $4,200.00; 18" - $5,300.00.

Parson-Jackson, baby: 14" - $475.00. **Toddler:** 15" - $600.00.

Recknagel: Marked "R.A." May have mold **#138.** 17" - $825.00; 23" - $1,500.00.

Sarg, Tony: Mammy doll. Composition/cloth. (See photo in Series 8, pg. 36.) 18" - $600.00 up.

Schoenau & Hoffmeister, #1909: (See photo in Series 5, pg. 29.) 16" - $525.00; 19" - $700.00.

Scowling Indian: (See photo in Series 6, pg. 41.) **Medium to poor quality:** 10" - $265.00; 13" - $375.00. **Excellent quality:** Probably by Simon and Halbig. (See photo in Series 11, pg. 33.) 15" - $1,350.00; 21" - $2,800.00.

Scootles, composition: 15" - $700.00 up. **Vinyl:** 14" - $265.00; 19" - $500.00; 27" - $625.00 up.

Simon & Halbig, #639: 14" - $6,800.00; 18" - $10,000.00. **#729, open mouth:** Smiling. 16" - $3,700.00 up. **#739, closed mouth:** (See photo in Series 6, pg. 38.) 16" - $2,500.00; 21" - $3,600.00. **#939, closed mouth:** (See photo in Series 5, pg. 28.) 19" - $3,400.00; 22" - $4,500.00. **#939, open mouth:** (See photo in Series 7, pg. 34.) 16" - $1,300.00; 22" - $2,200.00. **#949, closed mouth:** 17" - $3,200.00; 20" - $3,900.00. **#949, open mouth:** 17" - $1,600.00; 26" - $3,200.00. **Kid body:** 18" - $1,300.00; 21" - $1,750.00; 27" - $2,100.00. **#969, open mouth:** Puffed cheeks. (See photo in Series 10, pg. 37.) 17" - $1,800.00. **#1009, 1039, 1079:** (See photo in Series 8, pg. 35.) **Open mouth:** 12" - 1,200.00;

15" - $1,500.00; 18" - $1,800.00. **Pull string, sleep eyes:** 19" - $2,300.00. **#1248, open mouth:** 14" - $775.00; 17" - $1,000.00. **#1302, closed mouth:** Glass eyes, very character face. **Black:** 18" - $7,000.00. **Indian:** Sad expression. 18" - $7,400.00. **#1303 Indian:** Man or woman. Thin face. 16" - $6,900.00; 21" - $7,000.00. **#1339, 1358, 1368:** (See photo in Series 11, pg. 34.) 15" - $5,700.00; 19" - $7,200.00. **#1368:** (See photo in Series 6, pg. 37.) 14" - $3,700.00; 18" - $6,200.00; 22" - $6,800.00. **S.F.B.J., #226:** 17" - $3,100.00. **#301 or 60, open mouth:** 12" - $500.00; 16" - $650.00. **#301 or 60, closed mouth:** 12" - $675.00; 15" - $1,200.00. **#235, open/ closed mouth:** 16" - $2,800.00; 18" - $3,100.00. **#34.29, open mouth:** 17" - $4,700.00; 23" - $5,500.00.

S.P. mark: Toddler, glass eyes, open mouth: 15" - $585.00.

Steiner, Jules, "A" series: Open mouth: 12" - $3,800.00; 15" - $4,600.00; 18" - $5,200.00. **Closed mouth:** 17" - $5,800.00; 20" - $6,400.00. **"C" series:** 17" - $5,900.00; 20" - $6,200.00.

Stockinette: Oil-painted features. Excellent condition. 18" - $2,750.00; 20" - $3,000.00.

S & Q (Schuetzmeister & Quendt) #251, 252: Baby: 10" - $625.00; 16" - $2,000.00. **Child:** 19" - $2,400.00.

UNIS, #301 or 60: Open mouth. 14" - $450.00; 17" - $785.00.

12" closed mouth S.F.B.J. #301 has brown slim body and limbs without the extra joints at elbows and knees. $675.00. *Courtesy Kathy Riddick.*

BONNET DOLLS

Bonnet dolls date from the 1880s to the 1920s. They can be all bisque or have cloth or kid bodies. The lower limbs can be china, leather, or stone bisque. Most were made in Germany, but some were made in Japan. Also see under Goebel, Googly, and Recknagel sections.

All bisque: One-piece body and head, painted or glass eyes. Germany. 5" - $175.00; 7" - $235.00; 8" - $285.00; 10" - $375.00. **With swivel neck, glass eyes:** Germany. 5" - $325.00; 7" - $400.00 up.

Bisque head: Excellent bisque. Glass eyes, hat or bonnet, molded hair.

Five-piece papier maché, kid, or cloth body: 7" - $185.00; 9" - $300.00; 12" - $425.00; 15" - $650.00; 18" - $1,000.00; 21" - $1,250.00. **Fully jointed composition or kid or cloth body with bisque lower arms:** 8" - $225.00; 10" - $365.00; 12" - $485.00; 15" - $725.00; 21" - $1,200.00. **Molded shirt or top:** 14" - $825.00; 19" - $1,350.00.

Stone bisque: (See photo in Series 10, pg. 38.) 9" - $150.00; 12" - $185.00; 14" - $325.00; 17" - $550.00; 20" - $775.00.

Googly: See that section.
Japan: 8–9" - $75.00; 12" - $125.00.

19" bisque shoulderhead doll with modeled fur trimmed hat and blonde curls. Has modeled decorated shoulderplate and cloth body with leather arms. This particular size and model is rare. $1,350.00. *Courtesy Frasher Doll Auctions.*

BONNIE BABE

The "Bonnie Babe" was designed by Georgene Averill in 1926 with the bisque heads being made by Alt, Beck & Gottschalck and the cloth bodies made by the K & K Toy Co. (NY). The dolls were distributed by George Borgfeldt. The doll can have cloth body and legs or composition arms and legs with cloth body.

Marks: "Copr. by Georgene Averill/ Germany/1005/3652" and sometimes "1368."

All bisque: See the All Bisque section.

Bisque head: Crooked smile, open mouth. 12" - $425.00; 15" - $850.00; 18" - $1,050.00; 22" - $1,450.00; 24" - $1,650.00; 26" - $1,850.00.

Celluloid head: 10" - $385.00; 16" - $695.00.

Composition body: Bisque socket head. 12" - $1,150.00; 16" - $1,400.00.

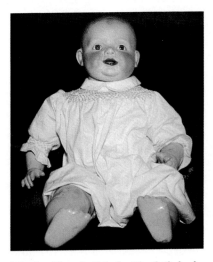

Life-size "Bonnie Babe" with cloth body, composition limbs, bisque head, and sleep eyes. Has open, lop-sided smiling mouth with two upper and two lower teeth. $1,850.00 up. *Courtesy Jeannie Mauldin.*

George Borgfeldt imported, assembled, and distributed dolls in New York. The dolls that he carried or had made ranged from bisque to composition. Many dolls were made for him in Germany. Many heads were made for this firm by Armand Marseille.

Marks:

G.B.

Child, mold #325, 327, 329, or marked "G.B.": 1910–1922. Fully jointed composition body, open mouth. No damage and nicely dressed. 12" - $285.00; 15" - $365.00; 17" - $475.00; 20" - $585.00; 22" - $625.00; 25" - $725.00 up.

Baby: 1910. Five-piece bent limb baby body, open mouth. 9" - $225.00; 15" - $450.00; 18" - $600.00; 20" - $685.00; 26" - $1,000.00 up.

Babykins: Made for G. Borgfeldt by Grace S. Putnam. Round face, glass eyes, and pursed lips. 1931. 13" - $900.00 up; 16" - $1,350.00 up.

24" George Borgfeldt doll with sleep eyes and open mouth. On fully jointed body. Has original wig, shoes, and dimity white dress. Coat and bonnet may be original. $650.00. *Courtesy Jeannie Nespoli.*

BOUDOIR DOLLS

Boudoir dolls are also called "flapper" dolls and were most popular during the 1920s and early 1930s, although they were made through the 1940s. Very rarely is one of these dolls marked with the maker or country of origin, but the majority were made in the United States, France, and Italy.

The most desirable boudoir dolls are the ones from France and Italy. (Lenci, especially. See that section.) These dolls will have a silk or velvet painted face mask, an elaborate costume, and be of excellent quality.

The least expensive ones have a full or half-composition head, some with glass eyes, and the clothes will be stapled or glued to the body. Boudoir dolls, except for Lenci, are not usually found with ears or earrings. If the doll does have earrings, they will be attached to a wig or directly to the head.

McCall patterns were available for dressing these dolls.

Boudoir dolls: Finely oil-painted features, excellent clothes. **Excellent quality:** 15" - $300.00 up; 28" - $475.00 up; 32" - $500.00 up. **Average quality:** 16" - $125.00; 28" - $165.00; 32" - $225.00. **Undressed:** 28–32" - $65.00 up. **With glass eyes:** 28–32" - $585.00 up. **Miniature:** 15" - $300.00 up.

Boudoir dolls: With composition head, stapled or glued-on clothes. No damage, and original clothes. 15" - $85.00; 28" - $145.00; 32" - $175.00.

Lenci: See that section.

Smoking doll: (See photo in Series 3, pg. 46; Series 5, pg. 32.) **Cloth:** 16–17" - $285.00 up; 25" - $465.00 up. **Composition:** 25" - $245.00 up; 28" - $375.00 up.

Printed-on clothes: 27" - $350.00 up. **Harem girl:** Has turban with spit curls around face. From lower torso to ankles, wears wide stuffed harem pants of colored material. 27" - $600.00 up. **Turkish, East Indian, Arabian:** 27" - $500.00 up.

26" "Coco Channel" with composition head and limbs and cloth body. Original. Coco Channel was the first popular, high-profile designer. She wore a slack suit in public, making it a "fad" during the 1920s. $350.00 up. *Courtesy Bonnie Stewart.*

38" 18th century Venetian lady dressed for Carnival. Missing black silk eye mask and diamond-shaped wide brimmed hat with large rose-colored flower in front. Made in France in 1924. $500.00 up.

Bru dolls will be marked with the name Bru or Bru Jne, Bru Jne R. Some will have a circle and dot or a half circle and dot. Some have paper labels – see marks. Prices are for dolls with no damage at all, very clean, and beautifully dressed. Add $2,000.00 up for all original clothes and marked shoes.

Marks:

Closed mouth, all kid body: Bisque lower arms. 15" - $8,500.00; 17" - $12,500.00; 23" - $23,500.00; 25" - $26,500.00.

Bru Jne: Ca. 1880s. Kid over wood, wood legs, bisque lower arms. 12" - $17,000.00; 14" - $13,500.00; 17" - $17,500.00; 20" - $21,500.00; 23" - $25,500.00; 27" - $31,500.00; 32" - $35,500.00. **All wood body:** 18" - $13,000.00; 21" - $19,000.00. **Key wound music box:** 16½" - $22,000.00.

Circle dot or half circle: Circa 1870s. Open/closed mouth, very slightly parted lips with molded or painted teeth. Kid body, bisque lower arms. 13" - $14,500.00; 15" - $17,500.00; 19" - $21,500.00; 24" - $25,000.00; 27" - $28,000.00; 30" - $34,000.00. **Key wound music box:** 16½" - $20,000.00.

Breveté: Circa 1870s. Swivel head, closed mouth with space between lips, full cheeks. Kid body, bisque lower arms. Sticker or stamp on body, size number on head. 13" - $15,000.00; 18" - $18,500.00; 22" - $23,000.00.

17" early Bru with all kid body and bisque lower arms. Has open/closed mouth with molded tongue. All original except wig. Marked with the full circle and dot. $18,500.00.

Bru Jne R., closed mouth: 18" - $9,000.00; 22" - $9,200.00.

Bru Jne R., open mouth: 1890s. Jointed composition body. First price for excellent quality bisque and second for poor quality bisque, poor artist workmanship, or high color. 12" - $2,300.00, $1,400.00; 14" - $6,800.00, $3,800.00; 16" - $7,500.00, $4,400.00; 19" - $8,000.00, $5,400.00; 23" - $8,800.00, $6,000.00.

Walker body: Throws kiss. 17" - $6,800.00; 21" - $7,400.00; 25" - $8,200.00.

Nursing Bru: 1878–1899. Operates by turning key in back of head. **Early, excellent quality:** 14" - $7,000.00 up; 17" - $9,200.00; 20" - $9,600.00. **Fair quality:** 15" - $5,800.00; 18" - $6,400.00. **High color, late S.F.B.J. type:** 15" - $4,500.00; 18" - $5,800.00.

Breathing, crying, kissing: (See photo in Series 7, pg. 41.) 19" - $15,000.00; 24" - $17,000.00.

Head of rubber/gutta percha: Original. Bru Jne R face, jointed body. Marked "Gomme Durée." 17" - $9,800.00. Redressed: $8,200.00.

Bru marked shoes: Size #1 to 4 (for 12–16" dolls) $600.00–800.00. Size #5 to 10 (for 17–25" dolls) $500.00–600.00. Size #11 to 12 (for 26–30" dolls) $800.00–1,000.00.

Right: 16" nursing Bru with open mouth, kid body, kid over wood upper arms, bisque lower arms, and wood lower legs. Metal wing screw in back of head activates the rubber ball in head and allows the doll to "nurse." Marked "Bru Jne 6" on head and shoulderplate and has Bru paper lable on torso. Left: 15½" Jumeau with closed mouth and original shoes. Marked "E. 6 J." Bru - $9,200.00. Jumeau - $6,200.00. *Courtesy Frasher Doll Auctions.*

17½" Bru Jne 7 has open/closed mouth with white space between lips. Marked on head and body. A very pretty example of a Bru Jne. $17,500.00. *Courtesy Frasher Doll Auctions.*

36" Bru Jne R 16 with deep shoulder-plate, modeled breast, and old mohair wig. Has bisque lower arms, jointed at elbows, and kid over wooden upper arms. Upper legs are kid over wood, and lower wooden legs are jointed at knees. Note beautiful toe detail. $12,000.00 up. *Courtesy Turn of Century Antiques.*

BYE-LO

The Bye-Lo baby was designed by Grace Storey Putnam, distributed by George Borgfeldt, and the cloth bodies were made by K & K Toy Co. of New York. Bisque heads were made by Kestner, Alt, Beck & Gottschalck and others. All bisque dolls were made by Kestner. The dolls date from 1922. Most dolls have celluloid or composition hands. Prices are for undamaged, clean and nicely dressed dolls.

Bisque head: Allow more for original clothes and pin. 8" - $450.00; 10" - $485.00; 12"- $525.00; 15" - $785.00; 17" - $1,150.00. **Black:** 16" - $2,800.00 up.

Mold #1415, smiling mouth: Very rare bisque with painted eyes. 14" - $5,000.00 up. **Composition head:** 14–15" - $900.00 up.

Marks:

1923 by
Grace S. Putnam
Made in Germany
7372145

Copy. By
Grace S. Putnam

Bye-Lo Baby
Pat. Appl'd For

Socket head: Bisque head on five-piece bent limb baby body. 14" - $1,400.00; 17" - $1,700.00.

Composition head: 1924. Must be in excellent condition and have good face color. 10" - $325.00; 14" - $450.00; 16" - $575.00.

Painted bisque: With cloth body, composition hands. 10" - $225.00; 14" - $400.00; 16" - $525.00.

Schoenhut, wood: 1925. Cloth body, wooden hands. 15" - $1,850.00 up.

All celluloid: 6" - $185.00. **Celluloid head/cloth body:** 12" - $350.00; 15" - $465.00.

All bisque: See All Bisque section, Characters.

Vinyl heads: Early 1950s. Cloth/stuffed limbs. Marked "Grace Storey Putnam" on head. 16" - $225.00.

Left: 14" "Bye-Lo" with bisque head, cloth body, and celluloid hands. Right: 16" "Bye-Lo" with composition head and very swollen "newborn" features that are more modeled than on the bisque version. Has never been played with and is all original with tagged baby blanket. Both dolls have brown eyes. 14" - $675.00. 16" (this condition) - $650.00. *Courtesy Turn of Century Antiques.*

Honey Child: Bye-Lo look-alike made by Bayless Bros. & Co. in 1926. 16" - $325.00; 20" - $465.00.

Wax Bye-lo: Cloth or sateen body. 16" - $2,200.00 up.

Basket with blanket and extra clothes: Five babies in basket, bisque heads: 12" - $4,400.00 up. Composition heads: 12" - $2,700.00 up.

Mold #1418, Fly-Lo Baby (Baby Aero): Bisque head, cloth body, celluloid hands, glass eyes. Closed mouth, deeply molded hair. Very rare. (See photo in Series 10, pg. 45.) 10" - $3,800.00; 13" - $5,000.00; 16" - $5,600.00. Composition head: 14" - $900.00 up.

5" all bisque "Bye-Lo" with sleep eyes and spray painted hair. Jointed at neck, shoulders, and hips. Original label on torso. $600.00 up. *Courtesy Ellen Dodge.*

17" "Peter Rabbit" was the subject of a comic strip by Harrison Cady. He was the illustrator for many authors as well as his own books. Rabbit has composition head and ears and straw stuffed body and limbs. Body is pin-jointed. Painted features with side glancing eyes. Professionally re-dressed to be an exact copy of original outfit. Dates from 1915. $600.00. *Courtesy Marianne's.*

CARTOON

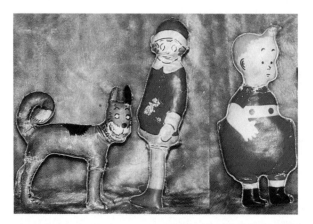

12" "Orphan Annie" and "Sandy" made of one-piece oilcloth. Dolls designed by Eileen Benoliel in 1929 from cartoon drawn by Harold Grey. Made by Live Long Toys. 14" "Skeezic" is also made of oilcloth and was first made in 1922. Cartoon drawn by Frank King. Trixy Toys made by Durrel Co. "Annie/Sandy" - $295.00 up for pair. "Skeezic" - $135.00 up. *Courtesy Susan Girardot.*

Catterfelder Puppenfabrik of Germany made dolls from 1902 until the late 1930s. The heads for their dolls were made by various German firms, including Kestner.

Marks:

26½" with open mouth and sleep eyes. On fully jointed body. Marked "C.P. 61 Germany." $900.00. *Courtesy Frasher Doll Auctions.*

Child: Ca. 1900s. Composition jointed body. Open mouth. **Mold #264:** Or marked "C.P." 17" - $625.00; 22" - $785.00; 34" - $1,800.00.

Character child: 1910 or after. Composition jointed body, closed mouth, and painted eyes. Can be boy or girl with character face. **Mold #207:** (See photo in Series 9, pg. 48.) 16" - $5,600.00; 20" - $7,000.00. **Mold #212:** Rare. Laughing wide open/closed mouth, painted teeth and eyes. 16" - $8,600.00. **Mold #215**: 16" - $4,900.00; 20" - $5,300.00. **Mold #217:** Rare. 24" - $9,300.00. **Mold #219:** 16" - $3,850.00; 20" - $4,600.00. **Glass eyes:** 22" - $6,300.00. **Mold #220: Glass eyes.** 17" - $7,300.00.

Babies: 1909 or after. Wig or molded hair, five-piece bent limb baby body, glass or painted eyes. Add more for toddler body.

Mold #200, 201, 207, 208, 209, 262, 263, 264: (See photo of #208 in Series 5, pg. 37.) 14" - $485.00; 16" - $600.00; 20" - $775.00; 23" - $985.00; 26" - $1,200.00.

CELLULOID DOLLS

Celluloid dolls date from the 1880s into the 1940s when they were made illegal in the United States because they burned or exploded if placed near an open flame or heat. Some of the makers were:

United States: Marks Bros., Irwin, Horsman, Averill, Parsons-Jackson, Celluloid Novelty Co.

France: Societe Industrielle de Celluloid (Sisoine), Petitcollin (eagle symbol), Societe Nobel Française (SNF in diamond), Jumeau/Unis (1950s), Neumann & Marx (dragon symbol).

Germany: Rheinische Gummi und Celluloid Fabrik Co. (turtle mark), Minerva (Buschow & Beck) (helmet symbol), E. Maar & Sohn (3 M's mark), Adelheid Nogler Innsbruck Doll Co. (animal with spread wings and a fish tail, in square), Cellba (mermaid symbol).

Poland: P.R. Zask ("ASK" in triangle).
England: Cascelloid Ltd. (Palitoy).

Prices for perfect, undamaged dolls.

All celluloid baby: 1910 on. **Painted eyes:** 8" - $75.00; 12" - $125.00; 14" - $175.00; 16" - $185.00; 19–20" - $300.00; 24" - $350.00; 26" - $450.00. **Glass inset eyes:** 14" - $200.00; 16" - $265.00; 20" - $425.00; 24" - $485.00. **Bye-Lo:** See that section.

All celluloid child dolls, painted eyes: Made in Germany. Jointed at neck, shoulders and hips. 6" - $45.00; 8" - $70.00; 12" - $125.00; 15" - $200.00; 18" - $375.00 up. **Jointed at neck and shoulders only:** 5" - $25.00; 7" - $45.00; 10" - $85.00. **Glass eyes:** 13" - $165.00; 15" - $225.00; 18" - $425.00. **Marked "France":** 8" - $150.00; 10" - $200.00; 16" - $300.00; 19" - $550.00 up.

All celluloid with molded-on clothes: Jointed at shoulders only. (See photo in Series 9, pg. 49.) 4" - $55.00; 6" - $70.00; 9" - $125.00.

All celluloid immobilies: No joints. 4" - $20.00; 6" - $35.00.

All celluloid Black dolls: See Black or Brown dolls section.

Carnival Dolls: Feathers glued to body and/or head. Some with top hats. (See photo in Series 7, pg. 45.) 7–8" - $40.00; 12" - $80.00; 17" - $175.00 up.

3" all celluloid "Happy Holligan," the comic character drawn by F. Opper. This rare figure has modeled cane and top hat with painted features. Was also made in felt with cloth clothes. Made in Germany and sold through George Borgfeldt, 1923–1927. $185.00 up. *Courtesy Shirley's Doll House.*

14" all celluloid baby with inset glass eyes has open mouth with tremble tongue and two upper teeth. On five-piece body. Head marked with helmet and "Minerva/Germany/5." Body marked "Minerva"/helmet mark/"80/Germany." $175.00.

Celluloid shoulder head: 1900–1912. Germany. Molded hair or wigged. Painted eyes, open or closed mouth. Kid, kidaleen, or cloth bodies. Can have any material for arms. 14" - $170.00 up; 17" - $225.00 up; 19" - $375.00. **Glass eyes:** 14" - $200.00; 16" - $325.00; 19" - $450.00; 23" - $500.00.

17" all celluloid with mohair wig, flirty glass eyes, and open mouth with two upper teeth. On unusual all celluloid toddler body. All original including glass beaded necklace. Marked "K✿R/728/0 Germany/ 25-27." This example - $850.00.
Courtesy Susan Girardot.

Celluloid socket heads: Made in Germany. Glass eyes. (Allow more for flirty eyes). Ball-jointed body or five-piece bodies. Open or closed mouths. 14" - $300.00; 18" - $425.00; 20" - $500.00; 25" - $700.00.

Celluloid/Plush: Early 1910s. Teddy bear body. Can have half or full celluloid body with hood half head. 12" - $650.00; 14" - $785.00; 17" - $925.00.

Bye-Lo: 4–4½" - $165.00; 6" - $200.00.

Jumeau: Marked on head, jointed body. (See photo in Series 4, pg. 41.) 12" - $450.00; 15" - $525.00.

Heubach Koppelsdorf, mold #399 (brown or black): See Black or Brown Dolls section.

Hitler youth group: (See photo in Series 5, pg. 39; Series 6, pg 53.) 8–9" - $175.00.

Kruse, Käthe: All original. 14" - $475.00; 17" - $675.00.

Kammer & Reinhardt (K✿R), mold #406, 700: Child or baby. (See photo in Series 4, pg. 40.) 14"- $475.00. **#701:** 14" - $950.00. **#714 or 715:** 15" - $685.00. **#717:** 15" - $475.00; 22" - $700.00. **#728, 828:** 16" - $500.00; 20" - $700.00. Toddler: 15" - $650.00. **All celluloid toddler body:** 15" - $725.00. **#826, 828, 406, 321, 255, 225: Baby:** 12" - $185.00; 14" - $365.00; 17" - $475.00; 20" - $600.00. **Child:** 14" - $350.00; 16" - $550.00; 20" - $650.00; 23" - $750.00.

Kewpie: See that section.

Konig & Wernicke (K&W), toddler: 15" - $325.00; 19" - $500.00.

Japan: 4" - $15.00; 7" - $30.00; 10" - $45.00; 14" - $100.00; 17" - $225.00; 19" - $350.00; 22" - $425.00.

Max and Moritz: 7", each - $300.00 up.

Parsons-Jackson: (See photo in Series 7, pg. 44.) **Baby:** 12" - $200.00; 14" - $285.00. **Toddler:** 15" - $385.00. **Black:** 14" - $485.00.

The Century Doll Company operated in New York City and used bisque heads made by Kestner. A marked Century infant can have a mold number 277 and were made from 1925 on. There are two infants that can be found — one with a frowning scowl and another with a smiling face.

Cloth body, closed mouth: Scowl: 14" - $650.00; 20" - $875.00. Smile: 14" - $750.00; 20" - $950.00.

Composition shoulder head doll: "Mama" style of the 1920s. Tin sleep eyes, open mouth. 16" - $245.00; 23" - $465.00.

20" character with scowling/frowning face. Has full closed mouth, sleep eyes, cloth body, and composition limbs. Made by Kestner for Century. Marked "Century Doll Co./Kestner Germany. $875.00.

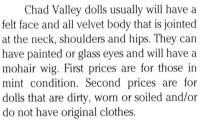

Chad Valley dolls usually will have a felt face and all velvet body that is jointed at the neck, shoulders and hips. They can have painted or glass eyes and will have a mohair wig. First prices are for those in mint condition. Second prices are for dolls that are dirty, worn or soiled and/or do not have original clothes.

Marks: "Hygienic Toys/Made in England by/Chad Valley Co. Ltd."

"The Chad Valley Hygienic Textile/ Toys/Made in England."

Child with painted eyes: 12" - $200.00, $60.00; 15" - $400.00, $100.00; 19" - $625.00, $225.00.

Child with glass eyes: 15" -$600.00, $165.00; 17" - $700.00, $200.00; 19" - $750.00, $300.00.

Child representing Royal Family: Four in set: **Princess Elizabeth, Princess Margaret Rose, Prince Edward, Princess Alexandra.** All four have glass eyes. (See photos in Series 5, pgs. 39–40; Series 10, pg. 50.) **Prince Edward as Duke of Kent:** (See photo in Series 11, pg. 45.) 15" - $1,500.00, $600.00; 18" - $1,800.00, $700.00. **As Duke of Windsor:** 15" - $1,500.00, $600.00; 18" - $1,800.00, $700.00. **Others:** 15" - $1,400.00 up, $500.00; 17" - $1,500.00 up, $500.00.

Characters (Long John Silver, Captain Bly, Train Conductor, Policeman, Pirate, Fisherman, etc.): Glass eyes: (See photo in Series 6, pg. 56.) 18" - $965.00 up, $300.00; 20" - $1,150.00 up. **Painted eyes:** 18" - $750.00; 20" - $850.00.

Storybook Dolls: Snow White: 17" - $950.00. **Dwarfs:** 9½" - $650.00 each. **Red Riding Hood:** 14" - $475.00. **Ding Dong Dell:** 14" - $450.00. **My Elizabeth, My Friend:** 14" - $650.00.

Ghandi/India: 13" - $650.00 up, $175.00. **Rahma-Jah:** (See photo in Series 9, pg. 53.) 26" - $875.00.

Golliwog: Disc eyes: 1920s–1930s. 13" - $500.00. **Post eyes:** World War II era. 1940s to 1950s. 10" - $150.00; 15" - $275.00.

Animals: Cat: 12" plush - $200.00 up; 6" cloth - $95.00 up. **Dog:** 12" plush - $250.00 up. **Bonzo:** Cloth dog with painted eyes almost closed and smile. 4" - $200.00; 13" - $400.00. Eyes open: 5½" - $265.00; 14" - $565.00.

Cute 10" Golliwog with clothes made as part of the body. Felt buttons and features. Mohair hair. Tagged: "Chad Valley. Made in England." $325.00. *Courtesy Ellen Dodge.*

17" "Bobby" (policeman) made of all felt with mohair wig and glass eyes. Original with suspender style pants with jacket and white gloves tucked in jacket front. Label on jacket: "Made in England." Label on bottom of foot: "The Chad Valley Ltd."/ English crown with lions/"By Appointment/Toymakers to H.M. the Queen." $950.00. *Courtesy Carmen Holshoe.*

10" tall chalk figure called "Miss Easy Street." Came with tag stating "Here I sit with time to think — should I buy a Silver Royce or a Golden Mink?" Dated 1930s and made by Jones-Moran Doll Mfg. Co. This company supplied novelty shops in Atlantic City and Coney Island and other large amusement areas/parks. $145.00. *Courtesy Diane Kornhauser.*

Lamp figure "Atlantic City Belle" was also sold separately. Made of chalk and painted with oil paints. If marked, it will read "A.T. Mfg. Co. for Atlantic Toy Mfg. Co. of New York." They made regular dolls and many of the souvenirs for Coney Island and Atlantic City. Figure - $85.00. As lamp - $125.00. *Courtesy Cindy Slator.*

Martha Jenks Chase of Pawtucket, Rhode Island, began making dolls in 1893, and they are still being made by members of the family. They all have oil-painted features and are made of stockinette and cloth. They will be marked "Chase Stockinette" on left leg or under the left arm. There is a paper label (often gone) on the backs with a drawn head, shown here. The words "Stockinette Doll" may also appear on brim of hat.

Mark:

The older Chase dolls are jointed at the shoulders, hips, knees, and elbows. Newer dolls are jointed at the shoulders and hips with straight arms and legs. Some after 1920 have sateen bodies. Prices are for very clean dolls with only minor wear.

OLDER DOLLS:

Babies: 16" - $575.00; 17" - $700.00; 22" - $825.00. Hospital used: 24" - $425.00; 29" - $575.00.

Child: Molded bobbed hair. 14" - $1,200.00; 16" - $1,350.00; 22" - $1,800.00; 23" - $2,300.00. **Solid dome, painted hair:** 15" - $485.00; 18" - $625.00; 22" - $725.00; 25" - $825.00. **Rare hairdo:** Such as molded oil-painted hair pulled back into bun, two sausage curls around face. 16" - $9,500.00 up.

Lady: 16" - $1,600.00; 19" - $1,850.00; 24" - $2,300.00. Life size, hospital used: $1,600.00.

Man: 15" - $2,000.00; 20" - $2,200.00. Life size: $1,800.00.

Black: 24" - $7,400.00 up; 26" - $9,200.00 up.

Alice In Wonderland: 15" - $1,700.00.

Frog Footman: 15" - $1,900.00 up.
Mad Hatter: 15" - $2,000.00 up.
Duchess: 15" - $2,000.00 up.
Tweedledum: 15" - $2,200.00 up.
George Washington: (See photo in Series 10, pg. 52.) Mint: 26" - $4,500.00 up. Played with: $1,800.00.
Chase Type: Child. 15" - $950.00 up; 18" - $1,500.00 up.

NEWER DOLLS:

Babies: 14" - $200.00; 16" - $275.00; 20" - $425.00.

Child, boy or girl: 14" - $265.00; 16" - $365.00.

20" Martha Chase with bobbed hair. Head made of oil-painted pressed stockinette. Oil-painted cloth body has stitched joints at shoulders and hips. $1,600.00. *Courtesy Frasher Doll Auctions.*

Almost all china heads were made in Germany between 1840 and the 1900s. Most have black hair, but blondes became popular by the 1880s. By 1900, one out of every three dolls was blonde. China dolls can be on a cloth or kid body with leather or china limbs. Generally, these heads are unmarked, but a few will have a number and/or "Germany" on the back shoulder plate. Prices are for clean dolls with no cracks, chips, or repairs on a nice body and nicely dressed. Also see Huret/Rohmer under "Fashions" and Alt, Beck & Gottschalck.

Alice In Wonderland: Snood, head band. (See photo in Series 1, pg. 75.) 13" - $225.00; 15" - $375.00; 19" - $650.00. **With flange neck:** Motschmann style body. 10" - $1,400.00; 13" - $2,200.00; 15" - $2,400.00.

Alice In Wonderland

Adelina Patti: 1860s. Center part, roll curl from forehead to back on each side of head and "spit" curls at temples and above exposed ears. 15" - $275.00; 19" - $475.00; 23" - $525.00.

Adelina Patti

Bald Head/Biedermeir: Ca. 1840. Has bald head, some with top of head glazed black, takes wigs. (See photo in Series 7, pg. 48.) **Excellent quality:** 13" - $600.00; 15" - $850.00; 17" - $1,000.00. **Medium quality:** 13" - $225.00; 15" - $400.00; 19" - $650.00. **Glass eyes:** 15" - $1,800.00; 20" - $2,400.00.

Bald Head/Biedermeir

Left to right: 26" pink luster china doll with Cover Wagon hairdo with sausage curls around head. Has all kid body. 25" china doll with Civil War wavy hair with deep modeling and molded eyelids. Has cloth body with china lower limbs. 27" Kling china child with curls deep on forehead and large painted eyes. Cloth with china lower arms. 26" - $850.00; 25" - $600.00; 27" - $550.00. *Courtesy Turn of Century Antiques.*

Bangs: Full across forehead. 1870s. **Black hair:** 13" - $245.00; 18" - $450.00; 22" - $525.00. **Blondes:** 14" - $265.00; 22" - $550.00; 24" - $650.00.

Brown eyes: (See photo in Series 5, pg. 43; Series 8, pg. 51.) Painted eyes, can be any hairstyle and date, but usually has short, "flat top" Civil War hairdo. 12" - $485.00; 16" - $575.00; 19" - $950.00; 23" - $1,100.00; 25" - $1,500.00.

Brown hair: Early hairdo with flat top or long sausage curls around head. Center part and smooth around face. 15" - $2,500.00; 21" - $3,200.00. **With bun:** 17" - $3,200.00 up.

Bun: 1830s–1840s. China with bun, braided or rolled and pulled to back of head. Usually has pink luster tint. Cloth

22" china doll with molded eyelids and an overall downcast look. Has Civil War/Covered Wagon hairdo with sausage curls around head. Cloth body with china lower limbs. (See photo on page 85 of three dolls with same face but with different hairdo and bright cheeks.) $800.00.

body, nicely dressed, undamaged. (See photo in Series 3, pg. 54; Series 10, pg. 55.) Prices depend upon rarity of hairdo and can run from $700.00–6,000.00.

Bun Hairdo

Early hairdo: Also see "Wood Body." 7" - $1,300.00 up; 14" - $1,800.00 up; 17" - $2,500.00 up; 23" - $3,200.00 up. **Double bun or any fancy bun:** 17" - $3,700.00; 23" - $5,200.00.

Common hairdo: Called "Lowbrow" or "Butterfly." Made from 1890, with most being made after 1900. Black or blonde hair. Wavy hairdo, center part with hair that comes down low on forehead. Also see "Pet Names." 9" - $70.00; 13" - $145.00; 15" - $165.00; 18" - $200.00; 22" - $285.00; 25" - $345.00. **With jewel necklace:** 14" - $225.00; 20" - $325.00. **With molded-on poke bonnet:** 9" - $175.00; 14" - $250.00. **Open mouth:** 15" - $485.00; 19" - $775.00.

Common Hairdo

Child: Swivel neck. China shoulder plate. May have china lower limbs and torso. 12" - $2,450.00.

Child or Boy: Short black or blonde hairdo, curly with partly exposed ears. 15" - $250.00; 21" - $500.00.

Covered Wagon: 1840s. Hair parted in middle with flat hairstyle. Has sausage-shaped curls around head. 9" - $175.00; 13" - $265.00; 16" - $485.00; 19" - $585.00; 23" - $875.00; 35–36" - $1,100.00 up.

Covered Wagon   Countess Dagmar

Countess Dagmar: Pierced ears. 15" - $575.00; 18" - $850.00.

Curly Top: 1845–1860s. Ringlet curls that are loose and over entire head. (See photo in Series 4, pg. 48.) 15" - $475.00; 18" - $685.00.

Curly Top

Currier & Ives: (See photo in Series 4, pg. 48.) 15" - $475.00; 21" - $675.00.

Currier & Ives

Dolly Madison: 1870–1880s. Loose curly hairdo with modeled ribbon and bow in center of the top of the head. Few curls on forehead. 13" - $275.00; 17" - $475.00; 20" - $550.00; 23" - $585.00; 27" - $725.00.

Dolly Madison

Early Marked China (Nuremberg, Rudolstadt, etc.): 16" - $2,600.00 up; 18" - $3,000.00 up.

Fancy Hairstyles: Flared sides, rolls of hair over top of head, long hair cascading down back, ringlet curls around face and full exposed ears. (See photos in Series 4, pg. 46; Series 9, pg. 57.) 15" - $550.00 up; 18" - $650.00 up; 22" - $800.00 up.

Flat Top, Civil War: 1850–1870s. Black hair parted in middle, smooth on top with short curls around head. 9" - $90.00; 13" - $165.00; 15" - $225.00; 18" - $300.00; 21" - $350.00; 25" - $400.00; 26" - $485.00; 30" - $600.00; 35" - $800.00. **Swivel neck:** 14" - $800.00 up; 21" - $1,500.00 up. **Molded necklace:** 21" - $700.00 up.

Flat Top, Civil War (1850–1870)

French: China shoulder head, painted eyes, cut pate with cork, wigged, fashion kid body. (See Fashions, Huret type.) 16" - $3,500.00; 19" - $4,400.00.

Glass eyes: 1840–1870s. Can have a variety of hairdos. 14" - $2,600.00; 18" - $3,600.00; 23" - $4,200.00.

Hat or bonnet: Molded on. 14" - $3,300.00; 17" - $4,000.00.

High Brow: 1860–1870s. Like Covered Wagon, but has very high forehead, smooth on top with a center part, curls over ears and around base of neck, and has a very round face. 14" - $475.00; 20" - $725.00; 24" - $925.00.

Highland Mary: (See photo in Series 7, pg. 50.) 15" - $350.00; 18" - $450.00; 22" - $550.00.

Highland Mary

Japanese: 1910–1920s. Can be marked or unmarked. Black or blonde and can have a "common" hairdo, or have much more adult face and hairdo. 12" - $125.00; 14" - $185.00.

Jenny Lind: Hair pulled back in bun. 17" - $1,750.00.

Jenny Lind

Kling: Number and bell. 14" - $365.00; 17" - $450.00; 22" - $675.00.

Man or boy: Excellent quality, early date, side part hairdo. Brown hair. 14" - $1,900.00; 17" - $2,600.00; 21" - $3,100.00 up.

Man hairdo with side part

Man or boy, glass eyes: (See photo in Series 4, pg. 45; Series 10, pg. 55.) 15" - $2,300.00; 17" - $3000.00; 21" - $3,800.00.

Man: Coiled, graduated size curl hairdo. 16" - $1,500.00; 20" - $2,000.00.

Man hairdo with curls

Mary Todd Lincoln: Has snood. 16" - $525.00; 20" - $825.00. Blonde with black snood: 18" - $1,700.00.

Mary Todd Lincoln

Morning Glory: Long neck, narrow at chin, wide at eyes. Very high forehead, brush strokes around face. Hair very flat, pulled back. Exposed ears. 21" - $5,600.00.

Open mouth: 1906. Common hairdo. Rare. 15" - $475.00 up; 19" - $875.00 up.

Pet Names: 1905. Same as "Common" hairdo with molded shirtwaist with the name on front: **Agnes, Bertha, Daisy, Dorothy, Edith, Esther, Ethel, Florence, Helen, Mabel, Marion, Pauline.** (See photo in Series 5, pg. 44; Series 9, pg. 59.) 10" - $125.00; 15" - $200.00; 17" - $225.00; 20" - $265.00; 22" - $300.00; 25" - $425.00.

Pierced ears: Can have a variety of hairstyles (ordinary hairstyle, flat top, curly, covered wagon, etc.) 13" - $425.00 up; 17" - $625.00 up. **Rare hairstyles:** 13" - $1,200.00 up; 17" - $1,800.00 up.

Snood, combs: Applied hair decoration. 15" - $625.00; 18" - $825.00. Grapes in hairdo: 18" - $1,850.00 up.

Sophia Smith: Straight sausage curls ending in a ridge around head rather than curved to head. 15" - $900.00; 17" - $1,300.00; 21" - $1,500.00 up.

Swivel flange neck: 8–9" - $1,800.00 up; 12" - $2,600.00 up.

Unusual: Such as gray hair, long thin face, downcast eyes, molded eyelids. Marked, such as "Nuremberg." (See Series 3, pg. 55; Series 6, pg. 59.) 18" - $3,200.00.

Whistle: Has whistle holes in head. 15" - $575.00; 17" - $700.00.

Wood body: Articulated with slim hips, china lower arms. 1840-1850s. Hair pulled back in bun or coiled braids. 6" - $1,200.00; 8" - $1,500.00; 12" - $1,650.00 up; 15" - $1,800.00 up; 18" - $3,600.00 up. **Same with Covered Wagon hairdo:** 8" - $775.00; 12" - $985.00; 16" - $1,400.00.

Young Queen Victoria: 16" - $1,600.00; 21" - $2,000.00; 25" - $3,200.00.

Sophia Smith

Spill curls: With or without headband. Many individual curls across forehead and over shoulders. Forehead curls continued to above ears. 15" - $400.00; 17" - $750.00; 22" - $850.00; 26" - $950.00.

Spill Curls

19" common pet name china doll. The name "Florence" is on front of shoulder plate. Cloth body with china lower limbs. $265.00. *Courtesy Kathy Tvrdik.*

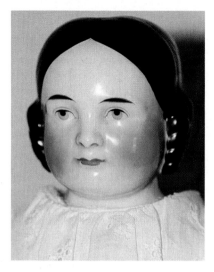

20" "Sophia Smith" has rare hairdo with 10 loose sausage curls around head — five rotate clockwise; five counterclockwise. Hairdo is flat with center part, but modeling makes hair appear more full. Note flat undersides to the eyebrows. (Wagner & Zetzsche painted their early turned head dolls this same way.) Doll's face is rather square with full cheeks. Has canvas-type cloth body with beautiful china hands. $1,500.00.

CLOTH DOLLS

Alabama Indestructible Doll: All cloth with head molded and painted in oils, painted hair, shoes and stockings. Marked on torso or leg "Pat. Nov. 9, 1912. Ella Smith Doll Co." or "Mrs. S.S. Smith/ Manufacturer and dealer/The Alabama Indestructible Doll/Roanoke, Ala./Patented Sept. 26, 1905 (or 1907)." A few rare dolls are marked "No. 1, Sept. 23, 1903." Prices are for clean dolls with only minor scuffs or soil. Allow more for mint dolls. **Child:** 15" - $1,600.00; 22" - $2,400.00. **Baby:** 15" - $1,700.00; 21" - $2,200.00. **Barefoot baby:** Rare. 23" - $3,000.00. **Black child:** 18" - $6,200.00; 23" - $6,800.00. **Black baby:** 20" - $6,200.00.

Art Fabric Mills: See Printed Cloth Dolls.

Averill Mfg. Co.: See Averill section.

Babyland: Made by E.I. Horsman from 1904 to 1920. Marked on torso or bottom of foot. Oil-painted features, photographic features or printed features. With or without wig. All cloth, jointed at shoulders and hips. First price for extra clean, original dolls; second price for dolls in fair condition that show wear and have slight soil. Allow more for mint dolls. **Oil-painted features:** 14" - $775.00, $275.00; 16" - $800.00, $350.00; 19" - $975.00, $400.00; 23" - $1,200.00, $500.00; 26" - $1,600.00, $700.00. **Black oil-painted features:** 15" - $800.00, $300.00; 19" - $1,100.00, $550.00; 24" - $1,550.00, $600.00. **Photographic face:** 15" - $525.00, $200.00; 18" - $825.00, $400.00. **Black photographic face:** 14–15" - $650.00, $275.00; 19" - $1,000.00, $450.00. **Photographic face, 1930s–1960s:** (See Series 10, pg. 59.) Mint and original. 16" - $265.00. Played with, little soil. 16" - $95.00. **Printed:** 14" - $225.00, $80.00; 17" - $365.00, $125.00; 20" - $600.00, $225.00. **Black printed:** 15" - $400.00, $150.00; 18" - $600.00, $150.00; 21" - $800.00, $300.00.

Topsy-Turvy: Two-headed doll. One black, other white. Oil painted: $650.00. Printed: $425.00.

Beecher (Missionary Babies): 1893–1910. Stuffed stockinette, painted eyes, needle sculptured features. Originated by Julia Jones Beecher of Elmira, N.Y., wife of Congregational Church pastor. Dolls made by sewing circle of church and all proceeds used for missionary work, so dolls can also be referred to as "Missionary Babies." Have looped wool hair. Extra clean: 16" - $2,650.00; 20" - $5,300.00. Slight soil and wear: 16" - $1,200.00; 20" - $2,300.00. **Black:** Extra clean: 15" - $3,000.00; 21" - $6,000.00 up. Soil and wear: 16" - $1,600.00; 23" - $2,900.00. **Beecher type:** 19" - $2,100.00.

Bing Art: By Bing Werke of Germany, 1921–1932. All cloth, all felt, or composition head with cloth body. Molded face mask, oil-painted feature, wig or painted hair, can have pin joints on cloth body, seams down front of legs, mitt hands with free formed thumbs. (See photo in Series 9, pg. 61.) **Painted hair, cloth or felt:** Unmarked or "Bing" on sole of foot. 12" - $500.00; 16" - $700.00. **Wig:** 10" - $350.00; 16" - $650.00. **Composition head:** 8" - $145.00; 12" - $175.00, 16" - $225.00.

Bruckner: Made for Horsman from 1901–on. Cloth with mask face stiffened and printed. Marked on shoulder "Pat'd July 8, 1901." Clean: 14" - $325.00 up. Soil and wear: 14" - $95.00 up. **Black:** Clean: 14" - $425.00 up. Soil and wear: 14" - $180.00.

Chad Valley: See that section.

Chase, Martha: See that section.

Columbian Doll: Ca. 1890s. Sizes 15–29". Stamped "Columbian Doll/Manufactured by/Emma E. Adams/Oswego Centre/N.Y." After 1905–1906, the mark was "The Columbian Doll/ Manufactured by/Marietta Adams Ruttan/Oswego, NY." All cloth with painted features and flesh-painted hands and feet. Stitched fingers and toes. (See photo in Series 5, pg. 63; Series 9, pg. 62.) Extra clean: 15" - $4,500.00; 21" - $6,300.00. Fair, with slight scuffs or soil, repainted: 16" - $2,600.00; 22" - $3,100.00. **Columbian type:** 15" - $1,200.00 up; 21" - $2,100.00 up.

Comic Characters: Extra clean: 15" - $450.00 up. Soil and wear: 15" - $150.00 up.

Middle: 14" all cloth doll with printed features and hair. Has stitched joints at shoulders and hips. Mitt hands have free standing thumbs. Original and in mint condition. Left: 11" Kestner baby marked "JDK 247. B made in Germany." Right: 7" "Chubby" with molded-on clothes, painted googly eyes, and molded hair with top knot. Has jointed shoulders only. Labeled "Chubby SHK Co. Germany. All cloth - $600.00. Kestner - $1,200.00. "Chubby" - $400.00. *Courtesy Frasher Doll Auctions.*

Deans Rag Book Dolls: Golliwogs (Black): (See photo in Series 6, pg. 65.) 13" - $250.00; 15" - $450.00. **Child:** 10" - $285.00; 16" - $550.00; 17" - $750.00. **Printed face:** 9" - $85.00; 15" - $165.00; 16" - $225.00. **Mask face:** Velvet and cloth body and limbs. 12" - $125.00; 18" - $265.00; 24" - $385.00; 30" - $475.00; 34" - $565.00; 40" - $695.00.

Drayton, Grace: Dolly Dingle. 1923 by Averill Mfg. Co. Cloth with printed features, marked on torso. 10" - $350.00; 14" - $500.00. **Two faced or two headed (one at each end):** 15" - $625.00. **Chocolate Drop:** 1923 by Averill. Brown cloth with printed features and three tufts of yarn hair. 10" - $400.00; 15" - $575.00. **Hug Me Tight:** By Colonial Toy Mfg. Co. in 1916. One-piece printed cloth with boy standing behind girl. 13" - $275.00; 15" - $400.00. **Kitty-puss:** All cloth, cat face, wired posable limbs and tail. 15" - $400.00.

Peek-A-Boo: Made by Horsman in 1913–1915. All cloth with printed features. 10" - $185.00; 12" - $225.00; 14" - $275.00.

Embroidered features, primitive: Home made, all cloth, yarn, lamb's wool or painted hair. **White:** 15" - $250.00 up; 20" - $465.00 up. **Black:** 15" - $365.00 up; 17" - $550.00 up.

Fangel, Maud Toursey: 1938 on. All cloth with printed features. Can have printed cloth body or plain body without "undies." Mitt-style hands with free-formed thumbs. Marked "M.T.F. 1938." (See photo in Series 5, pg. 58.) **Child:** "Snooks," "Sweets," "Peggy Ann," "Rosy," and others. Must be near mint condition. 10" - $350.00; 13" - $550.00; 16" - $675.00; 20" - $775.00. **Baby:** 15" - $500.00; 18" - $685.00.

16" "Humphery Pennyworth" from the "Joe Palooka" comics has felt clothes sewn onto cloth body. Mask face with reddish yarn hair. Tam is attached to hair. Lower arms are made of composition. All original and in mint condition. Made by Kem-Toy Amusement Co. in 1938. $625.00.
Courtesy Kay Bransky.

14" cloth doll with mask face from late 1930s. Dress is part of all cloth body with attached skirt. Hat and shoes are also a part of the doll. Hat is made of cream colored material with just an organdy ruffle framing around face. Doll is tagged on sole of foot: "Deans Rag Book Co. Ltd. London. Made in England." $325.00 up.

Farnell's Alpha Toys: Marked with label on foot "Farnell's Alpha Toys/Made in England." (See photo in Series 6, pg. 58.) **Child:** 15" - $475.00; 17" - $600.00. **Baby:** 15" - $475.00; 18" - $600.00. **King George VI:** 17" - $1,300.00. **Palace Guard/Beefeater:** 16" - $725.00. **Boudoir dolls:** Adult face. 26–28" - $800.00 up.

Georgene Novelties: See Averill, Georgene section.

Golliwog (Golliwogg): From English children's story, *The Adventures of Two Dutch Dolls and a Golliwogg.* Book published in 1895. Dolls were advertised after 1901. Early examples are rare. **Early doll:** 13" - $500.00 up. **1940s and later:** 13" - $165.00 up.

Kamkins: Made by Louise Kampes. 1928–1934. Marked on head or foot, also has paper heart-shaped label on chest. All cloth with molded face mask and painted features, wigs, boy or girl. Extra clean: 20" - $1,600.00; 25" - $2,000.00. Slight wear/soil: 20" - $800.00; 25" - $1,000.00.

Kewpie: Cloth. See Kewpie section.

Krueger, Richard: New York, 1917 on. All cloth, oil-painted mask face, yarn or mohair wig, oil cloth body. Clean and original. Marked with tag "Krueger, N.Y. Reg. U.S. Pat. Off. Made in USA. **Child:** 14" - $150.00; 17" - $200.00; 21" - $250.00. **Character:** 1940. Such as Pinocchio. 16" - $425.00 up.

Kruse, Käthe: See that section.

Leather dolls: 1890s on. Made in Germany. Oil-painted features, painted hair. **Lady:** Cloth body. 16" - $1,850.00. **Child or baby:** All leather, oil-painted features, jointed 10" - $950.00; 16" - $1,800.00.

Lenci: See Lenci section.

Liberty of London Royal Dolls: Marked with cloth or paper tag. Flesh-colored cloth faces with stitched and painted features. All cloth bodies. 10" Royal Portrait dolls from 1939 include Queen Mary, King George VI, Queen Victoria and Princess Elizabeth. (See photo in Series 7, pg. 53) Extra clean: 10" - $165.00.

Slight wear/soil: 10" - $65.00. **Other historical or coronation figures:** Extra clean: 10" - $165.00. Slight wear/soil: 10" - $65.00.

Madame Hendren: See Averill section.

Mammy style Black dolls: All cloth with painted or sewn features. **Circa 1910–1920s:** 10" - $165.00; 15" - $265.00; 18" - $445.00. **Circa 1930s:** 16" - $175.00 up.

Missionary Babies: See Beecher in this section.

Mollye: See Mollye in Modern section.

Mother's Congress Doll: Patented Nov. 1900. All cloth, printed features and hair. Mitt-style hands without formed thumbs. Designed and made by Madge Mead. Marked with cloth label "Mother's Congress Doll/Children's Favorite/Philadelphia, Pa./Pat. Nov. 6, 1900." Extra

25" all cloth doll with oil-painted mask face and swivel neck. Made to capitalize on the 1930s "Shirley Temple" craze. Has hairdo of auburn curls and Shirley Temple style dress tagged "NRA" and "Blossom Doll Company." $300.00. *Courtesy Susan Girardot.*

clean: 16" - $875.00 up; 23" - $1,000.00 up. Slight soil: 16" - $350.00; 23" - $475.00. **Oil-painted faces and hair:** Unidentified, cloth body and limbs. 22" - $650.00; 27" - $800.00.

Philadelphia Baby: Also called "Sheppard Doll." Made by J.B. Sheppard in late 1890s to early 1900s. Stockinette covered body with painted cloth arms and legs. Modeled cloth head is painted. (See photo in Series 9, pg. 64; Series 11, pg. 55.) Extra clean: 20" - $3,800.00. Slight soil and wear: 20" - $2,500.00. Very worn: 20" - $1,000.00.

Petzold, Dora: Germany, 1920s. Pressed paper head, painted features, wig, stockinette body filled with sawdust, short torso. Soft stuffed arms, free-formed thumbs, stitched fingers. Legs have formed calves. (See photo in Series 7, pg. 139.) 17" - $575.00; 20" - $750.00; 24" - $825.00.

Poir, Eugenie: 1920s, made in New York and France. All cloth body with felt face and limbs or can be all felt. Painted features, majority of eyes are painted to the side, mohair wig. Stitched four fingers together with free-standing thumb. Unmarked except for paper label. Extra clean: 17" - $675.00; 23" - $900.00. Slight soil and wear: 17" - $350.00; 23" - $400.00.

Photographic faces: (Also see Babyland in this section) Extra clean: 16" - $600.00. Slight soil and wear: 16" - $250.00.

Printed Cloth Dolls: 1903 on. All cloth with features and/or underwear and clothes printed. These dolls are cut and sew types. (See photos in Series 4, pg. 53; Series 5, pg. 46; Series 10, pg. 62.) **Rastus, Cream of Wheat:** 16" - $125.00. **Aunt Jemima:** Set of four dolls. Each - $100.00 up. **Printed-on underwear (Dolly Dear, Merry Marie, Flaked Rice, etc.):** Cut: 7" - $95.00; 16" - $175.00; 19" - $200.00. Uncut: 7" - $125.00; 16" - $200.00; 19" - $275.00. **Boys and girls with printed outer clothes:** Circa 1903. Cut: 9–10" - $100.00; 14" - $200.00; 19" - $325.00. Uncut: 9" - $125.00; 14" - $200.00; 19" - $300.00. **Black boy or girl:** 17" - $450.00; 21" - $625.00. **Brownies:** By Palmer Cox in 1892. 8" - $100.00; 14" - $200.00. Uncut, yard long: $350.00. **George/Martha Washington:** Art Fabric in 1901. Cut: $450.00. Uncut: Set of four - $850.00. **Punch and Judy:** 14" - $425.00 pair. **St. Nicholas/Santa Claus:** Marked "Pat. Dec. 28, 1886. Made by E.S. Peck, NY." One arm stuffed with toys and other arm holds American flag. Cut: 15" - $325.00. Uncut: 15" - $600.00.

7" tall members of the "Brownies" marked "Drawn & copyright Jan. 15, 1892." These are old, but collectors beware — reproductions exist. But their colors are brighter and the flour sack cloth will not be the same. Uncut, yard long - $350.00. Cut, sewn together - $100.00 each.

Raynal: Made in France by Edouard Raynal. 1920s. Cloth body and limbs (sometimes has celluloid hands), felt mask face with painted features. Eyes painted to side. Marked on soles of shoes or will have necklace imprinted "Raynal." Original clothes generally are felt, but can have combination felt/organdy or just organdy. (See photo in Series 5, pg. 123.) Extra clean: 15" - $550.00; 20" - $800.00. Slight soil and wear: 15" - $225.00; 20" - $375.00.

Rollinson dolls: Molded cloth with painted features, head and limbs. Molded hair or wig. Designed by Gertrude F. Rollinson, made by Utley Doll Co. Marked with a stamp of doll in a diamond and printed around border "Rollinson Doll Holyoke, Ma." (See photo in Series 7, pg. 52.) **Molded hair:** Extra clean: 20" - $1,150.00 up. Slight soil and wear: 20" - $450.00. **Wigged by Rollinson:** Extra clean: 17" - $1,450.00 up, 22" - $1,875.00. Slight soil and wear: 20" - $750.00; 26" - $925.00. **Toddler with wig:** 17" - $1,725.00.

Smith, Mrs. S.S.: See Alabama in this section.

Soviet Union: 1920–1930s. (See photo in Series 8, pg. 57.) All cloth with stockinette hands and head. Molded face mask with painted features. Dressed in regional costumes. Marked "Made in Soviet Union." Extra clean: 12" - $165.00, 15" - $265.00; 18" - $400.00. Slight soil and wear: 10" - $40.00; 14" - $85.00. **Tea cozies:** (See photo Series 8, pg. 57.) Doll from waist up with full skirt that is placed over teapot to keep contents warm. 18" - $185.00; 21" - $275.00; 29" - $345.00.

Steiff: See Steiff section.

Walker, Izannah: Made in 1870s and 1880s. Modeled head with oil-painted features, applied ears, cloth body and limbs, painted-on boots. Brushstroke or corkscrew curls around face over ears. Hands and feet are stitched. Marked "Patented Nov. 4, 1873." (See photo in Series 9, pg. 62.) Very good condition: 16" - $18,000.00; 19" - $27,000.00. Fair condition: 16" - $9,000.00; 19" - $10,000.00. Poor condition: 16" - $2,000.00; 21" - $3,200.00. **Two vertical curls in front of ears:** Very good condition: 19" - $21,000.00 up; 25" - $26,000.00 up. Fair condition: 19"- $13,000.00; 25" - $17,000.00.

Wellings, Norah: See Wellings section.

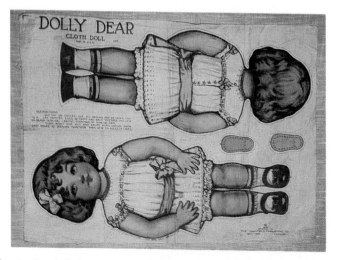

Uncut printed cloth panel for a 19" "Dolly Dear." $275.00. *Courtesy Susan Girardot.*

Wellington: 1883 on. All stockinette, oil-painted features, lower limbs. Features are needle sculpted. Hair is painted. Has distinctive buttocks; rounded. Label on back: "Pat. Jan. 8, 1883." Excellent condition: 24" - $15,000.00 up. Fair to poor condition: 24" - $6,000.00 up.

20" all cloth Rollinson doll made by Utley Doll Co., Holyoke, MA. Has hard pressed face with oil-painted features, hair, and single stoke eyebrows. Cloth body has oil-painted lower limbs and cotton sateen body cover. Limbs are stitch jointed. $1,200.00. *Courtesy Frasher Doll Auction.*

COMBS, I.C.

This 16" doll has a rubber head (gutta percha) and shoulder plate. Cloth body has leather arms and boots sewn to it. Has Griener hairdo. Made by and marked "I.C. Combs." Company name was India Rubber Comb Co. and was made under the rights of the Nelson Goodyear Rubber Co. $950.00.

Most German manufacturers made composition-headed dolls as well as dolls of bisque and other materials. Composition dolls were made in Germany before World War I, but the majority were made in the 1920s and 1930s. They can be all composition or have a composition head with cloth body and limbs. Prices are for excellent quality and condition.

Child: All composition with wig, sleep/flirty eyes, open or closed mouth and jointed composition body. Unmarked or just have numbers. 15" - $225.00; 19" - $385.00; 22" - $475.00; 24" - $600.00. **Marked:** Name of company (or initials). 15" - $325.00; 19" - $500.00; 24" - $625.00; 27" - $785.00.

Baby: All composition, open mouth. 15" - $175.00; 17" - $345.00; 20" - $450.00. **Toddler:** 19" - $500.00; 23" - $650.00.

Baby: Composition head and limbs with cloth body, open mouth, sleep eyes. 15" - $200.00; 21" - $300.00; 26" - $485.00.

Painted Eyes, child: 15" - $150.00; 17" - $250.00. **Baby:** 15" - $160.00; 17" - $275.00.

Shoulder Head: Composition shoulder head, glass eyes, wig, open or closed mouth, cloth or kidaleen body with composition arms (full arms or lower arms only with cloth upper arms), and lower legs. May have bare feet or modeled boots. Prices for dolls in extra clean condition and nicely dressed. Unmarked. (Also see Wax Section.) Excellent quality: Extremely fine modeling. 12" - $375.00; 15" - $475.00; 22" - $685.00; 23" - $725.00; 28" - $900.00. Average quality: May resemble a china head doll. 12" - $165.00; 14" - $200.00; 17" - $250.00; 22" - $325.00; 25" - $365.00; 29" - $500.00; 36" - $725.00.

Painted Hair: 12" - $145.00; 16" - $235.00; 18" - $425.00.

Swivel Neck: On composition shoulderplate. 15" - $425.00; 18" - $525.00; 24" - $725.00.

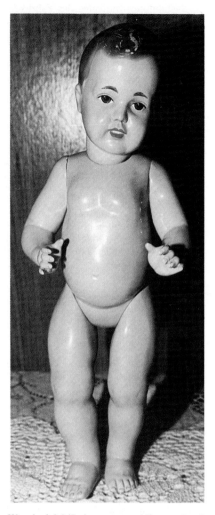

Wonderful 14" character toddler made of composition. This unmarked strung doll has typical German toddler body and limbs with detailed hands and feet, outlined nails, plus large molded breast. Hair is molded, and open/closed mouth has painted lower teeth. $565.00. *Courtesy Patricia Wood.*

Chambre Syndicates des Fabricants de Jouets et Jeux et Engins Sportif. One member was Societe du Caoutchouc Manufacture.

Child: Closed mouth. Excellent quality bisque. Allow more for original clothes. 12" - $925.00; 16" - $1,300.00.

12" bisque shoulder head with cloth body and bisque lower limbs. French Belton-type dome head with beautiful face and large eyes. Note painting of lips. Original. (See full-length photo in Series 11, pg. 59.) Made by C.S.F.J. which was a society of 47 doll/toymakers. This particular doll was made by Societe du Cautchouc, circa 1895. Marked with inverted triangle (▽). This quality - $1,100.00. Redressed - $900.00. *Courtesy Kathy Riddick.*

DEP

Many French and German dolls bear the mark "DEP" as part of their mold marks, but the dolls referred to here are marked *only with the* DEP *and a size number.* They are on French bodies with some bearing a Jumeau sticker. The early 1880s DEP dolls have fine quality bisque and artist workmanship, and the later dolls of the 1890s and into the 1900s generally have fine bisque, but the color will be higher, and they will have painted lashes below the eyes with most having hair eyelashes over the eyes. The early dolls will have outlined lips but the later ones will not. Prices are for clean, undamaged and nicely dressed dolls.

Marks:

27" doll with open mouth and French jointed body. Marked "DEP." She holds a watermelon colored "Cranberry Mountain Bear" muff. Doll - $2,350.00. Bear - unknown. *Courtesy Susan Girardot.*

Open mouth: 10" - $650.00; 15" - $775.00; 17" - $1,100.00; 20" - $1,350.00 up; 24" - $1,800.00 up; 29" - $2,600.00 up; 34" - $3,500.00 up. **Open mouth, very Jumeau looking, red marks (✔, ×, or artist's initials):** 17" - $1,550.00; 22" - $2,000.00; 30" - $3,200.00.

Closed mouth: 15" - $2,500.00; 17" - $3,200.00; 24" - $3,900.00; 27" - $4,400.00. Unusually fine example: 18" - $3,900.00; 28" - $5,000.00 up.

Walking, kissing (open mouth): 15" - $1,200.00; 18" - $1,550.00; 20" - $1,700.00; 25" - $2,400.00.

14" Jumeau type with French jointed body and straight wrist. Has open/closed mouth with space between lips. Marked "DEP/4." $1,200.00. *Courtesy Virgina Sofie.*

DOLL HOUSE DOLLS

Doll house man or woman: With molded hair/wig and painted eyes. 6–7" - $135.00–250.00.

Children: All bisque: 3½" - $75.00, 5½" - $135.00. Bisque/cloth: 3½" - $90.00; 5½" - $145.00.

Man or woman with glass eyes and wigs: 6–7" - $385.00–600.00.

Man or woman with molded hair: Glass eyes. 6–7" - $400.00.

Man with mustache: (See photo in Series 6, pg. 70.) 5½–6½" - $165.00–300.00.

Grandparents, old people, or molded-on hats: 6–7" - $265.00 up.

Military men: Have mustaches. Original. (See photo in Series 8, pg. 128; Series 9, pg. 68.) 6–7" - $500.00 up. **Molded helmet:** 6–7" - $600.00 up.

3" doll house china doll with flat top hair-do that flairs out at the sides. Has cloth body with china lower limbs. $165.00. *Courtesy Virginia Sofie.*

Black man or woman: Molded hair, all original. 6–7" - $475.00 up.

Chauffeur: Molded cap. 6–7" - $285.00 up.

Swivel neck: Wig or molded hair. 6–7" - $700.00 up.

China glaze with early hairdos: (See photo in Series 8, pg. 62.) 4–5" - $300.00-385.00. **Low brow/common hairdo:** 1900s and after. $45.00–145.00.

All composition doll house children from 1930s. Hair is molded and painted. Each have painted features and shoes. Original and marked "Germany." Mint condition - $135.00 pair. *Courtesy Kay Bransky.*

DRESSEL, CUNO & OTTO

Cuno & Otto Dressel operated in Sonneberg, Thuringia, Germany and were sons of the founder. Although the firm was in business in 1700, they are not listed as dollmakers until 1873. They produced dolls with bisque heads or composition over wax heads, which can be on cloth, kid, or jointed composition bodies. Some of their heads were made for them by other German firms, such as Simon & Halbig, Heubach, etc. They registered the trademark for "Jutta" in 1906 and by 1911 were also making celluloid dolls. Prices are for undamaged, clean and nicely dressed dolls.

Marks:

 C.O.D.   **C.O.D. 49 D.E.P.**
Made in Germany

Left: 19" character made by Cuno & Otto Dressel. Has open/closed mouth and protruding ears. Referred to as "Baby Perot." Right: 15½" Gebruder Heubach mold #8191 with molded hair and sideward laughing expression. Has open/ closed mouth with upper and lower teeth. On jointed body. Both dolls have painted features. 19" - $2,200.00; 15½" - $1,300.00. *Courtesy Turn of Century Antiques.*

Babies: 1910 on. Marked "C.O.D." but without the word "Jutta." Allow more for toddler body. 13" - $295.00. 16" - $450.00; 19" - $600.00; 25" - $800.00. **Child:** 1893 on. Jointed composition body. Open mouth. 16" - $350.00; 20" - $475.00; 23" - $550.00; 26" - $625.00; 30" - $1,200.00; 35" - $2,000.00. **Child:** Shoulder head or turned head on jointed kid body. Open mouth. 15" - $300.00; 18" - $550.00; 23" - $685.00. **Jutta baby:** 1910–1922. Open mouth. Five-piece bent limb body. 13" - $435.00; 15" - $500.00; 18" - $675.00; 22" - $950.00; 24" - $1,400.00; 27" - $1,800.00. **Jutta toddler:** 8" - $550.00; 15" - $675.00; 18" - $950.00; 22" - $1,250.00; 25" - $1,550.00; 27" - $1,850.00. **Jutta child:** Marked with "Jutta" or with **S&H #1914, #1348, #1349, etc.:** 1906–1921. (See photo in Series 8, pg. 67.) 14" - $425.00; 16" - $575.00; 20" - $700.00; 24" - $850.00; 26" - $950.00; 30" - $1,200.00; 38–39" - $2,500.00. **Lady doll:** 1920s. Flapper with adult face, closed mouth. On five-piece composition body with thin limbs and high heel feet. Hoses painted on entire leg. Original clothes. Marked **#1469.** (See photo in Series 8, pg. 66.) 13" - $3,600.00; 15" - $4,100.00. Redressed or nude: 13" - $2,600.00; 15" - $3,100.00. **Character dolls:** 1909 and after. Closed mouth. Molded hair or wig. May be glazed inside head. **Painted eyes:** 12" - $1,500.00; 14" - $2,300.00; 18" - $2,900.00; 22" - $3,300.00. **Glass eyes:** 15" - $2,500.00; 18" - $3,200.00; 24" - $3,500.00; 25" - $3,700.00. **Character dolls:** Marked with letter and number, such as **B/4, A/2, or A/16.** Jointed child or toddler body, painted eyes, closed mouth. No damage, ready to display. 12" - $1,400.00; 15–16" - $2,500.00; 18" - $2,800.00. **Composition:** 1870s. Shoulder head, glass or painted eyes, molded hair or wig. Cloth body with composition limbs with

Left: 26" Cuno & Otto Dressel "Jutta" toddler with open mouth. Center: 9" "George Washington" on horse candy container. Right: 11" Armand Marseille #240 googly on chubby five-piece body. All original. 26" - $1,850.00; 9" - $800.00– 1,100.00; 11" - $2,200.00–2,500.00. *Courtesy Frasher Doll Auctions.*

molded-on boots. Will be marked with Holz-Masse.
With wig: Glass eyes. 14" - $250.00; 16" - $325.00; 24" - $425.00. **Molded hair:** 13" - $250.00; 17" - $400.00; 24" - $565.00. **Portrait dolls:** 1896. Such as **Uncle Sam, The Farmer, Admiral Dewey, Admiral Byrd, Old Rip, Witch, etc.** Portrait bisque head, glass eyes, composition body. Some will be marked with a **"D"** or **"S."** Heads made for Dressel by Simon & Halbig. Prices for clean, undamaged and originally dressed. **Military dolls:** (See photo in Series 6, pg. 72) 9" - $750.00; 13" - $1,600.00; 16" - $2,000.00. **Old Rip, Farmer or Witch:** 9" - $725.00; 13" - $1,400.00; 16" - $1,700.00. **Uncle Sam:** 9" - $825.00; 13" - $1,500.00; 16" - $2,000.00. **Buffalo Bill:** 10–12" - $765.00.

Father Christmas: 10–12" - $1,500.00 up.
    Fur covered: Glued on body/limbs.
8–9" - $175.00; 12" - $265.00.

17" boy with painted features and serious expression. Has closed mouth and jointed body. Marked "C.O.D. A/16." $3,000.00. *Courtesy Frasher Doll Auctions.*

E.D.

E. Denamur of Paris made dolls from 1885 to 1898. The E.D. marked dolls seem to be accepted as being made by Denamur, but they could have been made by E. Dumont, Paris. Composition and wood jointed bodies. Prices are for excellent quality bisque, no damage and nicely dressed.

Marks:

E5D
DEPOSE

Closed or open/closed mouth: 14" - $2,200.00; 16" - $2,800.00; 23" - $3,500.00; 26" - $3,900.00; 28" - $4,400.00; 32" - $5,000.00.

Open mouth: 15" - $1,400.00; 17" - $1,700.00; 21" - $2,200.00; 24" - $2,500.00.
    Black: Open mouth. 15" - $2,100.00; 23" - $2,700.00.

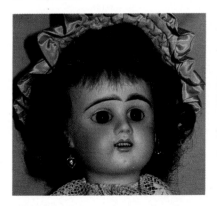

25" doll with heavy feathered eyebrows, open mouth, and composition and wood jointed body. Marked "E.D. 11 Depose." $2,600.00. *Courtesy Frasher Doll Auctions.*

Fleischmann & Bloedel of Fürth, Bavaria; Sonneberg, Thuringia; and Paris, France was founded in 1873 and making dolls in Paris by 1890. The company became a part of S.F.B.J. in 1899. Dolls have composition jointed bodies and can have open or closed mouths. Prices are for dolls with excellent color and quality bisque, no damage and nicely dressed.

Marks:

EDEN BÉBÉ PARIS

Closed or open/closed mouth: Pale bisque. 16" - $2,400.00; 19" - $2,900.00; 23" - $3,000.00; 26" - $3,600.00.

Closed mouth: High color bisque. Five-piece body. 12" - $1,000.00; 16" - $1,200.00; 17" - $1,600.00; 21" - $1,850.00; 25" - $2,400.00.

Open mouth: 16" - $1,100.00; 17" - $1,900.00; 21" - $2,300.00; 26" - $2,800.00.

Walking, kissing doll: Jointed body with walker mechanism, head turns and one arm throws a kiss. Heads by Simon & Halbig using mold **#1039** (and others).

Bodies assembled by Fleischmann & Bloedel. Price for perfect, working doll. 21" - $1,600.00 up.

This 27" doll with fully jointed French body has beautiful quality bisque and artist painting. Open mouth has "bow" painted upper lip and tiny teeth. Marked "Eden Bebe/Paris/14" $2,900.00. *Courtesy Jean Truman.*

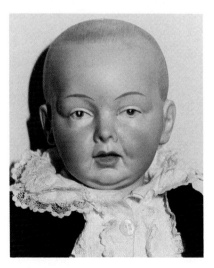

22" doll made by Joseph Eisenmann & Co. in Furth, Bavaria, ca. 1914. Has large, deep intaglio eyes, molded eyelids, and open/closed mouth. On five-piece bent limb baby body. Marked "EINCO/Germany." $5,300.00. *Courtesy Dorothy Rigg.*

Joel Ellis made dolls in Springfield, Vermont, in 1873 and 1874 under the name Co-operative Manufacturing Co. All wood jointed body has tenon and mortise joints, arms are jointed in same manner. The hands and feet are made of pewter. Has molded hair and painted features.

Springfield Wooden Doll: It must be noted that dolls similar to the Joel Ellis ones were made in Springfield, Vt. also by Joint Doll Co. and D.M. Smith & Co. They are very much like the Joel Ellis except when standing the knee joint will be flush with the method of jointing not showing. The hips are cut out with the leg tops cut to fit the opening, and the detail of the hands is not as well done. Prices are also for Mason-Taylor dolls. (See example under Bonnet dolls.)

Fair condition: Does not need to be dressed. 12" - $600.00; 14" - $775.00.

Excellent condition: 12" - $925.00 up; 14" - $1,200.00 up.

FASHION AND FORTUNE DOLLS, FRENCH

These "adult" style dolls were made by a number of French firms from about 1860 into the 1930s. Many will be marked only with a number or have a stamp on the body, although some of the stamps/labels may be the store from where they were sold and not the maker. The most available fashion doll seems to be marked F.G. dolls. Prices are for dolls in perfect condition with no cracks, chips, or repairs

18" French Fashion with wooden articulated body, swivel neck, and cobalt blue set eyes. Marked on shoulder plate "F.G." $8,200.00. *Courtesy Marcia Jarmush.*

and in beautiful old or newer clothes made of appropriate age materials.

Articulated wood: Marked or unmarked, or on blown kid bodies and limbs. Some have bisque lower arms. 15" - $6,400.00 up; 19" - $8,250.00 up.

Articulated: Marked or unmarked. With bisque lower legs and arms with excellent modeling detail. 15" - $8,200.00 up; 21" - $9,200.00 up.

Marked "Bru": (Also see Smiling Mona Lisa in this section.) 1860s. Round face, swivel neck, glass eyes: (See photo in Series 6, pg. 79.) 15" - $3,000.00; 18" - $4,600.00; 22" - $5,600.00 up. **Wood body:** 15" - $4,800.00.

Marked "Huret": Bisque or china glazed shoulder head, kid body with bisque lower arms. **Painted eyes:** 16" - $5,600.00; 19" - $6,600.00. **Glass eyes:** 15" - $6,200.00; 18" - $7,600.00. **Wood body:** 16" - $7,200.00 up; 19" - $8,800.00 up. **Gutta percha body:** 16" - $9,500.00 up; 19" - $12,000.00 up. **Portrait adult lady:** Painted eyes, articulated body with metal hands. (See photo is Series 4, pg. 64.) 18" - $17,500.00.

Huret Child: 17" - $25,000.00 up; 22" - $30,000.00 up.

Marked "Rohmer": (See photo in Series 7, pg. 65 and Series 8, pg. 71.) Bisque or china glazed shoulder head (can be jointed). Kid body with bisque lower arms (or china). **Glass eyes:** 15" - $6,800.00; 18" - $10,000.00; **Painted eyes:** 15" - $6,000.00; 18" - $8,500.00. **Wood body:** 16" - $7,400.00; 19" - $12,000.00.

Unmarked Rohmer or Huret type: Painted eyes. 15" - $4,400.00; 18" - $5,400.00; 24" - $6,200.00. **Wire controlled flat glass sleep eyes:** 26" - $11,500.00. **Painted black hair:** Kid body. 15" - $4,200.00.

Marked "Jumeau": Will have number on head and stamped body. (See photo in Series 7, pg. 79.) **Portrait-style head:** 16" - $3,600.00; 19" - $5,900.00; 22" - $6,400.00; 25" - $7,200.00. 28" - $8,350.00. **Wood body:** 16" - $6,000.00; 19" - $9,2000.00 up; 25" - $11,500.00 up.

Marked "Jumeau": Swivel head. 14" - $2,800.00; 16" - $3,400.00; 20" - $3,800.00. **Wood body:** Bisque limbs. 17" - $5,400.00; 21" - $6,500.00. **Very large eyes:** 11–12" - $2,200.00; 15–16" - $2,600.00.

Marked "F.G.": 1860 on. All kid body, one-piece shoulder and head. Glass eyes: 11" - $850.00; 14" - $1,100.00; 17" - $1,600.00. **Painted eyes:** 12" - $700.00; 14" - $1,000.00; 17" - $1,300.00.

Marked "F.G.": 1860 on. All kid body (or bisque lower arms), swivel head on bisque shoulder plate. **Glass eyes:** 12" - $1,400.00; 15" - $2,100.00; 18" - $2,600.00; 24" - $3,300.00; 26" - $4,400.00. **Black:** 15" - $3,200.00; 19" - $4,400.00.

Marked "F.G.": Gesland cloth-covered body with bisque lower arms and legs. Early face. 16" - $5,500.00; 19" - $6,500.00; 24" - $6,900.00; 25" - $7,300.00.

Marked "F.G.": Gesland cloth-covered body with composition or papier maché lower arms and legs. 16" - $4,100.00; 19" - $4,900.00; 24" - $5,400.00.

Smiling "Mona Lisa": After 1866. Now being referred to as made by Bru. (See photo in Series 8, pg. 72; Series 9. pg. 74.) Kid body with leather lower arms,

20½" Portrait Fashion by Jumeau has swivel bisque head on bisque shoulder plate, closed mouth, and large paperweight eyes. On stamped Jumeau body which is all kid with gusset jointing. $6,200.00 up. *Courtesy Frasher Doll Auctions.*

14" Fashion referred to as "Mona Lisa" because of her smile. Has swivel head and kid body. Appears to be all original. Incised with "C" on head. This doll has always been considered to be a Jumeau, but for past 10 years has been attributed to Bru. $4,000.00 up. *Courtesy Turn of Century Antiques.*

stitched fingers or bisque lower arms. Swivel head on bisque shoulder plate. Marked with letter (example: E, B, D, etc.) Allow more for wood body or arms. 12" - $2,700.00; 16" - $4,000.00; 19" - $5,400.00; 23" - $5,600.00; 27" - $6,700.00; 30" - $9,400.00.

Unmarked with numbers only: Kid body with one-piece bisque head and shoulder. Extremely fine quality bisque, undamaged. **Glass eyes:** 12" - $1,200.00; 14" - $1,400.00; 22" - $2,200.00. **Painted eyes:** 14" - $950.00; 17" - $1,400.00; 22" - $1,800.00. **Swivel neck, glass eyes:** Bisque

shoulder plate, kid body. Extremely fine quality bisque and undamaged. 15" - $2,600.00; 17" - $2,850.00; 19" - $3,500.00. **Black:** 14" - $1,800.00 up. **Wood or twill over wood body:** 15" - $3,800.00; 18" - $4,500.00.

Unmarked: Medium to fair quality. **One-piece head and shoulder:** 11" - $550.00; 15" - $725.00–1,000.00. **Swivel head:** On bisque shoulder plate. 16" - $1,000.00; 20" - $1,700.00 up.

Marked E.B. (E. Barrois): 1854–1877. (See photo in Series 7, pg. 67.) Allow more for bisque or wood arms. **Glass eyes:** 15" - $3,500.00; 19" - $5,000.00. **Painted eyes:** 16" - $2,900.00; 20" - $3,600.00. **China glaze:** (See photo in Series 8, pg. 73.) 16" - $6,000.00.

Marked "Simone": Glass eyes: 20" - $5,800.00; 24" - $6,900.00.

Factory original fashion clothes: Dress: $500.00 up. Wig: $250.00 up. Cape: $200.00 up. Boots: $250.00 up. Boots marked by maker: $500.00 up.

Fortune dolls: French fashion type head with swivel neck, painted or glass eyes, and kid body. Underskirt formed by many folded papers written in French. (See photo in Series 5, pg. 62; Series 8, pg. 82.) **Open mouth:** 19" - $3,200.00 up. **Closed mouth:** 19" - $5,200.00 up. **Wooden (German):** Tuck comb of mid-19th century. 17½" - $3,400.00 up. **China glazed:** 1870s–1880s hairdos. 16" - $1,800.00.

16" china fortune doll on stand has cloth body, china lower limbs, and curly top hairdo. Skirt is made of creased and folded papers with a different fortune on each. Originally, a silk material skirt covered the papers. Player puts hand under skirt and pulls out a folded fortune. After reading it, fortune was place back in skirt. $1,800.00. *Courtesy Diane Kornhauser.*

F. Gaultier (earlier spelled Gauthier) is the accepted maker of the F.G. marked dolls. These dolls are often found on the cloth-covered or all composition bodies that are marked "Gesland." The Gesland firm was operated by two brothers. One of them had the initial "F" (1887–1900).

Marks:

(1887–1900)

F. 8 G.
(1879–1887 Block Letter Mark)

Child with closed mouth (scroll mark): Excellent quality bisque, no damage and nicely dressed. 9" - $775.00; 13" - $1,400.00; 16" - $2,800.00; 18" - $3,600.00; 21" - $3,800.00; 24" - $4,900.00; 26" - $5,600.00; 30" - $5,200.00. **High face color:** No damage and nicely dressed. 14" - $1,200.00; 16" - $1,700.00; 19" - $1,900.00; 22" - $2,200.00; 25" - $2,600.00.

Child with open mouth (scroll mark): Excellent quality bisque, no damage and nicely dressed. 10–12" - $650.00; 15" - $1,700.00; 17" - $1,900.00; 20" - $2,200.00; 23" - $2,600.00; 27" - $3,000.00.

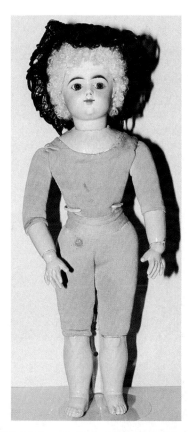

Tiny 13" doll with early pale bisque, Jumeau type body, closed mouth, and glass eyes. Marked "F 3 G" (called block F.G.) $3,800.00. *Courtesy Ellen Dodge.*

18" doll has Gesland cloth covered body and composition lower legs. Hands and lower arms are wood with composition. Has closed mouth and glass eyes. $5,400.00. *Courtesy Ellen Dodge.*

High face color: Very dark lips. No damage, nicely dressed. 14" - $900.00; 16" - $1,200.00; 19" - $1,600.00; 22" - $2,000.00; 25" - $2,400.00.

Marked "F.G. Fashion": See Fashion section.

Child on marked Gesland body: (See photo is Series 6, pg. 80; Series 8, pg. 80.) Bisque head on stockinette over wire frame body with composition limbs. **Closed mouth:** 15" - $4,800.00; 18" - $5,400.00; 24" - $6,000.00. **Open mouth:** 16" - $2,500.00; 20" - $3,000.00; 25" - $3,800.00.

Block letter (so called) F.G. child: 1879–1887. Closed mouth, chunky composition body, excellent quality and condition. 14" - $4,200.00; 17" - $5,000.00; 21" - $5,800.00; 24" - $6,200.00; 27" - $7,200.00; 34" - $10,000.00. **Gusseted kid body:** Bisque swivel head on bisque shoulder plate, bisque lower arms. 16" - $4,900.00; 20" - $5,200.00; 25" - $6,000.00.

Boy: Kid body, painted eyes, and closed mouth. Painted brown hair. (See photo in Series 8, pg. 75.) 12" - $1,800.00 up.

FRENCH BÉBÉ, MAKER UNKNOWN

A variety of French doll makers produced unmarked dolls from the 1880s into the 1920s. These dolls may only have a head size number or be marked "Paris" or "France." Many of the accepted French dolls that have a number are now being attributed to German makers and it will be questionable for some time.

Unmarked French Bébé: Closed or open/closed mouth, paperweight eyes. Excellent quality bisque and artistry on French body. Prices for clean, undamaged and nicely dressed dolls.

Early desirable, very French-style face: Marks such as "J.D." (maker probably J. DuSerre. See photo in Series 8, pg. 71), "J.M. Paris," numbers only, and "H.G." (probably made by Henri & Granfe-Guimonneau. See photo in Series 6, pg. 99). 15" - $9,500.00; 17" - $17,000.00 up; 23" - $22,000.00 up; 25" - $25,000.00 up.

Jumeau or Bru style face: Closed mouth. May be marked "W.D." or "R.R." (See photo in Series 8, pg. 76.) 16" - $3,000.00; 19" - $3,700.00; 22" - $4,600.00; 25" - $5,200.00; 28" - $5,800.00.

24" doll with almond cut paperweight eyes, closed mouth, and original wig. On French jointed body. Wears Jumeau marked shoes. Maker unknown. Marked "R. 11 R." Shown with costume for Bru #9. Dress tagged "Bébé Bru Margue Deposee Paris." Doll - $5,600.00. Dress - $900.00 up. Shoes - $500.00 up. *Courtesy Frasher Doll Auctions.*

Excellent quality, closed mouth:
Unusual face. Molds such as **F.1, F.2, J,** **#137, 136, etc.** (See photo in Series 8, pg. 79.) 12" - $1,800.00; 16" - $4,300.00; 19" - $4,900.00; 24" - $5,900.00; 28" - $7,400.00.

Standard French-looking head:
Excellent bisque, closed mouth. 14" - $2,600.00; 17" - $3,200.00; 22" - $4,200.00.

Medium quality: May have poor painting and/or blotches to skin tones. 14" - $1,150.00; 19" - $1,600.00; 25" - $2,200.00.

Excellent quality, open mouth:
1890s and later. Will be on French body. 16" - $1,650.00; 19" - $2,400.00; 23" - $2,600.00; 26" - $3,300.00.

Open mouth, high face color:
1920s. May have five-piece papier maché body. 16" - $650.00; 20" - $825.00; 24" - $1,000.00.

13" late French doll with open/closed mouth and space between lips. No double chin but has German style one-stroke eyebrows. Has large paperweight eyes, five-piece body with straight wrists, and painted-on boots. $850.00. *Courtesy Turn of Century Antiques.*

FREUNDLICH, RALPH

Freundlich Novelty Company operated in New York from 1923. Most of their dolls have a cardboard tag and will be unmarked or may have name on the head, but no maker's name.

Baby Sandy: 1939–1942. All composition with molded hair, sleep or painted eyes. Marked "Baby Sandy" on head. (See photo in Series 6, pg. 85; Series 11, pg. 71.) **Excellent condition:** No cracks, craze, or chips. Original or appropriate clothes. 8" - $200.00; 12" - $275.00; 16" - $400.00 up; 19" - $750.00. **With light crazing:** Clean, may be redressed. 8" - $90.00; 12" - $125.00; 16" - $145.00; 19" - $225.00.

General Douglas MacArthur: Circa 1942. Portrait doll of all composition with painted features. Molded hat. Jointed shoulders and hips. (See photo in Series 6, pg. 85.) **Excellent condition:** Original. 15" - $300.00; 17" - $350.00. **Light craze:** Clothes dirty. 16" - $100.00; 18" - $125.00.

Military dolls: Circa 1942 on. All composition with painted features and molded-on hats. Can be woman or man – W.A.V.E, W.A.A.C., sailor, Marine, etc. (See photo in Series 5, pg. 65; Series 6, pg. 85.) **Excellent condition:** Original and no crazing. 16" - $265.00 up. **Light craze:** Clothes in fair condition. 16" - $95.00.

Pinocchio: Composition/cloth with molded hair. Painted features with bright red cheeks. Large eyes, moderate size nose, and open/closed mouth. Tongue molded on one side of mouth. Tagged "Original as portrayed by C. Collodi." 17" - $500.00 up.

Storybook dolls: Orphan Annie/ Sandy, Red Riding Hood/Wolf/Grandma, etc. 13" - $425.00 up.

Ventriloquist Doll (Dummy Dan): (See photo in Series 7, pg. 73.) Looks like Charlie McCarthy. 16" - $185.00; 23" - $450.00 up.

Right: 18" "General Douglas MacArthur" portrait doll that is all original and all composition. Arm bent so he can salute. Center: 15" "Howdy Doody" marionette that is all original. Left: 18" all original "Shirley Temple" in tagged dress. "MacArthur" - $365.00. "Howdy Doody" - $175.00. "Shirley Temple" - $950.00.
Courtesy Turn of Century Antiques.

FROZEN CHARLOTTE AND CHARLIE

Frozen Charlotte and Charlie figures can be china, partly china (such as hair and boots), stone bisque or fine porcelain bisque. They can have molded hair, have painted bald heads, or take wigs. The majority have no joints, with hands extended and legs separate (some are together). They generally come without clothes and they can have painted-on boots, shoes and socks, or be barefooted. (See "The Ballad of Charlotte" in *Antique Collector's Dolls, Volume II;* pg. 107 and *Album of All Bisque Dolls,* pg. 92.)

It must be noted that in 1976 a large amount of the 15½–16" "Charlie" figures were reproduced in Germany and their quality is excellent. It is almost impossible to tell that these are reproductions.

Prices are for doll figures without any damage. More must be allowed for any with unusual hairdos, an early face or molded eyelids or molded-on clothes.

All china: Glazed with black or blonde hair, excellent quality of painting and unjointed. 2" - $45.00; 5" - $95.00; 7" - $125.00; 9" - $200.00 up; 11" - $250.00 up. **Bald head with wig:** 6" - $125.00; 8" - $150.00; 10" - $250.00. **Charlie:** Molded black hair, flesh tones to neck and head. (See photo in Series 3, pg. 67; Series 11, pg. 72.) 10" - $250.00 up; 15" - $450.00 up; 18" - $625.00 up. **All pink luster:** 12" - $425.00 up. Luster to head and neck only: $325.00. Blonde: 15" - $400.00 up.

Untinted bisque (Parian): Molded hair, unjointed. 4" - $145.00; 7" - $165.00.

Untinted bisque: 1860s. Molded hair, jointed at shoulders. 4" - $135.00; 7" - $160.00.

Stone bisque: Unjointed, molded hair, medium to excellent quality of painting. 3" - $25.00; 6" - $40.00; 8" - $55.00.

Black Charlotte or Charlie: Unjointed, no damage. 3" - $125.00; 5" -

$225.00; 7" - $325.00. Jointed at shoulders: 4" - $225.00; 7" - $425.00.

Molded headband or bow: Excellent quality: 5" - $175.00; 8" - $250.00. Medium quality: 5" - $100.00; 8" - $145.00.

Molded-on clothes, shorts, or bonnet: Unjointed, no damage and medium to excellent quality. (See photo in Series 4, pg. 33.) 3" - $250.00; 7" - $350.00; 9" - $475.00.

Dressed in original clothes: Unjointed Charlotte or Charlie. No damage and in overall excellent condition. 5" - $135.00; 7" - $185.00.

Jointed at shoulder: Original clothes and no damage. (See photo in Series 2, pg. 75.) 6" - $165.00; 8" - $250.00.

Molded-on, painted boots: Unjointed, no damage. 5" - $175.00; 7" - $225.00. Jointed at shoulders: 5" - $200.00; 7" - $300.00.

Unique hairdo and boots: 5" - $325.00 up.

Left: 5" "Frozen Charlotte" with pink skintones and a rare Sophia Smith hairdo. Barefooted. Right: 4½" with a low brow style hairdo. Has molded-on unpainted boots. Both have a china glaze finish. 5" - $325.00 up; 4½" - $165.00. *Courtesy Shirley's Doll House.*

Fulper Pottery Co. of Flemington, N.J. made dolls from 1918–1921. They made children and babies and used composition and kid bodies.

Marks:

Made in U.S.A.

25" Fulper with open mouth, feathered brows, and very good bisque. On fully jointed composition body. $675.00. *Courtesy Sylvia Bryant.*

Child: Fair to medium quality bisque head painting. No damage, nicely dressed. **Composition body, open mouth:** 15" - $325.00; 17" - $475.00; 21" - $625.00. **Kid body, open mouth:** 14" - $300.00; 16" - $375.00; 20" - $525.00.

Child: Poor quality (white chalky look, may have crooked mouth and be poorly painted.) **Composition body:** 15" - $225.00; 20" - $300.00. **Kid body:** 14" - $165.00; 20" - $250.00.

Baby: Bent limb body, open mouth. Near excellent to medium quality bisque. No damage and dressed well. Good artist work on features. 16" - $500.00; 17" - $600.00; 24" - $825.00. **Toddler:** Has toddler jointed or straight leg body. 18" - $700.00; 25" - $975.00 up.

Baby: Poor quality bisque and painting. 15" - $165.00; 26" - $450.00. **Toddler:** 18" - $350.00; 25" - $675.00.

GANS & SEYFARTH

Dolls with the "G.S." or "G & S" were made by Gans & Seyfarth of Germany who made dolls from 1909 into the 1930s. Some dolls will be marked with the full name.

Child: Open mouth, composition body. Good quality bisque, no damage and nicely dressed. (See photo in Series 9, pg. 82.) 13" - $325.00; 16" - $525.00; 17" - $650.00; 21" - $700.00; 26" - $825.00; 30" - $1,100.00.

Baby: Bent limb baby body. Perfect condition and nicely dressed. (Add more for toddler body.) 14" - $350.00; 17" - $550.00; 21" - $650.00; 24" - $750.00.

GERMAN DOLLS, MAKER UNKNOWN

Some of these unmarked dolls will have a mold number and/or a head size number and some may have the mark "Germany." Add more for original clothes.

Closed mouth child: 1880–1890s. Excellent bisque. No damage and nicely dressed. **Jointed composition body:** 13" - $750.00; 15" - $850.00; 22" - $1,600.00; 24" - $1,900.00. **Kid or cloth body:** May have slightly turned head. Bisque lower arms. 13" - $600.00; 15" - $750.00; 22" - $1,300.00; 24" - $1,500.00.

Closed mouth child on German body: Very French looking. No double chin or dimple in chin. Feathered eyebrows. (See photo in Series 11, pg. 80.) 20" - $2,500.00; 24" - $3,400.00.

Open mouth child: Late 1880s to 1900. Excellent pale bisque, glass eyes. No damage and nicely dressed. **Jointed composition body:** 12" - $185.00; 15" - $285.00; 20" - $450.00; 23" - $550.00; 26" - $650.00; 30" - $900.00. **Kid body:** Excellent quality bisque. Bisque lower arms. 15" - $175.00; 20" - $300.00; 23" - $425.00; 26" - $550.00.

Open mouth child: 1888–1920s. Very "dolly" type face. Overall excellent condition. **Jointed composition body:** 10" - $150.00; 13" - $185.00; 19" - $300.00; 23" - $425.00; 26" - $550.00; 28" - $675.00; 32" - $750.00. **Kid body:** 12" - $125.00; 15" - $150.00; 18" - $200.00; 22" - $350.00.

Belton type: May have **mold #132, 136, 137, 138, etc.** German composition jointed body, glass eyes. **Open mouth:** 13" - $1,300.00; 16" - $1,600.00; 21" - $2,200.00; 23" - $3,000.00. **Closed mouth:**

Excellent quality. 15" - $2,500.00; 18" - $3,000.00; 25" - $4,000.00.

Molded hair: See that section.

All bisque: See All Bisque – German section.

Infants: Bisque head with molded/painted hair and glass eyes. Cloth body has composition or celluloid hands No damage. 13" - $325.00; 16" - $475.00; 19" - $650.00.

Babies: Solid dome or wigged, five-piece baby body, open mouth. Nicely dressed and no damage. (Allow more for closed or open/closed mouth, very unusual face, or toddler doll.) **Glass eyes:** 10" - $245.00; 15" - $450.00; 18" - $625.00; 21" - $700.00. **Painted eyes:** 10" - $165.00; 15" -

$275.00; 18" - $425.00; 21" - $600.00. **Toddler:** 15" - $550.00; 18" - $675.00.

Bonnet or hat: See Bonnet Doll section.

Tiny unmarked doll: Head has very good quality bisque with glass eyes, open mouth. On five-piece papier maché or composition body. No damage. 7" - $185.00; 10" - $275.00; 13" - $400.00. Jointed body: 7" - $250.00; 10" - $375.00; 13" - $525.00. **Poorly painted bisque:** 6" - $85.00; 9" - $125.00; 12" - $175.00.

Tiny doll: Closed mouth, jointed body. 7" - $350.00; 10" - $500.00; 13" - $650.00. Five-piece body: 7" - $250.00; 10" - $350.00; 13" - $425.00.

Character child: Unidentified, closed mouth, **very character face.** May

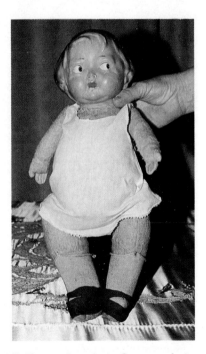

This 1920s bisque head with painted features is marked "Germany" with "W" in a diamond and "137-0". We know that "Just Me" made by Armand Marseilles came before the "Patsy" made by Effanbee, but this head fits into the pattern some place. $500.00. *Courtesy Ellen Dodge.*

14" "Grumpy" made in Germany during the early 1920s. Composition head, molded hair, and painted features. Cloth body and limbs with fingers sewn together and free standing thumb. Unmarked. $365.00. *Courtesy Bonnie Stewart.*

have wig or solid dome. Glass eyes, closed or open/closed mouth. Excellent quality bisque. No damage, nicely dressed. 15" - $3,800.00 up; 19" - $4,600.00 up.

Character: Mold #128, 134, and others of this quality. Closed mouth. Glass eyes: 15" - $7,200.00 up; 21" - $9,500.00 up. Painted eyes: 15" - $5,800.00 up; 21" - $8,300.00 up. **Mold #111:** (See photo in Series 8, pg. 82.) Glass eyes: 21" - $19,000.00

up. Painted eyes: 21" - $12,000.00 up. **Mold #116:** (Maybe made by Kämmer & Reinhardt.) 18" - $9,500.00. **Mold #163:** 17" - $1,100.00.

American Schoolboy: (so called) Side part painted hair swept across forehead like bangs. Glass eyes, closed mouth. **Jointed composition body:** 13" - $575.00, 17" - $750.00. **Kid or cloth body:** 13" - $425.00; 17" - $550.00; 21" - $700.00.

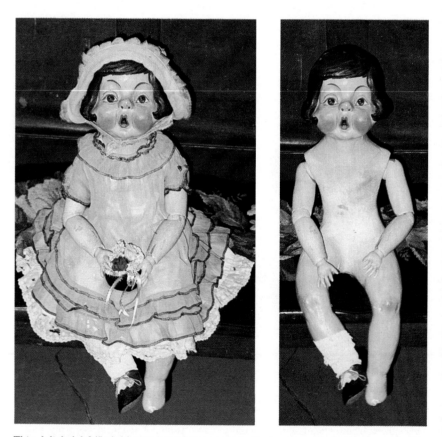

This delightful 24" child may have been made in Germany and is being shown in this section. She has oil-painted features and molded hair. The shoulder plate becomes part of the cloth body. German jointed arms and molded legs make her sit. She appears to be singing with wide open/closed style mouth. Original clothes are from the 1910s–1920s. Doll could also have been made in Spain, Mexico, or Italy. $600.00 up. *Courtesy Jackie Whitmarsh.*

11" composition shoulder head with painted eyes, cloth arms and upper half of body. Lower part is a key-wound metal clown that makes the little boy shake and move forward. The clown is 8" tall and both are unmarked. Top of boy sits on clown's head and shoulder. Original clothes cover all of the clown except feet. The clown is unpainted except feet which are painted red. Likely made in Germany. $200.00. *Courtesy Sandra Cummins.*

GLADDIE

Gladdie was designed by Helen Jensen in 1929. The German-made doll was distributed by George Borgfeldt. The cloth body has composition limbs, and the head has glass eyes. (See photos in Series 5, pg. 69; Series 6, pg. 92; Series 7, pg. 79; Series 11, pg. 76.)

Ceramic style or biscaloid head: 17" - $1,100.00; 20" - $1,400.00 up. **Unusual:** Teeth rest on molded tongue. (See photo in Series 6, pg. 92.) 19" - $2,100.00.

Bisque head, mold #1410: 17" - $4,200.00; 20" - $5,300.00; 25" - $6,600.00.

GOEBEL

The Goebel factory has been operating since 1879 and is located in Oeslau, Germany. The interwoven W.G. mark has been used since 1879. William Goebel inherited the factory from his father, Franz Detlev Goebel. About 1900, the factory only made dolls, dolls heads and porcelain figures. They worked in both bisque and china glazed items.

Child: 1895 and later. Open mouth, composition body, sleep or set eyes with head in perfect condition, dressed and ready to display. 7" - $175.00; 15" - $325.00; 20" - $525.00; 23" - $650.00.

Child: Open/closed mouth, wig, molded teeth, shoulder plate, kid body, bisque hands. 18" - $900.00; 21" - $1,200.00.

Child: Rare. Deeply molded hair; may have molded bows. Intaglio eyes, open/closed mouth, smile, jointed body. (See photo in Series 7, pg. 80.) 13" - $2,000.00; 16" - $3,500.00; 18" - $4,400.00.

Character: After 1910. Molded hair that can be in various styles, with or without molded flowers or ribbons, painted features and on five-piece papier maché body. No damage and nicely dressed. 8" - $365.00; 10" - $450.00; 13" - $575.00.

Character baby: After 1909. Open mouth, sleep eyes and on five-piece bent limb baby body. No damage and nicely dressed. 14" - $450.00; 17" - $575.00; 20" - $750.00; 25" - $950.00. Toddler: 15" - $600.00; 18" - $750.00; 23" - $1,100.00.

Molded-on bonnet: Closed mouth, five-piece papier maché body, painted features and may have various molded-on hats or bonnets and painted hair. 8" - $400.00; 10" - $550.00; 13" - $650.00.

Marks:

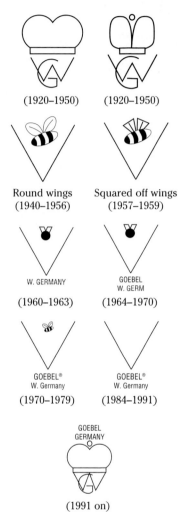

(1920–1950)   (1920–1950)

Round wings   Squared off wings
(1940–1956)   (1957–1959)

W. GERMANY   GOEBEL
                     W. GERM
(1960–1963)   (1964–1970)

GOEBEL®   GOEBEL®
W. Germany   W. Germany
(1970–1979)   (1984–1991)

GOEBEL
GERMANY

(1991 on)

Center right: 24" doll with glass eyes, open mouth, fully jointed body. Made by Goebel and marked with bee symbol/"WG 120/Germany 8½." Rear: 30" Simon & Halbig with open mouth and fully jointed body. Marked "1249/Santa/Germany/Halbig." 24" Cuno and Otto Dressel toddler with open mouth. Front: 17" Simon & Halbig #1428 with very character face, open/closed mouth, and molded tongue. Goebel - $650.00; 30" S&H - $1,900.00; 24" toddler - $850.00; 17" #1428 - $1,950.00. *Courtesy Frasher Doll Auctions.*

86

Bisque head with glass or set eyes to the side, closed smiling mouth, impish or watermelon-style mouth, original composition or papier maché body. Molded hair or wigged. 1911 and after. Not damaged in any way and nicely dressed.

All bisque: See All Bisque section.

Armand Marseille, #200: (See photo in Series 8, pg. 21.) 9" - $1,400.00; 13" - $2,200.00. **#210:** 9" - $2,100.00; 13" - $2,900.00. **#223:** 8" - $850.00; 12" - $1,050.00. **#240, 241:** (See photos in Series 3, pg. 35; Series 5, pg. 72.) Three tufts of molded hair, glass eyes. 12" - $2,200.00; 14" - $2,500.00. **#248:** 10" - $1,100.00. **#252:** Kewpie type baby. (See photo in Series 5, pg. 72.) 9" - $1,000.00; 13" - $1,900.00. **#253, 353:** 8" - $825.00; 10" - $1,250.00; 13" - $1,450.00. **#254:** 12" - $975.00. **#255–#310 (Just Me), fired-in color:** 9–10" - $950.00 up; 12–13" - $1,800.00 up. **#310, painted bisque:** 9" - $700.00; 12–13"- $1,100.00. **#320:** Glass eyes: 10" - $1,400.00. Painted eyes: 8" - $675.00; 11" - $875.00. **#323, fired-in color:** 8" - $1,000.00; 12" - $1,400.00; 14" - $1,600.00. On baby body: 12" - $850.00; 16" - $1,200.00. **Painted bisque baby:** 10" - $425.00; 15" - $625.00. **#325:** 8" - $650.00; 13" - $925.00.

B.P. (Bahr & Proschild), #686: 12" - $2,300.00; 14" - $2,800.00 Baby: 15" - $1,500.00. **#401:** 8" - $625.00.

Demalcol: (See photo in Series 7, pg. 82) 12" - $600.00; 15" - $800.00.

Elite: See end of this section.

Hansi: "Gretel." Molded hair, shoes and socks. Made of porcelain material called "prialytine." (See photo in Series 8, pg. 87.) 11" - $2,600.00.

Hertel Schwab: See that section.

Heubach Einco: 12" - $4,800.00; 16" - $7,400.00; 19" - $8,200.00.

Heubach (marked in square): 10" - $900.00; 14" - $1,850.00. **#8556:** 16" - $8,500.00 up. **#8676:** 8" - $765.00; 12" - $1,150.00. **#8723, 8995:** Glass eyes. 12" - $2,600.00. **#9056:** Full bangs, hair rolled under around head. 10" - $1,150.00 up; 13" -

16" googly with oversized round eyes, high arched eyebrows, round face, and sweet expression. Marked "Heubach" in square/"8723." $3,650.00. *Courtesy Ellen Dodge.*

9½" googly with glass eyes to side, full cheeks, and closed mouth grin. Five-piece body with painted-on shoes and socks. Marked "G.B. 253 Germany A 6/0 M." $1,250.00. *Courtesy Patricia Wood.*

$1,350.00 up. **#9573:** 9" - $875.00; 12" - $1,550.00; 14" - $1,900.00. **#9578, 11173:** Called "Tiss Me." (See photos in Series 6, pg. 96; Series 9, pg. 89.) 9" - $1,300.00; 13" - $1,500.00. **Winker:** One eye painted closed. (See photo in Series 8, pg. 85.) 12" - $1,875.00. **#9743:** Sitting. Wide open/closed mouth, top knot, and "star" shaped hands. 7" - $600.00.

Heubach Koppelsdorf: (See photo in Series 6, pg. 96.) **#260–264:** 9" - $450.00; 12" - $550.00. **#291:** Dimples, lower lip sucked up under upper lip. Glass eyes. 9" - $1,350.00. **#318:** 12" - $1,400.00; 15" - $2,200.00. **#319:** 9" - $650.00; 12" - $1,250.00. **#417:** 9" - $600.00; 14" - $1,300.00.

Kestner, #111: Jointed body. (See photo in Series 8, pg. 8.) 12" - $2,975.00; 15" - $3,550.00.

Kestner, #163, 165: This number now attributed to **Hertel Schwab.** 14" - $3,600.00; 16" - $5,200.00. **#172–173:** Attributed to **Hertel Schwab.** 12" - $3,200.00; 15" - $5,800.00. **#217, 221:** (See photo in Series 8, pg. 85.) 8" - $1,250.00; 12" - $2,700.00; 14" - $3,800.00.

Kammer & Reinhardt (K✿R): Five-piece body. 10" - $2,400.00. **#131:** 8" - $2,500.00; 12" - $5,100.00; 15" - $7,300.00.

Kley & Hahn (K&H), #180: 16" - $2,900.00; 18" - $3,600.00.

Oscar Hitt: 16" - $5,500.00; 18" - $7,500.00.

Our Fairy: See All Bisque section and Hertel, Schwab & Co. (See photo in Series 7, pg. 81.)

P.M. (Otto Reinecke), #950: 7" - $850.00; 10" - $1,000.00; 14" - $1,500.00; 17" - $1,700.00 up.

S.F.B.J., #245: (See photo in Series 6, pg. 96) Five-piece body: 9" - $1,450.00. Fully jointed body: 13" - $2,500.00; 16" - $4,700.00 up.

Steiner, Herm: 10" - $925.00; 13" - $1,150.00.

Composition face: Very round composition face mask or all composition head with wig, glass eyes to side and

15" googly with flirty glass eyes, open/closed watermelon mouth, and original wig. Has mold #165 which is now attributed to Hertel & Schwab. $4,900.00. *Courtesy Turn of Century Antiques.*

13" bisque head googly with modeled hair and ribbon, large glass disc eyes, and closed smiling mouth. Has cloth body with composition lower arms. Original provincial costume. Marked "D.R.G.M. 954647" (registration number). $2,800.00. *Courtesy Frasher Doll Auctions.*

closed impish watermelon-style mouth. Body is stuffed felt. In original clothes. (See photo in Series 10, pg. 86.) **Excellent condition:** 9" - $375.00; 13" - $675.00; 15" - $725.00; 17" - $1,100.00; 21" - $1,500.00. **Fair condition:** Cracks or crazing, nicely redressed. 9" - $170.00; 12" - $285.00; 14" - $450.00; 16" - $550.00; 20" - $775.00. **Composition head:** Can have plain cloth or corduroy stuffed body. Celluloid disc eyes: Made during World War II. (One maker was Freundlich.) 17" - $100.00; 21" - $125.00.

Painted eyes: Composition or papier maché body with painted-on shoes and socks. Bisque head with eyes painted to side, closed smile mouth and molded hair. Not damaged and nicely dressed. **A.M. 320, Goebel, R.A., etc.:** 7" - $285.00; 9" - $425.00; 12" - $600.00; 14" - $800.00. **Heubach, Gebruder:** 9" - $450.00 up.

Disc eyes: Bisque socket head or shoulder head with molded hair (can have molded hat/cap), closed mouth and inset celluloid discs in large googly eyes. (See photo in Series 8, pg. 85; Series 10, pg. 86.) 12" - $950.00; 15" - $1,250.00; 18" - $1,600.00; 22" - $2,000.00. **Black:** 14" - $1,600.00. **Molded hairbow:** 13" - $2,800.00.

Molded-on military hat: Marked **"Elite."** (See photo in Series 5, pg. 71; Series 7, pg. 82; Series 8, pg. 86.) 13" - $2,300.00; 17" - $3,600.00. **Japanese soldier:** 13" - $3,000.00. **Two faced:** 13" - $4,200.00.

Center: 9½" Gebruder Heubach with painted features, closed mouth, and five-piece toddler body. Hairdo has molded, coiled top knot and flared sides. Left: 6" Heubach cat with white bisque head, intaglio eyes, and open/closed mouth. Has jointed body with painted-on boots. Marked "9102/Heubach" in square. Right: 5" all bisque with painted features and open/closed mouth. Has mad expression and curled fists. Shoes and socks are painted on. Marked "791-3." 9½" - $1,600.00. 6" cat - $1,400.00. 5" - $400.00.
Courtesy Frasher Doll Auctions.

GREINER

Ludwig Greiner of Philadelphia, PA, made dolls from 1858 into the late 1800's. The heads are made of papier maché, and they can be found on various bodies. Some can be all cloth; many are homemade. Many have leather arms or can be found on Lacmann bodies that have stitched joints at the hips and the knees and are very wide at the hip line. The Lacmann bodies will be marked "J. Lacmann's Patent March 24th, 1874" in an oval. The Greiner heads will be marked "Greiner's Patent Doll Heads/Pat. Mar. 30, '58." Also "Greiner's/Improved/Patent

Heads/Pat. Mar. 30, '58." The later heads are marked "Greiner's Patent Doll Heads/ Pat. Mar. 30, '58. Ext. '72."

Greiner doll: Can have black or blonde molded hair, blue or brown painted eyes and be on a nice homemade cloth body with cloth arms or a commerical cloth body with leather arms. Dressed for the period and clean, with head in near perfect condition with no paint chips and not repainted.

With '58 label: 17" - $550.00; 23" - $725.00; 26" - $825.00; 30" - $975.00 up; 35" - $1,300.00; 38" - $1,800.00 up. **With chips/flakes or repainted:** 16" - $300.00; 22" - $400.00; 25" - $500.00; 28" - $625.00; 32" - $750.00; 36" - $825.00.

With '72 label: 18" - $450.00; 21" - $525.00; 26" - $650.00; 30" - $975.00. **With chips/flakes or repainted:** 18" - $225.00; 21" - $325.00; 26" - $425.00; 30" - $500.00.

Glass Eyes: 21" - $1,600.00; 26" - $2,300.00. **With chips, flakes or repainted:** 21" - $950.00; 26" - $1,100.00.

Unmarked: Circa 1850. So called "Pre-Greiner." Papier maché shoulder head, cloth body can be home made. Leather, wood or cloth limbs. Painted hair, black eyes with no pupils. Glass eyes, old or original clothes. **Good condition: Glass eyes:** 18" - $1,200.00; 26" - $1,600.00; 30" - $1,900.00. **Painted eyes:** 18" - $450.00; 26" - $650.00; 30" - $825.00.

31" papier maché with cloth body and leather arms. Has painted features and hair. Marked "Greiner's Improved Patent Heads. Pat. March 30th '58." $725.00. *Courtesy Frasher Doll Auctions.*

H

Dolls with an "H" mark are attribiuted to Halopeau (France), circa 1882. They have outlined eyes, blushed eyelids, open/closed mouths with white space between lips, and original human hair wigs. Original French bodies are of composition and wood with straight wrists. (See photos in Series 2, pg. 77; Series 3, pg. 72; Series 7, pg. 84; Series 10, pg. 88.) 21" - $72,000.00; 26" - $83,000.00. Unmarked: 22" - $30,000.00; 25" - $38,000.00.

Exceptional 20" French doll with closed mouth. On original wood/composition jointed body with straight wrists. Excellent quality. Marked "H." $70,000.00. *Courtesy Frasher Doll Auctions.*

HALF DOLLS

Half dolls can be made of any material including bisque, papier maché and composition. Not all half dolls were used as pincushions. They were also used for powder box tops, brushes, tea cozies, etc. Most date from 1900 into the 1930s. The majority were made in Germany, but many were made in Japan. Generally, they will be marked with "Germany" or "Japan." Some have numbers; others may have the marks of companies such as William Goebel or Dressel, Kister & Co.

The most desirable are the large figures, or any size for that matter, that have both arms molded away from the body or are jointed at the shoulder. Allow more if marked by maker. Very rare half figures can cost from $800.00 to $2,000.00.

Arms and hands extended: Prices can be higher depending on detail and rarity of figure. Marked; china or bisque.

4" - $165.00 up; 6" - $300.00 up; 9" - $675.00 up; 13" - $975.00 up.

Arms extended: Hands attached to figure. China or bisque: 4" - $85.00; 6" - $125.00; 9" - $175.00. Papier maché or composition: 5" - $45.00; 7" - $95.00. **Holding item:** Such as letter, flowers, etc. 5" - $225.00 up.

Bald head, arms away: 5" - $175.00 up. Arms attached: 5" - $90.00 up. **Holding item:** Such as flowers or animals. 5" - $285.00.

Common figures: Arms and hands attached. China: 3" - $22.00; 5" - $35.00; 8" - $45.00. Papier maché or composition: 3" - $20.00; 5" - $30.00; 8" - $40.00.

Jointed shoulders: China or bisque: 6" - $175.00; 9" - $250.00; 11" - $375.00. Papier maché: 4" - $60.00; 7" - $100.00. Wax over papier maché: 5" - $65.00; 8" - $125.00.

Children or men: 3" - $90.00; 5" - $135.00; 7" - $185.00. Jointed shoulders: 3" - $100.00; 5" - $145.00; 7" - $225.00.

Japan marked: 3" - $15.00; 5" - $30.00; 7" - $60.00. **Germany marked:** 3" - $150.00 up; 5" - $300.00 up; 7" - $600.00 up.

These half dolls with arms molded away from bodies are beautifully balanced and are from 2¾" to 4¾" tall. All are made in Germany. Note jewelry and modeled rib cage on lower right lady. Top row: left - $145.00; center - $125.00; right - $130.00. Bottom row: Left - $300.00; right - $285.00. *Courtesy Henrietta Fox.*

Ladies wearing hats were made in many designs, including the little girl wearing a Dutch cap. All were made in Germany. Ladies are 3½" to 4½" tall and girl is 2" tall. Top row: left - $300.00; child - $125.00; right - $100.00. Bottom row: left - $185.00; center - $225.00; right - $125.00. *Courtesy Henrietta Fox.*

Wonderful grouping of half dolls that range in size from 3¼" to 4" tall. All are from Germany. Note the 1920s Dutch hairdo on the first two on the top row and the 1920s bourdoir gown top on the first. Also note lady holding dog on bottom row. Top row, left to right: $100.00, $85.00, $90.00, $90.00. Bottom row, left to right: $80.00, $75.00, $145.00, $85.00, $85.00. *Courtesy Henrietta Fox.*

Hairstyle dictated the fashion in which half doll would be dressed. For example, the doll with the gray hair depicts the powdered effect of the late 1700s. The bald doll took a wig and is very unusual because of her parrot. Both figures mentioned have arms molded away from body. The dolls are 2¾" to 4½" tall and made in Germany. Top row: $285.00. Bottom row: left - $200.00; right - $160.00. *Courtesy Henrietta Fox.*

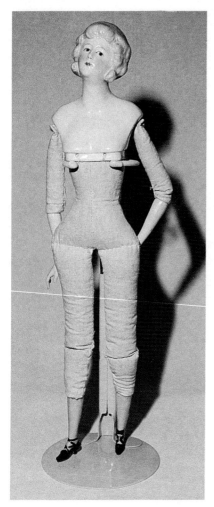

15" half doll with sew holes, formed busts, and molded eyelids. Head is modeled upward and has gray 1920s hairstyle. Two layers of bisque, square on all sides, lower part is white with the upper having slight flesh tones. Arms are wire jointed and hands are extremely delicate. Appears to be all original. Marked "#15837 Germany." $350.00.

China glazed half doll complete with rare original feather duster. Has original "clothes" and is silk wrapped down to blue feathers. Made in Germany. Being held by extremely rare #601 Simon & Halbig. See that section for description. Duster with half doll, in this condition - $225.00. *Courtesy Lois Thomas.*

Heinrich Handwerck began making dolls and doll bodies in 1876 at Gotha, Germany. The majority of their heads were made by Simon & Halbig. In 1897 they patented, in Germany, a ball jointed body #100297 and some of their bodies will be marked with this number.

Mold numbers include: **12x, 19, 23, 69, 79, 89, 99, 100, 109, 118, 119, 124, 125, 139, 152, 189, 199, 1001, 1200, 1290.**

Sample mold marks:

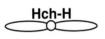

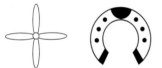

Child, no mold number: After 1885. Open mouth, sleep or set eyes, on ball jointed body. Bisque head with no cracks, chips or hairlines, good wig and nicely dressed. 15" - $375.00; 17" - $465.00; 20" - $575.00; 24" - $650.00; 27" - $800.00; 32" - $1,350.00; 36" - $1,800.00; 40" - $2,600.00. **Child with mold numbers:** 13" - $425.00; 15" - $450.00; 18" - $500.00; 22" - $625.00; 25" - $700.00; 29" - $950.00; 32" - $1,300.00; 36" - $1,550.00; 40" - $3,100.00.

Kid body: Bisque shoulder head, open mouth. All in good condition and nicely dressed. 15" - $250.00; 18" - $350.00; 24" - $450.00; 26" - $650.00.

Mold #79, 89: With closed mouth. 15" - $1,700.00; 18" - $2,000.00 up; 22" - $2,400.00 up.

Mold #189: With open mouth. 15" - $475.00; 18" - $850.00; 22" - $975.00.

Bear: Bisque head on teddy bear body of silver/blue mohair. 14" - $650.00 up.

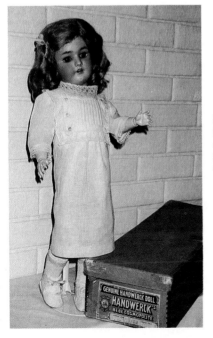

22" "Bebe Cosmpolite" in mint condition. Shown with original box. Has sleep eyes and open mouth. Marked "Heinrich Handwerck/ Simon Halbig/3" and body is also stamped with company name. Written on box "Bought in San Bernadino (CA) Feb. 21, 1913." In box - $900.00 up. Clean, redressed - $550.00. *Courtesy Pat Graff.*

Max Handwerck started making dolls in 1900 and his factory was located at Waltershausen, Germany. In 1901, he registered "Bébé Elite" with the heads made by William Goebel. The dolls from this firm are marked with the full name, but a few are marked with "M.H."

Child: Bisque head, open mouth, sleep or set eyes, on fully jointed composition body, no damage and nicely dressed. **Mold #283, 287, 291, etc.:** 15" - $375.00; 21" - $550.00; 25" - $650.00; 29" - $850.00; 32" - $1,100.00; 40" - $2,300.00.

Bébé Elite: Bisque heads with no cracks or chips, sleep or set eyes, open mouth. Upper teeth and smile. Can have a flange neck on cloth body with composition limbs or be on bent leg composition baby body. (See photo in Series 7, pg. 88.) 16" - $475.00; 22" - $700.00. **Toddler:** 18" - $775.00; 23" - $975.00; 27" - $1,400.00. **Socket head on fully jointed body:** 18" - $675.00; 22" - $875.00.

32" with good quality bisque, sleep eyes, and open mouth. On fully jointed body. Marked "Max Handwerck." $1,000.00. *Courtesy Ken Bowers.*

HANSI

9" "Hansi" made of prialytine with body left natural and head and limbs made in flesh tones. Shoes and socks are painted on. Has hole in one hand to attach original umbrella. Painted googly eyes and smile mouth. Original clothes included very large navy blue headpiece with the insignia fo the French Legion d'Honneur. Designed by L'Oncle Hansi, a painter and illustrator. Nude - $850.00; original - $1,900.00.

Hertel, Schwab & Co. has been recognized by the German authors Jurgen and Marianne Cieslik as the maker of many dolls that were attributed to other companies all these years. There does not seem to be a "common denominator" to the Hertel, Schwab doll lines and any style can be included. As of 1993, collectors believe that this company made heads of very poor to finest quality for major Germany dollmakers.

Babies: Bisque head, molded hair or wig, open or open/closed mouth, sleep or painted eyes, bent limb baby body. Good condition with no damage.

Mold #125, 127 ("Patsy"): 15" - $1,050.00; 18" - $1,500.00.

Mold #126 ("Skippy"): 13" - $1,150.00; 16" - $1,500.00.

Mold #121, 130, 136, 142, 150, 151, 152, 153, 154: 9" - $365.00; 14" - $485.00; 18" - $600.00; 19" - $775.00; 22" - $875.00; 25" - $1,200.00.

Child: Bisque head, painted or sleep eyes, closed mouth, jointed composition body, no damage and nicely dressed. **#119, 134, 140, 141, 149: Glass eyes:** 12" - $3,100.00; 16" - $4,700.00; 18" - $5,700.00; 22" - $6,900.00. **Painted eyes:** 12" - $2,900.00; 16" - $3,900.00; 18" - $5,000.00; 22" - $5,500.00.

#154, closed mouth: 15" - $2,400.00; 21" - $2,700.00. **Open mouth:** 17" - $1,100.00; 21" - $1,500.00.

#169, closed mouth: 17" - $3,200.00; 21" - $3,600.00. **Toddler:** 23" - $4,400.00; 28" - $5,800.00. **Baby:** Open mouth. 19" - $1,000.00; 23" - $1,350.00.

All bisque: One-piece body and head, glass eyes, closed or open mouth. All in perfect condition. **Prize Baby, #208:** Late 1920s. 6" - $325.00; 8" - $550.00. **Swivel neck:** (See #222 below.) 6" - $450.00; 8" - $700.00; 10" - $800.00.

Googly: These molds are now being attributed to Hertel, Schwab & Co. Large,

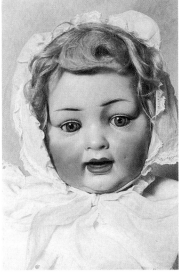

Left: 19½" mold #151 with bald head, painted hair, and sleep eyes. Has open/closed mouth with molded tongue and two modeled upper teeth. Right: 21" mold #152 with wig, sleep eyes, and small cheek dimples. Has open/closed mouth and two upper teeth. 19½"–21" - $775.00 each. *Courtesy Turn of Century Antiques.*

side glance sleep or set eyes. Wig or molded hair. Closed mouth, no damage and nicely dressed. **#163, 164, 165:** 13" - $2,800.00; 16" - $5,200.00. **Baby:** 14" - $2,900.00. **Toddler:** 16" - $5,900.00. **#168:** Looks like Campbell Kid. **Open/closed mouth:** 17" - $6,000.00. **Two-faced:** 15" - $7,000.00 up. **#172: Baby** body, glass eyes. 14" - $3,450.00. **Toddler:** 16" -

$5,900.00. **Child:** 18" - $6,000.00. **#173:** 13" - $3,300.00; 15" - $5,800.00. **#189:** 10" - $800.00. **#217:** 8" - $1,250.00. **#222 (Our Fairy):** Painted eyes, molded hair. 7" - $650.00; 10" - $1,275.00; 14" - $1,700.00 up. **Wig, glass eyes:** 11" - $1,850.00; 13" - $2,400.00 up. **Baby:** 17" - $4,400.00. **Toddler:** 17" - $5,000.00.

HEUBACH, GEBRÜDER

The Heubach Brothers (Gebrüder) made dolls from 1863 into the 1930's at Lichte, Thuringia, Germany. They started producing character dolls in 1910. Heubach dolls can reflect almost every mood and are often found on rather crude, poor quality bodies, and many are small dolls.

Marks:

#1017: Baby-faced toddler with open mouth. 17" - $1,500.00; 23" - $1,800.00; 29" - $2,300.00.

#2850, 8058: Open/closed mouth, two rows teeth. Molded braided hair, blue

Character dolls: Bisque head, open/closed or closed mouth. Painted eyes (allow more for glass eyes). Kid, papier maché or jointed composition bodies. Molded hair or wig. No damage and nicely dressed.
Marked "Heubach": No mold number. Open/closed mouth, deep dimples. (See photo in Series 9, pg. 98.) 19" - $4,700.00; 26" - $6,800.00. **Adult:** Open mouth, glass eyes. 15" - $4,800.00. **Slight smile:** Painted eyes. 16" - $3,800.00.

Left: 16½" "Dolly Dimple" character child made by Gebruder Heubach. Open mouth and dimples. Marked with "Heubach" in a square. Right: 19½" "Santa" made by Simon & Halbig. Has open mouth. Marked "S&H 1249." 16½" - $2,600.00; 19½" - $1,300.00. *Courtesy Frasher Doll Auctions.*

ribbon bow. 15" - $9,400.00 up; 19" - $10,000.00 up.

#5636: Laughing child. Two lower teeth, intaglio painted eyes. 10" - $925.00; 13" - $1,300.00. **Glass eyes:** 13" - $1,600.00; 17" - $2,400.00.

#5689: Open mouth, smiling. Glass eyes. (See photos in Series 5, pg. 82; Series 7, pg. 90.) 15" - $1,950.00; 19" - $2,600.00; 24" - $3,200.00.

#5730 (Santa): 15" - $1,600.00; 18" - $2,400.00; 25" - $2,700.00.

#5777, 7307, 9355 ("Dolly Dimples"): Ball-jointed body. Can be marked with "Heubach" in square. (See photo in Series 5, pg. 93; Series 9, pg. 97; Series 11, pg. 86.) 14" - $2,300.00; 17" - $2,700.00; 23" - $3,400.00; 25" - $3,600.00.

#6692: Shoulder head, smiling, intaglio eyes. 16" - $1,000.00 up.

#6736, 6894: Laughing, wide open/closed mouth, molded lower teeth. 12" - $1,000.00; 17" - $2,000.00.

#6894, 6898, 7759: Baby, closed mouth, pouty. (See photo in Series 6, pg. 107.) 5" - $200.00; 7" - $300.00; 10" - $475.00; 14" - $650.00.

#6896: Pouty, jointed body. 17" - $1,000.00; 21" - $1,400.00.

#6969, 6970, 7246, 7248, 7347, 7407, 7603, 7802, 8017, 8420: Pouty boy or girl with jointed body. **Painted eyes:** (See #6970 in Series 9, pg. 97.) 7" - $365.00; 12" - $675.00; 14" - $1,000.00; 16" - $1,300.00; 20" - $2,900.00. **Glass eyes:** 13" - $2,300.00; 15" - $2,700.00; 18" - $3,400.00; 21" - $4,200.00; 25" - $5,300.00. **Toddler, painted eyes:** 19" - $2,500.00; 23" - $3,000.00. **Toddler, glass eyes:** 22" - $3,100.00; 26" - $4,700.00.

#7134: See #7634.

#7172, 7550: 16" - $1,750.00.

#7246: 20" - $3,600.00; 25" - $5,400.00.

#7307: See #5777.

#7448: Open/closed mouth, eyes half shut. 16" - $2,900.00.

10½" Gebruder Heubach mold #6970 with glass eyes and closed mouth. On fully jointed body. $675.00. *Courtesy Ricki Small.*

17½" Heubach pouty with mold #7603. Has intaglio eyes, flocked hair, and all original clothes. An exceptional example of this mold number. $1,450.00. With flocked hair - $1,950.00. *Courtesy Turn of Century Antiques*

#7602: Painted eyes and hair. Long face pouty. Closed mouth. (See photo in Series 9, pg. 98.) 15" - $2,200.00; 19" - $2,800.00 up. **Glass eyes:** 17" - $2,700.00; 21" - $3,300.00.

#7604: Laughing expression. Jointed body, intaglio eyes. 9" - $500.00; 13" - $725.00; 15" - $900.00. **Baby:** 15" - $700.00. **Walker:** Key wound. 15" - $1,500.00.

#7606: Open/closed mouth. 15" - $975.00; 21" - $1,400.00.

#7616: Open/closed mouth with molded tongue. Socket or shoulder head. **Glass eyes:** 13" - $1,600.00; 17" - $2,200.00.

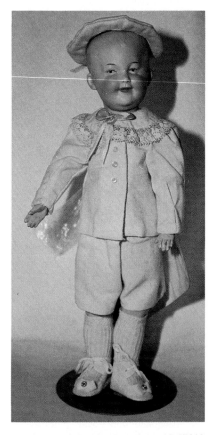

13" Gebruder Heubach with mold #7646. This character has intaglio eyes, wide open/closed laughing mouth, and solid dome with brush stroke hair. $1,450.00.
Courtesy Barbara Earnshaw-Cain.

#7620: Open/closed mouth, dimples, protruding ears. 21" - $1,600.00.

#7622, 8793, 76262: Molded hair, intaglio eyes. Closed mouth, light cheek dimples. (See photos in Series 7, pg. 91; Series 9, pg. 100.) 15" - $1,700.00; 17" - $1,950.00. **Pouty:** 15" - $950.00; 18" - $1,200.00.

#7623: Molded hair, intaglio eyes, open/closed mouth, molded tongue, on bent limb baby body. (See photo in Series 5, pg. 80.) 13" - $875.00; 17" - $1,400.00. **Jointed body:** 16" - $1,650.00; 22" - $2,250.00.

#7626: Deep intaglio eyes, open/closed mouth, molded tongue, large dimples. 18" - $2,000.00 up.

#7634, 7134: Crying, squinting eyes. Wide open/closed mouth. 15" - $1,100.00; 17" - $1,600.00.

#7636: 11" - $850.00; 14" - $1,050.00.

#7644: Slight smiling mouth, open/closed mouth, or can be laughing. Socket or shoulder head, small intaglio eyes. 15" - $925.00; 18" - $1,250.00.

#7646: Open/closed laughing mouth, full cheeks. 14" - $1,550.00.

#7665, 8724: Smile expression. 17" - $1,850.00.

#7666: Squinting eyes, crooked smile. 17" - $3,700.00 up.

#7661, 7686: Wide open/closed mouth, deeply molded hair. 15" - $2,500.00; 18" - $4,000.00.

#7669, 7679: Laughing expression with open/closed mouth, glass eyes. (See photo in Series 10, pg. 95.) 13" - $1,300.00; 16" - $1,800.00; 19" - $2,600.00. **Walker:** 15" - $2,000.00; 17" - $2,350.00.

#7668, 7671: See Black or Brown Doll section.

#7679: Whistler with socket head. (See photo in Series 8, pg. 75.) 11" - $800.00; 16" - $1,300.00; 18" - $1,800.00.

#7684: Screamer with molded tongue, painted eyes. Large open/closed mouth, wrinkles between eyes. 13" - $1,200.00; 17" - $2,200.00; 19" - $2,600.00.

#7686: See #7661.

#7701: Pouty with intaglio eyes. 16" - $1,500.00; 19" - $1,900.00.

#7703: "Coquette" type. Deep molded curls and headband. Smiling, open/closed mouth. Deep intaglio eyes. 14" - $1,950.00.

#7711: Open mouth, molded eyelids, glass eyes, jointed body. Indent in both lips. 13" - $475.00; 16" - $1,000.00; 23" - $1,800.00.

#7743: Girl singing. 17" - $4,600.00.

#7745, 7746: Wide open/closed mouth, two painted lower teeth, molded hair. **Baby or toddler:** 17" - $2,400.00.

#7748: Protruding ears, open/closed mouth, two lower teeth, dimples, painted laughing eyes partly closed. Row of baby fat on back of neck. Chunky **toddler** body. 15" - $5,000.00 up; 18" - $6,300.00 up.

#7751: Squinting eyes, open/closed mouth modeled as yawn. Molded hair, jointed body. 16" - $3,450.00; 19" - $4,250.00.

#7759: See #6894.

#7763: Same description as #7768, 7788.

#7764: Wide open/closed mouth, intaglio eyes to side, deeply sculptured hair, large molded bow. Five-piece body or **toddler** body. 15" - $1,400.00 up; 18" - $2,100.00 up.

#7768, #7788 "Coquette": Tilted head, molded hair and can have ribbon modeled into hairdo. (See photos in Series 7, pg. 93; Series 8, pg. 97.) 8½" - $485.00; 12" - $800.00; 16" - $1,150.00. **Swivel neck:** 9" - $625.00; 12" - $900.00. **All bisque:** 8" - $1,450.00 up.

#7781 baby: Squinted eyes, wide yawn mouth. 16" - $1,900.00.

#7820: Boy with molded hair, intaglio eyes. Open/closed mouth with two painted upper teeth. Slight smile, cheek dimples. 15" - $3,100.00; 18" - $3,900.00.

#7802: See #6969.

#7849: Closed mouth, intaglio eyes. 15" - $900.00.

Right: 15½" with open/closed mouth with two lower teeth, dimples, full cheeks, double chin, roll of baby fat at back of neck, and protruding ears. Has painted hair and eyes. On chubby toddler body. Marked "Heubach 7748/Germany." Left: 20" with very character face. Lips are slightly parted and mouth has six teeth. Has jointed body with straight wrists. 15½" - $5,000.00 up; 20" - $2,800.00 up. *Courtesy Frasher Doll Auctions.*

#7851: Same description as #7764. Cloth body, composition limbs. 13" - $1,300.00. **Without hairbow:** 13" - $1,100.00.

#7852, 7862, 119: Braids coiled around ear (molded), intaglio eyes. (See photo in Series 8, pg. 96.) 17" - $5,500.00 up; 19" - $5,900.00 up.

#7853: Shoulder head, downcast eyes. 15" - $1,550.00; 18" - $2,100.00.

#7865: 15" - $3,100.00.

#7877: See #7977.

#7911: Grin. (See photo in Series 11, pg. 88.) 16" - $1,400.00.

#7925 adult: Painted eyes: 16" - $3,200.00 up; 19" - $3,600.00. **Glass eyes:** 18" - $4,200.00.

#7926: Adult with pensive expression. Closed mouth, molded eyelids. **Glass eyes:** 17" - $4,700.00. **Painted eyes:** 17" - $4,200.00.

#7956: Girl with two patches of bangs almost to eyebrows. Deeply molded hair, intaglio eyes. 16" - $4,000.00.

#7958: Deeply modeled hair and bangs. Dimples, open/closed mouth, intaglio eyes. 16" - $4,500.00; 19" - $5,500.00.

#7959: Intaglio eyes, molded-on bonnet, deeply molded hair, open/closed mouth. (Also see under Babies.) 16" - $3,600.00; 20" - $4,400.00 up.

#7975 ("Stuart Baby"): Glass eyes, removable porcelain bonnet. 13" - $1,900.00.

#7977, #7877, 8228 ("Stuart Baby"): Molded baby bonnet. Painted eyes. (See photo in Series 7, pg. 93.) 12" - $1,200.00; 14" - $1,700.00; 16" - $2,100.00; 18" - $3,000.00. **Glass eyes:** 12" - $1,800.00, 14" - $2,200.00; 16" - $2,900.00.

#8017: See #6969.

#8022: Girl with hair pulled up into knot on top of head. Large intaglio eyes, fully closed mouth, one thick curl in middle of forehead. 12" - $1,000.00 up.

#8035: Boy with molded hair, painted eyes, and jointed body. Long cheeks, short chin, full lips (closed mouth). 18" - $9,500.00 up.

#8050: Lightly modeled hair, intaglio eyes, open/closed laugh mouth with two rows of teeth. 16" - $2,800.00. **Smiling girl:** Molded hairbow. 16" - $3,400.00; 17" - $5,900.00.

Very unusual Gebruder Heubach dolls – 8" boy and girl with mold #8178. (Girl is earlier than boy.) Both have *painted eyes* and single stroke eyebrows. Shoes and socks are painted-on. Both are on five-piece bodies. Boy has all original clothes. Boy - $925.00; girl - $800.00.
Courtesy Virgina Smith.

Mark on girl

Mark on boy

#8053: Round cheeks, closed mouth, painted eyes to side, large ears. 18" - $3,700.00.

#8058: Laughing expression. Open/closed mouth, two rows teeth, painted eyes, molded hair with ribbon around head. 18" - $9,500.00 up.

#8145: Toddler with closed smile mouth. Eyes painted to side. Painted hair. 15" - $1,500.00 up; 21" - $2,200.00 up.

#8178: Six modeled teeth. 12" - $850.00 up.

#8191: Smiling openly. Painted upper and lower teeth. Molded hair, intaglio eyes to side, jointed body. 13" - $950.00; 15" - $1,300.00; 18" - $1,600.00.

#8191: Dolly style face, glass eyes, open mouth. Composition jointed body. (See photos in Series 1, pg. 141; Series 4, pg. 86.) 15" - $550.00; 18" - $675.00; 23" - $785.00.

#8192: Open/closed smiling mouth. Tongue molded between teeth. (See photo in Series 6, pg. 109; Series 11, pg. 88.) 10" - $550.00; 13" - $875.00; 17" - $1,400.00; 24" - $2,000.00. **Open mouth, glass eyes:** Can also be marked "JGODI" with kid body. 16" - $875.00; 17" - $1,500.00; 24" - $2,200.00.

#8197: Deeply molded curls. Molded loop for bow. Pretty face with closed mouth and full lips. Shoulder head, kid body, bisque lower arms, composition legs. 18" - $9,200.00 up.

#8228: See #7977.

#8316: Smiling expression. Open/closed mouth, molded teeth, wig. **Glass eyes:** 17" - $3,600.00 up; 20" - $4,800.00 up. **Painted eyes:** 15" - $1,150.00 up.

#8381 (referred to as "Princess Juliana"): Closed mouth, pensive expression, painted eyes, molded hair, ribbon around head with bow, exposed ears. 18" - $8,500.00 up.

#8420: See #6969.

#8459, 8469: Wide open/closed laughing mouth, two lower teeth, glass eyes. (See photo in Series 6, pg. 109.) 13" - $2,500.00; 16" - $3,100.00.

#8793: See #7622.

#8850: Molded tongue sticking out. **Intaglio eyes:** 15" - $1,100.00. **Glass eyes:** 16" - $1,500.00.

#8555: Shoulder head, painted bulging eyes. (See photo in Series 8, pg. 97.) 15" - $4,950.00.

#8556: Bulging painted eyes to side and looking down. Very puckered small mouth. Deeply molded hair with top knot. Hair wave near front and onto forehead. 13" - $1,800.00; 15" - $2,400.00.

#8556: Open/closed mouth, two rows teeth, molded hair, ribbon. 19" - $8,500.00; 22" - $9,300.00.

#8590: Closed mouth, puckered lips. 15" - $1,500.00; 18" - $2,000.00. Baby: 15" - $1,300.00; 17" - $1,600.00.

#8596: Smile, intaglio eyes. 15" - $900.00; 17" - $1,200.00.

#8648: Extremely pouty closed mouth, intaglio eyes to side. 21" - $2,900.00; 25" - $3,700.00.

#8723: See Googly section.

#8724: See #7665.

#8774 ("Whistling Jim"): Eyes to side and mouth modeled as if whistling. (See photo in Series 7, pg. 92.) 13" - $800.00; 15" - $1,000.00; 18" - $1,500.00.

#8776: See Googly section.

#8868: Molded hair, glass eyes, closed mouth, very short chin. (See photo in Series 7, pg. 92.) 15" - $1,800.00; 19" - $2,500.00.

#8991: Molded hair, painted eyes to side, open/closed mouth with molded tongue, protruding ears. **Toddler body:** 10" - $1,800.00; 16" - $2,800.00. **Kid body:** 14" - $1,300.00.

#8995: Smile, large round glass eyes. Top knot on back of molded hair. Hair molded like flaps over ears. 14" - $2,800.00.

#9141: Winking. Glass eyes: 10" - $1,450.00. Painted eyes: 9" - $925.00.

#9145: Intaglio eyes to side. Molded hair. Open/closed mouth. **Toddler body:** (See photo in Series 10, pg. 94.) 22" - $7,000.00.

#9167: Molded wavy hair, crooked smile, intaglio eyes. Molded upper eyelids closed almost halfway. 9" - $950.00.

#9189: Same description as #7764 but no bow in molded hair. Cloth body, composition limbs. 13" - $1,200.00.

#9355: Shoulder head. Also see **#5777.** 18" - $1,000.00; 24" - $1,800.00.

#9457, 9467 (Indian): 15" - $2,500.00; 18" - $4,000.00.

#9891: Molded-on cap, intaglio eyes. **Aviator:** 14" - $1,700.00. **Sailor:** 14" - $1,800.00. **Farmer:** 14" - $1,300.00.

#10532: Open mouth, jointed body. 12" - $500.00; 15" - $750.00; 18" - $1,000.00; 21" - $1,400.00.

#10586, 10633: Child with open mouth, jointed body. (See #10586 in Series 7, pg. 93.) 15" - $625.00; 18" - $775.00; 24" - $975.00.

#11173 ("Tiss-Me"): Glass eyes, five-piece body, pursed closed mouth with large indented cheeks. 9" - $1,650.00 up; 13" - $1,950.00.

#76262: See #7622.

Child with dolly-type face (non-character): Open mouth, glass sleep or set eyes. Jointed body, bisque head with no damage. Nicely dressed. (Also see #5777 "Dolly Dimples" and #10586.) 15" - $475.00; 17" - $600.00; 20" - $775.00; 25" - $975.00; 28" - $1,200.00.

Googly: See that section.

Indian portrait, #8467: Man or woman. 15" - $4,400.00 up.

Babies or infants: Bisque head, wig or molded hair, sleep or intaglio eyes, open/closed pouty-type mouths.

#6894, #6898, #7602: 6" - $245.00; 9" - $385.00; 13" - $525.00; 16" - $650.00; 18" - $850.00; 23" - $1,200.00; 26" - $1,400.00; 28" - $1,800.00.

#7604: Laughing expression. 14" - $850.00.

#7745, 7746: Rare. Has laughing expression. 17" - $4,600.00 up.

#7959, molded bonnet: Deep modeling to pink or blue bonnet. Molded hair to front and sides of face. 13" - $2,100.00 up.

#7975: See #7977 "Stuart Baby."

Animals: Bisque head on five-piece body or fully jointed body. Usually smiling with painted teeth. 10" - $1,000.00 up.

Walking: Key wind. Price depends on head used. 16" - $800.00 up.

#8649: Same as #7959 but has open/closed mouth, two upper teeth resting on molded tongue, and intaglio eyes. 14" - $2,400.00.

HEUBACH, (ERNST) KOPPELSDORF

Ernst Heubach began making dolls in 1887 in Koppelsdorf, Germany. Marks of this firm can be the initials "E.H." or the dolls can be found marked with the full name, Heubach Koppelsdorf, or:

Child, #250, 275, 302 etc.: After 1888. Jointed body, open mouth, sleep or set eyes. No damage and nicely dressed. 9" - $185.00; 12" - $225.00; 15" - $250.00; 19" - $450.00; 23" - $575.00; 27" - $700.00; 32" - $950.00; 39" - $1,400.00.

Child: Kid or cloth body, bisque lower arms. Bisque shoulder head, some turned head. Open mouth. No damage, nicely dressed. 15" - $185.00; 21" - $325.00; 25" - $475.00; 32" - $800.00. **Painted bisque:** 9" - $125.00; 13" - $185.00.

Babies, #300, 320, 330, 342, etc.: 1910 and after. Five-piece bent limb baby body. Open mouth with some having wobbly tongue and pierced nostrils. Sleep eyes. No damage and nicely dressed. Allow more for toddler body. (See photo in Series 4, pg. 88.) 8" - $185.00; 12" - $250.00; 15" - $400.00; 17" - $525.00; 20" - $650.00; 27" - $975.00.

#300, 320: Fully jointed body. 19" - $575.00; 24" - $725.00.

Baby, #267: Typical baby with open mouth but has flirty eyes and metal eyelids that drop down over eyes. 15" - $500.00; 18" - $675.00; 21" - $800.00; 25" - $975.00. **Painted bisque:** 12" - $150.00; 17" - $265.00. **Toddler:** 17" - $485.00.

Infant: 1925 and after. Molded or painted hair, sleep eyes, closed mouth, flange neck bisque head on cloth body with composition or celluloid hands. No damage and nicely dressed.

#338, 340: 15" - $700.00; 17" - $800.00.

#339, 349, 350: 12" - $425.00; 14" - $575.00.

#320, 335, 339, 340, 349, 350, 399: See Black or Brown Doll section.

Character child: 1910 on. Molded hair, painted eyes and open/closed mouth. No damage. **#261, 262, 271, 330 and others:** 13" - $575.00; 17" - $1,000.00; 19" - $1,200.00; 21" - $1,550.00.

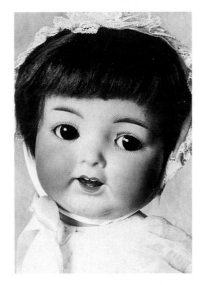

21" Heubach Koppelsdorf toddler with mold #342. Has flirty eyes, open mouth, and five-piece body. $875.00. *Courtesy Turn of Century Antiques.*

18½" Ernst Heubach of Koppelsdorf mold #275 with open mouth. Bisque shoulder head on kid body. Sleep eyes with hair lashes. On fully jointed body. $450.00. *Courtesy Kathy Riddick.*

Jullien marked dolls were made in Paris, France from 1875 to 1904. The heads will be marked Jullien and a size number. In 1892, Jullien advertised "L'Universal" and the label can be found on some of his doll bodies. (See photo in Series 7, pg. 96.)

Child, closed mouth: Paperweight eyes. French jointed body of composition and papier maché with some having wooden parts. Undamaged bisque head. Must have excellent condition, artist workmanship, and color. 13" - $2,500.00; 15" - $2,800.00; 17" - $3,800.00; 19" - $4,200.00; 23" - $4,700.00; 26" - $5,200.00; 30" - $5,600.00. **Open mouth:** 16" - $1,400.00; 18" - $1,800.00; 21" - $2,100.00; 23" - $2,300.00; 26" - $2,600.00; 30" - $3,400.00. **Poor quality, high color:** 16" - $950.00; 21" - $1,500.00; 21" - $1,600.00; 26" - $1,900.00; 28" - $2,400.00.

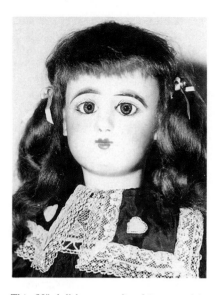

This 20" doll has very fine bisque and is on a five-piece French body. Good artist painting with heavy painted eyebrows and lashes. Marked "J. 6 J." Most likely made by Jeune Jullien but could have been made by Joseph Joanny of Paris, 1884–1921. $4,200.00.

JUMEAU

Known Jumeau Sizes: 0 - 8–9"; 1 - 10"; 2 - 11"; 3 - 12"; 4 - 13"; 5 - 14–15"; 6 - 16"; 7 - 17"; 8 - 19"; 9 - 20"; 10 - 21–22"; 11 - 24–25"; 12 - 26–27"; 13 - 29–30".

Tete Jumeau, closed mouth: 1879–1899 and later. Marked with red stamp on head and oval sticker on body. Paperweight eyes, jointed body with full joints or jointed with straight wrists. Pierced ears with larger sizes having applied ears. No damage at all to bisque head, undamaged French body, dressed and ready to place into collection. (Allow more for original clothes and marked shoes.) 9" - $3,800.00 up; 12" - $3,300.00; 15" - $3,500.00; 17" - $4,000.00; 19" - $4,300.00; 21" - $4,600.00; 23" - $4,800.00; 26" - $5,100.00; 29" - $5,900.00; 32" - $6,200.00; 34" - $7,200.00; 36" - $7,600.00.

Tete Jumeau, open mouth: Not incised "1907." May or may not have number. Will have marked Jumeau body. (See photo in Series 8, pg. 103, Series 9, pg. 105–107.) 17" - $2,300.00; 22" - $2,800.00; 25" - $3,200.00; 28" - $3,500.00; 32" - $4,000.00. **Pull string:** "Mama" cryer. 20" - $2,650.00; 27" - $3,350.00.

1907 Jumeau: Incised "1907," sometimes has the Tete Jumeau stamp. Sleep or set eyes, open mouth, jointed French body. No damage, nicely dressed. 15" - $1,700.00; 17" - $2,300.00; 20" - $2,800.00; 23" - $3,100.00; 26" - $3,500.00; 30" - $4,000.00; 34" - $4,300.00.

Tete Jumeau: Adult body, closed mouth. (See photo in Series 5, pg. 87.) Allow more for original clothes. 19–20" - $5,800.00; 25" - $6,400.00. **Open mouth:**

(See photo in Series 9, pg. 104.) Allow more for original clothes. 14" - $2,000.00; 16" - $2,500.00; 19" - $2,800.00; 20" - $3,000.00; 22" - $3,200.00; 24" - $3,400.00; 28" - $3,900.00; 30" - $4,300.00; 34" - $4,700.00.

E.J. child: Circa early 1880s. Head incised "Depose/E. 6 J." Paperweight eyes, closed mouth, jointed body with straight wrist (unjointed at wrist). Larger dolls will have applied ears. No damage to head or body and nicely dressed in excellent quality clothes. 10" - $5,400.00 up; 14" - $5,700.00; 16" - $6,200.00; 18" - $6,400.00; 22" - $7,300.00; 26" - $8,500.00 up. **Tete style (later dolls):** 18" - $5,000.00; 24" - $6,400.00; 27" - $7,600.00.

E.J. child: Mark with number over the E.J. (Example: $E.^{6}J.$) 17–18" - $10,000.00; 22–23" - $16,000.00.

E.J./A child: 19" - $14,000.00; 22" - $18,500.00; 26" - $26,500.00 up.

Depose Jumeau, incised: 1880. Head will be incised "Depose Jumeau" and body should have Jumeau sticker. Closed mouth, paperweight eyes and on jointed body with straight wrists, although a few may have jointed wrists. No damage at all and nicely dressed. 16" - $5,400.00; 19" - $6,200.00; 24" - $7,200.00.

Long Face (Triste Jumeau): 1870s. Closed mouth, applied ears, paperweight eyes and straight wrists on Jumeau marked body. Head is generally marked with a size number. No damage to head or body, nicely dressed. 20–21" - $24,000.00 up; 25–26"- $26,000.00 up; 29–30" - $30,000.00 up; 33–34" - $36,000.00.

Portrait Jumeau: 1870s. Closed mouth, usually large almond-shaped eyes.

27" Tete Jumeau has open mouth and fully jointed Jumeau body. Has two pull strings on side that make the doll cry "Mama." $3,350.00. *Courtesy Turn of Century Antiques.*

18½" with closed mouth and a beautiful Jumeau look. On marked Jumeau jointed body. Marked "Depose Tete Jumeau. Size 8." $4,300.00 up. *Courtesy Turn of Century Antiques.*

Jointed Jumeau body. Head marked with size number only. Body has Jumeau sticker or stamp. Allow more for original clothes. 10" - $5,600.00; 12" - $5,800.00; 15" - $6,400.00; 21" - $7,900.00; 25" - $11,000.00; 28" - $15,000.00. **Very early almond-shaped eyes:** 12" - $5,900.00; 15–16" - $7,000.00; 19" - $8,500.00; 24" - $12,500.00.

Phonograph Jumeau: Bisque head with open mouth. Phonograph in body. No damage, working and nicely dressed. 21" - $8,200.00; 26" - $11,000.00 up.

Wire Eye (Flirty) Jumeau: Lever in back of head operates eyes. Open mouth, jointed body, straight wrists. 19" - $7,000.00; 22" - $8,400.00; 27" - $9,800.00.

Very pretty 28" Tete Jumeau marked "Depose/Tete Jumeau/Bte S.G.D.G./13." Body marked "Jumeau/Medaille D'or/Paris. $5,900.00. *Courtesy Patty Martin.*

Walker: Open mouth. 21" - $2,500.00; 23" - $2,900.00. **Throws kisses:** 21" - $2,650.00; 23" - $3,000.00.

Celluloid head: Incised "Jumeau." (See photo in Series 3, pg. 85.) 15" - $650.00 up.

Mold #200 series: Examples: **201, 203, 205, 208, 211, 214, 223.** *Very character faces* and marked "Jumeau." Closed mouth. No damage to bisque or body. (See photo in Series 6, pg. 116; Series 7, pg. 100.) 15" - $36,000.00 up; 21" - $58,000.00 up. **At auction:** Original dressed African with scowl lines - $115,000.00. Smiling woman - $120,000.00.

Mold #230 series: Circa 1906. Open mouth. 15" - $1,350.00; 18" - $1,650.00; 21" - $1,900.00 up.

S.F.B.J. or UNIS: Marked along with Jumeau. No damage to head and on French body. Open mouth: 15" - $1,250.00; 21" - $1,750.00. Closed mouth: 15" - $2,200.00; 21" - $2,750.00.

Two-faced Jumeau: Two different faces on same head – one crying and one smiling. Open/closed mouths, jointed body. No damage and nicely dressed. 15" - $9,000.00 up.

Fashion: See Fashion section.

Mold #221: Circa 1930s. Small 10" dolls will have a paper label "Jumeau." Adult style bisque head on five-piece body with painted-on shoes. Closed mouth and set glass eyes. Dressed in original ornate gown. No damage and clean. 12" - $800.00 up.

Mold #306 ("Princess Elizabeth"): Jumeau made after formation of Unis and mark will be "Unis/France" in oval and "71" on one side and "149" on other, followed by "306/Jumeau/1939/Paris." Closed mouth, flirty or paperweight eyes. Jointed French body. No damage and nicely dressed. 21" - $2,500.00; 29" - $3,900.00.

Marked Shoes: #5 and up - $300.00 up. #7–10 - $400.00–600.00.

19" with open mouth and French jointed body. Marked "Jumeau/230 Paris." Shown with a miniature French Papeterie. Heavy covered cardboard with two inkwells and writing pen. Three flaps open for stationary and envelopes. Marked on back "Ruth from Bertha Muller 1902." Doll - $1,600.00. Desk - $775.00. *Courtesy Frasher Doll Auctions.*

26" with open/closed mouth with space between lips. On fully jointed Jumeau body. Marked "Depose Tete Jumeau/Bte S.G.D.G. 12." Shown with miniature leather French Necessaire case with inner compartments. Hinged case holds ivory button hook, brushes, and shoe horn. Also shown is a fabric valise with leather straps and a wooden handled umbrella. Marked "Bon Voyage." Doll - $5,100.00. Valise - $400.00. Umbrella - $385.00. *Courtesy Frasher Doll Auctions.*

KÄMMER & REINHARDT

Kämmer and Reinhardt dolls generally have the Simon and Halbig name or initials incised along with their own name or mark, as Simon & Halbig made most of their heads. They were located in Thüringia, Germany, at Waltershausen and began in 1895, although their first models were not on the market until 1896. The trademark for this company was registered in 1895. In 1909, a character line of fourteen molds (#100–#114) was exhibited at the Leipzig Toy Fair.

Marks:

CHARACTER BOY OR GIRL:

Closed or open/closed mouth. Jointed body or five-piece body. No damage and nicely dressed.

#101 ("Peter" or "Marie"): Five-piece body: 9" - $1,600.00; 12" -$2,400.00. **Fully jointed body:** 10"- $2,000.00; 12" - $2,500.00; 15" - $3,600.00; 17" - $4,000.00; 19" - $5,200.00; 23" - $6,000.00. **Glass eyes:** 15" - $6,700.00; 18" - $7,500.00; 22" - $9,850.00.

#102 ("Karl"): Extremely rare. 14" - $32,000.00 up; 17" - $37,000.00; 22" - $54,000.00. **Glass eyes:** 17" - $37,500.00 up.

#103: Closed mouth, sweet expression, painted eyes. 19" - $60,000.00.

#104: Open/closed mouth, dimples, mischievous expression, painted eyes. Extremely rare. 18" - $58,000.00 up; 21" - $72,000.00 up.

#105: Extremely rare. Open/closed mouth. Much modeling around intaglio eyes. 20" - $86,000.00 up.

23½" character child "Gretchen," mold number 114, with very pouty closed mouth and painted eyes. On fully jointed body. $8,200.00. *Courtesy Frasher Doll Auctions.*

#106: Extremely rare. Full round face, pursed closed full lips, intaglio eyes to side, and much chin modeling. 19" - $62,000.00 up.

#107: Pursed, pouty mouth. Intaglio eyes. 15" - $17,000.00 up; 22" - $42,000.00 up. **Glass eyes:** 17" - $48,000.00 up.

#108: One example sold at auction at over $240,000.00.

#109 ("Elise"): Very rare. (See photo in Series 8, pg. 105; Series 10, pg. 105.) 10" - $8,000.00; 16" - $20,000.00; 21" - $28,000.00. **Glass eyes:** 21" - $32,500.00.

#112, #112X, #112A: Very rare. Intaglio eyes, open/closed mouth with modeled tongue and upper teeth. (See photo in Series 5, pg. 91.) 16" - $11,000.00; 19" - $25,000.00; 24" - $32,000.00. **Glass eyes:** 16" - $16,000.00; 19" - $26,000.00; 25" - $34,000.00.

#114 ("Gretchen" or "Hans"): (See photo in Series 9, pg. 108.) 9" - $2,000.00; 12" - $2,800.00; 16" - $4,700.00; 20" - $5,700.00; 24" - $8,200.00. **Glass eyes:** 19" - $13,000.00 up; 25" - $19,000.00 up.

#117: Closed mouth. 10" (on five-piece body) - $2,400.00; 12" - $2,900.00; 15" - $3,900.00; 18" - $4,900.00; 23" - $6,100.00; 26" - $7,000.00; 29" - $8,300.00; 32" - $9,200.00.

#117A: Closed mouth. 16" - $4,100.00; 19" - $5,200.00; 23" - $6,400.00; 26" - $7,400.00; 29" - $8,500.00.

#117, 117N: Open mouth, flirty eyes. (Subtract $300.00 for sleep eyes only on #117N.) 17" - $1,400.00; 19" - $2,100.00; 22" - $2,400.00; 27" - $2,700.00; 30" - $2,900.00.

#123, #124 ("Max & Moritz"): (See photo in Series 8, pg. 107.) 18" - $29,500.00 up each.

#127: (Also see under babies.) Molded hair, open/closed mouth. Jointed body. 15" - $1,900.00; 21" - $2,700.00; 25" - $3,500.00.

#135, child: 15" - $1,850.00; 18" - $2,100.00.

CHARACTER BABY:

Open/closed mouth or closed mouth on five-piece bent limb baby body, solid dome or wigged. No damage and nicely dressed.

#100 ("Kaiser Baby"): Intaglio eyes, open/closed mouth. (See photo in Series 11, pg. 99.) 13" - $650.00; 16" - $850.00; 19" - $1,100.00; 22" - $1,600.00. **Glass eyes:** 15" - $2,200.00; 20" - $2,400.00. **Black:** (See photo in Series 1, pg. 176.) 16" - $1,200.00; 18" - $1,900.00.

#115, #115a ("Phillip"): (See photo in Series 11, pg. 98.) 15" - $4,200.00; 18" - $4,700.00; 24" - $5,500.00; 26" - $5,800.00. **Toddler:** 16" - $5,000.00; 18" - $5,400.00; 24" - $5,800.00.

#116, #116a: 16" - $3,600.00; 19" - $4,100.00; 24" - $4,800.00. **Toddler:** 17" - $4,200.00; 22" - $4,900.00; 26" - $5,200.00. **Open mouth:** 15" - $1,500.00; 19" - $2,400.00. **Toddler:** 22" - $3,800.00.

#127: (Also see Child.) 13" - $875.00; 17" - $1,500.00; 22" - $1,900.00; 25" - $2,200.00. **Toddler:** 16" - $1,800.00; 21" - $2,400.00; 27" - $2,800.00.

BABY WITH OPEN MOUTH:

Sleep eyes, wigs. On five-piece bent limb baby body. May have tremble tongues or "mama" cryer in body. No damage and nicely dressed. Allow more for flirty eyes.

#118a: 16" - $1,600.00; 19" - $2,400.00; 22" - $2,600.00.

#119: 15" - $3,900.00; 19" - $4,800.00; 23" - $5,250.00.

#121: (See photo in Series 10, pg. 107.) 13" - $585.00; 16" - $775.00; 19" - $1,200.00; 25" - $1,600.00. **Toddler:** 16"- $1,300.00; 22" - $1,800.00; 26" - $2,300.00; 29" - $2,700.00.

11" baby with sleep eyes and open mouth with two upper teeth. On five-piece bent limb baby body. Marked "K✿R 116A." $850.00. *Courtesy Frasher Doll Auctions.*

Adorable 10½" K✿R mold #126 with open/closed mouth, two molded upper teeth, sleep eyes, original mohair wig, and old clothing. On five-piece toddler body. $675.00. *Courtesy Joanna Brunken.*

#122, 128: 13" - $650.00; 16" - $850.00; 19" - $1,250.00; 23" - $1,600.00. **Toddler:** 15" - $1,250.00; 17" - $1,500.00; 25" - $2,100.00; 28" - $2,600.00.

#126: 10" - $450.00; 13" - $625.00; 17" - $775.00; 21"- $975.00; 25" - $1,300.00; 28" - $1,900.00. **Toddler:** 8" - $600.00; 10" - $675.00; 17" - $1,000.00; 22" - $1,400.00; 25" - $1,800.00; 30" - $2,200.00. **Child body:** 21" - $975.00; 35" - $1,900.00.

#135: 14" - $1,500.00; 20" - $2,500.00.

#172, 175: Circa 1925. Five-piece baby body. 17" - $3,000.00; 21" - $3,600.00. Cloth body: 13" - $1,000.00; 17" - $3,400.00.

CHILD DOLLS:

1895–1930s. Open mouth, sleep or set eyes. Fully jointed body. No damage, nicely dressed. Most often found mold numbers are: **#109, 191, 290, 400, 403:** Majority do not have a mold number but may have a number such as 32, 66, 99, etc. (below #100). These are size numbers equal to doll's height in centimeters. Add more for flirty eyes. Add more for all original clothes. (See photo in Series 8, pg. 105.) 9" - $465.00; 13" - $585.00; 16" - $675.00; 20" - $800.00; 23" - $985.00; 26" - $1,200.00; 30" - $1,500.00; 34" - $2,000.00; 39" - $2,800.00; 42" - $3,200.00.

#192: Closed mouth, sleep eyes, fully jointed body. No damage. 8" - $600.00; 15" - $2,400.00; 21"- $2,900.00; 24" - $3,400.00. **Open mouth:** 9" - $450.00; 13" - $800.00; 15" - $900.00; 21" - $1,200.00; 26" - $1,600.00; 29" - $2,000.00.

Small child doll: Open mouth, sleep eyes (some set). No damage. **Five-piece body:** 6" - $375.00; 8" - $475.00; 10" - $585.00. **Jointed body:** 9" - $585.00; 12" - $650.00. **Walker:** 9" - $575.00.

Small child doll: Flapper style. Open mouth, painted bisque. 9" - $525.00.

Small child doll: Closed mouth. 8" - $575.00; 10" - $675.00.

Googly: See Googly section.

Needle sculptured: 1927. Characters. Each - $185.00 up.

26" with open mouth and sleep eyes. On fully jointed German body. Head made for Kammer & Reinhardt by Simon & Halbig. $1,200.00. *Courtesy Virginia Sofie.*

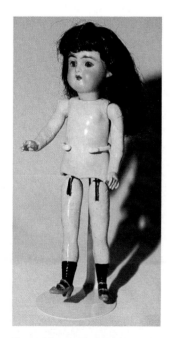

9" walker with metal walking mechanism that makes head turn and legs move. Has open mouth, glass eyes, and modeled-on heeled shoes. Head made by Simon & Halbig for Kammer & Reinhardt. Marked "S&H/K✿R/23." $575.00. *Courtesy Jean Truman.*

Celluloid: See Celluloid section.

Infant: 1924 on. Molded hair, glass eyes, open mouth. Cloth body with composition hands. 15" - $1,650.00; 18" - $2,500.00.

Composition, #926: Looks like mold #260. **Five-piece toddler body:** Allow more for flirty eyes. 16" - $625.00; 24" - $900.00. **Baby:** 17" - $475.00; 23" - $685.00.

Johannes Daniel Kestner's firm was founded in 1802, and his name was carried through the 1920s. The Kestner Company was one of the few that made entire dolls, both bodies and heads. In 1895, Kestner started using the trademark of the crown and streamers. (Also see German - All Bisque.)

Sample marks:

B MADE IN 6   **J.D.K.**
GERMANY   **208**
J.D.K.   **GERMANY**
126

F GERMANY 11

Child doll, closed mouth: Circa 1880. Some appear to be pouties, some may have very sweet expression. Sleep or set eyes, jointed body with straight wrist. No damage and nicely dressed.

#X, XII, XV, 1003: (See photo in Series 8, pg. 111.) 16" - $3,200.00; 19" - $3,800.00; 23" - $4,100.00; 26" - $4,500.00.

#XI, 103: Very pouty. (See photos in Series 6, pg. 122; Series 7, pg. 106.) Price will be less for kid body. 13" - $2,850.00; 17" - $3,500.00; 19" - $3,900.00; 23" - $4,200.00; 26" - $4,400.00; 34" - $5,200.00.

#128 pouty, #169, or unmarked pouty: #128 can have sweet pouty expression. Five-piece body. (See photo of #169 in Series 10, pg. 108.) 8½" - $985.00; 12" - $1,400.00; 14" - $1,700.00; 16" - $2,400.00; 18" - $2,700.00; 20" - $2,900.00; 24" - $3,300.00; 28" - $3,700.00.

Child, closed mouth: May be marked with a letter or number or be unmarked. **Not a pouty.** 16" - $2,200.00; 19" - $2,500.00; 21" - $2,700.00; 24" - $3,000.00; 28" - $3,400.00.

Turned shoulder head: Circa 1880s. Set or sleep eyes. Kid body with bisque lower arms. No damage and nicely dressed. (Allow more for swivel neck.) **Closed mouth:** 13" - $900.00; 17" - $1,200.00; 19" - $1,500.00; 24" - $2,000.00; 27" - $2,500.00. **Open mouth:** 17" - $700.00; 19" - $800.00; 24" - $950.00.

Beautiful 24" early Kestner with closed mouth and large paperweight eyes. On jointed body with straight wrists. Clothes and wig may be original. $3,000.00. *Courtesy Barbara Earnshaw-Cain*

Early child with square cut porcelain teeth: Jointed body. Marked with number and letter. 12" - $585.00; 16" - $850.00; 19" - $1,050.00; 23" - $1,450.00 up; 26" - $1,700.00 up.

A.T. type: Composition jointed body with straight wrists. (See photo in Series 8, pg. 111; Series 9, pg. 113.) **Closed mouth:** 12" - $3,600.00; 14" - $4,200.00; 16" - $4,900.00; 18" - $6,000.00. **Kid body:** 23" - $7,400.00. **Open mouth:** 14" - $2,200.00; 16" - $2,400.00; 18" - $3,000.00.

Bru type, open/closed mouth: Modeled teeth. Bulge in back of neck looks like roll of fat. (See photo in Series 7, pg. 107; Series 8, pg. 112.) **Composition lower arms, kid body:** 15" - $2,400.00; 21" - $3,100.00. **Bisque lower arms:** 18" - $4,800.00; 25" - $6,200.00. **Jointed composition body, straight wrists:** 17" - $5,000.00; 22" - $6,000.00; 25" - $6,600.00.

12" Kestner "A.T." type with sleep eyes and closed mouth. All factory original. $2,800.00. *Courtesy Turn of Century Antiques.*

CHARACTER CHILD:

1910 and after. Closed mouth or open/closed unless noted. Glass or painted eyes, jointed body. No damage and nicely dressed. (See photos in Series 4, pg. 102; Series 6, pg. 124, Series 9, pg. 114.)

#175, 176, 177, 178, 179, 180, 181, 182, 183, 184, 185, 187, 188, 189, 190: These mold numbers can be found on the boxed set doll that has one body and interchangable four heads. (See photos in Series 5, pg. 96; Series 6, pg. 124.) **Boxed set with four heads:** (See photo in Series 2, pg. 97.) 13" - $7,000.00 up. 15" - $9,000.00 up. **Larger size, painted eyes:** Closed or open/closed mouth: 16" - $4,000.00; 18" - $4,500.00; 20" - $5,000.00. **Glass eyes:** 13" - $3,200.00; 16" - $4,200.00; 19" - $4,900.00. **Glass eyes, molded-on bonnet:** 15" - $5,000.00 up.

#151: 15" - $3,600.00; 19" - $4,600.00.

#155: Five-piece body: 10" - $575.00. Jointed body: 10" - $775.00.

#206: Fat cheeks, closed mouth, glass eyes. (See photo in Series 8, pg. 112.) **Child or toddler:** 13" - $7,200.00; 16" - $9,500.00; 18" - $11,000.00; 22" - $16,500.00; 26" - $19,000.00.

#208: Painted eyes, full cheeks. 13" - $3,600.00; 17" - $6,200.00; 20" - $9,800.00; 25" - $12,000.00. **Glass eyes:** 17" - $9,600.00; 23" - $11,000.00.

#212: 12" - $2,200.00; 16" - $3,900.00.

#239: Child or toddler. (Also see Babies.): 18" - $3,600.00; 22" - $4,600.00; 27" - $6,200.00.

#241: Open mouth, glass eyes. (See photo in Series 7, pg. 108.) 17" - $4,200.00; 23" - $5,600.00.

#249: 18" - $1,600.00; 21" - $2,000.00.

#211, 260: Open/closed mouth. Jointed or toddler body. 10" - $675.00; 13" - $975.00; 17" - $1,800.00; 23" - $2,400.00.

CHILD DOLL:

Late 1880s to 1930s. Open mouth on fully jointed body, sleep eyes, some set, with no damage and nicely dressed.

#128, 129, 134, 136, 141, 142, 144, 146, 149, 152, 156, 159, 160, 161, 162, 164, 173, 174, 180, 208, 211, 215: (Allow 20% more for **#128, 129, 149, 152, 160, 161, 173, 174.**) 12" - $450.00; 16" - $525.00; 18" - $575.00; 22" - $725.00; 24" - $785.00; 26" - $950.00; 30" - $1,300.00; 32" - $1,500.00; 37" - $2,200.00.

#143, 189: Character face, open mouth. (See photo in Series 6, pg. 126.) 9" - $650.00; 13" - $850.00; 17" - $950.00 up; 19" - $1,550.00; 21" - $1,850.00; 26" - $2,700.00 up.

#192: 14" - $625.00; 17" - $725.00; 20" - $925.00.

CHILD WITH KID BODY:

Circa 1880s. "Dolly" face, open mouth, sleep or set eyes, bisque shoulder head, bisque lower arms. No damage and nicely dressed.

#145, 147, 148, 149, 155, 166, 167, 170, 195, etc.: (Add more for fur eyebrows.) 9" - $285.00; 13" - $325.00; 17" - $485.00; 20" - $625.00; 23" - $750.00; 26" - $925.00; 30" - $1,200.00.

#142, 144, 146, 154, 164, 167, 168, 171, 196, 214: Jointed body, open mouth. 9" - $650.00; 13" - $725.00; 16" - $825.00; 21" - $900.00; 24" - $1,100.00; 28" - $1,300.00; 32" - $1,850.00; 42" - $3,400.00 up. **Swivel bisque head:** Bisque shoulder head, open mouth. **Kid body:** 16" - $485.00; 20" - $685.00; 25" - $950.00. **Kid body, shoulder head:** 16" - $350.00; 20" - $485.00; 25" - $625.000.

#171 (Daisy), some #154: 18" only. (See previous listing for additional sizes.) Blonde, side part mohair wig. White dress, red hooded cape. Original - $925.00; redressed - $650.00.

CHARACTER BABIES:

1910 and later. Bent limb baby bodies, sleep or set eyes, open mouth. Can be wigged or have solid dome with painted hair. No damage, nicely dressed.

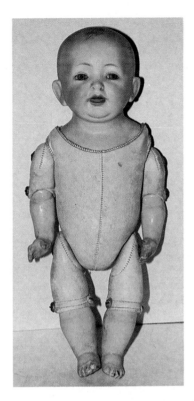

Cute 11½" Kester, mold #210, has jointed kid leather toddler/baby body with composition lower limbs. Has open/closed mouth and glass eyes. On this body - $625.00 up. *Courtesy Ellen Dodge.*

#121, 142, 150, 151, 152, 153, 154: Now attributed to Hertel, Schwab & Co. 9" - $365.00; 13" - $485.00; 16" - $550.00; 19" - $675.00; 23" - $900.00.

#211, 226, 236, 260, 262, 263: 10" - $525.00; 13" - $625.00; 16"- $725.00; 19" - $875.00; 21" - $1,200.00; 25" - $1,600.00.

#220: Glass eyes, open/closed mouth, deep dimples. (See photo in Series 8, pg. 109.) 16" - $4,900.00; 19" - $5,900.00. **Toddler:** 18" - $5,900.00; 26" - $6,800.00.

#234, 235, 238: 14" - $650.00; 17" - $850.00; 21" - $1,000.00; 25" - $1,200.00.

#237, 245, 1070 ("Hilda"): Patent/ registration number. Wigged or solid dome. 13" - $2,600.00; 17" - $4,000.00; 20" -

$4,800.00; 23" - $5,800.00; 25" - $6,800.00.
Toddler: 16" - $5,100.00; 18" - $5,500.00; 23" - $6,200.00.

#239: 16" - $2,100.00; 18" - $3,200.00; 24" - $3,500.00.

#247: 13" - $1,000.00; 15" - $1,500.00; 18" - $1,800.00; 23" - $3,000.00.

#249: 14" - $975.00; 17" - $1,650.00; 21" - $1,800.00.

#257: 10" - $525.00; 15" - $625.00; 19" - $825.00; 22" - $1,100.00; 26" - $1,600.00. **Toddler:** 21" - $1,600.00; 26" - $2,500.00.

#272 ("Siegfried"): Closed mouth, wide spaced eyes. 10" head circumference. $1,250.00 up.

#277 (Century Doll): Cloth body, closed mouth. **Scowl:** 14" - $650.00; 20" - $875.00. **Smile:** 14" - $750.00; 20" - $950.00. **Composition head:** Cloth body. 16" - $245.00; 23" - $465.00.

#279, 200 (Century Doll): Molded hair with part, bangs, cloth body, composition hands. 16" - $1,200.00; 19" - $2,300.00; 24" - $4,200.00.

#281 (Century Doll): Open mouth: 19" - $950.00.

J.D.K. marked baby: Called **"Sally," "Jean," or "Sammy."** Solid dome, painted eyes and open mouth. 13" - $950.00; 16" - $1,300.00; 22" - $1,800.00; 25" - $2,500.00.

Adult doll, #162: Sleep eyes, open mouth, adult jointed body (thin waist and molded breasts) with slender limbs. No damage and very nicely dressed. 13" - $1,500.00; 16" - $1,700.00; 21" - $2,400.00.

Adult #172 ("Gibson Girl"): 1910. Bisque shoulder head with closed mouth, kid body with bisque lower arms, glass eyes. No damage and beautifully dressed. (See photo in Series 8, pg. 115.) 12" - $1,000.00; 15" - $1,900.00; 17" - $2,500.00; 19" - $3,900.00.

Oriental #243: Olive fired-in color to bisque. Matching color five-piece bent limb baby body (or jointed toddler-style body). Wig, sleep or set eyes. No damage and dressed in oriental style. 15" - $4,400.00; 18" - $5,800.00. **Child:** On jointed Kestner olive-toned body. 16" - $5,000.00; 19" - $6,500.00. **Molded hair baby:** 15" - $4,600.00; 18" - $6,000.00.

13" character babies with different wigs. The one on the left has a mohair wig; the one on the right is fur. Both are marked "J.D.K./211." Each - $625.00. *Courtesy Kris Lundquist.*

Small dolls, open mouth: Five-piece bodies or jointed bodies. Wigs, sleep or set eyes. No damage and nicely dressed. 8" - $500.00; 10" - $585.00. **Closed mouth:** 10" - $850.00 up.

#133: 10" - $875.00.

#155: Five-piece body: 10" - $585.00. Jointed body: 10" - $700.00.

19" "Gibson Girl," mold #172, has up tilt head and nose with thin features, closed mouth, glass eyes, and original mohair wig. Bisque shoulder head on kid body with bisque lower arms. $3,900.00. *Courtesy Frasher Doll Auctions.*

Designed by Rose O'Neill and marketed from 1913. All prices are for dolls that have no chips, hairlines or breaks. *See Modern section for composition and vinyl Kewpies.*

Labels:

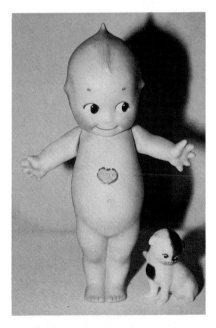

All bisque: One-piece body and head, jointed shoulders only. Blue wings, painted features with eyes to one side. 2½" - $115.00; 5" - $145.00; 7" - $225.00; 8" - $300.00; 9" - $450.00; 10" - $625.00; 12" - $950.00. **With any article of clothing:** 3" - $225.00; 5" - $275.00; 7" - $325.00; 9" - $550.00 up.

8" all bisque Kewpie with remains of paper label. Shown with 2½" "Doodle Dog" marked "Rose O'Neill" on bottom of back feet. Kewpie - $300.00. Dog - $1,350.00.

All bisque: Jointed at hips and shoulders. 4" - $425.00; 6" - $650.00; 9" - $825.00; 12" - $1,200.00 up. **Painted shoes and socks:** 4–5" - $500.00; 10" - $1,200.00.

Shoulder head: Cloth or stockinette body. 8" - $650.00. **Head only:** 3" - $165.00 up.

Action Kewpie: Arms folded. 5" - $500.00.

Confederate soldier: 4½" - $450.00.

Cowboy: Big hat, gun. Made as lamp. (See photo in Series 7, pg. 11.) 10½" - $825.00. Kewpie only - $800.00.

Farmer: 4" - $400.00.
Gardener: 4" - $425.00.
Governor: 4" - $400.00.
Groom with bride: 4" - $350.00.
Guitar player: 3½" - $325.00.

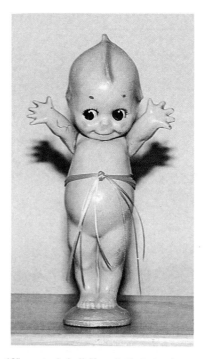

13" carnival chalk Kewpie that stands on a base and is jointed at the shoulders only. Was very popular during the 1910s to 1930s at such places as Atlantic City Boardwalk, Coney Island, and carnivals. $165.00. *Courtesy Carmen Holshoe.*

Holding pen: (See photo in Series 5, pg. 100.) 3" - $350.00.

Holding cat: (See photo in Series 9, pg. 117.) 4" - $450.00.

Holding butterfly: 4" - $550.00.

Hugging: 3½" - $275.00.

On stomach: Called **"Blunderboo."** (See photo in Series 7, pg. 117.) 4" - $450.00.

Soldier: 4½" - $550.00.

Thinker: 4" - $250.00; 6" - $450.00.

Traveler: Tan or black suitcase. (See photo in Series 5, pg. 101.) 3½" - $350.00.

With broom: 4" - $425.00.

With dog, "Doodle": (See photo in Series 7, pg. 117.) 3½" - $1,350.00 up.

With helmet: (See photo in Series 5, pg. 101.) 6" - $575.00.

With outhouse: 2½" - $1,300.00.

With pumpkin: 4" - $400.00.

With rabbit: 2½" - $400.00.

With rose: 2½" - $275.00. **Vase attached to back:** $350.00.

With teddy bear: 4" - $525.00.

With turkey: 2" - $375.00.

With umbrella and dog: 3½" - $1,650.00.

Kewpie soldier and nurse: 6" - $2,500.00 up.

Kewpie tree or mountain: 17 figures. $20,000.00 up.

Kewpie driving chariot: $2,800.00 up.

Kewpie on inkwell: Bisque: 3½" - $600.00. Cast metal: (See photo in Series 9, pg. 118.) 3½" - $375.00; 6" - $600.00.

Kewpie in basket with flowers: 3½" - $725.00 up.

Kewpie with drawstring bag: 4½" - $600.00.

Buttonhole Kewpie: $145.00.

Reading book: 3½" - $850.00.

Sitting in chair: Arms crossed. (See photo in Series 8, pg. 96.) 3½" - $550.00.

At tea table: 4" - $1,800.00 up.

Kewpie and dog on bench: 4" - $2,700.00 up.

Kewpie Doodle Dog: (See photo in Series 8, pg. 117.) 1½" - $700.00; 3" - $1,350.00.

Hottentot (Black Kewpie): 3½" - $425.00; 5" - $575.00; 9" - $950.00; 12" (rare) - $4,500.00 up.

Kewpie perfume bottle: 3½" - $400.00 up; 4½" - $550.00.

Pincushion Kewpie: 2½" - $350.00.

Paperweight: 1935. Kewpie in center. (See photo in Series 10, pg. 114.) $325.00.

Celluloid Kewpies: 2" - $45.00; 5" - $90.00; 9" - $175.00. Black: 5" - $140.00. **Jointed shoulders:** 3" - $75.00; 5" - $125.00; 9" - $185.00; 12" - $265.00; 16" - $650.00 up; 22" - $950.00 up. **Soldier or Action:** 4" - $125.00 up.

Chalk/plaster carnival Kewpie: On base, jointed shoulders only. In good condition: 13" - $165.00; 15" - $185.00 up; 17" - $300.00 up.

Cloth body Kewpie: Bisque head, painted eyes. (See photo in Series 4, pg. 106.) 10" - $1,600.00; 14" - $1,900.00. **Glass eyes:** 12" - $2,700.00 up; 16" - $4,800.00 up. Composition head and half arms: 13" - $365.00.

Glass eyed Kewpie: Chubby jointed toddler body, bisque head. Marked "Ges. Gesch./O'Neill J.D.K." 10" - $3,800.00; 12" - $5,100.00; 16" - $6,400.00; 20" - $8,100.00.

All cloth ("Cuddle Kewpie"): Made by Krueger. All one-piece with body forming clothes, mask face. (See photo in Series 7, pg. 117.) Mint condition: 9" - $185.00; 13" - $300.00; 15" - $475.00; 21" - $725.00; 26" - $1,300.00. Fair condition: 12" - $100.00; 15" - $175.00; 21" - $275.00; 26" - $500.00. **Plain cloth body, removable clothes:** Original, mint condition. 14" - $525.00; 20" - $750.00; 25" - $1,300.00; 20" - $2,300.00. Fair condition: 16" - $175.00; 20" - $300.00.

Kewpie tin or celluloid talcum container: Excellent condition: 8½" - $200.00.

Kewpie soaps: 4" - $90.00 each. Boxed set of five: $600.00.

Japan: Bisque. 2" - $40.00; 3" - $60.00; 4" - $85.00; 5" - $95.00; 6" - $125.00.

KLEY & HAHN

Kley & Hahn operated in Ohrdruf, Germany from 1895 to 1929. They made general dolls as well as babies and fine character dolls.

Marks:

K & H

CHARACTER CHILD:

Boy or girl. Painted eyes (some with glass eyes), closed or open/closed mouth; on jointed body. No damage and nicely dressed. **#320, 520, 523, 525, 526, 531, 535, 536, 546, 547, 548, 549, 552:** (See photos in Series 1, pg. 187; Series 3, pg. 93; Series 7, pg. 89, 115; Series 10, pg. 115; Series 11, pg. 107.) 13" - $3,000.00; 16" -

$3,600.00; 19" - $4,500.00; 23" - $5,400.00; 26" - $6,500.00. **Child with glass eyes:** 15" - $4,200.00; 19" - $6,400.00; 22" - $7,000.00; 26" - $7,800.00. **Toddler bodies:** 17" - $3,200.00; 21" - $4,200.00; 25" - $5,100.00. **Bent limb baby body:** 15" - $1,400.00; 17" - $2,200.00; 21" - $3,000.00; 24" - $3,400.00.

CHARACTER BABY:

Molded hair or wig, glass sleep eyes or painted eyes. Can have open or open/closed mouth. On bent limb baby body, no damage and nicely dressed. (Allow more for flirty eyes.) **#130, 132, 138, 142, 150, 151, 158, 160, 161, 162, 167, 176, 199, 458, 585, 680:** 12" - $485.00; 17" - $685.00; 21" - $975.00; 25" - $1,200.00; 28" - $1,600.00. **Toddler bodies:**

17" - $875.00; 21" - $1,200.00; 25" - $1,400.00; 27" - $1,900.00.

#547: Closed mouth, glass eyes. 16" - $2,8000.00; 18" - $3,000.00. **Baby:** 16" - $1,600.00.

#538, 568: (See photo in Series 8, pg. 118.) 16" - $750.00; 18" - $900.00; 21" - $1,000.00. **Toddler:** 23" - $1,600.00; 27" - $2,000.00. **Baby:** 16" - $475.00; 18" - $575.00; 21" - $685.00.

#162 with talker mechanism in head: 18" - $1,600.00; 24" - $2,400.00; 26" - $2,900.00.

#162 with flirty eyes and clockworks in head: 19" - $1,700.00; 25" - $3,000.00.

#680: 15" - $825.00. **Toddler:** 21" - $1,450.00.

#153, 154, 157, 166, 169: Child, closed mouth. (See photo in Series 7, pg. 114.) 15" - $2,800.00; 21" - $3,600.00. **Open mouth:** 15" - $1,200.00; 21" - $1,600.00. **Baby:** 19" - $1,150.00.

#159, two-faced doll: (See photo in Series 4, pg. 110.) 13" - $1,700.00; 16" - $2,200.00.

#166: Molded hair, open mouth. 18" - $1,400.00; 24" - $1,800.00. **Baby:** 19" - $1,250.00. **Closed mouth:** 19" - $2,800.00.

#169: Closed mouth. (See photo in Series 8, pg. 118.) **Toddler:** 16" - $2,500.00; 19" - $3,200.00. **Open mouth:** 21" - $1,500.00.

#119: Child, glass eyes, closed mouth. 19" - $4,900.00. **Painted eyes:** 19" - $3,400.00. **Toddler, glass eyes:** 19" - $4,600.00.

Child dolls, Walküre, and/or #250: Sleep or set eyes, open mouth, jointed body. No damage and nicely dressed. 9" - $385.00; 15" - $465.00; 18" - $625.00; 21" - $700.00; 25" - $850.00; 30" - $950.00; 32" - $1,100.00; 36" - $1,700.00; 42" - $3,000.00.

16" Kley & Hahn mold #167 with sleep eyes, open mouth, five-piece bent limb baby body. Old clothes made by nuns who did wonderful needle and handwork. $625.00. *Courtesy Jeanne Venner.*

28" Kley & Hahn Walküre with mold #282. Has sleep eyes and open mouth. On fully jointed body. $885.00. *Courtesy Turn of Century Antiques.*

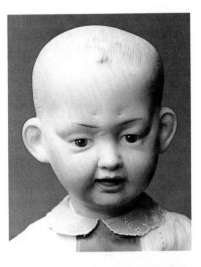

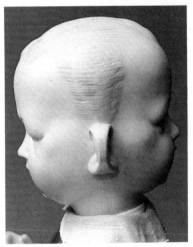

19" two-faced baby by Kley & Hahn with very protruding ears and brush stroke hair. One side has glass eyes and the other has painted eyes. $3,400.00. *Courtesy Frasher Doll Auctions.*

Kling & Co. was in Ohrdurf, Germany, from 1836 to 1927 and produced bisque and china dolls from 1870 to 1927.

Marks:

Bisque head: Jointed body, open mouth. No damage and nicely dressed. 15" - $450.00; 18" - $600.00; 23" - $800.00.

Bisque shoulder head: Wig or molded hair, painted eyes. Cloth body with bisque lower limbs. 14" - $365.00; 18" - $585.00; 23" - $700.00. **Glass eyes:** 12" - $485.00. **#123:** Closed mouth. Original clothes: 12" - $685.00. Re-dressed: 12" -

$300.00. **#131, 166, 176, 186:** Closed mouth. 16" - $1,150.00. **#182, 370, 372, 373, 377, 182:** 17" - $550.00; 24" - $785.00.

China shoulder head: Cloth or kid body, china limbs. Can have blonde or black molded hair with many having bangs. **#188, 189, 200, 202** and others: 14" - $300.00, 17" - $425.00; 23" - $525.00.

15" Kling shoulder head with kid body, bisque lower arms, and open mouth. $345.00.

Marked:  *Courtesy Kathy Riddick.*

KNOCH, GEBRUDER

Gebruder Knoch porcelain factory operated in Neustadt, Germany, from 1887 into the 1920's. Most of their dolls have bisque shoulder heads and kid or cloth bodies, but some will be on jointed bodies and/or have kid bodies with composition jointed limbs.

Marks:

Character doll: No damage and ready to display in collection.

#206: 12" - $925.00 up; 16" - $1,250.00 up.

#216, 218: Girl or boy with modeled hairdo, wide open/closed mouth, and molded lower teeth. 15" - $2,400.00; 19" - $4,800.00.

#246: Winking, has molded cap. 15" - $3,300.00.

#237: Molded decorated bonnet. 12" - $825.00; 15" - $1,300.00.

#3920: Closed mouth. (See photo in Series 10, pg. 116; Series 11, pg. 109.) 10" - $825.00; 14" - $985.00.

Child doll: Perfect, no damage, nicely dressed. Sleep eyes, wig, open mouth, ball-jointed body. 15" - $285.00; 18" - $450.00; 21" - $575.00.

Konig & Wernicke's doll factory was in Walterhausen, Germany, and began making dolls in 1912. They made dolls with composition heads along with dolls with composition bodies with bisque heads. The bisque heads were made for them by Bahr & Proschild. Those heads will be marked "K&W." Allow more for flirty eyes or toddler body.

Bisque head: Sleep eyes, open mouth, composition toddler or baby body. All in very good condition. 9" - $275.00; 11" - $435.00; 15" - $575.00; 20" - $785.00; 23" - $950.00.

Child or toddler: Character with closed mouth and glass eyes. 23" - $3,450.00.

Child: Ca. 1920s–1930s. All composition, open mouth. Five-piece or fully jointed body. (Allow more for flirty eyes.) 15" - $325.00; 17" - $485.00.

17" Konig & Wernicke has composition character head, flirty eyes, and open mouth with teeth. On five-piece chunky body. All fingers curled and has free standing thumbs. Clothes maybe original. With flirty eyes - $575.00. Without flirty eyes - $485.00. *Courtesy Ellen Dodge.*

17" Konig & Wernicke has open mouth with tremble tongue. Has character face, sleep eyes, and five-piece bent limb baby body. Marked "42 99/10 Made in Germany." $650.00. *Courtesy Virginia Sofie.*

Käthe Kruse began making dolls in 1910. In 1916, she obtained a patent for a wire coil doll, and in 1923 she registered a trademark of a double "K" with the first one reversed, along with the name Käthe Kruse. The first heads were designed after her own children and copies of sculptures from the Renaissance period. The dolls have molded muslin heads that are handpainted in oils, and jointed cloth bodies. These early dolls will be marked "Käthe Kruse" on the foot and sometimes with a "Germany" and number.

In 1911, doll had disc-jointed bodies with wide hips and a double seam down the center of the bodies. Thumbs were sewn on individually. From 1911 to 1912, the dolls had swivel heads and ball-jointed knees. The bodies were short with long legs. These dolls are rare.

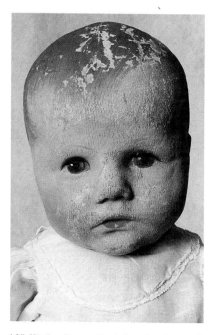

19" Käthe Kruse that has been much loved. This face is more scare than others in the period (1922–1924). Has oil-painted features. Fair condition - $2,800.00. Good condition - $3,600.00. *Courtesy Turn of Century Antiques.*

Early marked dolls, Model I: 1910. Wide hips, painted hair. In excellent condition and with original clothes. (See photo in Series 7, pg. 116; Series 8, pg. 120; Series 10, pg. 117.) 17" - $3,600.00; 21" - $4,400.00. **Fair condition:** Not original. 17" - $1,300.00; 21" - $1,800.00. **Ball-jointed knees:** (See photo in Series 8, pg. 120.) 18" - $5,200.00; 22" - $6,000.00. **Later model:** Slim hips. Mint condition: 17" - $2,800.00. Fair condition: 17" - $1,800.00.

Model II: 1922–1936. Smiling baby with tricot covered body and limbs. 14" - $2,700.00.

Model III, IV: 1923 on. Serious child. (See photo in Series 7, pg. 116.) 17" - $2,000.00 up.

Model V, VI: 1925 on. Typical Kruse. (See photo in Series 8, pg. 121.) 17" - $1,400.00; 21" - $1,900.00. Baby: **"Traümchen"** has painted closed eyes; **"Du Mein"** has open eyes. Has weighted tricot-covered body and limbs with sewn on navel. 21" - $3,200.00 up.

Model VII: 1927–1952. Reduced body same as model I with wide hips. Larger size has a thin body and swivel head. (See photo in Series 7, pg. 116; Series 8, pg. 120.) 14" - $1,800.00; 21" - $2,400.00. Fair condition: 14" - $950.00.

Model VIII: 1929 on. Wigged. (See series 9, pg. 123.) 16" - $1,650.00; 21" - $2,300.00. **Good condition:** 21" - $1,150.00. Ball-jointed knees: Slim hips. **Mint condition:** 17" - $2,800.00. **Fair condition:** 17" - $1,800.00.

Model IX: 1929. Wigged. 14" - $1,800.00. Good condition: 15" - $1,150.00.

Model X: 1935 on. 15" - $1,300.00.

1920s dolls, Model IH and others: (See photo in Series 7, pg. 116; Series 8, pg. 121.) Molded hair or wigged, hips are wide. **Excellent condition:** Original. 16" - $2,100.00; 21" - $2,700.00. **Fair condition:** Not original. 16" - $1,200.00; 21" - $1,700.00.

U.S. Zone: Germany, 1945–1951. Has turtle mark. (See photo in Series 6,

pg. 133.) 14" - $850.00; 17" - $975.00. Cloth head: 14" - $1,300.00.
Hard plastic dolls: 1952–1975. Glued-on wigs, sleep or painted eyes. Pink muslin body. Mint condition: 14" - $400.00; 17" - $550.00.

Celluloid: 1936–1939, 1945–1958. 12" - $285.00; 16" - $450.00.
1975 to date: Retail store prices could be higher. 9" - $165.00; 13" - $345.00; 17" - $465.00.

17" boy and girl dolls (Model I) made by Käthe Kruse. Both have cloth bodies with wide hips. Girl is all original, and boy is beautifully re-dressed. Original - $3,100.00. Re-dressed - $2,200.00. *Courtesy Frasher Doll Auctions.*

KUHNLENZ, GEBRÜDER

Kuhnlenz made dolls from 1884 to 1930 and was located in Kronach, Bavaria. Marks from this company include the "G.K." plus numbers such as **31.42, 32.14, 34.32, 38.27, 41.28, 41.72, 41.77, 44.15, 44.26, 44.27, 44.30,**

56.18, 56.38, 61.24. Other marks now attributed to this firm are:

Child with closed mouth, mold #31, 32, : Bisque head in perfect condition, jointed body and nicely dressed. (See photo in Series 4, pg. 75.) 10" - $750.00, 12" - $875.00; 16" - $1,400.00; 18" - $1,800.00; 22" - $2,200.00.

Mold #34: Bru type. (See photo in Series 4, pg. 75.) 14" - $1,450.00; 18" - $2,750.00.

Mold #38: Kid body, bisque shoulder head. (See photo in Series 9, pg. 124.) 16" - $650.00; 21" - $1,050.00.

Child with open mouth, mold #41, 44, 56: Bisque head in perfect condition, jointed body and nicely dressed. (See photo in Series 6, pg. 134; Series 10, pg. 118; Series 11, pg. 112.) 16" - $650.00; 18" - $850.00; 22" - $1,100.00.

Mold #61: Shoulder head, kid body. 19" - $775.00.

Mold #165: Bisque head in perfect condition, jointed body and nicely dressed. 17" - $475.00; 23" - $650.00.

Tiny dolls, mold #44, 46 and others: Bisque head in perfect condition, five-piece body with painted-on shoes and socks, open mouth. (See photo in Series 6, pg. 134.) 9" - $225.00. Closed mouth: 9" - $475.00. Fully jointed body: 9" - $300.00 up.

19" closed mouth doll with set eyes. On kid body with bisque lower arms. Made by Gebrüder Kuhnlenz. Marked "38.27." $925.00. *Courtesy Sharon Caldwell.*

LANTERNIER (LIMOGES)

A. Lanternier & Cie of Limoges, France, made dolls from about the 1890's on into the 1930s. Before making dolls, they produced porcelain pieces as early as 1855. Their doll heads will be fully marked and some carry a name such as "LaGeorgienne Favorite," "Lorraine," "Cherie," etc. They generally are found on papier maché bodies but can be on fully jointed composition bodies. Dolls from this firm may have nearly excellent quality bisque to very poor quality.

Marks:

FABRICATION
FRANCAISE

AL & CIE
LIMOGES

Child: 1915. Open mouth, set eyes on jointed body. No damage and nicely dressed. Good quality bisque with pretty face. 14" - $550.00; 19" - $750.00; 23" - $950.00; 26" - $1,200.00. **Poor quality bisque:** Very high coloring or blotchy color bisque. 15" - $400.00; 19" - $485.00; 23" - $550.00; 26" - $675.00.

Jumeau style face: Has a striking Jumeau look. Good quality bisque. 17" - $1,400.00; 20" - $1,700.00. **Poor quality bisque:** 18" - $650.00; 22" - $850.00.

Character: 1915. Open/closed mouth with teeth, smiling fat face, glass eyes, on jointed body. No damage and nicely dressed. Marked "Toto." 16" - $975.00; 20" - $1,450.00.

Lady: 1915. Adult-looking face, set eyes, open/closed or closed mouth. Jointed adult body. No damage and nicely dressed. 14" - $900.00; 16" - $1,200.00.

Left: 15" Lanternier with open and fully jointed body. Marked "Fabrication Francaise Limoges France. J.B." Right: 15½" Gebruder Heubach with open mouth and jointed body with straight wrists. Marked "8192 Made in Germany" with Heubach sunburst mark. 15" - $675.00; 15½" - $875.00. *Courtesy Frasher Doll Auctions.*

LENCI

Lenci dolls are all felt with a few having cloth torsos. They are jointed at neck, shoulders and hips. The original clothes will be felt, organdy, or a combination of both. Features are oil painted and generally eyes are painted to the side. Other characteristics are sewn together middle and fourth fingers and the steam-molded head is seamless with sewn-on felt ears. Size can range from 5" to 45". (Mint or rare dolls will bring higher prices.)

Marks: On cloth or paper label "Lenci Torino Made in Italy." "Lenci" may be written on bottom of foot or underneath one arm.

Child: No moth holes, very little dirt, doll as near mint as possible and all in **excellent condition.** 15" - $800.00 up; 17" - $1,100.00 up; 19" - $1,300.00 up; 21" - $1,500.00 up. **Dirty,** original clothes in poor condition or redressed: 15" - $250.00; 17" - $425.00; 19" - $600.00; 21" - $700.00. Very pouty child: (See photo in Series 6, pg. 13.)

Baby: (See photos in Series 5, pg. 108.) 15" - $1,600.00; 19" - $2,100.00. **Fair condition:** $750.00–1,000.00.

Tiny dolls (called Mascottes): (See photos in Series 7, pg. 120; Series 8, pg. 126.) **Excellent condition:** 6" - $225.00; 8" - $325.00. **Dirty,** redressed, or original clothes in **poor condition:** 6" - $70.00; 8–9" - $125.00. **Unusual costume:** 9" - $375.00.

Ladies with adult faces: "Flapper" or "boudoir" style with long limbs. (See photos in Series 5, pg. 107, Series 6, pg. 136; Series 10, pg. 121.) **Excellent condition:** 16" - $1,000.00; 25" - $1,900.00 up; 28" - $2,300.00 up; 33" - $2,700.00; 35" - $2,900.00; 42" - $3,700.00; 48" - $5,000.00. **Dirty** or in poor condition: 23" - $800.00; 27" - $900.00.

Aviator: Girl with felt helmet. Referred to as "Amelia Earhart." 18" - $3,200.00 up.

Characters: 1926. **Tom Mix or Jack Dempsey.** Both fat-faced. 18" - $3,500.00 each.

Clowns: (See photo in Series 4, pg. 99.) **Excellent condition:** 19" - $1,800.00; 28" - $2,300.00. **Poor condition:** 19" - $450.00; 28" - $785.00.

Sailor: 17" - $1,450.00.

Indians or Orientals (Thailand): (See photo in Series 2, pg. 112.) **Excellent condition:** 16" - $3,400.00. **Dirty** and poor condition: 16" - $800.00.

Lady with papoose: 17" - $4,200.00.

Golfer or other sports: (See photo in Series 2, pg. 112.) **Excellent, perfect condition:** 15" - $2,500.00. **Poor condition:** 15" - $750.00.

Mozart, Bach, Mendel: 19" - $3,200.00 up.

Pinocchio: All wood and felt. Label on back. (See photo in Series 8, pg. 125.) 14–15" - no price known.

Pan: Has hooved feet. (See photo in Series 9, pg. 127.) 10" - $1,950.00. **Dirty** and fair condition: 10" - $425.00.

Shirley Temple type: Excellent condition: 22" - $1,850.00. **Dirty** and poor condition: 22" - $600.00.

Bali dancer: Excellent condition: 15" - $1,500.00. **Poor condition:** 15" - $550.00. **South Seas girl:** Long thin limbs. 17" - $2,200.00 up.

Smoking doll: Painted eyes. (See photo in Series 1, pg. 192.) **Excellent condition:** 24" - $2,000.00 up. **Poor condition:** 24" - $800.00. **Glass eyes:** Excel-

18" all felt Lenci has oil-painted features and mohair wig that is sewn in strips. Has felt clothes. All original. $850.00 up. *Courtesy Carmen Holshoe.*

lent condition: 16" - $2,700.00; 21" - $3,400.00. Poor condition: 16" - $950.00; 21" - $1,050.00.

"Surprise Eyes" doll: Very round painted eyes and O-shaped mouth. (See photo in Series 4, pg. 99; Series 9, pg. 128.) 16" - $1,200.00; 20" - $1,800.00; 22" - $2,200.00. **Glass eyes:** 16" - $1,800.00; 20" - $2,400.00; 22" - $3,000.00. **Flirty glass eyes:** 15" - $2,200.00; 20" - $2,800.00.

Widow Allegra: Dressed in black, holds dog. (See photo in Series 9, pg. 128.) Painted eyes: 16" - $1,500.00. Glass eyes: 16" - $2,250.00.

Teenager: Long-legged child. 15" - $1,100.00 up; 24" - $1,500.00; 34" - $2,200.00.

Boys: Side part hairdo. **Excellent** condition: 17" - $1,900.00 up; 22" - $2,400.00. **Poor condition:** 17" - $800.00; 22" - $900.00. **In Fascist uniform:** (See photo in Series 8, pg. 124.) 16" - $1,700.00 up. **Hitler Youth:** 16" - $1,500.00 up. **Winking:** 1920s. Open/closed mouth, painted teeth. (See photo in Series 9, pg. 127.) 12" - $1,000.00; 15" - $1,800.00.

Lenci type: Can be made in Italy, Germany, France, Spain, or England. 1920s through 1940s. Felt and cloth. **Child:** Felt or cloth, mohair wig, cloth body. Original clothes. 15" - $600.00; 17" - $725.00. **Small dolls:** Dressed as child. 8" - $45.00; 11" - $80.00. In foreign costume: 8" - $35.00.

Lenci catalogs: From the 1920s. $650.00–1,100.00.

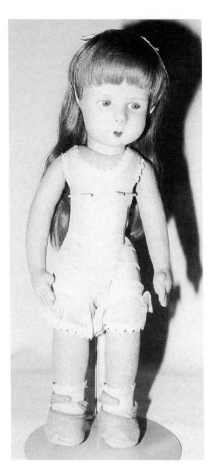

17" Lenci with very unusual face and human hair wig in "Alice in Wonderland" style. Ears have never been attached. All fingers are sewn together with free standing thumb. Original one-piece teddy and felt. Note tag below on back of doll. Nude - $650.00.

20" Lenci boy with composition face mask, disc eyes, and original clothes in mint condition. Rest of the doll is made of felt. Tag on pants. Circa late 1940s to 1950s. $600.00 up. *Courtesy Ellen Dodge.*

LIMBACH

These dolls were made mostly from 1893 into the 1920s by Limbach Porzellanfabrik, Limbach, Germany. Allow more for excellent bisque and artist workmanship.

Mark:

MADE IN GERMANY

Child: 1893–1899, 1919 and after. Incised with clover mark. Bisque head, glass eyes, jointed body. No damage and nicely dressed. **Open mouth:** 15" - $425.00; 16" - $550.00; 22" - $700.00; 25" - $900.00. **Closed mouth:** 16" - $1,200.00; 18" - $1,600.00; 21" - $2,200.00; 24" - $2,600.00. **Incised name:** Circa 1919. Incised names such as "Norma," "Rita," "Wally," etc. (See photo in Series 11, pg. 116.) 15" - $575.00; 20" - $750.00; 23" - $800.00.

MASCOTTE

Bébé Mascotte dolls were made by May Fréres Cie. They operated from 1890 to 1897, then became part of Jules Steiner in 1898. This means the dolls were made from 1890 to about 1902, so the quality of the bisque as well as the artist painting can vary greatly. Dolls will be marked "BÉBÉ MASCOTTE PARIS" and some will be incised with "M" and a number.

Child: Closed mouth. Excellent condition and no damage. (See photo in Series 8, pg. 128.) Marked "Mascotte": 15" - $3,400.00; 19" - $4,500.00; 22" - $4,900.00; 25" - $5,500.00; 29" - $6,000.00. Marked with "M" and a number: 15" - $2,700.00; 18" - $3,900.00; 20" - $4,400.00; 24" - $5,300.00; 28" - $5,800.00.

METAL HEADS

Metal heads made in Germany, 1888–on; United States, 1917 on.

Marks:

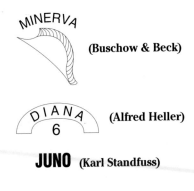

MINERVA (Buschow & Beck)

DIANA 6 (Alfred Heller)

JUNO (Karl Standfuss)

Metal shoulder head: Cloth or kid body. Molded hair, painted eyes. 15" - $150.00; 18" - $225.00. **Molded hair, glass eyes:** 15" - $200.00; 18" - $250.00. **Wig, glass eyes:** 15" - $250.00; 18" - $275.00; 22" - $350.00.

All metal child: Wig or molded hair, fully jointed. Some are also jointed at wrist, elbow, knee, and ankle. Open/closed mouth with painted teeth. Some have metal hands and feet with composition body. 16" - $475.00; 19" - $600.00.

All metal jointed dolls: Made in Switzerland. Patented 1921–1940. Metal ball joints. **Man:** 8" - $165.00; 12" - $225.00.

Comic character: 8" - $175.00. **Hitler:** 8" - $265.00; 12" - $325.00. **Chauffeur:** 8" - $150.00; 12" - $225.00. **Animal head:** 8" - $175.00; 12" - $250.00. **With composition hands, and feet:** 8" - $95.00 up; 12" - $145.00 up.

Metal baby: All metal bent baby body. Some are spring jointed. Painted features, wig or molded hair. (See photo in Series 9, pg. 134.) 15" - $165.00. Glass eyes: 15" - $250.00.

Cloth body, metal head: Composition limbs. Sleep eyes. 14" - $150.00; 17" - $225.00.

12" all metal baby with bent legs. Has open mouth and unusual painted sleep eyes. Original wig plugs into hole in top of head. Teddy may be original. $165.00. *Courtesy Virginia Sofie.*

The molded hair bisque dolls are just like any other flesh-toned dolls, but instead of having wigs, they have molded hair, glass set eyes or finely painted and detailed eyes, and generally they will have closed mouths. They almost always are one-piece shoulder heads on kid or cloth bodies with bisque lower arms. Some will have compostion lower legs. These dolls are generally very pretty. Many molded hair dolls are being attributed to A.B.G. (Alt, Beck & Gottschalck) but are recognizably Kling dolls. (See photo in Series 9, pg. 135.) Such dolls are from mold **#890, 1000, 1008, 1028, 1064, 1142, 1256, 1288, etc.** (See photos in Series 7, pg. 125; Series 9, pg. 135; Series 11, pg. 119 in lower photo.)

Child: Closed mouth. Glass eyes: 8" - $150.00; 12" - $250.00; 15" - $550.00; 20" - $900.00; 23" - $1,400.00; 25" - $1,800.00. **Painted eyes:** 12" - $145.00; 16" - $350.00; 22" - $525.00; 25" - $825.00.

21" molded hair bisque lady with glass eyes, pierced ears, decorated dress top, and flowers in hair. Has muslin body with leather arms. Made by Kling & Co. of Germany and marked "135-8." This example - $3,200.00. *Courtesy Frasher Doll Auctions.*

MOLDED HAIR BISQUE

Boy: Glass eyes: 16" - $800.00; 19" - $950.00; 22" - $1,200.00. **Painted eyes:** 16" - $600.00; 19" - $800.00; 22" - $975.00.

Decorated shoulder plate: Glass eyes, elaborate hairdo. 18" - $2,400.00 up; 21" - $3,200.00. **Painted eyes:** 19" - $1,400.00.

Bonnet or hat: Circa 1880–1920. Molded hair and bonnet. Some with bows, ribbons or feathers. (Allow more for unusual hairdo or hat.) **Glass eyes:** 13 - $850.00; 16" - $1,400.00; 19" - $1,700.00; 23" - $1,900.00. **Painted eyes:** 10" - $400.00; 14" - $750.00; 18" - $950.00.

Japan: Marked 𝒯𝓎 or ⊕ . Bows on sides of head. Cloth body, long legs, black silk feet, oilcloth arms. 16" - $265.00; 19" - $300.00.

MOTHEREAU

Alexandre Mothereau made dolls in Paris, France from 1880 to 1895. Dolls are marked "B.M." with size number and trademarked "Bébé Mothereau." (See photos in Series 9, pg. 135; Series 10, pg. 127.) 19" - $18,000.00; 24" - $26,000.00; 29" - $30,000.00.

MOTSCHMANN (SONNEBERG TÄUFLING)

Charles Motschmann has always been credited as the manufacturer of a certain style doll, but now his work is only being attributed to the making of the voice boxes in the dolls. Various German makers such as Heinrich Stier and others are being given the credit for making the dolls. They date from 1851 into the 1880s.

The early dolls were babies, children and Orientals. They have glass eyes, closed mouths, heads of papier maché, wax over papier maché or wax over composition. They can have lightly brush stroked painted hair or come with a wig. If the mouth is open, the doll will have bamboo teeth. The larger dolls will have arms and legs jointed at wrists and ankles. The lower torso and lower arms and legs are composition or wood; the upper torso and upper arms and legs are twill cloth. The mid-section will also be cloth. If the doll is marked, it can be found on the upper cloth of the leg and will be stamped:

Baby: Motschmann marked or type. Extremely fine condition: 14" - $700.00; 17" - $950.00; 21" - $1,500.00; 25" - $2,200.00. **Fair condition:** 14" - $450.00; 17" - $550.00; 21" - $700.00; 26" - $950.00.

Child: Extremely fine condition: 13" - $850.00; 16" - $1,200.00; 19" - $1,700.00; 24" - $2,200.00. **Fair condition:** 16" - $400.00; 19" - $700.00; 24" - $800.00.

Child: Bisque with cloth at waist and mid-limbs. (See photo in Series 9, pg. 136.) 17" - $6,950.00 up.

Munich Art character dolls are very rare and were designed by Marion Kaulitz, 1908–1912, who had them modeled by Paul Vogelsanger. Dolls have composition or fabric heads, painted features, and are on fully jointed bodies. (See photo in Series 11, pg. 121.)

Excellent condition: 15" - $2,600.00; 20" - $3,600.00.

Fair condition: 15" - $1,000.00; 20" - $1,500.00.

ORIENTAL DOLLS

Bisque dolls with fired-in Oriental color and on jointed yellowish tinted bodies were made in Germany by various firms. They could be children or babies and most were made after 1900. Must be in excellent condition and in Oriental clothes with no damage to head.

All bisque, marked "Kestner": 7" - $1,650.00; 9" - $1,800.00. **S&H:** 7" - $1,500.00; 8" - $1,650.00. **BSW:** 7" - $950.00. **Unknown marker:** 7" - $650.00; 9" - $900.00. Chinese man with mustache: 10" - $1,200.00.

Amusco, mold #1006: Bisque head. (See photo in Series 9, pg. 138.) 17" - $1,200.00.

Armand Marseille: Girl or boy marked only "A.M." 7" - $575.00; 10" - $775.00. **Painted bisque:** Excellent condition. 9" - $285.00; 13" - $500.00. **#353 baby:** 13" - $1,200.00; 16" - $1,400.00; 18" - $1,550.00. **Painted bisque:** 16" - $625.00. **Cloth body:** 12" - $850.00.

Belton type, #193, 206, etc.: Closed mouth. Small doll may have painted-on slippers. 12" - $2,500.00 up; 15" - $2,900.00 up; 18" - $4,000.00 up.

Bru: Olive-toned bisque. Bru Jne: 17" - $22,000.00 up; 24" - $30,500.00 up. Eyebrows painted into hairline: 17" - $28,000.00; 24" - $37,500.00.

Bruno Schmidt (BSW), #220: Closed mouth. 15" - $2,800.00; 18" - $4,000.00. **#500:** 15" - $2,300.00; 17" - $2,600.00.

Jumeau: Very rare. Closed mouth, very almond-shaped angled eyes, and upward painted eyebrows. Early body with straight wrists. 19" - $46,000.00; 26" - $58,000.00 up.

Kestner (J.D.K.), #243: Baby: 15" - $4,550.00; 18" - $6,200.00. **Molded hair baby:** 15" - $4,900.00. **Child:** 16" - $5,400.00; 19" - $6,900.00.

13½" Kestner with glass eyes. Open mouth has tongue and two upper teeth. On five-piece baby body. Marked "F. Made in Germany 10/243 J.D.K." $4,350.00.
Courtesy Frasher Doll Auctions.

Schoenau & Hoffmeister, #4900: Marked "S" PB in star "H." (See photo in Series 5, pg. 116.) 10" - $750.00; 15" - $1,750.00; 19" - $2,300.00.

Simon & Halbig (S&H), #164: (See photo in Series 5, pg. 116.) 15" - $2,400.00; 20" - $2,900.00 up. **#220:** (See photo in Series 6, pg. 145.) Solid dome or "Belton" type. Closed mouth. 12" - $1,500.00; 17" - $3,600.00. **#1099, 1129, 1159, 1199:** (See photo in Series 7, pg. 129; Series 8, pg. 132; Series 9, pg. 138.) 16" - $3,300.00; 20" - $3,800.00. **#1329:** (See photo in Series 7, pg. 129.) 16" - $2,200.00; 21" - $3,400.00.

Unmarked: Open mouth: 15" - $1,400.00; 19" - $2,100.00. **Closed mouth:** 15" - $1,900.00; 19" - $2,700.00. **All bisque:** Glass eyes. 7" - $525.00; 12" - $850.00 up. **Tiny dolls: Glass eyes:** 16" - $450.00; 11" - $850.00. **Painted eyes:** 6" - $275.00; 10" - $525.00.

Nippon (Caucasian dolls made in Japan): 1918–1922. Most made during World War I. These dolls can be near excellent quality to very poor quality. Morimura Brothers mark is ⊕, which is the *komaru* or clan crest of the family. (The Morimura family were the founders of Noritake.) Dolls marked 𝒯𝓎 were made by Yamato. Others will just be marked with NIPPON along with other marks such as "J.W."

Nippon or Japan marked baby: Good to excellent bisque, well painted, nice body and no damage. 10" - $165.00; 12" - $225.00; 16" - $325.00; 20" - $550.00; 23" - $750.00. **Poor quality:** 10" - $100.00; 15" - $150.00; 19" - $250.00; 23" - $400.00. **"Hilda" look-alike:** (See photo in Series 11, pg. 123.) **Excellent quality:** 16" - $750.00; 19" - $975.00. **Medium quality:** 16" - $475.00; 19" - $725.00. **Pouty:** Closed mouth. (See photo in Series 1, pg. 119.) 14" - $750.00.

Nippon child: Good to excellent quality bisque, no damage and nicely dressed. 15" - $275.00; 18" - $350.00; 23" -

12½" Oriental Simon & Halbig, mold #1129. Has bisque head with slanted glass eyes and open mouth. On fully jointed body. Completely original. $2,400.00. *Courtesy Turn of Century Antiques.*

Nippon marked child with glass eyes and open mouth on fully jointed German composition body. Eyelashes added. 18" - $350.00. *Courtesy Frasher Doll Auctions.*

$575.00. **Poor quality:** 16" - $125.00; 20" - $250.00; 24" - $350.00. **Mold #600:** Marked 𝒯𝓎. 15" - $385.00; 18" - $500.00; 23" - $650.00.

Molded hair: 1920–1930s. Molded bows on side, cloth body, oilcloth lower arms, silk feet. Marked 𝒯𝓎 or ⊛. 15" - $350.00; 18" - $550.00.

Traditional doll: Made in Japan. Papier maché swivel head on shoulder plate, cloth mid-section and upper arms and legs. Limbs and torso are papier maché, glass eyes, pierced nostrils. The early dolls will have jointed wrists and ankles and will be slightly sexed. **Early fine quality:** Original dress, 1890s. 15" - $375.00; 20" - $575.00; 27" - $1,200.00. **Early Boy:** With painted hair. 16" - $600.00; 21" - $1,000.00; 25" - $1,400.00 up. **1930s or later:** 15" - $165.00; 18" - $285.00. **1940s:** 14" - $95.00. **Lady:** 1920s. All original and excellent quality. 13" - $250.00; 17" - $350.00. **Later lady:** 1940s–1950s. 13" - $90.00; 15" - $125.00.

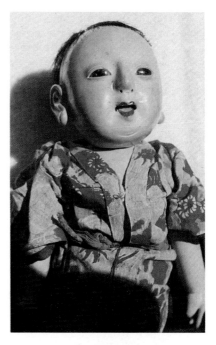

16" composition doll with jointed flange neck, wrists, and ankles. Papier maché chest and torso with cloth body. Upper limbs are also made of cloth. $750.00.
Courtesy Marcia Piecewicz.

Emperor or Empress in sitting position: 1890s: 9" - $650.00 up. **1920s–1930s:** (See photo in Series 10, pg. 133.) 6" - $175.00 up; 9" - $250.00 up; 13" - $400.00 up.

Warrior: 1880s–1890s. 17" - $700.00 up. **On horse:** 15" - $1,100.00 up. **Early 1920s:** 13" - $350.00 up. **On horse:** 13" - $850.00 up.

Japanese baby: Bisque head, sleep eyes, closed mouth, and all white bisque. **Papier maché body:** Original and in excellent condition. Late 1920s. 9" - $80.00; 13" - $125.00. **Glass eyes:** 9" - $145.00; 13" - $250.00.

Japanese baby: Head made of crushed oyster shells painted flesh color, papier maché body, glass eyes and original. 9" - $60.00; 13" - $90.00; 17" - $165.00; 20" - $250.00.

11" wooden figures that are carved in one piece. They are two of the seven Chinese gods, Han Chang Li and Chang Kuo Lao. One on left has exposed upper body. Shoes and features are painted on. Each - $300.00. *Courtesy Virginia Sofie.*

Oriental dolls: All composition, jointed at shoulder and hips. Painted features and hair. Can have bald head with yarn braid down back with rest covered by cap, such as "Ling Ling" or "Ming Ming" made by Quan Quan Co. in 1930s. Painted-on shoes. 12" - $165.00.

4" all bisque immobiles marked "Made in Japan." Each - $42.00. *Courtesy Lynn Dowdy.*

8" Chinese man with head of hardened clay and soft wood body. Upper arms are muslin with wooden lower arms and very long fingers of rolled paper. Tin upper legs are jointed at hips and knees with thin wire. Slippers cover wooden feet and lower legs. Wears original costume. $365.00.

Baby Butterfly: 1911–1913. E.I. Horsman. Composition and cloth. Painted hair and features. 15" - $550.00.

Chinese traditional dolls: Man or woman. Composition-type material with cloth-wound bodies or can have wooden carved arms and feet. In traditional costume and in excellent condition. 10" - $325.00; 13" - $500.00.

Door of Hope Dolls: Created at the Door of Hope Mission in China from 1901 to 1910s. Cloth bodies with head and limbs carved of wood by carvers who came from Ning-Po providence. Chinese costume. (See photo in Series 7, pg. 59; Series 8, pgs. 63–65; Series 9, pg. 68.) **Adult:** 10" - $625.00; 12" - $700.00 up. **Child:** 7" - $400.00; 9" - $500.00. **Mother/ baby:** 12" - $650.00. **Man:** 10" - $650.00. **Carved flowers in hair:** 12" - $675.00. **Bride or bridesmaid:** 12" - $625.00. **Groom:** $625.00. **Widow:** $675.00. **Mourner:** $625.00. **Grandfather:** $725.00. **Amah (Governess):** $600.00. **Manchu:** Mandarin man or woman. Ornate clothes. 12" - $1,000.00 up.

11" oriental baby with crushed oyster shell paste and tinted flesh color over papier maché. Has glass eyes and open/closed mouth. This type of doll had a hole in the tummy that held a voice cryer box. $95.00. *Courtesy Joan Newton.*

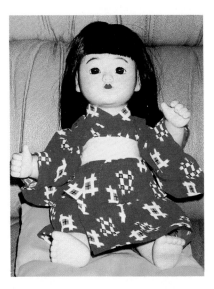

11½" Japanese doll purchased in San Francisco in 1993. Made of all rigid vinyl with jointed elbows and knees. Looks just like the older dolls with the flesh tones painted over oyster shell. Purchase price - $97.60. *Courtesy Theo Lindley.*

P.D.

P.D. marked dolls were made in Paris, France by Petit & DuMontier, 1878–1890. (See Series 8, pg. 77; Series 10, pg. 134.)

Child: Closed mouth, jointed body, **metal hands.** No damage, nicely dressed. 16" - $9,600.00; 19" - $14,500.00; 22" - $17,000.00; 24" - $19,000.00; 28" - $23,000.00.

P.G.

Pintel & Godchaux of Montreuil, France made dolls from 1890 to 1899. They held one trademark – "Bébé Charmant." Heads will be marked "P.G."

Child, closed mouth: 17" - $2,800.00; 22" - $3,200.00; 26" - $4,200.00.
Child, open mouth: 17" - $1,400.00; 21" - $2,200.00; 24" - $2,800.00.

24" P.G. doll with closed mouth and French jointed body. Has a "look" of an F.G. doll. Marked "P 11 G." $3,500.00. *Courtesy Ellen Dodge.*

PAPIER MACHÉ

Papier maché dolls were made in U.S., Germany, England, France and other countries. Paper pulp, wood and rag fibers containing paste, oil or glue are formed into a composition-like moldable material. Flour, clay and/or sand is added for stiffness. The hardness of papier maché depends on the amount of glue added.

Many so called papier maché parts were actually laminated paper with several thicknesses of molded paper bonded (glued) together or pressed after being glued.

"Papier maché" means "chewed paper" in French, and as early as 1810,

dolls of papier maché were being mass produced by using molds.

Marked "M&S Superior": Made by Muller & Strassburger. Papier maché shoulder head with blonde or black molded hair, painted blue or brown eyes, old cloth body with kid or leather arms and boots. Nicely dressed and head not repainted, chipped or cracked. 17" - $425.00; 19"- $625.00; 25" - $785.00. **Glass eyes:** 21" - $825.00. **With wig:** 19" - $775.00. **Repainted** nicely: 15" - $285.00; 20" - $425.00. Chips, scuffs or not repainted well: 15" - $85.00; 20" - $100.00.

French or French type: (See photos in Series 5, pg. 151; Series 7, pg. 133; Series 9, pg. 142.) Painted black hair, some with brush marks, on solid dome. Some have nailed-on wigs. Open mouths have bamboo teeth. Inset **glass eyes.** All leather/kid body. Very good condition, nice old clothes. 15" - $1,350.00; 18" - $1,850.00; 22" - $2,200.00; 25" - $2,300.00; 29" - $2,700.00. **Wooden jointed body:** 9" - $865.00. **Painted eyes:** 16" - $685.00; 19" - $975.00.

Early papier maché: 1840s–1860s. Cloth body and wooden limbs. Early hairdo with top knots, buns, puff curls or braiding. Not restored and dressed in original or very well made clothes. Very good condition; may show a little wear. (See photo in Series 6, pg. 153.) 10" - $450.00; 13" - $725.00; 17" - $985.00; 20" - $1,100.00; 24" - $1,200.00; 30" - $1,850.00. **Glass eyes:** 21" - $1,900.00; 25" - $2,400.00. **Flirty eyes:** 21" - $2,200.00 up; 25" - $2,700.00 up.

Long curls: 10" - $525.00; 14" - $650.00; 24" - $1,400.00.

Covered Wagon or Flat Top hairdo: 8" - $265.00; 12" - $375.00; 16" - $575.00.

Milliner's models: 1820s–1860s. (See photos in Series 6, pg. 153; Series 8, pg. 137; Series 10, pg. 135.) **Braided bun, side curls:** 8" - $800.00; 12" - $1,300.00. **Side curls, high Apollo top knot (beehive):** 13" - $1,050.00; 16" - $1,950.00; 17" - $2,250.00. **Coiled braids over ears, braided bun:** 17" - $1,800.00; 19" - $2,100.00 up. **Center part:** Sausage curls. 16" - $675.00; 19" - $850.00. **Center part with molded bun:** 8" - $575.00; 12" - $925.00. **Molded bonnet:** Very rare. Kid body, wood limbs, bonnet painted to tie under chin. 16" - $1,800.00 up. **Side curls, braided coronet, molded comb:** 17" - $3,500.00 up.

Marked Greiner: See Greiner section.

Motschmann types: With wood and twill bodies. Separate hip section, glass eyes, closed mouth and brush stroke hair on solid domes. Nicely dressed and ready to display. 16" - $700.00; 22" - $850.00; 26" - $1,300.00.

German papier maché: 1870–1900s. Various molded hairdos, painted eyes and closed mouth. May be blonde or black hair. Nicely dressed and not repainted. (See photos in Series 2, pg. 133, Series 4, pg. 124, Series 7, pg. 135.) 15" - $250.00; 18" - $375.00; 26" - $475.00; 24" - $525.00; 26" - $575.00; 32" - $800.00. **Glass eyes:** 15" - $550.00; 18" - $800.00. Showing **wear and scuffs,** but not touched up: 18" - $200.00; 22" - $275.00; 26" - $325.00; 32" - $425.00; 36" - $675.00.

Wax over papier maché: See Wax section.

9" early papier maché doll head with rolled bun hairdo. On stuffed kid body with wooden lower limbs. Greenish-blue leather bands attach limbs to body. Shoes seem to be carved separately, then glued to legs. $875.00. *Courtesy Virginia Sofie.*

Turned shoulder head: Solid dome, glass eyes, closed mouth. Twill cloth body with composition lower arms. Very good condition and nicely dressed. (See photo in Series 3, pg. 114.) 18" - $775.00; 23" - $975.00.

German character heads: Heads are molded just like the bisque ones. Glass eyes, closed mouth. On fully jointed body. Excellent condition and nicely dressed. (See photo in Series 6, pg. 152.) 16" - $1,100.00 up; 22" - $1,700.00 up.

Papier maché, 1920s on: Head usually has bright coloring and wigged. Usually dressed as a child or in provincial costumes. Stuffed cloth body and limbs or have papier maché arms. Excellent overall condition. (See photo in Series 5, pg. 119.) 9" - $70.00; 13" - $125.00; 15" - $165.00. Marked by maker: **German:** 9" - $85.00; 13" - $145.00. **French:** 9" - $125.00; 13" - $200.00; 15" - $285.00.

Close-up of 25" doll made of wax covered papier maché or composition. Shoulder head on straw stuffed body with glass eyes and mohair wig. Composition lower arms and cloth legs with sewn-on leather boots. Made in the tradition of the German Patent Washable dolls. $600.00. *Courtesy Janet & Bob Slivka.*

26" papier maché doll with very thin wax overlay. Has excelsior stuffed body, glass eyes, mohair wig, and leather limbs. Clothes and wig are original. This example - $700.00. *Courtesy Ellen Dodge.*

Two papier maché dolls with cloth bodies, attached at arms. All original with stitched fingers, posable wire limbs, and painted features. He is "Carnival Man," the German equivalent of Charlie Chaplin's "Little Tramp." He has painted hair, and girl has mohair. From late 1920s or early 1930s. Marked "Germany." Pair - $725.00. *Courtesy Pat Graff.*

Clowns: Papier maché head with painted clown features. Open or closed mouth. Molded hair or wigged. Cloth body with some having composition or papier maché lower arms or five-piece body. (See photo in Series 10, pg. 136.) Excellent condition. 9" - $265.00; 13" - $450.00; 19" - $745.00; 25" - $885.00.

PARIAN-TYPE (UNTINTED BISQUE)

Parian-type dolls were made from the 1850s to the 1880s, with the majority being made during the 1870s and 1880s. There are hundreds of different heads, and all seem to have been made in Germany. If there is a mark, it will be found on the inside of the shoulder plate. It must be noted that the very rare and unique unglazed porcelain dolls are difficult to find and their prices will be high.

Parian-type dolls can be found with every imaginable thing applied to the head and shirt tops – flowers, snoods, ruffles, feathers, plumes, etc. Many have inset glass eyes, pierced ears and most are blonde, although some will have from light to medium brown hair, and a few will have glazed black hair.

Fancy hairstyles: With molded combs, ribbons, flowers, head bands, or snoods. Cloth body with cloth/ Parian-type limbs. Most have pierced ears. Perfect condition and very nicely dressed. (See photo in Series 5, pg. 121.) **Glass eyes:** 15" - $1,600.00 up; 20" - $2,800.00 up. **Painted eyes,** pierced ears: 17" - $975.00 up; 21" - $1,650.00 up. **Painted eyes:** Decoration but unpierced ears. 19" - $11,000.00.

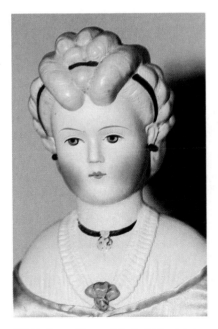 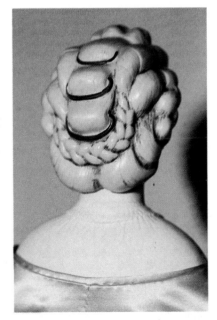

22" Parian with modeled shirtwaist top and necklace. Ears are pierced. Beautifully detailed molded hair with braid and rows in back. $1,500.00.

Swivel neck: Glass eyes. 16" - $2,800.00; 20" - $3,200.00; 22" - $3,500.00.

Molded necklaces: Jewels or standing ruffles, undamaged. (See photo in Series 5, pg. 121; Series 11, pg. 128.) **Glass eyes,** pierced ears: 17" - $1,800.00 up; 22" - $2,300.00 up. **Painted eyes,** unpierced ears: 17" - $1,000.00; 21" - $1,500.00. **Necklace** with multiple large stones: scenes of Paris in them. 17" - $9,700.00 up.

Bald head: Solid dome, takes wigs, full ear detail. 1850s. Perfect condition and nicely dressed. 15" - $800.00; 19" - $1,000.00; 23" - $1,500.00.

Molded head band or comb (called "Alice"): (See photo in Series 5, pg. 121; Series 7, pg. 137; Series 9, pg. 146.) 13" - $425.00; 16" - $625.00; 19" - $750.00.

Very plain style: No decoration in hair or on shoulders. No damage and nicely dressed. 12" - $165.00; 16" - $325.00; 22" - $450.00; 26" - $550.00. With applied flowers: 19" - $900.00.

Men or boys: Hairdos with center or side part, cloth body with cloth/Parian-type limbs. Decorated shirt and tie. 15" - $900.00; 18" - $1,200.00. **Glass eyes:** 18" - $2,400.00 up.

Molded hat: Blonde or black hair. (See photos in Series 8, pg. 140.) **Painted eyes:** 16" - $2,300.00; 19" - $2,900.00 up. **Glass eyes:** 15" - $2,650.00; 17" - $3,200.00; 22" - $3,950.00.

PARIS BÉBÉ

These dolls were made by Danel & Cie in France from 1889 to 1895. The heads will be marked "Paris Bébé" and the body's paper label will be marked with a drawing of the Eiffel Tower and "Paris Bébé/Brevete."

Paris Bébé Child: Closed mouth, no damage and nicely dressed. 15" - $4,400.00; 19" - $5,000.00; 23" - $5,300.00; 26" - $5,800.00. **Late doll:** High color to bisque, closed mouth: 16" - $2,300.00; 20" - $2,900.00; 24" - $3,650.00; 26" - $4,000.00.

19" doll made by Danel & Cie, ca. 1889, with courturior costume of silk. Has open/closed mouth with space between lips and human hair wig. On French jointed body. Marked "Tete Depose/Paris Bébé/8." $5,000.00. *Courtesy Frasher Doll Auctions.*

Bébé Phénix dolls were made by Henri Alexandre of Paris who made dolls from 1885 to 1901. The company was sold to Tourel in 1892 and Jules Steiner in 1895.

Mark:

(1885–1891)

Child, closed mouth: #81: 12" - $1,700.00. **#85:** 15" - $2,900.00. **#88:** 18" - $4,100.00. **#90:** 19" - $4,300.00. **#91:** 18" - $4,500.00. **#93:** 20" - $5,200.00. **#94:** 22" - $5,500.00. **#95:** 24" - $5,700.00.

Child, open mouth: 16" - $1,700.00; 18" - $2,000.00; 22" - $2,300.00; 24" - $2,600.00.

1885–1891: (Also see under Alexandre, Henri.) Perfect, early jointed body, beautiful clothes, closed mouth, glass eyes. Marked: H⊠A 16" - $5,400.00; 19" - $6,250.00; 23" - $7,000.00.

20" Phenix with large almond cut eyes and eyebrows that almost meet. Has open mouth with upper teeth. On jointed French body. Incised with "92" and five point star. $4,400.00. *Courtesy Virginia Sofie.*

PIANO BABIES

Piano babies were made in Germany from the 1880s into the 1930s. One of the finest quality makers of piano babies was Gebruder Heubach. They were also made by Kestner, Dressel, Limbach, etc. A number of these figures were reproduced in the late 1960s to late 1970s. Painting and skin tones will not be as "soft" as old ones.

Piano Babies: All bisque with molded hair and painted features. Unjointed with molded-on clothes. Figures come in a variety of poses.

Excellent quality or marked "Heubach": Extremely good artist workmanship and excellent detail to modeling.

5" - $225.00; 7" - $475.00; 9" - $675.00 up; 13" - $775.00 up; 17" - $1,200.00 up.

Medium quality: May not have painting finished on back side of figure. 5" - $125.00; 9" - $225.00; 13" - $325.00; 17" - $450.00.

With animal, pot, flowers, on chair, or with other items: (See photos in Series 6, pg. 158; Series 7, pg. 141.) Excellent quality. 5" - $225.00; 9" - $425.00; 13" - $775.00 up; 17" - $1,150.00 up.

Black: Excellent quality: 4" - $350.00; 8" - $425.00; 12" - $775.00; 16" - $1,000.00 up. **Medium quality:** 4" - $165.00; 8" - $175.00; 12" - $300.00; 16" - $700.00.

PIANO BABIES

Lower right: 12" piano baby of excellent quality and detail. Has molded eyelids and cheek dimples. Lower left: 10½" bust of boy that is incised "1523." Made very well. Background: 7½" bust of boy with dark brown hair. He is incised "M.352." Piano baby - $675.00. 10½" bust - $700.00. 7½" bust - $450.00. *Courtesy Frasher Doll Auctions.*

RABERY & DELPHIEU

26" marked "R.D." with all the characteristics of an "F.G." Has very pale bisque and beautiful artist painting. On fully jointed French body. Has closed mouth and certainly is not like a typical R.D. doll. $4,600.00. *Courtesy Susan Cap.*

Rabery & Delphieu began making dolls in 1856. The very first dolls have kid bodies and are extremely rare. Most of their dolls are on French jointed bodies and are marked "R.D." A few may be marked "Bébé de Paris."

Child, closed mouth: Pretty face. Body in overall good condition and nicely dressed. Excellent condition with no chips, breaks or hairlines in bisque. 13" - $2,400.00; 17" - $3,400.00; 20" - $3,800.00; 23" - $4,000.00; 25" - $4,400.00; 28" - $5,300.00. **Child, open mouth:** 16" - $1,350.00; 20" - $1,900.00; 23" - $2,400.00; 25" - $2,800.00; 29" - $3,300.00. **With two rows of teeth:** Excellent condition. 20" - $2,800.00. **Bisque lower arms:** 26" - $4,750.00; 30" - $5,000.00.

Child, high color: Lesser quality, poor artist workmanship. **Closed mouth:** 15" - $1,700.00; 18" - $2,200.00; 21" - $2,300.00. **Open mouth:** 16" - $725.00; 20" - $925.00; 23" - $1,000.00.

Walker: Head turns. Closed mouth: (See photo in Series 10, pg. 141.) 22" - $4,600.00. In original box: 22" - $4,800.00.

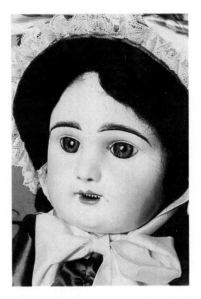

26" with open mouth and small teeth. On French jointed body. Has original mohair wig. Marked "R.D." $3,000.00. *Courtesy Turn of Century Antiques.*

Bernard Ravca made dolls in Paris from 1924 to the mid-1930s when he moved to New York. The dolls were stitched stockinette characters and personalities. If made in France, doll will bear a label marked "Original Ravca/Fabrication Francaise" or a wrist tag "Original Ravca" plus handwritten name of doll. Some of the dolls will be cloth and stockinette, some with cloth body and limbs, and others will be a gesso/papier maché combination. His dolls can range in size from 7" to 35."

Peasants/Old People: 7" - $95.00; 9" - $125.00; 12" - $165.00; 15" - $225.00 up.

Character from books/poems: (See photo in Series 11, pg. 133.) 7" - $125.00 up; 9" - $150.00 up; 12" - $200.00 up; 15" - $225.00 up; 17" - $350.00 up.

Gesso, papier maché, and cloth dolls: Personality figures. (See photo in Series 11, pg. 143.) 12" - $425.00; 15" - $600.00; 17" - $995.00; 20" - $1,500.00.

Military Figures: Such as Hitler, Mussolini. 17" - $1,200.00; 20" - $2,500.00; 27" - $5,000.00 up.

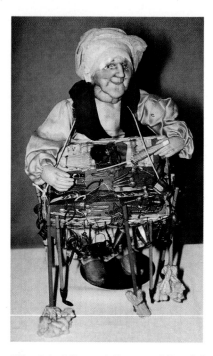

16" original Bernard Ravca peddler doll made while he was still living in Paris during the 1920s. Has sewn features using stocking material. $285.00 up. *Courtesy Shirley's Doll House.*

17" cloth Ravca-type "Fishing Lady" with stitched facial features and highly painted face. White floss hair, large wooden shoes. All original. Marked on bottom "Made in Italy." $225.00. *Courtesy Patricia Wood.*

RECKNAGEL OF ALEXANDRINENTHAL

Dolls marked with "R.A." were made by Recknagel of Alexandrinenthal, Thuringia, Germany. The R.A. dolls date from 1886 to after World War I. Bisque quality and artist workmanship can range from very poor to excellent. Prices are for dolls with good artist workmanship, such as nice lips and eyebrows painted straight, feathered, and not off center. Original or nicely dressed and no damage.

Child: 1890s–1914. Set or sleep eyes, open mouth. Small dolls have painted-on shoes and socks. 9" - $125.00; 13" - $225.00; 17" - $350.00; 21" - $475.00; 24" - $625.00. Covered with rabbit fur: (See Series 6, pg. 160.) 12" - $300.00.

#1907, 1909, 1914, etc.: 9" - $145.00; 12" - $250.00; 15" - $325.00; 21" - $525.00; 24" - $675.00.

Baby: Circa 1909–1910 on. Five-piece bent limb baby body or straight leg, curved arm toddler body and with sleep or set eyes. No damage and nicely dressed. 8" - $165.00; 10" - $200.00; 13" - $300.00; 17" - $450.00; 21" - $525.00.

Character, painted eyes: Has modeled bonnet or large hair bow. Open/closed mouth with some dolls smiling and others with painted-in teeth. No damage and nicely dressed. (See photo in Series 9, pg. 152.) 10" - $825.00; 13" - $985.00. Molded ribbon and two side bows: (See photo in Series 7, pg. 146.) 15" - $900.00 up.

Character, glass eyes: Closed mouth, composition bent limb baby body. 8" - $650.00; 12" - $725.00; 16" - $975.00.

12" bisque head with open mouth, one stoke eyebrows, and fully jointed body. Marked "Made in Germany ⚔ D 4/0." $200.00. *Courtesy Kathy Riddick.*

REINECKE, OTTO

Dolls marked "P.M." were made by Otto Reinecke of Hof-Moschendorf, Bavaria, Germany, from 1909 into the 1930s. The mold number found most often is the **#914** baby or toddler. (See photo in Series 7, pg. 144.)

Child: Bisque head with open mouth. On five-piece papier maché body or fully jointed body. Can have sleep or set eyes. No damage and nicely dressed. 9" - $145.00; 12" - $185.00; 15" - $265.00; 18" - $400.00; 22" - $485.00.

Character child: Molded hair, open/closed or fully closed mouth. 8" - $350.00.

Baby: Open mouth, sleep eyes or set eyes. Bisque head on five-piece bent limb baby body. No damage and nicely dressed. Can be incised "DEP - P.M. - Grete." 9" - $225.00; 12" - $285.00; 14" - $365.00; 16" - $500.00; 22" - $645.00; 25" - $985.00.

SCHMIDT, BRUNO

Bruno Schmidt's doll factory was located in Waltershausen, Germany and many of the heads used by this firm were made by Bahr & Proschild, Ohrdruf, Germany. They made dolls from 1898 on into the 1930s.

Mark:

2033-6

Child: Bisque head on jointed body, sleep eyes, open mouth, no damage and nicely dressed. 15" - $475.00; 19" - $650.00; 24" - $925.00. **Flirty eyes:** 20" - $875.00; 28" - $1,400.00.

Character baby, toddler or child: Bisque head, glass eyes or painted eyes, jointed body, no damage and nicely dressed.

#2025, 2026: Closed mouth, glass eyes. (See photo in Series 9, pg. 146; Series 10, pg. 146.) 19" - $4,000.00; 22" - $4,500.00. **Painted eyes:** 15" - $1,800.00; 21" - $3,800.00.

#2052: Intaglio eyes with molded eyelids, glass eyes. Closed smile mouth. Molded hair or wig. 18" - $5,500.00 up.

#2069: Closed mouth, glass eyes, sweet face, jointed body. 14" - $4,000.00; 18" - $6,500.00.

#2048, 2094, 2096 ("Tommy Tucker"): Molded, painted hair. (See photo in Series 6, pg. 163; Series 8, pg. 146; Series 11, pg. 135.) **Open mouth:** 11" - $950.00; 15" - $1,300.00; 19" - $1,600.00; 22" - $1,900.00; 25" - $2,100.00. **Closed mouth:** (See photo in Series 8, pg. 146.) 15" - $1,950.00; 19" - $2,600.00; 24" - $3,200.00. **Toddler:** 18" - $2,900.00; 21" - $3,400.00.

#2072: Closed mouth, glass eyes, wig. 19" - $3,800.00. **Toddler:** 23" - $4,200.00.

#2097, toddler: 16" - $725.00; 22" - $1,050.00. **Baby:** (See photo in Series 6, pg. 164.) 16" - $575.00; 20" - $875.00.

Character child: Closed mouth, painted eyes or glass eyes, jointed child body, no damage and nicely dressed.

Marked "BSW" in heart: No mold number. (See photo in Series 6, pg. 164.) 16" - $2,600.00; 20" - $3,200.00.

#529: Marked with "BSW" in heart. Closed mouth, painted eyes, molded eyelids. (See photo in Series 9, pg. 154.) 15" - $5,600.00 up; 20" - $6,450.00 up.

#2033, 531, 537 "Wendy": (See photo in Series 6, pg. 163; Series 9, pg. 154.) 12" - $8,500.00; 14" - $15,000.00; 17" - $18,000.00 up; 21" - $20,000.00 up.

SCHMIDT, FRANZ

Franz Schmidt & Co. began in 1890 at Georgenthal, near Waltershausen, Germany. In 1902, they registered the cross hammers with a doll between and also the F.S.&Co. mark. (Also see Swaine & Co.)

Mark:

1310
F.S. & Co.
Made in
Germany
10

S. & Co.

Baby: Bisque head on bent limb baby body, sleep or set eyes, open mouth and some may have pierced nostrils. No damage and nicely dressed.

#1255, 1271, 1272, 1295, 1296, 1297, 1310: 10" - $325.00; 15" - $475.00; 21" - $725.00; 25" - $1,300.00. **Toddler:** 10" - $685.00; 16" - $1,050.00; 22" - $1,400.00; 24" - $1,700.00.

#1267: Painted eyes, open/closed mouth. (See photo in Series 5, pg. 126; Series 10, pg. 147.) 15" - $2,950.00; 20" - $3,900.00. **Glass eyes:** 15" - $3,500.00; 20" - $4,500.00.

#1270: Painted eyes, open/closed mouth with painted teeth. Bald head with very protruding ears. 15" - $825.00. With two faces: 15" - $1,350.00.

#1285: (See photos in Series 1, pg. 253; Series 4, pg. 133.) 15" - $800.00; 21" - $950.00.

Child: Papier maché and composition body with walker mechanism with metal rollers on feet. Open mouth, sleep eyes. Working and no damage to head, nicely dressed. (See photos in Series 4, pg. 173; Series 8, pg. 148.) **#1250:** 15" - $675.00; 21" - $925.00.

#1262, 1912: Child with closed mouth, almost smiling. Painted eyes, wig, jointed body. 15" - $6,200.00; 20" - $10,500.00 up. **Glass eyes:** 17" - $8,400.00.

#1263: Closed mouth, wide spaced painted eyes. Can have sweet expression or downcast expression. 19" - $9,500.00 up; 23" - $13,000.00 up.

#1266: Child with open mouth and sleep eyes. 20" - $2,450.00.

#1286: Molded hair, ribbon, open mouth smile, glass eyes. 14" - $3,850.00.

Child: Open mouth, dolly face. Jointed body. Marked with "S & Co.," "F.S. & Co.," or mold number. No damage, clean, and nicely dressed. 15" - $475.00; 20" - $685.00; 24" - $875.00; 28" - $1,100.00.

15" Franz Schmidt child with sleep eyes and hair lashes. Has open mouth with two upper teeth and pierced nostrils. $485.00. *Courtesy Turn of Century Antiques.*

Right front: 13" Franz Schmidt with pierced nostrils, open mouth, upper teeth. Left front: 11" Armand Marseille "Dream Baby." Left rear: 14" "Bye-Lo." Right rear: 17" "Dream Baby." 13" Franz Schmidt - $595.00; 11" "Dream Baby" - $295.00; 14" "Bye-Lo" - $495.00; 17" "Dream Baby - $575.00. *Courtesy Turn of Century Antiques.*

Schmitt & Fils produced dolls from the 1870s to 1891 in Paris, France. The dolls have French jointed bodies and came with closed or open/closed mouths.

Mark:

Child: 1880–on. Bisque head with long face. Jointed body with closed mouth or open/closed mouth. No damage and nicely dressed. Marked on head and body. (See photo in Series 8, pg. 149; Series 9, pg. 156.) 11" - $9,600.00; 15" - $14,000.00 up; 17" - $16,000.00 up; 21" - $20,000.00 up; 24" - $24,000.00 up; 27" - $28,000.00 up.

Child: Early round face, full cheeks. (See photo in Series 6, pg. 166.) 13" - $9,400.00; 16" - $1,550.00; 19" - $17,000.00 up; 24" - $22,500.00 up.

17" Schmitt Bebe with long face modeling. Closed mouth and on Schmitt marked jointed body with straight wrists. Marked with crossed hammers and "Sch" within a shield. $16,000.00. *Courtesy Frasher Doll Auctions.*

SCHOENAU & HOFFMEISTER

Schoenau & Hoffmeister began making dolls in 1901 and were located in Bavaria. The factory was called "Porzellanfabrik Burggrub" and this mark will be found on many of their doll heads.

Mark:

HANNA

PORZELLANFABRIK BURGGRUB

Princess Elizabeth: Smiling open mouth, set eyes, bisque head on jointed five-piece body and marked with name on head or body. 15" - $1,800.00; 21" - $2,450.00; 24" - $2,900.00.

Hanna: Child with black or brown fired-in color to bisque head. Sleep or set eyes, five-piece body or jointed body. Marked with name on head. 9" - $325.00; 15" - $675.00.

Hanna Baby: White bisque head, open mouth, sleep eyes. On five-piece bent limb baby body. 8" - $285.00; 12" - $425.00; 15" - $650.00; 17" - $750.00; 21" - $1,200.00; 23" - $1,400.00. **Toddler:** 9" - $375.00; 16" - $850.00; 20" - $1,400.00.

Character baby, #169, 769, 1271, etc.: 1910–on. Bisque head on five-piece bent limb baby body. Can also be marked with **"Burggrub."** 14" - $365.00; 17" - $575.00; 19" - $685.00; 23" - $825.00. **Toddler:** 22" - $1,000.00; 25" - $1,300.00.

Child, #1800, 1906, 1909, 5500, 5700, 5800, 5900, etc. Bisque head with open mouth, sleep or set eyes, jointed body. No damage and nicely dressed. 12" - $250.00; 15" - $325.00; 19" - $450.00; 22" - $550.00; 26" - $800.00; 29" - $1,000.00; 32" - $1,300.00; 36" - $1,600.00; 40" - $3,000.00 up. **Kid body:** Open mouth. 15" - $250.00; 18" - $375.00; 22" - $450.00.

Character child, #4000: "Long" face, open mouth. 13" - $365.00; 17" - $650.00; 20" - $975.00; 24" - $1,200.00; 27" - $1,400.00.

Painted bisque: Painted head on five-piece body or jointed body. 10" - $175.00; 13" - $300.00.

Das Lachende Baby (The Laughing Baby): 22" - $2,300.00; 25" - $2,800.00.

Pouty baby: Closed mouth, very small sleep eyes, and painted hair. Cloth body, composition limbs. 13" - $825.00.

23" with very "long" character face with short chin. Character modeling around open mouth. On fully jointed German body. Marked "S" and "H" with "PB" inside star, "4000-11." $1,150.00.

14" "Hanna" character baby with open mouth, sleep eyes, and painted lashes below eyes. On five-piece bent limb baby body. Marked "S," "PB" inside star, "H/0x/ Germany." $625.00. *Courtesy Virginia Sofie.*

20" Schoenau & Hoffmeister with sleep eyes and open mouth. On fully jointed body. Marked "S," "PB" in star, "H. 1923." $475.00. *Courtesy Virginia Sofie.*

Albert Schoenhut & Co. was located in Philadephia, PA, from 1872 until the 1930s. The dolls are all wood with spring joints, have holes in the bottoms of their feet to fit in a metal stand.

Marks:

(1911–1913)   **(1913–1930)**

SCHOENHUT DOLL
PAT. JAN. 17, '11, USA
& FOREIGN COUNTRIES
(Incised 1911–on)

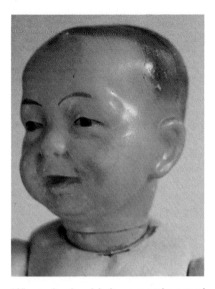

13" wooden head baby, correctly named "Bauz," but referred to by collectors as the "Kaiser Baby" because the arms are bent and the hand turned inward. Kaiser Wilhelm of Germany had a slightly deformed hand, thus the name. This is a very rare Schoenhut model. They also made a model #101 "Marie" (See Series 8, pg. 152.) Only value known - $2,000.00. *Courtesy Ken Bowers.*

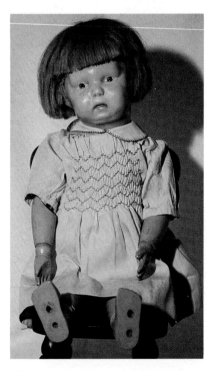

17" "baby face" Schoenhut that comes with wig and painted hair. Holes in bottom of feet and through original shoes are for the Schoenhut stand. $750.00. *Courtesy Barbara Earnshaw-Cain.*

Child with carved hair: May have comb marks, molded ribbon, comb or bow. Closed mouth. Original or nice clothes. **Excellent condition:** 15" - $2,600.00; 20" - $2,800.00. Very good condition: **Some wear.** 15" - $1,500.00; 18" - $1,650.00; 20" - $2,100.00. **Poor condition:** With chips and dents. 15" - $550.00; 20" - $650.00.

Child (rare): 1911. Looks exactly like Kammer & Reinhardt's #101 pouty. (See photo in Series 8, pg. 152.) 23" - $5,800.00 up. **Baby, #100:** 14" - $1,300.00.

Man with carved hair: Mint: 20" - $2,800.00 up. **Some wear:** 20" - $1,700.00. Chips, dirty: 20" - $850.00.

Baby head: Can be on regular body or bent limb baby body. Bald spray painted hair or wig, painted decal eyes. Nicely dressed or original. **Excellent condition:**

13" - \$525.00; 15" - \$685.00; 17" - \$750.00. **Good condition:** 15" - \$375.00; 17" - \$485.00. **Poor condition:** 17" - \$150.00; 20" - \$200.00. **Toddler:** Excellent condition. 13" - \$875.00; 17" - \$975.00.

Child, character face: 1911–1930. Wig, intaglio eyes. Open/closed mouth with painted teeth. Suitably redressed or original. **Excellent condition:** 15" - \$1,500.00; 19" - \$1,650.00; 22" - \$1,900.00. **Good condition:** 15" - \$850.00; 19" - \$985.00; 22" - \$1,100.00. **Poor condition:** 15" - \$300.00; 19" - \$425.00; 22" - \$500.00.

Cap molded to head: (See photo in Series 8, pg. 152.) 15" - \$3,700.00 up.

Snickelfritz: Some wear. 16" - \$2,600.00 up.

Tootsie Wootsie: Molded, painted hair, open/closed mouth with molded tongue and two upper teeth. Toddler or regular body. (See photo in Series 6, pg. 170.) 15" - \$2,000.00; 19" - \$2,300.00; 22" - \$2,500.00 up.

"Dolly" face: 1915–1930. Common doll that is wigged. Open/closed mouth with painted teeth. Decal painted eyes. Original or nicely dressed. **Excellent condition:** 15" - \$650.00; 18" - \$725.00; 21" - \$850.00. **Good condition:** 15" - \$425.00; 18" - \$600.00; 21" - \$725.00. **Poor condition:** 15" - \$165.00; 17" - \$250.00.

Sleep eyes: 1920–1930. Has lids that lower down over the eyes. Open mouth with teeth or just slightly cut open mouth with carved teeth. Original or nicely dressed. **Excellent condition:** 15" - \$1,150.00; 18" - \$1,350.00; 23" - \$1,550.00. **Good condition:** 15" - \$650.00; 19" - \$775.00. **Poor condition:** 19" - \$245.00; 21" - \$325.00.

Walker: 1919–1930. One-piece legs with "walker" joints in center of legs and torso. Painted eyes, open/closed or closed mouth. Original or nicely dressed. **Excellent condition:** 16" - \$925.00; 19" - \$1,200.00; 20" - \$1,500.00. **Good condi-**

8" tall German comic characters "Max and Moritz" made by Schoenhut. All original. Original - \$800.00 each; re-dressed - \$625.00 each. *Courtesy Ellen Dodge.*

tion: 16" - $600.00; 19" - $700.00; 22" - $875.00. **Poor condition:** 16" - $145.00; 19" - $225.00; 22" - $300.00.

All composition: 1924. Molded curly hair, "Patsy" style body, paper label on back. (See photo in Series 7, pg. 153.) 14" - $650.00.

Circus animals: (See photo in Series 9, pg. 161.) $95.00–500.00.

Circus parade set, #18: 1950s. Tent and all figures/animals - $1,600.00.

Circus Humpty Dumpty: Tent, figures, and animals. (See photo in Series 9, pg. 161.) $2,600.00 up.

Clowns: $150.00–300.00.

Felix The Cat: Copyright on foot. 8" - $650.00.

Ringmaster and bareback rider: $200.00–350.00.

Roly-Poly figures: 1914. Figures are marked. (See photo in Series 8, pg. 155.) $325.00 up.

Teddy Roosevelt: Circa 1920. Portrait head with glass eyes. Original in hunting gear. 10" - $2,300.00 up.

Maggie and Jiggs: 9" and 7" figures from the comic, "Bringing Up Father." She has tall top knot. Each - $525.00 up.

Max & Moritz: 8" carved figures with painted hair. Dowel legs with carved shoes. Each - $625.00 up.

Dancing doll: Constructed like a marionette. Made of wood and papier maché. Attached by wire to wooden base. Excellent condition. (See photo in Series 9, pg. 160.) Single figure: $500.00 up. Double figure: $785.00 up.

SCHUETZMEISTER & QUENDT

Schuetzmeister & Quendt made dolls from 1898 to 1910s. This short term factory was located in Boilstadt, Germany.

Marks:

SQ &Q $\frac{S}{Q}$

Child, mold #101, 251, 252, etc.: Can have cut pate or be a bald head with two string holes. No damage and nicely dressed, open mouth. 13" - $400.00; 19" - $500.00; 22" - $600.00.

Baby, includes mold #201, 301: Five-piece bent limb baby body. Not damaged and nicely dressed. Open mouth. 12" - $300.00; 14" - $375.00; 17" - $475.00; 22" - $650.00. **Toddler:** 16" - $800.00; 20" - $975.00; 24" - $1,200.00.

SIMON & HALBIG

Simon & Halbig began making dolls in the late 1860s or early 1870s and continued until the 1930s. Simon & Halbig made many heads for other companies and they also supplied some doll heads from the French makers. They made entire dolls, all bisque, flange neck dolls, turned shoulder heads and socket heads.

Marks:

1279-3
DEP

S 11 H
729

SH
GERMANY

All prices are for dolls with no damage to the bisque and only minor scuffs to the bodies, well dressed, wigged and with shoes. Dolls should be ready to place in a collection.

CHILD:

#130, 530, 540, 550, 570, 600, etc: 1890 to 1930s. Open mouth. (Add more for flirty eyes.) 13" - $450.00; 17" - $575.00; 20" - $675.00; 24" - $865.00; 28" - $1,200.00; 30" - $1,650.00; 35" - $2,200.00; 40" - $3,000.00 up. **#1039 walker:** See end of this section.

#1039, 1040, 1049, 1059, 1069, 1078, 1079, 1099: Open mouth, jointed body. 13" - $525.00; 16" - $625.00; 20" - $725.00; 23" - $800.00; 27" - $1,250.00; 30" - $1,300.00; 35" - $2,300.00; 42" - $3,400.00. **Pull string sleep eyes:** 18" - $975.00 up.

#1009: Kid body: 15" - $750.00; 20" - $950.00; 25" - $1,250.00; 27" - $1,500.00. **Jointed body:** 12" - $900.00; 20" - $1,200.00; 22" - $1,400.00; 25" - $1,700.00.

#1019, open mouth: Smiling. Jointed body. 15" - $6,100.00. Composition shoulder plate, ball-jointed arms, cloth body and upper legs. Ball-jointed lower legs. 17" - $7,300.00.

#1010, 1029, 1040, 1080, 1170, etc: Open mouth and **kid body.** 12" - $350.00; 15" - $485.00; 22" - $675.00; 26" - $825.00; 29" - $1,050.00.

#1109: 15" - $725.00; 22" - $975.00.

#1250, 1260: Open mouth, **kid body.** 15" - $525.00; 20" - $650.00; 26" - $900.00.

CHARACTERS:

1910 and after. Wig or molded hair. Glass or painted eyes. Open/closed, closed, or open mouth. On jointed child bodies.

S & H, no mold number: Closed or open/closed mouth. 15" - $1,500.00; 17" - $1,700.00. Shoulder head: 12" - $875.00; 16" - $1,200.00; 18" - $2,200.00. Fashion type: 15" - $3,600.00.

24" with beautiful bisque, very large eyes, and open mouth. On French style jointed body with straight wrists. Marked "12 S&H 1039 DEP." $825.00. *Courtesy Virginia Sofie.*

Extremely rare 13" character by Simon & Halbig, mold #150. Closed mouth, molded eyelids, and jointed body. All original. This example - $12,000.00. Not original and played with - $10,000.00. *Courtesy Frasher Doll Auctions.*

#IV: Closed mouth. Thoughtful, serious expression. 19" - $18,000.00 up. Open mouth: 17" - $16,000.00 up. **Dolly face:** Open mouth. 23" - $800.00 up.

#120: 16" - $1,800.00; 24" - $2,950.00; 29" - $3,850.00.

#150: Full, closed mouth. Intaglio eyes. (See photo in Series 7, pg. 155; Series 9, pg. 163.) 15" - $13,000.00 up; 20" - $17,000.00 up; 24" - $22,000.00 up; 27" - $25,000.00 up.

#151, 1388: Open/closed mouth, painted teeth. (See photo in Series 7, pg. 155; Series 9, pg. 163.) 16" - $5,400.00; 21" - $7,500.00.

#153 ("Little Duke"): (See photo in Series 8, pg. 157.) 14" - $24,000.00; 16" - $31,000.00; 18" - $39,000.00; 22" - $42,000.00 up.

#540, 550, 570, Baby Blanche: 18" - $650.00; 24" - $800.00.

#600: 15" - $985.00; 19" - $1,500.00; 23" - $2,000.00. **Open mouth:** 18" - $700.00; 22" - $875.00.

#601: Full cheeks, open mouth, blub-like chin. 31" - $10,000.00 up (estimate value).

#603: 13" - $5,700.00.

#718, 719, 720: 15" - $2,300.00; 21" - $3,500.00. **Open mouth:** (See photo in Series 9, pg. 164.) 14" - $1,250.00; 19" - $1,850.00; 26" - $2,300.00.

#729: Slight open mouth, smiling. 15" - $2,400.00 up; 18" - $2,600.00. **Closed mouth:** 17" - $3,200.00; 21" - $3,900.00. **Kid body:** 15" - $1,300.00; 19" - $1,750.00; 24" - $2,100.00.

#739: 14" - $1,500.00; 19" - $2,600.00; 27" - $3,200.00. **Open mouth:** 18" - $1,300.00; 22" - $1,600.00; 27" - $1,750.00.

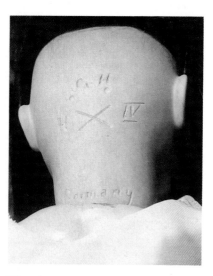

23" with very rare mold mark called "Ivy." This doll *does not* have the true "IV" look which is a closed mouth child with a very thoughtful, serious expression. This model has what is termed a "dolly face." She is a mystery! Marked "S&H/H, large X, IV/Germany." $800.00 up. *Courtesy Virginia Sofie.*

#740: Kid or cloth body, closed mouth. 12" - $600.00; 17" - $1,500.00; 19" - $1,700.00. **Jointed body:** 12" - $675.00; 18" - $1,900.00; 22" - $2,400.00.

#749: Closed mouth, jointed body. 19" - $3,000.00; 23" - $3,600.00. **Open mouth:** 13" - $1,450.00; 19" - $2,300.00; 26" - $2,800.00. **Kid body:** Open mouth. 18" - $1,800.00; 22" - $2,300.00.

#758: Full cheeks, open mouth. 20" - $800.00; 23" - $900.00. **Pull string talker:** 21" - $850.00.

#759: Open mouth, deep cheek dimples, rare. (See photo in Series 9, pg. 164.) 16" - $7,000.00; 19" - $9,200.00.

#769: Open mouth. 13" - $1,400.00; 19" - $2,300.00; 26" - $3,000.00.

#905, 908: (See photo in Series 6, pg. 173.) Closed mouth. 15" - $2,800.00; 18" - $3,200.00. **Open mouth:** 15" - $1,700.00; 19" - $1,900.00; 24" - $2,400.00.

#919: Open/closed mouth with protruding upper lip. 16" - $8,100.00 up; 20" - $9,000.00 up.

21" Simon & Halbig, mold #758, is a pull string talker with full cheeks, large round eyes, and open mouth. On fully jointed body. $850.00. *Courtesy Virginia Sofie.*

#929: Closed mouth. 18" - $3,650.00; 23" - $4,600.00. **Open mouth:** 17" - $2,100.00; 22" - $3,100.00.

#939: Closed mouth. (See photo in Series 6, pg. 173.) Composition body: 16" - $2,500.00; 19" - $2,800.00; 22" - $3,500.00; 27" - $4,800.00; 30" - $5,400.00. **Kid body:** Closed mouth. 17" - $2,000.00; 22" - $2,400.00; 26" - $2,900.00. **Open mouth:** 14" - $1,200.00; 17" - $1,900.00; 25" - $2,600.00; 29" - $3,400.00.

#939, 949: See Black or Brown Doll section.

#940, 950: Kid body. (See photo in Series 7, pg. 156; Series 11, pg. 144.) 12" - $565.00; 16" - $1,400.00; 22" - $1,800.00. **Jointed body:** 12" - $725.00; 16" - $1,800.00; 22" - $2,400.00.

#949: Closed mouth. (See photo in Series 9, pg. 165.) 15" - $2,200.00; 22" - $2,800.00; 26" - $3,300.00; 30" - $4,100.00. **Open mouth:** (See photo in Series 9, pg. 164.) 17" - $1,500.00; 20" - $1,800.00; 25" - $2,300.00. **Kid body:** (See photo in Series

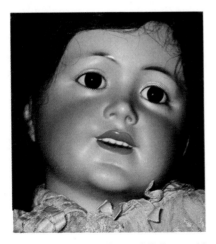

Very rare 31" doll by Simon & Halbig, mold #601, along with the initials "S&H." Wonderful face modeling of very character face. Chin is modeled differently than any other known German character child. Her jointed body is marked "Germany/6½" in red on hip. Estimated value - $10,000.00 up. *Courtesy Lois Thomas.*

9, pg. 165.) 16" - $1,200.00; 19" - $1,600.00; 22" - $2,100.00.

#969, 970: Slighty open mouth grin, square cut teeth, puffed cheeks. 14" - $3,600.00; 18" - $7,200.00; 22" - $9,600.00.

#979: Closed mouth. (See photo in Series 8, pg. 157.) 14" - $2,600.00; 17" - $3,400.00; 20" - $3,700.00. **Open mouth:** Square cut teeth, slight smile. 15" - $1,800.00; 20" - $2,600.00; 23" - $2,900.00; 27" - $3,400.00. **Kid body:** 18" - $1,800.00; 22" - $2,400.00.

#1148: Open/closed smiling mouth with teeth showing, dimples, glass eyes. 14" - $5,400.00; 17" - $6,900.00.

#1247, 1248, 1249, 1250, 1260 Santa: 15" - $1,000.00; 18" - $1,200.00; 23" - $1,400.00; 27" - $1,800.00; 32" - $2,400.00; 36" - $3,000.00.

#1269, 1279: (See photo in Series 5, pg. 134; Series 9, pg. 166.) 13" - $1,600.00;

23" Simon & Halbig child, mold #939, with sleep eyes, heavy feathered eyebrows, open mouth, and original wig. On fully jointed body. $1,850.00. *Courtesy Turn of Century Antiques.*

16" - $2,400.00; 19" - $3,000.00; 23" - $3,400.00; 27" - $3,900.00; 32" - $5,300.00; 36" - $5,600.00.

#1299: 15" - $1,300.00; 18" - $1,700.00; 22" - $2,200.00.

#1302: See Black or Brown Dolls section.

#1303: Closed mouth, thin lips. Adult body. (Also see Black or Brown Dolls section.) 17" - $7,700.00 up. Man: (See photo in Series 8, pg. 161.) 17" - $8,500.00.

#1304: 15" - $6,400.00; 18" - $8,100.00.

#1305: Open/closed smiling mouth, dimples, long nose. 17" - $18,000.00 up.

#1308: 21" - $6,500.00 up.

#1309: Character with open mouth. 12" - $1,600.00; 17" - $2,100.00; 21" - $3,200.00.

#1310: Open/closed mouth, modeled mustache. 18" - $18,000.00.

#1338: Open mouth, jointed body. 17" - $1,600.00; 23" - $2,700.00; 27" - $3,200.00.

#1339: Character face, open mouth. (See photos in Series 5, pg. 135; Series 7, pg. 157.) 19" - $1,800.00; 25" - $3,200.00.

#1339, 1358: See Black or Brown Dolls sections.

#1345: 16" - $2,800.00; 18" - $4,200.00.

#1388, 1398: See Ladies.

#1428: Very character face. Open/closed mouth, glass eyes. 17" - $1,950.00; 23" - $2,900.00.

#1448: Full closed mouth. Serene expression. 16" - $17,000.00 up; 20" - $21,500.00 up. **Open/closed mouth:** Laughing. Modeled teeth. 15" - $15,000.00 up; 20" - $21,000.00 up.

#1478: 16" - $9,600.00 up.

#1488: Child with closed mouth. (See photos in Series 4, pg. 139; Series 6, pg. 175.) 15" - $3,200.00; 19" - $4,100.00; 23" - $5,200.00.

CHARACTER BABIES:

1909 to 1930s. Wigs or molded hair, painted or sleep eyes, open or open/closed mouth and on five-piece bent limb baby bodies. (Allow more for toddler body or flirty eyes.)

18" character child with open mouth and large expressive eyes. On fully jointed body. Made for Louis Lindner & Sohne by Simon & Halbig. Marked "1339/S&H/ L.L. & S/8." $1,650.00. *Courtesy Virigina Sofie.*

#1294: 15" - $625.00; 18" - $800.00; 22" - $1,000.00; 25" - $1,600.00. **With clockwork** in head to move eyes: 26" - $2,500.00. **Toddler:** 24" - $1,700.00.

#1299: Open mouth. 12" - $525.00; 15" - $925.00. **Toddler:** 17" - $1,400.00; 19" - $1,600.00.

#1428, toddler: (See photo in Series 7, pg. 158.) 13" - $1,400.00; 17" - $2,300.00; 21" - $2,500.00; 27" - $3,000.00. **Baby:** 13" - $1,300.00; 16" - $1,700.00; 20" - $2,200.00.

#1488 toddler: (See photo in Series 6, pg. 175.) 16" - $2,500.00; 19" - $4,100.00; 23" - $4,700.00. **Baby:** 16" - $1,600.00; 19" - $3,200.00; 23" - $4,000.00; 27" - $4,500.00.

#1489 Erika baby: (See photos in Series 6, pg. 176; Series 7, pg. 159; Series 11, pg. 146.) 19" - $3,600.00; 21" - $4,600.00 up; 25" - $5,200.00 up.

#1498 toddler: (See photo in Series 6, pg. 175.) 17" - $5,800.00; 21" - $6,800.00. **Baby:** 15" - $5,100.00; 19" - $5,800.00.

MECHANICAL:

#1039 walker: Open mouth. Key wound. 17" - $1,600.00; 21" - $1,900.00; 24" - $2,300.00. **Walking/kissing:** 21" - $1,500.00; 25" - $2,200.00.

Edison, Thomas: Metal body with phonograph. Uses S&H head (mold #719, etc.) Open mouth. 17" - $2,800.00 up; 23" - $3,500.00 up.

MINIATURE DOLLS:

Tiny dolls with open mouth on jointed body or five-piece body with some having painted-on shoes and socks.

#1078, 1079, etc.: Fully jointed: 8" - $475.00; 12" - $575.00. **Five-piece body:** 8" - $350.00; 12" - $450.00. **Walker:** 12" - $645.00.

#1160: "Little Women" type. Closed mouth and fancy wig. 7" - $425.00; 12" - $625.00. **Head only:** 2–3" - $70.00–150.00.

LADIES:

#1159, 1179: Circa 1910. Open mouth, molded lady-style slim body with slim arms and legs. (See photo in Series 9, pg. 167.) 13" - $1,100.00; 16" - $1,650.00; 20" - $2,200.00; 24" - $2,700.00; 27" - $3,200.00.

#1303: Circa 1910. Closed mouth with character lines around mouth and eyes. Adult slim limb body. 16" - $12,000.00; 18" - $14,000.00.

#1305: Open/closed mouth with full row of teeth, long nose. 17" - $9,800.00 up; 21" - $15,000.00 up.

#1307: Lady with long face. 19" - $16,000.00 up; 22" - $21,000.00; 25" - $23,000.00 up.

#1308: Man. 14" - $6,200.00; 16" - $7,800.00. **Molded mustache:** Original. 15" - $12,000.00 up.

#1388: Thin face with dimples and open/closed smile mouth. Glass eyes with heavy upper molded eyelids. Adult composition and wood body. 21" - $17,500.00 up; 26" - $27,000.00 up.

#1398, 1399: 18" - $15,000.00 up.

#1468, 1469: Sweet expression. Closed mouth, glass eyes. 15" - $2,600.00; 17" - $3,100.00.

#1527: 17" - $9,400.00 up; 21" - $10,000.00 up.

#152: Lady with long Roman nose, molded eyelids, closed mouth. 16" - $18,000.00 up; 22" - $30,000.00 up.

22" Simon & Halbig fashion lady with mold #1159. Has sleep eyes and open mouth. On jointed adult body. Wig and clothes may be original. $2,500.00. *Courtesy Turn of Century Antiques.*

S.F.B.J.

The Société Française de Fabrication de Bébés et Jouets (S.F.B.J.) was formed in 1899 and known members were Jumeau, Bru, Fleischmann & Bloedel, Rabery & Delphieu, Pintel & Godchaux, P.H. Schmitz, A. Bouchet, Jullien, and Danel & Cie. By 1922, S.F.B.J. employed 2,800 people. The Society was dissolved in 1958. There is a vast amount of "dolly-faced" S.F.B.J. dolls, but some are extremely rare and are character molds. Most of the characters are in the 200 mold number series.

Marks:

S.F.B.J.
239
PARIS

DÉPOSÉ
S.F.B.J.
301

S	F
B	J

CHILD:

1899. Sleep or set eyes, open mouth and on jointed French body. No damage and nicely dressed.

#60: 13" - $575.00; 15" - $625.00; 21" - $825.00; 27" - $1,250.00.

#301: 9" - $400.00; 13" - $650.00; 15" - $800.00; 21" - $1,000.00; 27" - $1,650.00; 34" - $2,800.00. **Lady body:** 22" - $1,800.00.

Bleuette: 1930s–1960s. Exclusively made for Gautier-Languereau and their newspaper for children, La Semaine de Suzette. (Just as "Betsy McCall" was used by McCall's magazine.) Marked "SFBJ" or "71 Unis France 149 301" with "1½" at base of neck socket. Body marked "2" and feet marked "1." Sleep eyes, open mouth. (See photo in Series 7, pg. 36.) 10" - $775.00 up.

Jumeau type: 1899–1910. Open mouth. (See photo in Series 7, pg. 163; Series 8, pg. 164; Series 9, pg. 170.) 12" -

$825.00; 16" - $1,100.00; 19" - $1,500.00; 23" - $1,9500.00; 27" - $2,400.00. **Closed mouth:** 16" - $2,400.00; 20" - $3,100.00; 24" - $3,500.00.

Lady #1159: Open mouth, adult body. (See photo in Series 10, pg. 159.) 25" - $3,000.00 up.

CHARACTER:

Sleep or set eyes, wigged, molded hair, jointed body. (Allow more for flocked hair. Usually found on mold #227, 235, 237, 266.) No damage and nicely dressed.

#211: 16" - $5,000.00 up.

#226: (See photo in Series 4, pg. 144; Series 11, pg. 148.) **Glass eyes:** 16" - $1,750.00; 18" - $2,200.00. **Painted eyes:** 16" - $1,350.00.

#227: (See photo in Series 5, pg. 136.) 15" - $2,200.00; 21" - $2,700.00.

22" with very charcter face. Has high color bisque, sleep eyes, and open mouth. On jointed toddler body. Marked "SFBJ 247." $3,000.00. *Courtesy Barbara Earnshaw-Cain.*

#229: 17" - $3,700.00.

#230: 16" - $1,600.00; 19" - $2,100.00; 21" - $2,400.00.

#233: Screamer. (See photo in Series 4, pg. 143.) 13" - $1,900.00; 16" - $3,000.00; 19" - $3,300.00.

#234: 16" - $2,900.00; 22" - $3,400.00.

#235: Glass eyes: 15" - $1,600.00; 23" - $2,300.00. **Painted eyes:** 16" - $1,300.00; 23" - $2,000.00.

#236, 262 toddler: 13" - $1,200.00; 15" - $1,600.00; 19" - $1,800.00; 23" - $2,300.00; 25" - $2,600.00. **Baby:** 14" - $800.00; 18" - $1,450.00; 24" - $1,950.00.

#237: (See photo in Series 7, pg. 161.) 14" - $1,900.00; 19" - $2,300.00.

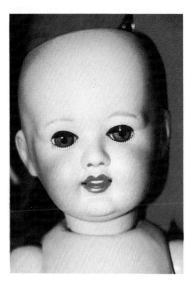

15" with rare mold number and character modeling. Modeled tongue extends over lower lip and two painted teeth. There are cut-out holes at the edge of the mouth. Head pate area is cut almost straight, rather than slanted. Has sleep eyes with lashes and painted lashes below eyes only. Marked "SFBJ/246/Paris/6." $2,500.00. *Courtesy Susan Cap.*

#238: (See photo in Series 3, pg. 134.) 15" - $3,600.00; 23" - $4,200.00. **Lady:** 23" - $3,800.00.

#239 Poulbot: (See photo in Series 10, pg. 159.) 17" - $8,200.00 up.

#242: (See photo in Series 5, pg. 137.) 15" - $2,600.00; 18" - $2,900.00 up. Nursing baby: 15" - $3,000.00.

#246: Modeled tongue and two teeth with open space on each side. Light cheek dimples. **Excellent bisque:** 15" - $2,500.00. **High color:** Orangish skin tones. 14" - $1,350.00.

#247 toddler: 17" - $2,600.00; 21" - $2,900.00; 27" - $3,400.00.

#248: Very pouty, glass eyes. 15" - $4,200.00; 20" - $5,800.00.

#251 toddler: 16" - $1,300.00; 19"- $1,800.00; 23" - $2,400.00; 27" - $2,750.00. **Baby:** 16" - $1,200.00; 22" - $1,800.00; 26" - $2,300.00.

#252 toddler: 14" - $5,300.00; 17" - $5,700.00; 21" - $7,200.00; 27" - $8,000.00. **Baby:** 13" - $1,600.00; 17" - $5,000.00; 23" - $6,900.00; 27" - $7,900.00.

#257: 17" - $2,750.00.

Large 28" toddler with sleep eyes and closed pouty mouth. Marked "SFBJ 252 Paris." Shown with 25" French toy stove and miniature blue granite dishes. Doll - $7,900.00. Store - $1,500.00 up. Dishes - $300.00 up. *Courtesy Frasher Doll Auctions.*

#266: 21" - $4,300.00.

#306 ("Princess Elizabeth"): See Jumeau section.

Googly: See Googly section.

Kiss throwing, walking doll: (See photo in Series 5, pg. 138; Series 9, pg. 170.) Composition body with straight legs and walking mechanism. When it walks, arm goes up to throw kiss. Head moves from side to side. Flirty eyes, open mouth. In working condition, no damage to bisque head and nicely dressed. 20" - $1,900.00. All original - $2,500.00 up.

These 11" and 13" dolls both have the same mark, "SFBJ/Paris/3." The 11" doll is also stamped "Jumeau" in red and has set eyes. 13" has sleep eyes. Both have open mouthes and are on fully jointed bodies. 11" $625.00; 13" - $825.00. *Courtesy Viriginia Sofie.*

Skookums have mask faces with wigs. Wool blankets form the bodies that are stuffed with twigs, leaves, and grass. Wooden dowel rods form the legs and they have suede over wooden feet. They were made from 1920 to 1940s. After 1949, they have plastic feet. (Allow more for original box.)

Squaw with baby: 10" - $165.00; 15" - $250.00; 18" - $450.00; 22" - $650.00 up.

Portrait chief: 10" - $175.00; 15" - $300.00; 18" - $450.00; 22" - $650.00; 30" - $900.00.

Sitting squaw: 8" - $145.00; 12" - $185.00.

Child: 8" - $80.00–95.00 up.

Plastic feet: 4" - $20.00; 6" - $30.00; 12" - $65.00; 15" - $150.00; 18" - $185.00; 22" - $300.00; 30" - $450.00; 36" - $600.00.

6" "Skookum" googly. Has a box form that extends to end of blanket. Dress is about 2" longer. Mask face with Indian blanket folded to form arms. Most likely made by Georgene Averill, because she used this head for other dolls. $145.00. *Courtesy Jeannie Venner.*

16" and 14" "Skookums" in mint condition and with their original boxes. Both have paper with painted decorations covering their wooden feet. 16" - $325.00; 14" - $250.00. *Courtesy private collection.*

Snow babies have fired-on "pebble-textured" clothing and were made in Germany and Japan. German-made babies were made as early as the 1880s and have excellent details. These early ones had no shoes or mittens, and these "stubs" were covered with all-white pebbly "snow." In the 1890s, some snow had a blue-grey appearance. Those babies are of excellent quality but did not remain on the market long.

After 1900, the hands and feet of the snow babies became defined. Early ones had beautiful painted features, but the later ones tended to have high color and poor artist workmanship. Japan reproduced snow babies in 1971 and they are stamped "Japan."

Snow babies can be excellent to poor in quality from both countries. Many are unmarked. Prices are for good quality painted features, rareness of pose, and no damage to the piece.

Single figure: 1½" - $55.00 up; 3" - $125.00–175.00 up.

Two figures: Molded together. 1½" - $125.00; 3" - $250.00.

Three figures: Molded together. 1½" - $145.00–250.00; 3" - $195.00–350.00.

One figure on sled: 2–2½" - $200.00. With reindeer: $300.00 up. Pulled by dogs: 3" - $375.00.

Two figures on sled: 2–2½" - $275.00.

Three figures on sled: (See photo in Series 6, pg. 180.) 2–2½" - $350.00.

Jointed shoulders and hips: (See photo in Series 5, pg. 139.) 3¼" - $225.00 up; 5" - $400.00 up; 7" - $500.00 up.

Shoulder head: Cloth body with china limbs. 5" - $200.00; 9" - $350.00; 12" - $450.00.

On sled in glass: "Snow" scene. $225.00 up. Sled/dogs: 3–4" - $400.00.

With bear: Child or baby. $375.00 up.

With snowman: 2½" - $250.00.

With musical base: $250.00 up.

Laughing child: 3" - $265.00 up.

Snow bear: 2" - $95.00 up. With Santa: $400.00.

With reindeer: $350.00

Snow baby riding polar bear: 3" - $400.00.

Snow angel: White texturing. Pink feathered smooth bisque wings. 3" - $500.00 up.

Snowman alone: 3" - $125.00.

Tumbling figure: 3" - $350.00.

Sliding on cellar door: 2½" - $450.00.

Dog with Santa: 2½" - $400.00.

Santa going down chimney: $325.00.

Igloo: $125.00.

Ice skater: 3" - $200.00 up.

In airplane: 4½" - $500.00.

Mother: Pushing two babies in red sled carriage. 4½" - $400.00 up.

Rolling snowball: 5" - $300.00.

Pushing carriage with twins: $400.00.

Snow babies, new: Presently being produced but they have a different look and color than old ones. Majority of new figures are not doing the same activities as the old ones. Many marked "Dept. 56."

Steiff started business in 1894. This German maker is better known for their well-crafted plush stuffed animals than for their dolls.

Steiff dolls: Felt, velvet or plush with seam down middle of face. Button-style eyes, painted features and sewn-on ears. The dolls generally have large feet so they stand alone. Prices are for dolls in excellent condition and with original clothes. Second prices are for dolls that are soiled and may not be original.

Adult dolls: (See photo in Series 7, pg. 165.) 19" - $2,600.00 up; 23" - $3,100.00 up.

Military men or uniforms: Policemen, conductors, etc. (See photo in Series 7, pg. 165.) 16" - $3,800.00 up; 18" - $4,200.00 up; 22" - $5,400.00 up.

Above: 18" German school teacher, "Ichabod." All felt with very thin limbs and body, large nose, and applied ears. Seam line down middle of face, black glass eyes, and original clothes. $4,200.00.

Left: 18" felt doll, most likely a military officer or official of some sort. Felt with pin-jointed arms, disc-jointed hips and neck, and hinged knees. Black glass eyes, center face seam, and applied ears. Has Steiff metal button on soles of boots. $4,200.00. *Both dolls courtesy Evelyn Krouse.*

Onkel Sam: From 1904. Long skinny legs, velvet face, felt body. 17" - $4,500.00. **Reissued as "Uncle Sam"** in 1994 and limited to 1,000.

Children: (See photo in Series 6, pg. 181.) 13" - $1,100.00 up; 16" - $1,700.00; 19" - $2,000.00 up.

Made in U.S. Zone Germany: Has glass eyes. 13" - $850.00 up; 17" - $1,100.00 up.

Comic characters: Such as chef, musician, etc. 15" - $2,600.00 up; 17" - $3,400.00 up.

Golliwog: 17" - $3,600.00.

Mickey Mouse: 9–10" - $1,200.00 up. **Minnie Mouse:** 9–10" - $1,800.00 up.

Clown: 17" - $2,600.00 up.

Leprechaun, elf, or gnome: All felt, straw stuffed, carries felt cloverleaf. Red mohair beard. 13" - $750.00 up; 18" - $1,400.00.

Max and Moritz: Circa 1960. "Bendy" type with felt costumes. Each - $200.00. All felt: 16" - $5,800.00 pair.

20" all felt Steiff clown with applied ears. Mohair wig is in poor condition, otherwise, doll in very good shape. Has seam down face and black glass eyes. $3,000.00.
Courtesy Margaret Mandel.

STEINER, HERM

Hermann Steiner of Sonneburg, Germany made dolls from 1921 on. Dolls come in various sizes, but are usually small.

Marks:

Child: Sleep eyes, open mouth, composition body. Perfect condition. 9" - $175.00; 16" - $325.00. Molded hair: 8" - $275.00. **#128:** Special eye movement. 15" - $400.00 **#401:** Shoulder head. 16" - $500.00.

Baby: Bisque character head with sleep eyes and open mouth. Cloth or composition body. All in good condition. 12" - $300.00; 16" - $400.00. **#240:** 17" - $675.00; 20" - $875.00.

Infant: Bisque head with molded hair, sleep eyes, and closed mouth. Cloth or composition body. All in good condition. 9" - $250.00; 12" - $300.00. **#246:** Holds pacifier and when bounced, hand moves to open mouth. 16" - $675.00.

Jules Nicholas Steiner operated from 1855 to 1892 when the firm was taken over by Amedee LaFosse. In 1895, this firm merged with Henri Alexandre, the maker of Phenix Bébé and a partner, May Freres Cie, the maker of Bébé Mascotte. In 1899, Jules Mettais took over the firm and in 1906, the company was sold to Edmond Daspres.

In 1889, the firm registered the girl with a banner and the words "Le Petit Parisien" and in 1892, LaFosse registered "Le Parisien."

Steiner body: All fingers are nearly same length. (See photo in Series 8, pg. 167.)

Marks:

J. STEINER	STE C3
STE. S.G.D.G.	J. STEINER
FIRE A12	B. S.G.D.G.
PARIS	

Bourgoin

23½" Steiner with extremely fine bisque. Has closed mouth and on marked Steiner jointed body with straight wrists. Marked "Steiner Bte SGDG Paris A-17." Shown with French toilette set. Doll - $6,500.00. Box set - $400.00. *Courtesy Frasher Doll Auctions.*

"A" Series child: 1885. Has paperweight eyes, jointed body, and cardboard pate. No damage and nicely dressed. (Also see "Le Parisien – "A" Series in this listing.) Closed mouth: 9" - $3,100.00; 12" - $3,400.00; 16" - $4,500.00; 23" - $6,500.00; 26" - $6,900.00; 29" - $7,500.00. **Open mouth:** 9" - $1,250.00; 12" - $1,500.00; 15" - $1,650.00; 19" - $2,400.00; 23" - $2,800.00.

"B" Series: Closed mouth. 23" - $6,800.00; 29" - $8,900.00; 33" - $10,500.00. **Open mouth: Two rows of teeth.** 23" - $7,000.00; 28" - $9,400.00. **Lever sleep eyes:** 18" - $6,800.00; 24" - $8,200.00.

"C" Series child: Circa 1880. Round face, paperweight eyes. No damage, nicely dressed. (See photo in Series 9, pg. 173.) Closed mouth: 17" - $6,000.00; 22" - $6,400.00; 28" - $8,850.00; 31" - $9,400.00 up. **Open mouth:** Two rows teeth. 23" - $6,200.00; 28" - $7,600.00; 34" - $8,400.00.

Bourgoin Steiner: 1870s. With "Bourgoin" incised or in red stamp on head along with the rest of the Steiner mark. No damage, nicely dressed. Closed mouth: 17" - $5,200.00; 21" - $6,300.00; 26" - $7,400.00.

Wire-eye Steiner: Closed mouth, flat glass eyes that open and close by moving wire in back of the head. Jointed body, no damage and nicely dressed. **Bourgoin:** 18" - $5,600.00; 22" - $6,300.00; 27" - $7,700.00. **"A" series:** 18" - $5,400.00; 22" - $6,400.00; 27" - $7,600.00. **"C" series:** 18" - $5,400.00; 22" - $6,300.00; 27" - $7,600.00.

"Le Parisien" - "A" Series: 1892. Closed mouth: 10" - $2,600.00; 15" - $4,200.00; 18" - $5,400.00; 22" - $6,200.00; 25" - $6,500.00; 29" - $7,000.00. **Open mouth:** 17" - $2,100.00; 23" - $2,500.00; 26" - $3,100.00.

Mechanical, Kicking Steiner: Composition torso, chest, and lower limbs. Kid or twill covered sections between parts of body. Open mouth with two rows of teeth. Key wound. Cries, head moves, legs kick. 18" - $2,800.00; 25" - $3,600.00.

Bisque hip Steiner: Bisque head, Motschmann-style body with shoulders, lower arms and legs and bisque torso sections. No damage anywhere. 17" - $6,900.00 up.

Early white bisque Steiner: Round face, open mouth with two rows of teeth. On jointed Steiner body. Pink wash over eyes. Unmarked. No damage, nicely dressed. (See Series 8, pg. 167; Series 9, pg. 174.) 17" - $4,650.00; 21" - $5,700.00.

Pretty 13" Steiner with round face, open mouth, and two rows of teeth. A unique feature of Steiner bodies is that all the fingers are the same length. Marked head and body. $1,600.00. *Courtesy Ellen Dodge.*

18" key wound mechanical Jules Steiner that kicks and screams. Arms go up and down, legs kick, and head moves from side to side as she cries. $2,800.00. *Courtesy Turn of Century Antiques.*

33" Steiner with round face, open mouth, and two rows of tiny teeth. On jointed Steiner body stamped "LePetite Parisien." Head marked with rare number: "Figure B No 7/3 Steiner Bte SGDG/Paris." Shown beside wicker carriage with metal wheels and framework. All original upholstery. Doll - $8,400.00. Buggy - $700.00. *Courtesy Frasher Doll Auctions.*

The "Lori Baby" was made by Swaine & Co. and can be marked "232," "DIP," "DV," "DI," "Geschutz S & Co." with green stamp or incised "D Lori 4." It has lightly painted hair, sleep eyes, open/closed mouth, and is on five-piece bent limb baby body.

Incised "Lori": 1910. Open/closed mouth, glass eyes. 13" - $1,100.00; 17" - $1,600.00; 21" - $2,600.00; 24" - $3,200.00; 27" - $3,700.00.

Intaglio eyes: (See photo in Series 6, pg. 138; Series 11, pg. 156.) 19" - $2,100.00; 23" - $2,600.00.

Flocked hair: 15" - $1,950.00; 19" - $2,800.00; 24" - $3,500.00.

#232: Open mouth. (See photo in Series 9, pg. 130.) 14" - $950.00; 21" - $1,500.00.

DIP: Closed mouth, wig, and glass eyes. 13" - $975.00; 17" - $1,500.00. **Toddler:** 20" - $2,500.00.

DV: Open/closed mouth, molded hair, glass eyes. 13" - $1,400.00; 16" - $1,600.00.

DI: Intaglio eyes, molded hair, open/closed mouth. 15" - $1,400.00.

S&C child with B.P.: Made for Bahr & Proschild. Smiling open/closed mouth. Very character face. (See photo in Series 10, pg. 165.) 15" - $6,400.00 up; 18" - $7,800.00 up; 22" - $9,200.00 up.

Lower right: 25" baby made by Swaine & Co. Has closed mouth and bent limb baby body. Marked "D Lori 4/Geschuzt S & Co. Germany." Center: 13" googly made by Kestner, mold #221. Left: 24" "Hilda" baby by Kestner. Standing: 25" S.F.B.J. toddler, mold #236. "Lori" - $3,200.00. Googly - $2,800.00. "Hilda" - $5,850.00. S.F.B.J. - $2,600.00. *Courtesy Frasher Doll Auctions.*

Child marked "S&C": 8" - $325.00; 15" - $525.00; 18" - $700.00; 23" - $800.00; 26" - $900.00; 31" - $1,300.00; 39" - $2,300.00.

TYNIE BABY

"Tynie Baby" was made for Horsman Doll Co. in 1924. Doll will have sleep eyes, closed pouty mouth and "frown" between eyes. Its cloth body has celluloid or composition hands. Markings will be "1924/E.I. Horsman/Made in Germany." Some will also be incised "Tynie Baby." Doll should have no damage and be nicely dressed.

Bisque head: 11" - $400.00; 13" - $475.00; 16" - $750.00. Original with pin: 16" - $925.00.

Composition head: 15–16" - $295.00.

All bisque: Glass eyes, swivel neck. 6" - $1,200.00; 9" - $1,800.00. Painted eyes: 6" - $600.00.

Vinyl/cloth: 1949. Crying face. 15" - $90.00–110.00.

Vinyl/cloth (J.C. Penney's): 1993. Sleep eyes. 13" - $80.00 (retail).

"UNIS, France" was a type of trade association or a "seal of approval" for trade goods to consumers from the manufacturers. This group of businessmen, who were to watch the quality of French exports, often overlooked guidelines and some poor quality dolls were exported. Many fine quality UNIS marked dolls were also produced.

UNIS began right after World War I and is still in business. Two doll companies are still members, Poupee Bella and Petitcollin. Other manufacturers in this group include makers of toys, sewing machines, tile, and pens.

Marks:

#60, 70, 71, 301: Bisque head, composition jointed body. Sleep or set eyes, open mouth. No damage, nicely dressed. (Allow more for flirty eyes.) 10" - $425.00; 16" - $600.00; 19" - $675.00; 23" - $825.00; 26" - $925.00. **Closed mouth:** 17" - $2,300.00; 19" - $2,700.00. **Composition head:** 13" - $185.00; 20" - $425.00. **Black or brown:** See that section.

#60, 70, 71, 301 with glass eyes: On five-piece body. 8" - $265.00; 13" - $385.00; 15" - $475.00.

Bleuette: See S.F.B.J section.

Provincial costume doll: Bisque head, painted, set or sleep eyes, open mouth (or closed on smaller dolls.) Five-piece body. Original costume, no damage. 8" - $250.00; 13" - $425.00; 15" - $525.00.

#272 baby with glass eyes: Open mouth, cloth body, celluloid hands. (See photo in Series 5, pg. 143.) 16" - $625.00; 19" - $985.00. **Painted eyes:** Composition hands. 15" - $325.00; 19" - $525.00.

#251 toddler: 16" - $1,350.00 up; 25" - $2,300.00. Composition head: 20" - $675.00.

Princess Elizabeth: (See photo in Series 6, pg. 185; Series 11, pg. 158.) 1938. Jointed body, closed mouth. (Allow more for flirty eyes.) 19" - $1,850.00; 24" - $2,450.00; 30" - $3,400.00 up.

Princess Margaret Rose: (See photo in Series 11, pg. 158.) 1938. Closed mouth. 17" - $1,950.00; 24" - $2,600.00; 33" - $3,650.00.

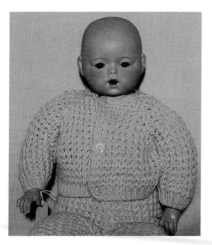

17" baby with bisque head, sleep eyes, and wide open mouth. Has chunky cloth body with delicate celluloid hands. Marked "Paris 272/Unis France" with a "71" on one side and "149" on the other. $850.00. *Courtesy Turn of Century Antiques.*

Closed mouth: 15" - $625.00; 20" - $850.00; 23" - $1,200.00; 26" - $1,450.00.

Open mouth: 15" - $375.00; 20" - $485.00; 23" - $625.00; 26" - $800.00.

Harald: Closed mouth. (See photo in Series 1, pg. 202.) Bisque head: 15" - $800.00. Celluloid head: 15" - $375.00 up.

Max, Hansi, Inge: Incised. 13" - $925.00.

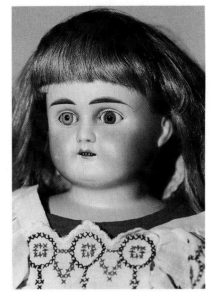

20" turned head doll with open mouth, kid body, bisque lower arms, and muslin lower legs. Note how flat underside of eyebrows are and how close brows are to eyes. Made by Wagner & Zetzsche. $545.00.

WAX

Poured wax: Cloth body with wax head, limbs and inset glass eyes. Hair is embedded into wax. Nicely dressed or in original clothes, no damage to wax, but wax may be slightly discolored evenly all over. Not rewaxed. (See photos in Series 5, pg. 144; Series 7, pg. 174.) 15" - $1,200.00; 18" - $1,700.00; 21" - $1,900.00; 24" - $2,200.00. **Lady:** 19" - $2,700.00 up; 23" - $3,800.00. **Man:** Mustache embedded into wax. 18" - $2,800.00.

Wax over papier maché or composition: Cloth body with wax over papier maché or composition head and with wax over composition or wood limbs. Only minor scuffs with no chipped out places, good color and nicely dressed. (See photo in Series 6, pg. 189.)

11" wax over papier maché baby with glass eyes, open mouth, and two upper and lower teeth. Has wooden torso and upper legs. Upper arms are wire with wax over lower arms. Kicks arms and legs and cries "Mama" when pull string is operated. Shown with 21" closed mouth Kestner with fully jointed body. Baby - $800.00. 21" - $2,700.00. *Courtesy Frasher Doll Auctions.*

Early dolls: 1860 on. **Sleep eyes:** Pull string to move eyes. 17" - $900.00. **Molded hair:** 15" - $300.00; 22" - $500.00; 25" - $600.00. **Squeaker body:** 15" - $350.00; 18" - $600.00. **Motschmann:** See that section. **"Alice":** Headband hairdo: 15" - $500.00; 18" - $600.00. **With wig:** Excellent quality. Heavy wax. 13" - $285.00; 17" - $450.00; 22" - $600.00; 25" - $675.00; 30" - $825.00. **Lever-operated eyes:** 1850s. 18" - $825.00. **Common quality:** Wax worn or gone. 13" - $165.00; 17" - $350.00; 22" - $375.00; 25" - $485.00.

Later dolls: 13" - $275.00; 17" - $450.00.

Bonnet or cap: 1860–1880. (See photo in Series 6, pg. 190.) **Hat** molded on forehead: 15" - $2,500.00. **Derby-type** hat: 23" - $2,200.00. **Bonnet-style** hat: 21" - $2,300.00. Round face, **poke bonnet:** 23" - $3,300.00. **Baby:** 17" - $1,500.00.

Pumpkin: Hair laced over ridged raised front area. 17" - $450.00; 21" - $550.00.

Slit head wax: English, 1830–1860s. Glass eyes, some open and closed by an attached wire. (See photo in Series 6, pg. 189.) In extra good condition: 15" - $1,050.00 up; 19" - $1,800.00; 22" - $2,100.00; 26" - $3,400.00 up.

Two-faced doll: 1880–1890s. Body stamped "Bartenstein" (Fritz). One side laughing, other crying. 16" - $1,200.00.

24" doll with wax over composition head and arms. Body and legs are cloth. Has human hair wig and glass eyes. All original. $585.00. *Courtesy Sandra Cummins.*

WELLINGS, NORAH

Norah Wellings's designs were made for her by Victoria Toy Works in Wellington, Shropshire, England. These dolls were made from 1926 into the 1960's. The dolls are velvet as well as other fabrics, especially felt and velour. They will have a tag on the foot "Made in England by Norah Wellings."

Child: All fabric with stitch jointed hips and shoulders. Molded fabric face with oil-painted features. Some faces are papier maché with a stockinette covering. All original felt and cloth clothes, clean condition. (See photo in Series 2, pg. 132.) **Painted eyes:** 13" - $400.00; 18" - $675.00; 22" - $975.00; 24" - $1,300.00. **Glass eyes:** 15" - $650.00; 18" - $850.00; 22" - $1,300.00.

Babies: Same description as child and same condition. (See photo in Series 4, pg. 158.) 16" - $625.00; 23" - $1,000.00.

Black islander ("Tak-uki") and Scots: These are most commonly found dolls. Must be in same condition as child. 9" - $90.00 up; 13" - $185.00 up; 16" - $225.00 up.

Characters: Mounties, Bobbies (policemen), and others. 13" - $385.00; 17" - $650.00; 24" - $1,100.00. **Glass eyes:** 17" - $900.00.

Characters from novels: (See photo in Series 11, pg. 161.) **Man:** 25" - $900.00. **Woman:** 23" - $850.00. **Child:** 17" - $575.00.

Child with glass eyes: White: 15" - $350.00; 18" - $550.00. **Black:** 15" - $275.00; 21" - $375.00; 25" - $625.00.

12" "Scot Lad" made by Norah Welling. Has molded farbic face with painted hair and dimples. Eyes are painted to the side. Body and limbs are made of felt and velvet. All original. $185.00. *Courtesy Virginia Sofie.*

11" child made by Hugo Wiegand. Has sleep eyes, open mouth, and all kid body with bisque lower arms. All original.

Marked

11" - $285.00; 16" - $395.00; 20" - $685.00; 24" - $800.00; 28" - $985.00. *Courtesy June Murkins.*

The Adolf Wislizenus doll factory was located at Waltershausen, Germany, and the heads he used were made by Bahr & Proschild, Ernst Heubach of Koppelsdorf, and Simon & Halbig. The company was in business starting in 1851, but it is not known when they began to make dolls.

Marks:

GERMANY
A.W.

26" doll made by Adolf Wislizenus. She has an open mouth with four teeth and is on a fully jointed body. Marked "Special 62." $750.00.

Child: 1890s into 1900s. Bisque head on jointed body, sleep eyes, open mouth. No damage and nicely dressed. Average quality: 13" - $185.00; 15" - $300.00; 18" - $425.00; 23" - $550.00; 26" - $650.00. **Excellent quality:** 13" - $425.00; 16" - $550.00; 18" - $650.00; 23" - $800.00; 28" - $1,200.00.

Walker: Open mouth, one-piece legs. Head turns as legs move. 21" - $725.00.

Baby: Bisque head in perfect condition and on five-piece bent limb baby body. No damage and nicely dressed. 17" - $500.00; 20" - $600.00; 26" - $985.00.

#110, 115: 15" - $1,200.00. **Glass eyes:** 17" - $3,900.00 up.

WOODEN DOLLS

English, William & Mary Period, 1690s–1700: Carved wooden head and eyes. Eyebrow and eyelashes are painted with tiny lines. Colored cheeks, human hair or flax wig. Wooden body with carved wooden hands shaped like forks. Legs are wood and jointed. Upper arms are cloth. In medium to fair condition: 14" - $52,000.00 up.

English, Queen Anne Period. Early 1700s: Eyebrows and lashes made of dots. Glass pupiless eyes (some paint-ed). Carved wooden egg-shaped head. Jointed wooden body, cloth upper arms. Back (including hips) was planed flat. Nicely dressed, in overall good condition. 13" - $9,400.00 up; 17" - $14,000.00 up; 23" - $23,000.00 up.

English, Georgian Period, 1750s–1800: Round wooden head with gesso coating, inset glass eyes. Eyelashes and eyebrows made of dots. Human or flax wig. Jointed wood body with pointed torso. Medium to fair condition. 12" -

$2,800.00; 16" - $4,400.00; 19" - $5,000.00; 25" - $6,500.00.

English, 1800s–1840s: Gesso coated wooden head, painted eyes. Human hair or flax wig. Original gowns generally longer than wooden legs. 14" - $1,500.00; 16" - $2,000.00; 21" - $3,000.00.

German, 1810s–1850s: Hair is delicately carved and painted with little spit curls around face. Some have decorations carved in hair such as yellow tuck comb. Features are painted. All wood doll with pegged or ball-jointed limbs. 9" - $825.00; 14" - $1,500.00; 18" - $1,800.00. **Exceptional:** All original. 16" - $3,000.00 up.

20" unjointed wooden doll with inset glass eyes. Natural wood finish. Origin unknown. $400.00. *Courtesy Frasher Doll Auctions.*

One of four wooden soldiers dressed in gold uniforms from original box set that also included four soldiers dressed in blue and two cannons. May represent Army and Navy academies. Ca. 1930s. Each - $65.00; box set - $275.00. *Courtesy Ellen Dodge.*

German, 1850s–1900: All wood with painted plain hairstyle. Some may have spit curls around face. 6" - $150.00; 9" - $225.00; 13" - $365.00. **Wooden shoulder head:** Same but with more elaborate carved hair such as buns. Wood limbs and cloth body. 11" - $450.00; 18" - $650.00; 24" - $900.00.

German, after 1900: Turned wood head with carved nose and painted hair. Painted lower legs with black shoes. Peg jointed. 12" - $85.00. **Child:** All wood, fully jointed body. **Glass eyes, open mouth:** 16" - $475.00; 19" - $650.00; 24" - $850.00.

Nesting Dolls ("Matryoshka"): Prices are for the set. **Old:** 1930s and before. 3" - $70.00 up; 6" - $125.00 up; 8" - $200.00 up. **New:** 4" - $12.00; 6" - $22.00. **Political:** Includes Gorbachev, Yeltsin. 4½" - $30.00; 6½" - $50.00.

Swiss: Carved wooden dolls. Dowel jointed all wood bodies. Jointed elbows, hips, and knees. 9" - $475.00.

Fortune tellers: Wooden half or full doll with multi-folded papers for skirt. Paper pulled outward to allow fortune to be read. 18" - $2,600.00; 21" - $3,200.00.

Left: 15" Mason-Taylor wooden doll with pewter hands and feet. Note how shoulders are extended beyond shoulder plate and the arms are jointed from the middle of this rod. Center: 11" Ella Smith "Alabama Baby" in rare small size. Has oil-painted hair and features. Right: 16" wax over papier maché doll with inset glass eyes and straw stuffed cloth body and limbs. Clothes may be original. 15" - $775.00; 11" (fair condition) - $900.00; 16" - $450.00. *Courtesy Turn of Century Antiques.*

W.P.A

President Franklin D. Roosevelt's Works Projects Administration (W.P.A.), allowed people to work and earn wages during the Depression from 1935 until the program's end in 1943. Out-of-work artisans made dolls, and those dolls are usually tagged or marked on their wooden stand with a number and the production location. (Example: #196, Kearny, Neb.) W.P.A. dolls were used as school teaching aids and are often found in school storerooms.

Composition type, bald: Finely detailed facial features, unjointed adult body. Good quality original clothes representing history or various nationalities. 16" pair - $725.00 up.

Plastic type composition: Molded heads have little detail, cloth body. Wears international costumes. 15" - $85.00 up.

Cloth dolls: Cloth body, stockinette head, yarn hair, molded mask face with oil-painted features. International style clothes. 22" - $1,200.00 up.

22" W.P.A. doll from 1937. All original in Dutch girl costume. Marked, from the W.P.A. Milwaukee Project. $1,200.00 up. *Courtesy Peggy Pergande.*

Modern Dolls

Background: 34" mohair teddy bear made by Knickerbocker in 1950, 24" "Marilee" by Effanbee. Foreground: 17" "Canadian Mountie" by Reliable of Canada, "Poor Pitaful Pearl" by Horsman, 15" "Brother" with yarn hair made by Effanbee, composition "Buddy Lee" with cowboy outfit, 14" "Polly Pigtails" by Madame Alexander, and all original "Majorette" by Mary Hoyer. In front: Original "Beatles" dolls. Teddy bear - $900.00. "Marilee" - $400.00 up. "Mountie" - $450.00. "Pearl" - $150.00. "Brother" - $300.00. "Buddy Lee" - $250.00. "Polly Pigtails" - $425.00. "Majorette" - $495.00. Beatles set - $395.00. *Courtesy Turn of Century Antiques.*

8" "Mindy" made by the Active Doll Co. Has large round sleep eyes, mohair wig, and jointed knees. Unmarked. In box - $75.00 up.
Courtesy Maureen Fukushima.

ADVANCE DOLL CO.

18" battery-operated "Wanda, the Walking Wonder" with plastic shoes attached with rollers on bottom of feet. All hard plastic with sleep eyes. Clothes and wig are original. Made by Advance Doll Co. from 1955 to 1959. Mint - $200.00 up. *Courtesy Frasher Doll Auctions.*

The author's separate price guide covering over 1,000 Madame Alexander dolls is available from book dealers or Collector Books.

1953–1954: 7½–8" straight leg non-walker. Heavy hard plastic. **Party dress:** Mint, all correct - $500.00 up. Soiled, dirty hair, mussed, or parts of clothing missing - $85.00. **Ballgown:** Mint and correct - $900.00 up. Soiled, dirty, bad face color, not original - $125.00. **Nude:** Clean, good face color. $250.00. Dirty, bad face color - $40.00.

1955: 8" straight leg walker. **Party dress:** Mint, all correct - $450.00 up. Soiled, dirty, parts of clothes missing - $50.00. **Ballgown:** Mint, all correct - $950.00 up. Dirty, part of clothing missing, etc. - $125.00. **Basic sleeveless dress:** Mint - $250.00. Dirty - $35.00. **Nude:** Clean, good face color - $125.00. Dirty, not original, faded face color - $25.00.

1956–1965: Bend knee walker. **Party Dress:** Mint, all correct - $375.00 up. Dirty, part of clothes missing, etc. - $60.00. **Ballgown:** Mint, correct - $650.00 up. Soiled, dirty, parts missing, etc. - $125.00. **Nude:** Clean, good face color - $225.00. Dirty, faded face color - $45.00. **Basic sleeveless dress:** Mint - $250.00. Dirty,

faded face color - $45.00. **Internationals:** $225.00 up. Dirty, parts missing - $40.00.

1965–1972: Bend knee non-walker. **Party Dress:** Mint, original - $275.00 up. Dirty, missing parts - $45.00. **Internationals:** Clean, mint - $60.00. Dirty or soiled - $20.00. **Nude:** Clean, good face color - $85.00. Dirty, faded face color - $20.00.

1973–1976 ("Rosies"): Straight leg non-walker. Rosy cheeks. Marked "Alex." $60.00. **Bride or ballerina:** Bend knee walker - $145.00 up. Bend knee only - $125.00. Straight leg - $60.00. **Internationals:** $50.00. **Storybook:** $60.00.

1977–1981: Straight leg non-walker. Marked "Alexander." **Ballerina or bride:** $45.00–55.00. **International:** $45.00– 55.00. **Storybook:** $50.00–60.00.

1982–1987: Straight leg non-walker. Deep indentation over upper lip that casts a shadow, makes doll look like it has mustache. **Bride or ballerina:** $35.00– 45.00. **International:** $35.00–40.00. **Storybook:** $35.00–45.00.

1988–1989: Straight leg, non-walker with new face. Looks more like older dolls but still marked with full name "Alexander." **Bride or ballerina:** $35.00– 45.00. **International:** $40.00–50.00. **Storybook:** $45.00–55.00.

Left to right: 8" "Thailand" (1966–1989), "Japan" (1968 to date), and "India" (1965–1988). Each - $60.00.

Prices are for mint condition dolls.

Baby Brother or Sister: 1977–1982. 14" - $80.00; 20" - $85.00.

Baby Ellen: 1965–1972. 14" - $125.00.

Baby Lynn: (Black "Sweet Tears") 1973–1975. 20" - $125.00.

Baby McGuffey: Composition. 22" - $195.00. Soiled - $65.00.

Baby Precious: 1975 only. 14" - $80.00.

Bitsey, Little: 1967–1968 only. All vinyl. 9" - $125.00.

Bonnie: 1954–1955. Vinyl. 19" - $95.00. Soiled - $20.00.

Genius, Little: Composition. 18" - $150.00. Soiled - $50.00.

Genius, Little: Vinyl. May have flirty eyes. 21" - $150.00. Soiled - $50.00.

Genius, Little: 8" - $245.00 up. Soiled - $40.00.

Happy: 1970 only. Vinyl. 20" - $250.00. Soiled - $65.00.

Hello Baby: 1962 only. 22" - $175.00.

Honeybun: 1951. Vinyl. 19" - $175.00. Soiled - $40.00.

Huggums, Big: 1963–1979. 25" - $90.00. **Lively:** 1963. 25" - $145.00.

20" "Happy" was made in 1970 only and is scarce in number. Has vinyl head and limbs with cloth body. She has a laughing expression and sleep eyes. All orginal. $250.00.

Kathy: Vinyl. 18" - $125.00; 26" - $150.00. Soiled: 18" - $25.00; 26" - $40.00.

Kitten, Littlest: Vinyl. 8" - $150.00 up. Soiled - $30.00.

Mary Cassatt: 1969–1970. 14" - $165.00; 20" - $245.00.

Mary Mine: 14" - $80.00. Soiled - $20.00.

8" original "Fischer Quints" using "Little Genuis" dolls with hard plastic heads and vinyl bodies and limbs. The set came with four pink and one blue baby bottle. Tagged "Original Quints." Original, from 1964. Set - $525.00 up. *Courtesy Mary Williams.*

Pinky: Composition. 23" - $225.00. Soiled - $95.00.

Precious: Composition. 12" - $200.00. Soiled - $60.00.

Princess Alexandria: Composition. 24" - $225.00. Soiled - $75.00.

Pussy Cat: Vinyl. 14" - $85.00. Soiled - $20.00. Black: 14" - $110.00. Soiled - $35.00.

Rusty: Vinyl. 20" - $325.00. Soiled - $75.00.

Slumbermate: Composition. 21" - $475.00. Soiled - $150.00.

Sweet Tears: 9" - $65.00. Soiled - $20.00. With layette: $165.00.

Victoria: 20" - $80.00. Soiled - $30.00.

MADAME ALEXANDER – CISSETTE

This 10–11" doll with high heel feet was made from 1957 to 1963, but the mold was used for other dolls later. She is made of hard plastic, and clothes will be tagged "Cissette."

The first price is for mint condition dolls and the second price is for soiled, dirty or faded clothes, tags missing and hair messy.

Street dresses: $265.00, $65.00
Ballgowns: $375.00, $100.00.
Ballerina: $350.00 up, $125.00.
Gibson Girl: $700.00, $165.00.
Jacqueline: $650.00 up, $125.00.
Margot: $425.00 up, $125.00.
Portrette: $425.00 up, $125.00.
Wigged in case: $800.00 up, $275.00.
Slacks or pants outfits: $250.00.
Queen: $350.00 up.

Three all original "Cissette" dolls made between 1957 and 1960. Made of hard plastic. Each - $250.00. *Courtesy Sally Bethschieder.*

"Cissy" was made 1955–1959 and had hard plastic with vinyl over the arms, jointed at elbows, and high heel feet. Clothes are tagged "Cissy." Prices are for excellent face color and clean dolls.

Street dress: $325.00 up.
Ballgown: $800.00 up.
Bride: $475.00 up.
Queen: $850.00.
Portrait: "Godey," etc. 21" - $1,000.00 up.
Scarlett: $1,300.00.
Flora McFlimsey: Vinyl head, inset eyes. 15" - $575.00.
Pant suit: $250.00 up.

Beautiful 20" "Cissy" in ankle length ballgown. Made of hard plastic with vinyl arms that are jointed at the elbow. Has high heel feet. $800.00. *Courtesy Jeannie Nespoli.*

MADAME ALEXANDER – CLOTH DOLLS

The Alexander Company made cloth/plush dolls and animals and oil cloth baby animals in the 1930s, 1940s and early 1950s. In the 1960s, only a few were made.

First prices are for mint condition dolls; second prices are for ones in poor condition, dirty, not original, played with or untagged.

Animals: $250.00 up, $70.00.
Dogs: $285.00 up, $80.00.
Alice in Wonderland: Has flat face. $800.00 up, $150.00. Mask face with formed nose: $650.00.
Clarabelle The Clown: 19" - $325.00, $95.00.
David Copperfield or other boys: $750.00 up.
Funny: $65.00, $10.00.
Little Shaver: 7" - $350.00 up; 12" - $275.00 up.
Little Women: Each - $625.00 up, $125.00.

26" "Mary Muslin" from 1951 is all original except for missing pansies from middle of eyes and her mouth. All cloth with felt features. Came in 19" and 40" sizes. 26" - $575.00. *Courtesy Green Museum.*

Muffin: 14" - $90.00, $30.00.
So Lite Baby or Toddler: 20" - $400.00 up, $125.00.
Susie Q: $650.00, $160.00.
Tiny Tim: $700.00, $225.00.
Teeny Twinkle: Has disc floating eyes. $525.00 up, $125.00.

Both of these "Muffins" with sapphire blue eyes are from 1965. Doll also came with button eyes and round felt eyes. Dress on left was first used on "Muffin" in 1963. Each - $90.00 up. *Courtesy Green Museum.*

MADAME ALEXANDER – COMPOSITION

First prices are for mint condition dolls; second prices are for dolls that are crazed, cracked, dirty, soiled clothes or not original.
Alice in Wonderland: 9" - $325.00, $90.00; 14" - $425.00, $125.00; 21" - $875.00, $150.00.
Babs Skater: 1948. 18" - $650.00 up, $150.00.
Baby Jane: 16" - $900.00, $325.00.
Brides or bridesmaids: 7" - $250.00, $65.00; 9" - $325.00, $75.00; 15" - $325.00, $90.00; 21" - $525.00, $165.00.
Dionne Quints: 8" - $175.00, $60.00. Set of five - $1,200.00. 11" - $350.00, $125.00. Set of five - $2,000.00. **Cloth baby:** 16" - $850.00, $200.00; 24" - $1,200.00, 350.00.
Dr. DeFoe: 14–15" - $1,250.00 up, $500.00.
Fairy Princess: 1939. 15" - $650.00; 21" - $975.00 up.
Flora McFlimsey: Has freckles. Marked "Princess Elizabeth." 15" - $525.00, $125.00; 22" - $800.00, $250.00.

9" all composition "Dutch" with painted features and mohair wig. All original. Made from 1936 to 1941. $300.00. *Courtesy Patricia Wood.*

Flower Girl: 1939–1947. Marked "Princess Elizabeth." 16" - $525.00, $100.00; 20" - $625.00, $175.00; 24" - $750.00 up, $300.00.

Internationals/Storybook: 7" - $285.00, $50.00; 9" - $300.00, $80.00.

Jane Withers: 13" - $1,000.00 up, $400.00; 18" - $1,300.00, $500.00.

Kate Greenaway: Very yellow blonde wig. Marked "Princess Elizabeth." 14" - $650.00, $150.00; 18" - $775.00, $265.00.

Little Colonel: 9" (rare size) - $600.00, $200.00; 13" - $575.00, $165.00; 23" - $900.00, $375.00.

Madelaine DuBain: 1937–1944. 14" - $500.00, $165.00; 17" - $600.00, $225.00.

Margaret O'Brien: 15" - $725.00, $275.00; 18" - $850.00, $250.00; 21" - $1,000.00, $450.00.

Marionettes by Tony Sarg: 12" - $325.00, $95.00. Disney: $375.00, $165.00. Others: 12" - $265.00, $95.00.

McGuffey Ana: Marked "Princess Elizabeth." 13" - $675.00, $175.00; 20" - $825.00, $325.00.

Military dolls: 1943–1944. 14" - $750.00, $300.00.

Nurse: 1936–1940. 14–15" - $575.00 up.

Portrait dolls: 1939–1941, 1946. 21" - $1,800.00 up, $950.00.

Princess Elizabeth: Closed mouth. 13" - $575.00, $175.00; 18" - $700.00, $250.00; 24" - $850.00, $350.00.

Scarlett: 9" - $475.00, $150.00; 14" - $750.00, $175.00; 18" - $1,200.00, $500.00; 21" - $1,600.00, $650.00.

Snow White: 1939–1942. Marked "Princess Elizabeth." 13" - $450.00, $150.00; 18" - $700.00, $225.00.

Sonja Henie: 17" - $950.00, $350.00; 20" - $1,100.00, $450.00. Jointed waist: 14" - $750.00, $250.00.

Wendy Ann: 11" - $450.00, $150.00; 15" - $575.00, $175.00; 18" - $775.00, $225.00.

18" all composition "Sonja Henie" with open mouth, dimples, and brown sleep eyes. Hair in original set. All original and in mint condition. From 1939. $1,000.00. *Courtesy Pat Graff.*

MADAME ALEXANDER – HARD PLASTIC

First prices are for mint condition dolls; second prices are for dolls that are dirty, played with, soiled clothes or not original.

Alice in Wonderland: 14" - $600.00, $200.00; 17" - $650.00, $225.00; 23" - $850.00, $300.00.

Annabelle: 15" - $550.00, $200.00; 18" - $650.00, $225.00; 23" - $800.00, $275.00.

Babs: 20" - $700.00, $225.00.

Babs Skater: 18" - $700.00, $225.00; 21" - $765.00, $250.00.

Ballerina: 14" - $375.00, $150.00.

Brenda Starr: 1964 only. Dress: 12" - $200.00. Gown: $350.00 up. Bride: $325.00.

Binnie Walker: 15" - $165.00, $50.00; 25" - $485.00, $175.00.

Cinderella: In ballgown: 14" - $800.00, $225.00. "Poor" outfit: 14" - $625.00, $165.00.

Cynthia: Black doll. 15" - $800.00, $300.00; 18" - $950.00, $400.00; 23" - $1,200.00, $500.00.

Elise: In street dress: 16½" - $325.00, $100.00. Ballgown: $650.00 up, $225.00.

Bride: 16" - $350.00, $150.00.

Fairy Queen: 14½" - $700.00,

Godey Lady: 14" - $875.00, $275.00.

Man/Groom: 14" - $950.00, $350.00.

Kathy: 15" - $550.00, $175.00.

Kelly: 12" - $450.00, $145.00.

Lissy: Street dress: 12" - $250.00, $125.00. Bride: $275.00, $125.00. Ballerina: $325.00, $150.00.

Little Women: 8" - $135.00, $60.00. Set of five with bend knees - $700.00; Set of five with straight legs - $300.00. Using Lissy

doll: 12" - $250.00, $90.00. Set of five - $1,400.00. 14" - $450.00. Set of five - $1,800.00. **Laurie:** Bend knee. 8" - $150.00 up, $50.00; 12" - $350.00, $125.00.

Madeline: 1950–1953. Jointed knees and elbows. 18" - $875.00 up, $250.00.

Maggie: 15" - $550.00, $175.00; 17" - $650.00, $225.00; 23" - $775.00, $300.00.

Maggie Mixup: 8" - $450.00 up, $150.00; 16½" - $400.00, $125.00. Angel: 8" - $685.00, $150.00.

Margaret O'Brien: 14½" - $850.00, $350.00; 18" - $975.00, $450.00; 21" - $1,100.00, $525.00.

Marybel: Doll only: $165.00. In case: $325.00.

Mary Martin: Sailor suit or ball-gown. 14" - $800.00 up, $400.00; 17" - $975.00, $425.00.

McGuffey Ana: 1948–1950. Hard plastic. 21" - $875.00, $325.00.

18" "Alice In Wonderland" with "Margaret" face from 1951. Has blue flannel wool dress, white pinafore, and mohair wig. $675.00. *Courtesy Glorya Woods.*

17" all hard plastic "Margot Ballerina" has "Margaret" face and was made from 1953 to 1955. $500.00. *Courtesy Jeannie Nespoli.*

Peter Pan: 15" - $700.00 up, $300.00.

Polly Pigtails: 14" - $500.00, $150.00; 17" - $625.00, $175.00.

Prince Charming: 14" - $700.00, $250.00; 18" - $825.00, $275.00.

Queen: 18" - $700.00 up, $300.00.

Shari Lewis: 14" - $500.00, $175.00; 21" - $800.00, $275.00.

Sleeping Beauty: 16½" - $600.00, $165.00; 21" - $950.00, $425.00.

Wendy (Peter Pan set): 15" - $500.00, $200.00.

Wendy Ann: 14½" - $725.00, $250.00; 17" - $850.00, $350.00; 22" - $975.00, $425.00.

Winnie Walker: 15" - $250.00, $80.00; 18" - $350.00, $100.00; 23" - $425.00, $125.00.

14" "Story Princess" is made of all hard plastic and all original. Made from 1954 to 1956. A very rare doll. $725.00 up. *Courtesy Jeannie Nespoli.*

MADAME ALEXANDER – PLASTIC AND VINYL

First prices are for mint condition dolls; second prices are for dolls that are played with, soiled, dirty and missing original clothes.

Bellows' Anne: 1987 only. 14" - $70.00.

Bonnie Blue: 1989 only. 14" - $80.00.

Bride: 1982–1987. 17" - $135.00.

Caroline: 15" - $300.00, $100.00.

Cinderella: Pink: 1970–1981. Blue: 1983–1986. 14" - $70.00.

Edith The Lonely Doll: 1958–1959. 16" - $225.00; 22" - $275.00.

Elise: Street dress: Made in 1966. 17" - $225.00. Formal: 1966, 1976–1977. $165.00. Bride: 1966–1986. $150.00.

First Ladies: First set of six - $700.00. Second set of six - $500.00. Third set of six - $500.00. Fourth set of six - $550.00. Fifth set of six - $475.00. Sixth set of six - $700.00.

Grandma Jane/Little Granny: 1970–1972. 14" - $250.00, $85.00.

14" "Jenny Lind and Listening Cat." Cat made by Schuco and is 3½" tall. All original. $325.00. *Courtesy Glorya Woods.*

Ingres: 1987 only. 14" - $70.00.

Isolde: 1985 only. 14" - $70.00.

Jacqueline: Street Dress: 21" - $575.00, $200.00. Ballgown: $750.00 up, $300.00. Riding Habit: $575.00, $200.00.

Janie: 12" - $265.00, $95.00.

Joanie: 36" - $425.00, $165.00.

Leslie: Black doll. Ballgown: 17" - $300.00, $150.00. Ballerina: $300.00, $150.00. Street dress: $285.00, $100.00.

Little Shaver: 1963 only. Made of vinyl. 12" - $275.00, $95.00.

Nancy Drew: 1967 only. 12" - $325.00, $100.00.

Napoleon: 1980–1986. 12" - $65.00.

Marybel: 16" - $175.00, $75.00. In case: $325.00 up; $150.00.

Mary Ellen: 31" - $450.00 up, $175.00.

Melinda: 14" - $300.00, $125.00; 16" - $350.00, $150.00.

Michael with bear: Peter Pan set. 11" - $325.00, $100.00.

Peter Pan: 14" - $225.00, $95.00.

Polly: 17" - $300.00, $100.00.

Renoir Girl: 14" - $150.00–55.00. With watering can: 1986–1987. $70.00–25.00. With hoop: 1986–1987. $70.00–25.00.

Scarlett: White gown, green ribbon. 1969–1986. 14" - $75.00, 35.00.

Smarty: 12" - $250.00, $125.00.

Sound of Music: Small set: $1,200.00. Large set: $1,500.00. **Liesl:** 10" - $200.00, $95.00; 14" - $165.00, $80.00. **Louisa:** 10" - $250.00, $100.00; 14" - $250.00, $100.00. **Brigitta:** 10" - $175.00, $85.00; 14" - $165.00, $75.00. **Maria:** 12" - $250.00, $125.00; 17" - $325.00, $150.00; **Marta:** 8" - $200.00, $80.00; 11" - $165.00, $95.00. **Gretl:** 8" - $150.00, $80.00; 11" - $165.00, $85.00. **Friedrich:** 8" - $200.00, $90.00; 11" - $165.00, $90.00.

Wendy: Peter Pan set. 14" - $250.00, $90.00.

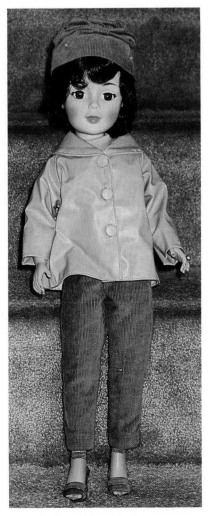

21" "Jacqueline" dressed in hard-to-find outfit. All original, including hose. Yellow top under jacket. Made in 1961 and part of 1962 only. ("Jacqueline" has been used as Portraits from 1965 to date.) $550.00 up.

Courtesy Jeannie Nespoli.

Prices are for mint condition dolls. There are many 21" portrait dolls and all use the Jacqueline face. The early ones have jointed elbows; later dolls have one-piece arms. All will be marked "1961" on head.

Agatha: 1967–1980. $350.00.

Bride: 1965. $1,000.00 up.

Coco: 1966. Portrait: 21" - $2,200.00. Street dress: $1,700.00. Ballgown: $1,900.00.

Cornelia: 1972–1978. $250.00–375.00.

Gainsborough: 1968–1978. $300.00–500.00.

Godey: 1965, 1967–1977. $375.00, $485.00.

Jenny Lind: 1969. $1,400.00.

Lady Hamilton: 1968: $450.00.

Madame Pompadour: 1970. $1,300.00.

Magnolia: 1977: $525.00. 1988: $300.00.

Manet: 1982–1983. $225.00.

Melanie: 1967–1989. $275.00–485.00.

Mimi: 1971. $500.00.

Monet: 1984. $265.00.

Morisot: 1985–1986. $250.00.

Queen: 1965. $800.00 up.

Renoir: 1965–1973. $375.00–500.00.

Scarlett: 1965–1989. $325.00–975.00 up.

Toulouse-Lautrec: 1986–1987. $225.00.

21" "Agatha" from 1976. All vinyl with one-piece arms. Has high heel feet. Uses the "Jacqueline" doll of 1961, and head will be marked "1961." $350.00.

AMERICAN CHARACTER DOLL COMPANY

All American Character dolls are very collectible and all are above average in quality of doll material and clothes. Dolls marked "American Doll and Toy Co." are also made by American Character, and this name was used from 1959 until 1968 when the firm went out of business. Early dolls will be marked "Petite." Many will be marked "A.C."

First prices are for mint dolls; second prices are for dolls that have been played with, dirty, with soiled clothes or not original.

"A.C." marked child: Composition. In excellent condition. 15" - $185.00, $65.00; 21" - $265.00, $110.00.

Annie Oakley: 1955. Hard plastic. Original. 17" - $450.00, $165.00.

Betsy McCall: See Betsy McCall section.

Butterball: 1961. 18" - $145.00, $65.00.

Campbell Kid: 1929–1931. Composition toddler. Curl in middle of forehead. Marked "Petite." (Allow more for original dress with tag.) 12" - $325.00.

Carol Ann Beery: Daughter of Wallace Beery. All composition, sleep eyes, closed mouth. Mohair wig with braid over top of head. Marked "Petite Sally" or "Petite." 14" - $425.00; 17" - $625.00; 20" - $800.00.

Cartwrights: Ben, Hoss, Little Joe: 1966. 8" - $135.00, $55.00.

Chuckles: 1961. 23" - $150.00, $60.00. Baby: 20" - $150.00, $60.00.

Composition babies: 1930s–1940s. Cloth bodies, marked "A.C." In excellent condition. 17" - $225.00, $85.00. 24" - $300.00, $65.00. Marked **"Petite":** 1920s–1930s. 15" - $175.00, $60.00; 23" - $275.00, $80.00.

Cricket: 1964. 9" - $35.00, $15.00. Growing hair: $40.00, $15.00.

Eloise: 1950s. Cloth character with yarn hair and crooked smile. (See photo in Series 7, pg. 212.) 16" - $250.00; 20" - $350.00 up. Christmas dress: (See photo in Series 11, pg. 176.) 15" - $400.00; 21" - $500.00.

Freckles: 1966. Face changes. 13" - $35.00, $20.00.

Hedda-Get-Betta: 1960. 21" - $105.00, $50.00.

Little Miss Echo: Talker, 1964. (See photo in Series 8, pg. 190.) 30" - $275.00, $80.00.

"Petite" marked child: Composition. 17" - $275.00, $85.00; 20" - $325.00, $100.00; 23" - $265.00, $150.00.

Preteen Tressy: 14" child marked "AM. Char. 63." (1963) **Grow hair:** $65.00, $25.00.

30" battery-operated "Little Miss Echo" records your voice and repeats it back to you. Has sleep eyes and open/closed mouth with upper teeth. Head and arms are vinyl. Body and legs are plastic. All original with box. No marks but made by American Character Doll & Toy Corp. in 1962. $275.00 up. *Courtesy Jeannie Mauldin.*

15" all vinyl "Newborn Baby" with sleep eyes, rooted hair, and closed mouth. Marked "American Character" on head. From 1958. $80.00. *Courtesy Pat Graff.*

14" all composition "Puggy" with molded hair, painted eyes to side, and scowling expression. Jointed at neck, shoulders, and hips. All original cowboy outfit with gun. Marked "A/Petite/Doll." Made from 1928 to 1930. $550.00. *Courtesy Helen McCorkel.*

Puggy: 1929–1931. All composition, painted eyes, frown. Has pug nose. Marked "Petite." 12" - $450.00, $165.00; 14" - $550.00, $175.00.

Ricky, Jr.: 1955–1956. (See photo in Series 11, pg. 176.) 14" - $45.00, $15.00; 21" - $85.00, $35.00. Hand puppet: $20.00.

Sally: 1929–1935. Composition, molded hair in "Patsy" style. Painted eyes. 12" - $175.00, $70.00; 14" - $200.00, $70.00. 16" - $250.00, $70.00; 18" - $300.00, $130.00. **Sally Joy:** 24" - $350.00 up.

Sally: Shirley Temple look-alike with full bangs and ringlet curls around head. Composition/cloth with sleep eyes and open mouth. 15" - $225.00; 17" - $275.00; 23" - $350.00. **Painted eyes, molded hair:** 17" - $245.00; 23" - $325.00.

Sally Says: 1965. Talker, plastic/vinyl. 19" - $65.00, $30.00.

Sweet Sue/Toni: 1949–1960. Hard plastic, some walkers, some with extra joints at knees, elbows and/or ankles, some combination hard plastic and vinyl. Marked "A.C. Amer. Char. Doll," or "American Character" in circle. **Must have excellent face color and be original. Ballgown:** 1958. 10½" - $160.00, $50.00; 14" - $245.00, $75.00; 18" - $300.00, $120.00; 24" - $475.00, $150.00; 30" - $650.00 up, $275.00. **Street dress:** 1958. 10½" - $145.00, $60.00; 15" - $250.00, $80.00; 18" - $325.00, $100.00; 22" - $375.00, $130.00; 24" - $400.00, $165.00;

13" "Tiny Tears" with hard plastic head and all rubber body. Open mouth/nurser. When stomach is pressed, doll cries tears through holes in side of eyes. Has rooted hair and sleep eyes. Wearing original dress and bonnet. $145.00 up. *Courtesy Glorya Woods.*

30" - $600.00, $225.00. **Vinyl:** 10½" - $160.00, $45.00; 14" - $165.00, $60.00; 18" - $250.00, $75.00; 21" - $350.00, $125.00; 25" - $425.00, $180.00; 30" - $575.00 up, $200.00. **Groom:** 20" - $450.00, $150.00. **Mint in box:** 14" - $350.00 up; 18" - $425.00 up; 20" - $475.00 up.

Talking Marie: 1963. Record player in body, battery operated. Vinyl/plastic. 18" - $85.00, $35.00.

Tiny Tears: 1955–1962. **Hard plastic/vinyl:** 9" - $65.00, $30.00; 12" - $145.00, $50.00; 18" - $225.00, $100.00. **All vinyl:** 1963. 9" - $35.00, $15.00; 13" - $45.00, $25.00; 17" - $60.00, $30.00. **Mint in box:** 13" - $300.00 up. **Teeny Tiny Tears:** 1964. All vinyl with sleep eyes. (See photo in Series 10, pg. 192.) 8" - $45.00.

Toni: Vinyl head. 10½" - $160.00, $50.00; 14" - $200.00, $75.00; 20" - $300.00, $100.00.

Toodles: 1956–1960. **Baby:** (See photo in Series 11, pg. 177.) 14" - $100.00, $35.00; 18" - $200.00, $80.00. **Tiny:** 10½" - $150.00, $40.00. **Toddler:** With "follow me eyes." 22" - $250.00, $80.00; 24" - $265.00, $95.00; 28" - $325.00, $130.00; 30" - $350.00, $165.00. **Mint in box:** 28–30" - $475.00 up.

Toodle-Loo: 1961. 18" - $185.00, $65.00.

Tressy: 12½". **Grow Hair:** 1963–1964. (#1 heavy makeup). $40.00, $15.00. **#2 Mary/Magic Makeup:** 1965–1966. Pale face, no lashes, bend knees. $35.00, $10.00. **Miss America:** 1963. $50.00 up. **Preteen:** 14" - $45.00, $20.00.

Whimette/Little People: 1961–1962. Pixie, Swinger, Granny, Jump'n, Go Go. 7½" - $30.00, $12.00.

Whimsies: 1960. Strongman, Wheeler the Dealer, Polly the Lolly, Miss Take, Zack, Simon, Dixie, Fanny (Angel), Tillie, Bessie Bride, Raggie, Susie, Zero (football), Lena the Cleaner, Monk. 19" - $85.00, $40.00. **Hilda the Hillbilly or Devil:** $130.00.

Group of 10½" all vinyl "Toni" dolls made by American Character. All are original and in mint condition. Each - $160.00 up. *Courtesy Sandy Johnson Barts.*

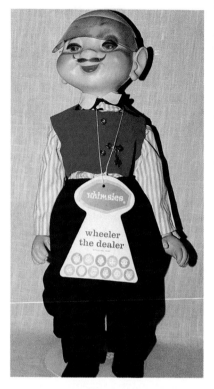

14" plastic and vinyl "Preteen Tressy" with sleep eyes. Rooted hair has grow hair mechanism in her back at the waist to shorten hair. Original clothes have hole for knob. Jumper and blouse are sewn together. (Outfit came in other colors.) Marked "Am.Char. 63" on head. $45.00. *Courtesy Ellen Dodge.*

19" "Wheeler the Dealer" is one of the dolls from the "Whimsies" collection. Made of stuffed all vinyl with painted-on mustache, molded eyelids, and painted eyes. All original. $105.00 up. *Courtesy Susan Girardot.*

ANNALEE MOBILITEE DOLLS

The first Annalee tags were red woven lettering on white linen tape. Second tags were made of white rayon with red embroidered lettering. The third tags, around 1969, were red printing on white satin tape. The fourth tags, about 1976, had red printing on gauze-type cloth. The hair on dolls from 1934–1963 was made of yarn. From 1960–1963, it was made of orange or yellow chicken feathers. Since 1963, the hair has been made of synthetic fur.

Animals became part of the line in 1964. On the oldest models, tails were made of the same materials as the body. During the mid-1970s, cotton bias tape was used and the ones made during the 1980s are made of cotton flannel.

Child: 1950s, Skier: boy or girl. 10" - $900.00 up. **1960s:** 10" - $450.00 up. **1970s:** 10" - $250.00 up. **1980s:** $150.00 up. **1990: Shepherd boy with lamb:** $250.00.

Adults: **1950s:** 10" - $1,600.00 up. **1970s:** 7" - $600.00. **1980s: Wisemen:** 1989. 18" - $250.00. **State policeman:** 1987. 10" - $600.00.

Babies: Usually angels. (See photo in Series 10, pg. 194.) **1960s:** 7–8" - $300.00. **1970s:** 7" - $250.00. **1980s:** 7" - $175.00.

Clowns: (See photo in Series 11, pg. 180.) **1970s:** 18" - $465.00; 10" - $135.00. Baggy pants: 1978. 42" - $900.00.

Elf/Gnome: (See photo in Series 11, pg. 180.) **1970s:** 7" - $200.00; 12" - $275.00. **1980s:** 7" - $80.00; 12" - $125.00; 16" - $175.00; 22" - $215.00.

Indians: 1970s: 7" - $200.00. **1980s:** 8" - $165.00 up; 18" - $225.00 up.

Merlin: 1989. Only 3,565 made. 10" - $300.00 up.

Monks: 1970s: 8" - $75.00 up.

7" Annalee "Santa Mouse" made of all felt with felt covered tail. Ca. 1970s. $85.00.
Courtesy Kris Lundquist.

22" Annalee elf dolls – two have closed smiling mouthes and the other two have painted open/closed smiling mouths. Made of stuffed felt with felt over wire arms and legs for posing. Tagged "1971." Each - $200.00. *Courtesy Jessie Smith.*

Santa/Mrs. Claus: (See photo in Series 11, pg. 181.) **1968:** 29" - $500.00. **1970s:** 7" to 26" - $85.00–600.00. **1980s:** 7 to 30" - $50.00–500.00. 1984: 30" - $450.00. **Mrs. Claus:** 1989. Carries turkey on tray. $185.00. **Santa** in chair: 10" - $250.00. **Santa Fox:** 1981. (See photo in Series 10, pg. 195.) 18" - $295.00 up.

Skiers: 1960s: 7" - $500.00 up. **1970s:** 7" - $250.00. **1980s:** 7" - $85.00 up.

Bears: 1970s: 7" - $165.00 up; 10" - $200.00 up; 18" - $300.00 up. **1980s:** (See photo in Series 10, pg. 194.) 7" - $90.00 up; 10" - $160.00 up; 18" - $200.00 up.

Mice: (See photo in Series 11, pg. 181.) **1970s: Fireman:** $275.00. **Groom:** $160.00. **1991: Desert Storm:** $85.00.

ARRANBEE DOLL COMPANY

The Arranbee Doll Company began making dolls in 1922 and was purchased by the Vogue Doll Company in 1958. Vogue used the Arranbee marked molds until 1961. Arranbee used the initials "R & B."

First prices are for mint condition dolls; second prices are for dolls that have been played with, are cracked, crazed, dirty or do not have original clothes.

Babies: Bisque heads. See Armand Marseille section.

Babies: Original. 1930s–1940s. Composition/cloth bodies. 15" - $100.00, $35.00; 20" - $135.00, $50.00.

Bottletot: 1932–1935. Has celluloid bottle molded to celluloid hand. 17" - $245.00, $90.00.

Debu-Teen: 1940. Composition girl with cloth body. 12" - $150.00, $50.00; 14" - $175.00, $65.00; 18" - $250.00, $85.00; 21" - $350.00, $125.00.

Dream Baby, My: (See Armand Marseille section for bisque heads.) **Composition:** 1934–1944. 14" - $245.00 up, $95.00; 16" - $285.00 up; 19" - $475.00 up. **Vinyl/cloth:** 1950. 15" - $75.00, $40.00; 23" - $165.00, $65.00.

Kewty: 1934–1936. Original. Composition "Patsy" style molded hair. Marked "R&B." (Kewty marked with name on back made by Domec toy Co., 1930.) 10" - $150.00, $50.00; 17" - $225.00, $90.00.

Lil' Imp: 1960. Hard plastic with red hair and freckles. 10" - $70.00, $30.00.

10" all hard plastic "Littlest Angel" was made by Arranbee from 1956 to 1959. She is a walker with jointed knees. All original, excellent condition. $50.00. *Courtesy Pat Graff.*

Littlest Angel: 1956. All hard plastic. 10" - $50.00, $20.00. **Vinyl head:** 10" - $35.00, $15.00.

Miss Coty: 1958. Vinyl, marked " Ⓟ ." (" Ⓟ " dolls also dressed and marketed by Belle Doll Co.) 10" - $95.00, $27.00.

My Angel: 1961. Plastic/vinyl. 17" - $40.00, $15.00; 22" - $65.00, $30.00; 36" - $150.00, $75.00. Walker: 1957–1959. 30" - $135.00. Oil cloth body/vinyl: 1959. 22" - $50.00.

Nancy: 1936–1940. Composition, molded hair or wig. Sleep eyes, open mouth. 12" - $185.00, $75.00; 17" - $325.00, $135.00; 19" - $400.00, $140.00. **Hard plastic:** Vinyl arms/head: 1951–1952 only. **Wig:** 14" - $145.00, $65.00; 18" - $185.00, $85.00. **Walker:** 24" - $275.00, $125.00. **Cloth body:** Rest is composition. Molded wavy hair combed to side. 12" - $165.00; 14" - $200.00; 17" - $275.00.

Nancy Lee: 1939. **Composition:** 12" - $185.00; 14" - $250.00, $85.00; 17" - $325.00, $100.00; 20" - $400.00, $135.00. **Hard plastic:** 1950–1959. 14" - $275.00, $90.00; 20" - $450.00, $135.00.

17" all hard plastic "Nanette" with floss wig, sleep eyes, and original pinafore dress. $325.00 up. *Courtesy Jeannie Nespoli.*

Nancy Lee: 1934–1939. Baby with composition head and limbs, open mouth with upper and lower teeth. 25" - $300.00, $125.00.

Nancy Lee: 1952. Baby, painted eyes, "crying" look. 16" - $125.00, $65.00. **Glass eyes:** 16" - $90.00, $45.00.

Nancy Lee: 1954. Vinyl with unusual eyebrows. 15" - $175.00, $80.00.

Nanette: 1949–1959. Hard plastic or composition. Original clothes, excellent face color. 14" - $235.00 up, $85.00; 17" - $300.00 up, $95.00; 21" - $375.00 up, $135.00; 23" - $475.00 up, $165.00. **Walker:** 1957–1959. Jointed knees. 18" - $325.00 up, $135.00; 25" - $500.00 up, $200.00. **Plastic/vinyl walker:** 1955–1956. 30" - $200.00 up, $100.00. **Hard plastic:** Mint in box. 17" - $550.00 up.

Sonja Skater: 1945. Composition. Some have "Debu-Teen" tag. 10–12" - $185.00; 14" - $265.00, $85.00; 17" - $300.00, $90.00; 21" - $400.00, $125.00.

15" "Nanette" is made of all hard plastic with sleep eyes and saran hair piled on head with flowers. Wears strapless ballgown. All original and in mint condition. $265.00. *Courtesy Jeannie Nespoli.*

Storybook dolls: 1930–1936. All composition. Molded hair, painted eyes. 9–10" - $185.00, $50.00. **Mint in box:** $285.00 up.

Taffy: 1956. Looks like Alexander's "Cissy." 23" - $165.00, $50.00.

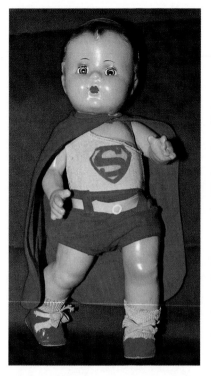

12" "Super Boy" made of all composition and on toddler body. Has dark molded hair and sleep glassene eyes with hair lashes. All original with one bare shoulder. Cape snaps on. Also came with blue top and socks. Maker was likely Arranbee Dolls, but doll is unmarked. In mint condition - $400.00 up. *Courtesy Carmen Holshoe.*

ARTISAN NOVELTY CO.

20" "Raving Beauty" made of all hard plastic with sleep eyes and open mouth. Dress and bonnet may be original. Made by Artisan Novelty Co. in 1953. In this condition - $100.00. In mint condition - $285.00. 19–20" walker - $325.00 up. *Courtesy Kathy Tvrdik.*

First prices are for mint dolls; second prices are for dolls in average condition, dirty, soiled, or not original.

Alfred E. Newman: Vinyl head. 20" - $175.00, $115.00.

Captain Kangaroo: 19" - $135.00, $85.00; 24" - $235.00, $90.00.

Christopher Robin: 18" - $165.00, $65.00.

Daisy Mae: 14" - $185.00, $60.00; 21" - $250.00, $80.00.

Emmet Kelly (Willie the Clown): (See photo in Series 10, pg. 199.) 15" - $175.00, $60.00; 24" - $265.00, $90.00.

Lil' Abner: 14" - $185.00, $60.00; 21" - $250.00, $80.00.

Mammy Yokum: 1957. (See photo in Series 9, pg. 203.) Molded hair: 14" - $150.00, $80.00; 21" - $250.00, $100.00. **Yarn hair:** 14" - $175.00, $60.00; 21" - $275.00, $125.00. **Nose lights up:** 23" - $300.00, $125.00.

Pappy Yokum: 1957. 14" - $125.00; 21" - $250.00, $100.00. Nose lights up: 23" - $300.00, $125.00.

Prices are as accurate as possible, but one must remember a price guide is just a "guide," and prices vary from coast to coast. Barbie® is a registered trademark of Mattel Inc. See related dolls, such as "Midge," "Ken," etc. in Mattel section.

These prices are based on mint in box doll and accessories. (Must be *mint*, but may have been removed from box.) Second price, when indicated, is for mint condition doll only.

American Girl: $850.00 up, $400.00. **Side part:** $3,200.00, $2,000.00.

Angel Face: $35.00.

Astronaut: $125.00 up.

Baby Sits: 1963–1965: $300.00 up. 1974–1976: $85.00.

Baggies: Doll in plastic bag. $55.00–95.00.

Ballerina: $50.00.

Beautiful Bride: $250.00. With hair lashes: $300.00 up.

Beauty Secrets: $60.00.

Bendable legs: 1965: Center part. $900.00. 1966: Side part. $2,000.00.

Bild Lilli: German. Mint - $750.00 up.

Bubble cut: $250.00; $115.00. Brunette: $700.00, $350.00.

Busy: $250.00 up.

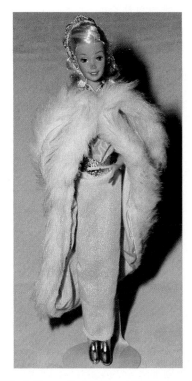

"Magic Moves Barbie" from 1986 has cape that will fit over head and long skirt that makes into mini skirt. Has silver shoes and headpiece. $35.00. *Courtesy Kathy Tvrdik.*

Busy Talking: $300.00 up.
Color Magic: $1,200.00, $400.00 up.
Crystal: $35.00.
Day to Night: $30.00.
Dream Date: $35.00.
Dream Glow: $25.00.
Dreamtime: $20.00.
Dressed boxed doll: $400.00 up. Pink Silhouette: $900.00 up. Wedding Day set: $1,800.00 up.
Fashion Jeans: $25.00.
Fashion Photo: $85.00.
Fashion Queen: $350.00 up, $175.00.
Feelin' Groovy: $200.00.
Free Moving: $60.00.
Fun Time: $20.00.
Gift Giving: $20.00.
Gift sets: See separate listing.
Golden Dream: $35.00.

Gold Medal: $85.00. Skater: $40.00. Skier: $20.00.
Great Shape: $15.00.
Growing Pretty Hair: 1971: Pink. $250.00. 1972: Blue. $300.00.
Hair Fair: $90.00, $40.00.
Hair Happenin's: $485.00, $250.00.
Happy Birthday: White or pink. $45.00.
Hawaiian: $75.00.
Hispanic: $65.00.
Horse Lovin': Formerly Western. $45.00.
Jewel Secrets: $25.00.
Kissing: $45.00. With bangs: $60.00.
Live Action: $125.00, $50.00. On stage: $170.00, $85.00.
Living: $200.00.
Loving You: $75.00.
Magic Curl Moves: $35.00.

"Barbie Skier" has lavender painted eyes. Made in Malaysia in 1990. $20.00. *Courtesy Kathy Tvrdik.*

11½" "UNICEF Barbie" from 1989. $20.00. *Courtesy Kathy Tvrdik.*

Malibu: 1971. $25.00.
Miss Barbie: Sleep eyes. $1,400.00, $650.00.
 My First: $22.00.
 Newport: $125.00.
 Peaches & Cream: $40.00.
 Pink & Pretty: $30.00.
 Plus Three: $60.00.
 Ponytail: First price for MIB dolls; second price for clean, near mint, doll with original swimsuit and shoes. **#1:** Blonde: $3,500.00, $2,000.00. Brunette: $3,700.00; $2,300.00. **#2:** Blonde: $3,300.00, $1,800.00. Brunette: $3,400.00, $2,300.00. **#3:** (See photo in Series 11, pg. 185.) $700.00, $400.00. **#4:** $575.00, $300.00. **#5:** Blonde: $400.00, $195.00. Redhead: $425.00, $215.00. **1962–1965:** $400.00, $200.00.
 Pretty Changes: $30.00.
 Quick Curl: $65.00. Deluxe: $85.00.
 Rocker Barbie: 1986–1987. $45.00.
 Roller Skating: $65.00.
 Sears Celebration: $70.00.
 Sleep eyes: See "Miss Barbie."
 Standard: 1967–1972. $400.00.
 Sun Gold Malibu: $20.00.
 Sun Lovin': $20.00.
 Sunsational: $20.00.
 Sun Valley: $145.00.
 Super Hair: $30.00.
 Super Size: Bridal: $185.00. Super Hair: $165.00.
 Super Star: $165.00. Fashion Change Abouts: $100.00. In The Spotlight: $85.00.
 Sweet Sixteen: $80.00.
 Swirl Ponytail: $475.00; $245.00.
 Talking: $275.00. Spanish speaking: $350.00.
 Tropical: $20.00.
 Twirly Curls: $30.00.
 Twist N' Turn: $325.00; $100.00. Redhead: $495.00, $195.00.
 Walk Lively: $200.00.
 Ward's Anniversary: $350.00 up.
 Western: $35.00.
 Wig Wardrobe: $225.00.

GIFT SETS:
 NRFB prices. **Barbie Hostess:** (See photo in Series 11, pg. 186.) $2,000.00 up. **Barbie & Ken Little Theatre:** $3,000.00. **Barbie, Ken & Midge Pep Rally:** $1,800.00. **Barbie, Ken & Midge on Parade:** $2,200.00. **Barbie Movie Groovy (Sears):** $400.00. **Barbie Perfectly Plaid (Sears):** $400.00. **Barbie Round The Clock:** $1,000.00. **Barbie Sparkling Pink:** $900.00. **Barbie Travels In Style (Sears):** $800.00. **Barbie & Ken Tennis:** $1,600.00. **Barbie Color Magic (Sears):** $1,700.00. **Fashion Queen & Friends:** $900.00. **Fashion Queen & Ken Trousseau:** $1,900.00. **Mix & Match (ponytail or bubble cut):** $1,100.00. **Party Set:** $1,900.00. **Trousseau Set:** $2,500.00. **Wedding Party:** 1964. Four dolls in set. $4,000.00 up.

"Flight Time Barbie" gift set from 1989. Doll came in black or white in airline outfit. Paper doll wears date clothes. $65.00.
Courtesy Kathy Tvrdik.

"Ken's Sports Plane" is made of all plastic and is extremely difficult to find. Marked "Irwin Corp./Custom Designed for/Barbie & Ken & Midge/Mattel/1964." (Dolls were not included with plane.) $2,000.00 up. *Courtesy Joan Ashabraner.*

BARBIE ITEMS:

Travel trailer: $60.00. **Silver Vette:** $75.00. **Roadster:** $250.00 up. **Sports car:** $200.00 up. **Sports car:** Orange. $90.00. **Ferrari:** White. $45.00. **Motor bike:** Pink. $50.00. **Splash cycle:** $45.00. **Speed boat:** $250.00 up. **Dune buggy:** $100.00 up. **Airplane:** $900.00 up. **"Dancer":** Brown horse. $250.00. **"Prancer":** All white horse. $150.00. **"Dallas":** Palomino horse. $55.00. **"Dixie":** Pony. $35.00. **"Blinking Beauty":** All white horse with extremely long mane and tail. $45.00. **"Midnight":** All black horse. $45.00.

INTERNATIONAL SERIES:

Since Mattel has begun to make Barbie in series, which is same as the "mints" and "galleries," the doll has become a "non-Barbie" and the name of the doll in the series is important. Example: The Scarlett Series using the Barbie doll.

The name of the International Collection Series was changed to Dolls of the World Collection and Mattel reissued a few of the earlier dolls such as "Eskimo" and "Parisian."

1980: **Italian:** $175.00. **Parisian:** $150.00. **Royal (England):** $275.00.

1981: **Oriental:** $165.00. **India:** $135.00. **Scottish:** $175.00.

1982: **Eskimo:** $200.00. **India:** $135.00.

1983: **Spanish:** $125.00. **Swedish:** $80.00.

1984: **Irish:** $85.00. **Swiss:** $80.00.

1985: **Japanese:** $125.00.

1986: **Greek:** $70.00. **Peruvian:** $85.00.

1987: **German:** $85.00. **Icelandic:** $70.00.

1988: **Canadian:** $60.00. **Korean:** $75.00.

1989: **Mexican:** $80.00. **Russian:** $85.00.

1990: **Brazilian:** $75.00. **Nigerian:** $65.00.

1991: **Malaysian:** $80.00. **Czechos- vakian:** $75.00.

1992: **Native American (#1):** $125.00 up.

1993: **Kenya:** $60.00.

**SPECIAL EDITIONS AND
STORE SPECIALS:**

Does not include all, just ones that are most likely to increase in value at a steady rate.

1988: Equestrienne: Toys 'Я Us. $40.00. **Lilac & Lovely:** Sears. $75.00. **Frills & Fantasy:** Wal-mart. $60.00. **Mardi Gras:** $150.00. **Tennis Barbie & Ken:** Toys 'Я Us. $45.00. **Sweet Dreams:** Toys 'Я Us. $40.00.

1989: Army: $35.00. **Dance Club:** Children's Palace. $70.00. **Denim Deluxe:** Toys 'Я Us. $30.00. **Evening Enchantment:** Sears. $60.00. **Golden Greeting:** FAO Schwarz. $250.00. **Gold n' Lace:** Target. $40.00. **Lavender Look:** Wal-Mart. $50.00. **Lavender Surprise:** Sears. $55.00. **Party Lace:** Hills. $45.00. **Party Pink:** Winn-Dixie. $35.00. **Peach Pretty:** K-Mart. $45.00. **Pepsi Set:** Toys 'Я Us. $45.00. **Pink Jubilee:** $1,800.00. **Special Expressions:** Woolworth. $35.00. **Sweet Roses:** Toys 'Я Us. $35.00. **Sweet Treats:** Toys 'Я Us. $40.00. **UNICEF:** Four nations. Each - $40.00.

1990: Air Force: $40.00. **Barbie Style:** Applause. $45.00. **Dance Magic set:** $40.00. **Disney's Barbie:** Children's Palace. $45.00. **Dream Fantasy:** Wal-Mart. $40.00. **Evening Sparkle:** Hills. $40.00. **Party Pretty:** Target. $35.00. **Party Sensation:** Wholesale Clubs. $60.00. **Pink Sensation:** Winn-Dixie. $30.00. **Special Expressions:** Second for Woolworth. $25.00. **Summit:** Four nations. Each - $30.00. **Wedding Fantasy:** $35.00. **Western Fun-Sun Runner Gift Set:** $65.00. **Winter Fantasy:** FAO Schwarz. $250.00.

1991: All American: Wholesale Clubs. $60.00. **Ballroom Beauty:** Wal-Mart. $40.00. **Barbie Collector Doll:** Applause. $40.00. **Barbie & Friends Gift Set:** Disney and Toys 'Я Us. $60.00. **Blossom Beauty:** Shopko/Venture. $35.00. **Blue Rhapsody:** Service Merchandise. $250.00. **Cute & Cool:** Target. $25.00.

Dream Bride: $45.00. **Earring Magic:** Radio Shack. $135.00. **Enchanted Evening:** J.C. Penney. $30.00. **Evening Flame:** Home Shopping Club/Special Shops. $145.00. **Golden Evening:** Target. $40.00. **Holiday Doll:** Applause. $45.00. **Hot Looks:** Ames. $30.00. **Jewel Jubilee:** Sam's Club. $75.00. **Madison Avenue:** FAO Schwarz. $175.00. **Moonlight & Roses:** Hills. $30.00. **Navy:** $25.00. **Night Sensation:** FAO Schwarz. $150.00. **Party In Pink:** Ames. $35.00. **Pretty Hearts:** Supermarkets. $25.00. **School Fun:** Toys 'Я Us. $35.00. **Southern Beauty:** Winn-Dixie. $30.00. **Southern Belle:** Sears. $45.00. **Special Expressions:**

Porcelain Barbie in "Enchanted Evening." Made in 1987. All original. $850.00 up.
Courtesy Shirley's Doll House.

Woolworth. $25.00. **Star Stepper Gift Set:** Wholesale Clubs. $65.00. **Sterling Wishes:** Spiegel. $150.00. **Swan Lake Gift Set:** Wholesale Clubs. $65.00. **Sweet Romance:** Toys 'Я Us. $30.00. **Sweet Spring:** Supermarkets. $25.00.

1992: Anniversary Star: Wal-Mart. $40.00. **Back To School:** Ames. $25.00. **Barbie For President:** Toys 'Я Us. $50.00. **Blossom Beauty:** Sears. $375.00. **Blue Elegance:** Hills. $35.00. **Cool Look:** Toys 'Я Us. $30.00. **Cool 'N Sassy:** Toys 'Я Us. $25.00. **Country Looks:** Ames. $25.00. **Dazzlin' Date:** Target.

"Parisian Barbie," a 1981 department store special. Made in Taiwan and body will be marked "1966." $150.00. *Courtesy Renie Culp.*

$30.00. **Denim 'N Lace:** $30.00. **Disney Fun Barbie:** $45.00. **Dream Princess:** Sears. $45.00. **Evening Sensation:** J.C. Penney. $55.00. **Dr. Barbie:** Toys 'Я Us. $30.00. **Fantastica:** Pace. $50.00. **Holiday Gowns Collection:** Wholesale Clubs. $75.00. **Holiday Hostess:** Supermarkets. $45.00. **Kraft Treasures:** Kraft premium Barbie. $75.00. **Marine Corps:** $25.00. **Marine Barbie & Ken Gift Set:** $55.00. **My Size:** Three feet tall. $160.00. **Nutcracker:** $125.00. **100 Piece Gift Set:** Wholesale Clubs. $55.00. **Party Premiere:** Supermarkets. $25.00. **Party Perfect:** Shopko/Venture. $45.00. **Peach Blossoms:** Sam's Club. $55.00. **Picnic Pretty:** Osco. $25.00. **Pretty in Plaid:** Target. $25.00. **Pretty in Purple:** K-Mart. $45.00. **Radiant in Red:** Toys 'Я Us. $40.00. **Red Romance:** Supermarkets. $25.00. **Regal Reflections:** Spiegel. $300.00. **Rollarblade Gift Set:** Wholesale Clubs. $55.00. **Royal Romance:** Price Clubs. $55.00. **Satin Nights:** Service Merchandise. $65.00. **School Fun:** Toys 'Я Us. $25.00. **Something Extra:** Meijers. $35.00. **Sparkle Eye Gift Set:** Wholesale Clubs. $65.00. **Special Expressions:** Woolworth. $25.00. **Spring Bouquet:** Supermarkets. $25.00. **Special Parade:** Toys 'Я Us. $25.00. **Sun Sensations - Spray & Play Gift Set:** Wholesale Clubs. $65.00. **Sweet Lavender:** Woolworth. $40.00. **Very Violet:** Pace. $50.00. **Wacky Warehouse #1:** Kool-Aid. $70.00. **Wild Style:** Target. $20.00.

1993: Army Desert Storm: $25.00. **Army Barbie & Ken Gift Set:** $60.00. **Back To School:** Supermarkets. $25.00. **B-Mine:** Supermarket. $30.00. **Baseball:** Target. $25.00. **Beach Fun Gift Set:** Wholesale Clubs. $35.00. **Disney Fun:** Disney. $40.00. **Dressing Fun Gift Set:** Wholesale Clubs. $55.00. **Easter Fun:** Supermarkets. $35.00. **Festiva:** Wholesale Clubs. $35.00. **Gibson Girl:** $55.00. **Golf Date:** Target. $25.00. **Golden Winter:** J.C. Penney. $55.00. **Holiday Hostess:** Supermarkets. $25.00. **Holiday Gown Collection #2:** Wholesale Clubs. $55.00. **Hollywood Hair Gift Set:** Wholesale Clubs. $35.00. **Island Fun Gift Set:** Wholesale Clubs. $35.00. **Love To Read:** Toys 'Я Us. $30.00. **Little Debbie:** Little Debbie Cakes. $50.00. **Malt Shop:** Toys 'Я Us. $25.00. **Moonlight Magic:** Toys 'Я Us. $45.00. **1920s Flapper:** $75.00. **Paint 'n Dazzle Gift Set:** Wholesale Club. $35.00. **Police Officer:** Toys 'Я Us. $30.00. **Radiant In Red:** Toys 'Я Us. $35.00. **Rockette:** FAO Schwarz. $95.00. **Romantic Bride:** $40.00. **Royal Invitation:** Spiegel. $100.00. **School Spirit:** Toys 'Я Us. $25.00. **Secret Hearts Gift Set:** Wholesale Clubs. $55.00. **Shopping Fun:** Meijer. $30.00. **Special Expressions:** Woolworth. $25.00. **Sparkling Splendor:** Service Merchandise. $35.00. **Spring Bouquet:** Supermarkets. $25.00. **Spots 'n Dots:** Toys 'Я Us. $25.00. **Super Star:** Wal-Mart. $30.00. **Toothfairy:** Wal-mart. $25.00. **Wedding Fantasy Gift Set:** Wholesale Clubs. $95.00. **Western Horse Gift Set:** Toys 'Я Us. $60.00. **Western Stampin' Gift Set:** Wholesale Clubs. $45.00. **Winter Royal:** Wholesale Clubs. $65.00. **Winter Princess:** Home Shopping Club. $500.00.

BOB MACKIE COLLECTION:

Designer Gold: 1990. $725.00, $285.00. **Platinum:** 1991. $450.00; $225.00. **Starlight Splendor:** 1991. $450.00, $225.00. **Empress Bride:** 1992. $475.00, $250.00. **Neptune's Fantasy:** 1992. $400.00, $285.00. **Masquerade Ball:** 1993. Harlequin costume. $175.00. **Queen of Hearts:** 1994. $165.00.

OTHER DESIGNERS:

Feelin' Groovy: 1986. BillyBoy. $175.00. **Nouveau Theatre dé la Mode:** 1987. BillyBoy. $300.00. **Benefit Ball:** 1992, Carol Spencer. $85.00. **Opening Night:** 1993, Janet Goldblatt. $80.00. **City Style:** 1993, Janet Goldblatt. $80.00.

HAPPY HOLIDAY BARBIE:

1988: $625.00. 1989: $450.00. 1990: White - $275.00; Black - $195.00. 1991: White - $175.00; Black - $150.00. 1992: White - $100.00; Black - $75.00. 1993: White or Black - $100.00.

CLOTHING (1959–1963):

Prices are for mint in box outfits only. If out of box or pack, deduct 20%. If played with, deduct 65%. *Must have all accessories to bring top prices.*

After 5: $150.00. **Apple print sheath:** $200.00. **American Airlines:** $200.00. **Ballerina:** $250.00. **Barbie Baby Sits:** With apron - $300.00. With layette - $350.00. **Barbie-Q outfit:** $200.00. **Bride's Dream:** $350.00. **Busy Gal:** $250.00. **Busy Morning:** $250.00. **Candy Striper:** $200.00. **Career Girl:** $175.00. **Cheerleader:** $150.00. **Commuter set:** $900.00 up. **Cotton Casual:** $200.00. **Cruise Stripe dress:** $200.00. **Dinner at Eight:** $175.00. **Drum Majorette:** $200.00. **Easter Parade:** $2,800.00 up. **Enchanted Evening:** $350.00. **Evening Splendor:** $250.00. **Fancy Free:** $125.00. **Fashion undergarments:** $175.00. **Floral petticoat:** $175.00. **Friday Night:** $200.00. **Garden Party:** $150.00. **Gay Parisienne:** $2,000.00 up. **Golden Elegance:** $200.00. **Golden Girl:** $200.00. **Graduation:** $100.00. **Icebreaker:** $175.00. **It's Cold Outside:** $150.00. **Knitting Pretty:** Blue - $200.00; pink - $175.00. **Let's Dance:** $175.00. **Masquerade:** $175.00. **Mood For Music:** $175.00. **Movie Date:** $150.00. **Nighty-Negligee:** $175.00. **Open Road:** $200.00. **Orange Blossom:** $200.00. **Party Date:** $175.00. **Peachy Fleecy coat:** $200.00. **Picnic Set:** $250.00. **Plantation Belle:** $300.00. **Red Flair:** $150.00. **Registered Nurse:** $250.00. **Resort Set:** $200.00. **Roman Holiday:** $2,500.00 up. **Senior Prom:** $175.00. **Sheath Sensation:** $150.00. **Silken Flame:** $150.00. **Singing in the Shower:** $150.00. **Ski Queen:** $175.00. **Solo in the Spotlight:**

$350.00. **Sophisticated Lady:** $350.00. **Sorority Meeting:** $150.00. **Stormy Weather:** $175.00. **Suburban Shopper:** $200.00. **Sweater Girl:** $200.00. **Sweet Dreams:** Yellow - $150.00. Pink - $300.00. **Swingin' Easy:** $150.00. **Tennis Anyone:** $150.00. **Theatre Date:** $175.00. **Wedding Day Set:** (See photo in Series 11, pg. 185.) $700.00. **Winter Holiday:** $200.00.

CLOTHING (1964–1966):

Aboard Ship: $275.00. **Barbie Learns To Cook:** $275.00. **Beautiful Bride:** $1,800.00. **Beau Time:** $200.00. **Benefit Performance:** $1,000.00. **Black Magic:** $225.00. **Brunch Time:** $275.00. **Campus Sweetheart:** $500.00. **Caribbean Cruise:** $200.00. **Club Meeting:** $250.00. **Coffee's On:** $250.00. **Country Club Dance:** $275.00. **Country Fair:** $150.00. **Crisp 'n Cool:** $175.00. **Dancing Doll:** $300.00. **Debutante Ball:** $800.00 up. **Disc Date:** $275.00. **Dogs 'n Suds:** $275.00. **Dreamland:** $300.00. **Evening Enchantment:** $1,000.00. **Evening Gala:** $600.00. **Fabulous Fashion:** $600.00. **Fashion Editor:** $275.00. **Fashion Luncheon:** $600.00 up. **Floating Gardens:** $900.00. **Formal Occasion:** $1,000.00. **Fraternity Dance:** $300.00. **Fun At The Fair:** $200.00. **Fun 'n Games:** $175.00. **Garden Tea Party:** $125.00. **Garden Wedding:** $600.00. **Golden Evening:** $200.00. **Golden Glory:** $600.00. **Gold 'n Glamour:** $600.00. **Here Comes The Bride:** $2,000.00. **Holiday Dance:** $500.00. **International Fair:** $250.00. **Invitation To Tea:** $300.00. **Junior Designer:** $250.00. **Junior Prom:** $300.00. **Knit Hit:** $150.00. **Knit Separates:** $125.00. **Little Theater:** Arabian Nights - $350.00; Cinderella - $350.00; Guinevere - $300.00; Red Riding Hood/Wolf - $350.00. **London Tour:** $500.00. **Lunch Date:** $125.00. **Lunch on the Terrace:** $250.00. **Lunchtime:** $250.00. **Magnificence:** $600.00. **Matinee Fashion:** $500.00. **Midnight Blue:** $500.00. **Miss Astronaut:** $600.00. **Modern Art:** $300.00.

Music Center Matinee: $600.00. **On the Avenue:** $600.00. **Outdoor Art Show:** $275.00. **Outdoor Life:** $250.00. **Pajama Party:** $75.00. **Pan Am Airways:** $2,700.00. **Poodle Parade:** $600.00. **Pretty as a Picture:** $250.00. **Reception Line:** $250.00. **Riding In The Park:** $500.00. **Satin 'n Rose:** $325.00. **Saturday Matinee:** $500.00. **Shimmering Magic:** $1,000.00. **Skater's Waltz:** $275.00. **Skin Diver:** $100.00. **Sleeping Pretty:** $250.00. **Sleepytime Gal:** $300.00. **Slumber Party:** $400.00. **Sorority Tea:** $175.00. **Student Teacher:** $200.00. **Sunday Visit:** $600.00. **Travel outfits:** Hawaii - $300.00; Holland - $350.00; Japan - $300.00; Mexico - $300.00; Switzerland - $300.00. **Underfashions:** $450.00. **Vacation Time:** $175.00. **White Magic:** $175.00.

CLOTHING (1967–1971):

Plain street length dresses that have only a few accessories such as Knit Hit, Midi Magic, Snap Dash, etc. $75.00 up.

Elaborate dresses with lots of accessories that have a "mod" look such as Zokko, All That Jazz, Sparkle Squares, etc. $125.00 up.

Formals and brides such as Romatic Ruffles, Silver Serenade, Winter Wedding, Let's Have A Ball, etc. $175.00 up.

CLOTHING (1972–1976):

The outfits that will continue to climb in value are the ones that reflect the times, such as granny dresses, bell bottoms, peasant dresses, and clothing with a "flower child" look. Most are priced between $20.00 and $45.00.

CLOTHING (1980–1990):

Most clothing sets are only worth the purchase price, but you should try to keep your collection current and they will rise in value as time goes by. The following have increased in value. Collector series: $45.00 up. Oscar de la Renta collector series: $45.00 up.

First prices are for mint condition dolls; second prices are for played with, dirty, soiled or not original dolls.

8": All hard plastic, jointed knees. Made by American Character Doll Company 1957–1960. **Street dress:** $170.00, $65.00. **Ballgown:** $225.00 up, $85.00. **Bathing suit** or romper: $125.00, $45.00. **Ballerina:** $185.00; $60.00. **Riding habit:** $185.00, $60.00. **Original shoes and socks:** $25.00.

11½": Vinyl/plastic with brown or blue sleep eyes, and rooted hair. Three hair colors. Original. Made by Uneeda in 1964, but unmarked. $125.00, $50.00.

13": Made by Horsman in 1974–1975, but doll is marked "Horsman Dolls, Inc. 1967" on head. $85.00, $40.00.

14" American Character "Betsy McCall" dressed in hard-to-find outfit "School Days #2." All original and mint. $285.00 up. *Courtesy Peggy Pergande.*

8" all original "Betsy McCall" in very rare cowgirl outfit. Made by American Character. This example - $200.00 up. *Courtesy Peggy Pergande.*

14": Vinyl with slender body, medium high heels, rooted hair, and round sleep eyes. Made by American Character Doll Company in 1961. Marked "McCall 1958." $285.00 up, $95.00.

14": Vinyl head, hard plastic body and limbs. Rooted hair, sleep eyes. Marked "P-90" body. Made by Ideal Doll Company in 1952. $285.00 up, $95.00.

22": Extra joints at waist, ankles, wrists and above knees. Unmarked. Made by American Character Doll Company in 1961–1962. $265.00, $90.00. **29":** $425.00 up.

20": Vinyl with slender limbs. Rooted hair in three hair colors. Can have blue or brown sleep eyes. Made by American Character Doll Company. (Allow more for flirty eyes.) $285.00, $90.00.

22": Vinyl/plastic with extra joints. Made by Ideal Doll Company. $300.00 up, $125.00.

29-30": All vinyl with rooted hair. Made by American Character Doll Company. $425.00, $175.00.

30": Extra joints at ankles, knees, waist and wrists. Three hair colors. Blue or brown sleep eyes. Made by American Character Doll Company. Marked "McCall 1961." $450.00 up, $150.00.

29": Marked "B.M.C. Horsman 1971." $185.00, $65.00.

36": All vinyl with rooted hair. Made by American Character Doll Company. $600.00 up, $275.00.

36": Made by Ideal Doll Company. Marked "McCall 1959." $600.00 up, $250.00.

38": Boy called "Sandy McCall." Made by American Character. Marked "McCall 1959." $700.00 up, $350.00.

14" all vinyl "Betsy McCall" by American Character. Original and mint. $285.00. *Courtesy Patricia Wood.*

29" all original "Betsy McCall" with extra joints at knees, wrists, waist, and elbows. Has large, slightly slanted sleep eyes. Made by American Character with purchased molds of Ideal's "Miss Ideal" and "Terry Twist." Never played with and in mint condition. $425.00 up. *Courtesy Peggy Pergande.*

36" plastic and vinyl "Betsy McCall" and "Sandy McCall" made by Ideal Doll Co. "Betsy" - $600.00 up. "Sandy" - $700.00 up. *Courtesy Doris Richardson.*

BLOCK DOLL COMPANY

10–12" all hard plastic doll made by Block Doll Company. This doll was also made as an "answer" doll with lever on back that moved the doll's head. (See *Modern Collector's Dolls, Fifth Series*, pg. 60 for additional original outfits.) $65.00. *Courtesy Kathy Tvrdik.*

BONNYTEX

9½" "Red Riding Hood and Wolf" made of all rigid vinyl with painted clothes and features. Turn knob on head and wolf face appears. Marked "Bonnytex Prod. 1956." $60.00. *Courtesy Carmen Holshoe.*

BREYER

7½" all vinyl "Brenda Breyer" has posable arms and legs. Breyer horses are exceptional and sold through toy stores. This is the first doll made for them. She has outfits for all horse occasions. Doll is unmarked but made by Unger Toys. $20.00. *Courtesy Kathy Tvrdik.*

"Buddy Lee" dolls were made in composition to 1949, then changed to hard plastic and discontinued in 1962–1963. "Buddy Lee" came dressed in two Coca-Cola® uniforms. The tan with green stripe outfit matched the uniforms worn by delivery drivers while the white with green stripe uniforms matched those of plant workers. (Among Coca-Cola employees the white uniform became more popular and in warmer regions of the country, the white outfit was also worn by outside workers.)

"Buddy Lee" came in many different outfits.

Engineer: $300.00 up.

Gas station attendant: $275.00 up.

Cowboy: $325.00 up.

Coca-Cola uniform: White with green stripe - $450.00 up. Tan with green stripe - $500.00 up.

Other soft drink companies uniforms: $300.00 up.

Hard plastic: Original clothes. $375.00 up.

"Buddy Lee" in engineer outfit is made of all composition with one-piece body, legs, and head. Has jointed shoulders and painted features. All original. $300.00.
Courtesy Susan Girardot.

CAMEO DOLL COMPANY

Annie Rooney, Little: 1926. All composition with legs painted black and molded shoes. 12" - $465.00 up; 17" - $675.00 up.

Baby Bo Kaye: 1925. Bisque head: See Antique section. **Celluloid head:** 12" - $400.00; 15" - $650.00. **Composition head:** Mint condition: 14" - $450.00. Light craze: Not original. 14" - $175.00.

Baby Mine: 1962–1964. Vinyl/cloth, sleep eyes. **Mint:** 16" - $95.00; 19" - $115.00. **Slightly soiled:** Not original. 16" - $35.00; 19" - $50.00. On "Miss Peep" hinged body: 16" - $125.00.

Bandy: Wood/composition. Ad doll for General Electric. Large ears. Painted-on majorette uniform. Non-removable tall hat. 17" - $500.00 up.

Betty Boop: 12" with composition legs and molded clothes. Excellent: $625.00. Fair: $125.00.

Champ: 1942. Composition with freckles. **Mint:** 16" - $575.00. **Light craze:** Not original. 16" - $200.00.

Giggles: 1946. Composition with molded loop for ribbon. **Mint:** 11" - $325.00; 14" - $600.00. **Light craze:** 11" - $150.00; 14" - $225.00.

Group of vinyl "Kewpies." Two in back on right are "Ragsy Kewpies" with molded-on clothes. The small one in lower middle is a "Thinker." $10.00–$65.00. *Courtesy Sally Bethschieder.*

18" "Baby Blossom" is a really cute baby doll from Cameo. All vinyl with deeply molded hair, sleep eyes, and open mouth. Fully jointed. $85.00. *Courtesy Jeannie Mauldin.*

Ho-Ho: 1940. **Plaster:** Excellent condition. 4" - $55.00. **Vinyl:** Excellent condition: 4" - $12.00.

Joy: 1932. Composition with wood jointed body. **Mint:** 10" - $285.00; 15" - $450.00. **Slight craze:** 10" - $130.00; 15" - $165.00.

Kewpie: See Kewpie section.

Margie: 1935. **Composition:** Mint condition. 6" - $185.00; 10" - $275.00. **Slight craze:** Not original. 6" - $90.00; 10" - $135.00. **Segmented wood/composition:** 1929. Mint. 9½" - $300.00, $135.00.

Miss Peep: 1957 and 1970s. Pin-jointed shoulders and hips. **Vinyl:** Mint condition and original. 1960s. 15" - $40.00; 18" - $55.00. **Black:** 18" - $65.00. Slightly soiled, not original. 18" - $20.00. Black, from 1972: 18" - $25.00. **Ball-jointed** shoulders and hips: 1970s–1980s. 17" - $45.00; 21" - $65.00.

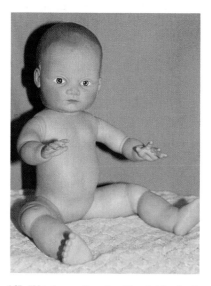

16" "Newborn Peep" with rigid plastic body and vinyl head and limbs. $45.00. *Courtesy Phyllis Kates.*

Miss Peep, Newborn: 1962. Vinyl and plastic. **Mint:** Original. 18" - $40.00. Slight soil: Not original. 18" - $20.00.

Pete the Pup: 1930–1935. Composition with wood jointed body. **Mint:** 9" - $250.00. Slight craze: Few paint chips. 9" - $100.00.

Pinkie: 1930–1935. Composition: Mint: Original. 10" - $275.00. Slight craze: 10" - $135.00. **Wood jointed body:** 10" - $365.00. **Vinyl/plastic:** 1950s. Mint condition: 10–11" - $135.00. Slight soil: Not original. 10–11" - $60.00.

Pretty Bettsie: Composition one-piece body and limbs. Separate wooden neck joint. Has molded hair. and smile mouth. Molded-on yellow, pink, or blue short dress with white ruffles at hem. Painted-on shoes and socks. Chest paper label marked "Pretty Bettsie/Copyright J. Kallus." 9" - $200.00; 14" - $285.00 up.

Scootles: 1925, 1930s. **All cloth** with fat legs, yarn hair, and dimples. No toe detail. $700.00. **Composition:** Mint condition: Original. 8" - $345.00 up; 12" - $450.00 up; 15" - $600.00 up; 20" - $725.00; 23" - $800.00 up. Light craze: Not original. 8" - $100.00; 12" - $225.00; 15" - $285.00; 20" - $350.00; 22" - $385.00. **Composition/ sleep eyes:** Mint condition: 15" - $650.00; 21" - $725.00 up. Slight craze: 15" - $250.00; 21" - $350.00. **Black, composition:** Mint: 15" - $650.00. Slight craze: 15" - $250.00. **Vinyl:** 1964. Mint: Original. 14" - $185.00 up; 19" - $350.00 up; 27" - $525.00 up. Lightly soiled: Not original. 14" - $75.00; 19" - $115.00; 27" - $175.00. **All bisque:** See that section.

18" all composition "Pretty Bettsie" with one-piece body, molded-on clothes, molded hair, and painted features. Has original lace collar and paper label on bodice. This rare doll was designed by Joseph Kallus. $500.00. *Courtesy Susan Girardot.*

10" all composition "Scootles" with deeply molded hair and painted features. This is a very rare tiny size. All original. This size - $450.00. *Courtesy Shirley's Doll House.*

11½" "John Travolta" made by Chemtoy when tie-die jeans were popular. Has extra joints at waist and knees only, long molded hair, and painted features. Marked "32/Hong Kong/1977." $30.00. *Courtesy Don Tvrdik.*

CLOTH

12" "Mr. Met" made of all printed cloth. $25.00. *Courtesy Sandra Cummins.*

9½" "Troll" and "Leperchaun" made of felt with stitch sculpting. Molded stockinette is formed over a hard clay-like material. Date unknown but probably ca. 1965. Stickers are marked "KIS/West Germany/Berlin." Each - $70.00. *Courtesy Marla Mikesh.*

15" "Dixie Anna" was a child nurse doll made by The Polk Co. of Atlanta, Georgia. Has cloth mask face with oil-painted features and hair. Nurse cap and cape sewn onto stuffed chenille body and limbs. On market in 1943, and original price tag is surprisingly high ($4.98) for that date. Tag marked "Red Cross Nurse #7C-11." Mint with tag - $125.00. *Courtesy Cindy Young.*

26" "Joe Montana" cloth doll in San Francisco 49ers uniform. (One of the finest quarterbacks in the history of football.) Made of all printed cloth and has printed autograph on one arm and real signature on other. Tagged "Ace Novelty Co./Los Angeles/Chicago/Seattle. 1991." $45.00 up.

COSMOPOLITAN

7½" straight leg and bend knee "Ginger" dolls shown with Little Golden Activity Book, *Ginger Paper Doll*. Both dresses are tagged, and both dolls are all original and in mint condition. Straight leg - $85.00 up; bend knee - $45.00. *Courtesy Ciny Young.*

10½" all vinyl "Miss Ginger" with rooted hair, sleep eyes, and tagged clothes. All original and excellent quality. $185.00 up.
Courtesy Maureen Fukushima.

8" "Ginger" dressed in one of her rarest and cutest outfits. (There is a matching outfit for her older sister, "Miss Ginger.") All hard plastic doll has large round sleep eyes. All original. This example - $165.00.
Courtesy Maureen Fukushima.

CREATA

6" "Today's Girl" doll made of vinyl with blue star-painted eyes. This one is "Sports Kids - Kelly." Marked "1988 Creata. Made in China." $16.00. *Courtesy Kathy Tvrdik*

This company also used the names Topper Toys and Topper Corp. They were well known for making dolls that did things and were battery operated during the 1960s and 1970s. These dolls have become highly collectible as they were well played with and not many dolls survived.

Baby Boo: Battery operated, 1965. 21" - $40.00.

Baby Catch A Ball: Battery operated, 1969. 18" - $50.00.

Baby Magic: 1966. 18" - $45.00.

Baby Peek 'N Play: Battery operated, 1969. 18" - $40.00.

20" plastic and vinyl "Tickles" by Deluxe Reading in 1962. Has sleep eyes and rooted hair. Battery operated. She laughs and cries. $30.00. *Courtesy Jeannie Mauldin.*

Baby Tickle Tears: 14" - $30.00.

Betty Bride: Also called "Sweet Rosemary." 1957. One-piece vinyl body and limbs. 30" - $85.00 up.

Dawn: 6". Mint - $15.00. In original box - $30.00. Played with - $6.00 up.

Dawn Model Agency dolls: Mint - $20.00. In box - $45.00. Played with - $8.00.

Dawn Series, boys: Mint - $20.00. In box - $40.00. Played with - $10.00.

Lil' Miss Fussy: Battery operated. 18" - $30.00.

Party Time: Battery operated, 1967. 18" - $40.00.

Penny Brite: 8" child. (See photo in Series 10, pg. 216.) Mint - $15.00. Played with - $4.00 up.

Private Ida: One of "Go Go's" from 1965. (See photo in Series 9, pg. 217.) Mint condition. 6" - $40.00.

Rosemary or Betty Bride: 1950s. 28–30" one-piece vinyl stuffed body and limbs. Sleep eyes, rooted hair. Dressed as bride or in blue, pink, yellow, or green long gown trimmed in silver. $85.00–125.00.

Smarty Pants and other mechanicals: Battery operated, 1971. 19" - $30.00.

6" original "Daphne" with jointed waist, snapping knees, and painted green eyes. Marked "H11A" on head; "1970/Topper Corp/Hong Kong" on back. Heads can also be marked "11C," "A11A," "K-10," "H-7/110," "11-7," "878/K11A," "2/H-11," "A8-10," "H-17," "4/H 72," "543/H11a," "92/H-17," "154/S11," "51/D10," "4/H86" and maybe other numbers. MIB - $45.00. Doll only - $20.00. Played with - $8.00. *Courtesy Gloria Anderson.*

Susie Homemaker: (See photo in Series 11, pg. 201.) 22" - $40.00.

Suzy Cute: Move arm and face changes expressions. (See photo in Series 10, pg. 216.) 7" - $25.00.

Tom Boy: One of the "Go-Go's" in 1965. (See photo in Series 10, pg. 216.) Mint condition. 6" - $40.00.

DOLL ARTISTS

33" "Swan" by Charleen Thanos in 1995. Cloth and porcelain with glass eyes and beautiful complexion. With hat off, she has a very Oriental look. $3,000.00. *Photo courtesy of Charleen Thanos.*

33" "Amber Lauren" by Charleen Thanos and what a beauty she is! She is an original with a small edition. Also available in blue with wide brimmed hat. This artist is one of the finest, and she has captured a look that will last and be hunted 100 years from now. Her dolls reflect not the look of yesterday, but the look of today, and will be remembered tomorrow. $3,000.00. *Photo courtesy of Charleen Thanos.*

22" "Adam" is the first in a series of "Bible Babies" created by Paul Spencer Wood Originals. He is one-of-a-kind and made of all hand carved wood, including the beautiful tug boat. Has blue glass eyes and is jointed at neck, shoulder, elbows, knees, and hips. $1,500.00.

Above: 7½" "Getsya Googlies" made by Pat Robinson, member of the National Institute of American Doll Artists (N.I.A.D.A.) All bisque dolls with mohair wigs — one has a very pouty mouth; the other has an impish smile. Made in late 1970s. Each - $200.00. *Courtesy Frasher Doll Auctions.*

Right: 13" all porcelain "Rosie" made by Robert Tonner. She has green eyes and a mohair wig. Signed limited edition of 50 was made in 1993. Mint - $700.00. *Courtesy Pat Graff.*

DUTCHESS

The two dolls on the right are Dutchess Doll with sleep eyes. The one on the left was made by Active Doll Co. and has painted eyes. (Active also made dolls with sleep eyes.) All three dolls are made of hard plastic with painted-on slippers and stapled-on clothes. Jointed at shoulders only. Each - $2.00. *Courtesy Gloria Anderson.*

The "Eegee" name was made up from the name of company founder E.G. Goldberger. Founded in 1917, the early dolls were marked "E.G.", then "E. Goldberger." Now the marks "Eegee" and "Goldberger" are used.

Andy: Teen type. (See photo in Series 9, pg. 221.) 12" - $35.00.

Annette: Teen type. 11½" - $50.00. Child: 1966, marked "20/25M/13." (See photo in Series 9, pg. 221.) 19" - $45.00. **Walker:** 1966. Plastic/vinyl. 25" - $45.00; 28" - $60.00; 36" - $80.00.

Baby Luv: 1973. Cloth/vinyl. Marked "B.T. Eegee." 14" - $30.00.

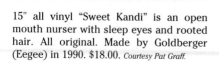

15" all vinyl "Sweet Kandi" is an open mouth nurser with sleep eyes and rooted hair. All original. Made by Goldberger (Eegee) in 1990. $18.00. *Courtesy Pat Graff.*

Baby Susan: 1958. Name marked on head. 8½" - $15.00.

Baby Tandy Talks: 1960. Pull string talker. Foam body/vinyl. $50.00.

Babette: 1962. Barbie look-alike. 11½" - $60.00 up.

Ballerina: 1958. Hard plastic/vinyl head. 20" - $40.00.

Ballerina: 1964. Hard plastic/vinyl head. 31" - $70.00.

Ballerina: 1967. Foam body and limbs, vinyl head. 18" - $25.00.

Boy dolls: Molded hair, rest vinyl. 13" - $30.00; 21" - $40.00 up.

Cartland, Barbara: Painted features, adult. (See photo in Series 9, pg. 222.) 15" - $45.00.

Composition: Open mouth child. Sleep eyes. 14" - $150.00 up; 18" - $200.00 up. **Babies:** Cloth/composition. 16" - $95.00 up; 20" - $130.00 up.

Debutante: 1958. Vinyl head, rest hard plastic. Jointed knees. 28" - $75.00.

Flowerkins: 1963. Plastic/vinyl. Marked "F-2" on head. Seven in set. 16", in box - $55.00. Played with, no box - $20.00.

Gemmette: 1963. Teen type. (See photo in Series 8, pg. 216.) 14" - $40.00 up.

Georgie or Georgette: 1971. Cloth/vinyl red-headed twins. (See photo in Series 10, pg. 221.) 22–23" - $40.00.

Gigi Perreaux: 1951. Hard plastic, early vinyl head. Open/closed smile mouth. Must have good face color. 17" - $700.00 up.

Granny: Old lady modeling. Grey rooted hair, painted or sleep eyes. From "Beverly Hillbillies." 14" - $60.00.

Miss Charming: 1936. All composition Shirley Temple look-alike. (See photo in Series 10, pg. 222.) 19" - $375.00 up. Pin - $45.00.

Miss Sunbeam: 1968. Plastic/vinyl, dimples. 17" - $25.00.

Musical baby: 1967. Key wind music box in cloth body. 17" - $15.00.

My Fair Lady: 1956. Adult type. All vinyl, jointed waist. 10½" - $50.00; 19" - $80.00.

Parton, Dolly: 1980. 12" - $20.00; 18" - $45.00.

Posey Playmate: 1969. Foam and vinyl. 18" - $15.00.

Puppetrina: 1963. (See photo in Series 11, pg. 205.) 22" - $30.00.

Shelly: 1964. "Tammy" type. Grow hair. 12" - $15.00.

Sniffles: 1963. Plastic/vinyl nurser. Marked "13/14 AA-EEGEE." 12" - $15.00.

Susan Stroller: 1955. Hard plastic with vinyl head. (See photo in Series 9, pg. 222.) 15" - $30.00; 20" - $40.00; 23" - $50.00; 26" - $30.00.

Tandy Talks: 1961. Pull string talker. Plastic with vinyl head and freckles. 20" - $45.00.

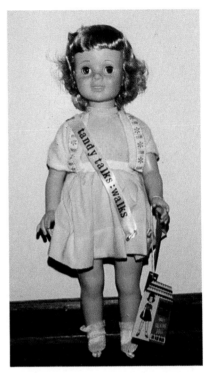

20" "Tandy Talks" is a pull string talker made of plastic with vinyl head. Has freckles and is all original. Made in 1961. Mint condtion - $45.00. *Courtesy Jeannie Mauldin.*

EFFANBEE DOLL COMPANY

First prices are for mint condition dolls; second prices for dolls that are played with, soiled, dirty, cracked or crazed or not original. Dolls marked with full name or "F & B."

Alice In Wonderland (Honey): Hard plastic. 16" - $375.00, $145.00.

Alyssia: 1958–1962. All hard plastic **walker** with vinyl head. Must have good face color. (See photo in Series 11, pg. 206.) 20" - $200.00, $80.00. (**Alicia** has rigid vinyl unjointed arms.)

American Children: (See photos in Series 8, pgs. 217–218.) 1938. All composition with painted or sleep eyes. Marked with that name. Some have "Anne Shirley" marked bodies; others are unmarked. **Closed mouth girls:** Sleep or painted eyes. 19–21" - $1,300.00. **Closed mouth boy:** 15" - $950.00; 17" - $1,400.00. **Barbara Joan:** Open mouth girl. 15" - $650.00. **Barbara Ann:** Open mouth. 17" - $750.00. **Barbara Lou:** Open mouth. 21" - $850.00 up.

Animals: Uses "Patsyette" body. Wolf, sheep, etc. $200.00 up.

Anne of Green Gables: 1937. Composition. 14" - $500.00.

Anne Shirley: 1936–1940. All composition. Marked with name. 16" - $250.00; 17" - $325.00; 22" - $425.00; 28" - $525.00.

Armstrong, Louis: 1984–1985 only. 15½" - $85.00.

Babyette: 1946. Cloth/composition sleeping baby. 12" - $250.00, $100.00; 16" - $325.00; $150.00. In box: 12" - $400.00.

12" composition "Babyette" with cloth body. Has closed eyes and painted features. Original clothes and layette. Basket may also be original. Made in 1946. Doll only - $250.00. With layette and basket - $500.00. *Courtesy Turn of Century Antiques.*

Babykin: 1940. All composition: 9–12" - $200.00, $90.00. All vinyl: 10" - $35.00.

Baby Cuddleup: 1953. Oil cloth body. Vinyl head/limbs. Two lower teeth. 20" - $45.00, $15.00; 23" - $65.00, $30.00.

Baby Dainty: 1912–1922. Cloth/composition. Marked with name. 15" - $225.00, $75.00; 17" - $275.00, $95.00.

Baby Effanbee: 1925. Marked on head. 12–13" - $150.00.

Baby Evelyn: 1925. Composition/cloth. Marked with name. 17" - $265.00, $125.00.

Baby Grumpy: See Grumpy.

Baby Tinyette: 1933–1936. Composition. 7–8" - $250.00, $95.00. Toddler: 7–8" - $275.00; $125.00.

Betty Brite: 1933. All composition. Fur wig, sleep eyes. Marked with name. 16–17" - $275.00, $95.00.

Bright Eyes: 1938, 1940s. Composition/cloth, flirty eyes. Same doll as "Tommy Tucker" and "Mickey." 16" - $285.00; 18" - $325.00; 22–23" - $425.00.

Brother or Sister: 1943. Composition head and hands, rest cloth. Yarn hair, painted eyes. 12" - $165.00, $60.00; 16" - $225.00, $85.00.

Bubbles: 1924. Composition/cloth. Marked with name. 16" - $345.00, $135.00; 19" - $400.00, $150.00; 22" - $485.00, $200.00; 25" - $525.00, $275.00. **Black:** 16" - $500.00; 20" - $800.00.

Button Nose: 1936–1943. (See photo in Series 8, pg. 218.) **Composition:** 8–9" - $235.00, $85.00. **Vinyl/cloth:** 1968. 18" - $30.00, $15.00.

19" Lawerence Welk's "Champagne Lady" made of all vinyl with sleep eyes, rooted hair, and high heel feet. Original and in mint condition. Marked "Effanbee" on head. $250.00. *Courtesy Jeannie Nespoli.*

Candy Kid: 1946. All composition toddler. 12" - $285.00, $100.00. Black: 12" - $365.00, $125.00.

Champagne Lady: From Lawrence Welk's Show. "Miss Revlon" type. 19" - $250.00.

Churchill, Sir Winston: 1984. $75.00.

Charlie McCarthy: 1929–1934. Composition/cloth. Mint condition. 15" - $525.00; 20" - $725.00. In box with button: Mint condition. 17" - $875.00.

Coquette: Composition with molded hair. Some have loop for hair ribbon. Painted eyes, smile. 10" - $250.00; 14" - $325.00.

Composition dolls: 1930s. All composition. Jointed neck, shoulders and hips. Molded hair. Painted or sleep eyes. Open or closed mouth. Original clothes. Marked "Effanbee." Perfect condition. 9" - $145.00, $70.00; 15" - $225.00, $100.00; 18" - $285.00, $125.00; 21" - $350.00, $135.00.

Composition dolls: 1920s. Composition head/limbs with cloth body. Open or closed mouth. Sleep eyes. Original clothes. Marked "Effanbee." Perfect condition. 18" - $185.00, $90.00; 22" - $225.00, $125.00; 25" - $325.00, $135.00; 28" - $385.00, $150.00.

Currier & Ives: Plastic/vinyl. 12" - $35.00, $10.00.

Disney dolls: 1977–1978. "Snow White," "Cinderella," "Alice in Wonderland" and "Sleeping Beauty." 14" - $200.00 up, $90.00.

Dydee Baby: 1933 on. Hard rubber head. Rubber body and ears. Later versions had hard plastic head. Perfect condition. 14" - $165.00 up, $45.00; 23" - $285.00, $100.00.

Dydee Baby: 1950 on. Hard plastic/vinyl. 15" - $150.00 up, $45.00; 24" - $225.00 up, $125.00.

Emily Ann and other character puppets: 1937. Composition puppet. 13" - $150.00, $50.00.

Fields, W.C.: 1938. Composition/cloth. 22" - $550.00, $135.00. **Plastic/vinyl:** See Legend Series.

Fluffy: 1954. All vinyl. 10" - $30.00, $10.00. **Girl Scout:** 10" - $55.00, $25.00. **Black:** 10" - $40.00, $10.00. **Katie:** 1957. Molded hair. 8½" - $45.00, $15.00.

Garland, Judy: See Legends Series.

Gumdrop: 1962 on. Plastic/vinyl. 16" - $30.00, $15.00.

Grumpy: 1912. Frowns. Cloth/composition. Painted features. German molds #172 through #176. 12" - $265.00, $80.00; 14" - $300.00, $100.00. Others: 14" - $235.00. **Black:** 12" - $300.00, $165.00; 15" - $375.00, $150.00.

Hagara, Jan: Designer. **Laurel:** 1984. 15" - $145.00. **Cristina:** 1984 only. $195.00. **Larry:** 1985. 15" - $95.00. **Lesley:** 1985. $85.00. **Originals:** George Washington, Uncle Sam, Amish, etc. 12" - $200.00 up.

Half Pint: 1966 on. Plastic/vinyl. 10" - $25.00, $10.00.

14" all composition "Plymouth Historical Doll" with painted eyes and human hair wig. All original, from 1939. Mint - $465.00 up. *Courtesy Jeannie Nespoli.*

Happy Boy: 1960. All vinyl. Molded tooth and freckles. (See photo in Series 10, pg. 225.) 10½" - $45.00, $20.00.

Hibel, Edna: Designer. 1984 only. **Flower girl:** $165.00. **Contessa:** (See photo in Series 11, pg. 208.) $185.00.

Historical Dolls: 1939. All composition, painted eyes. Original. "Little Lady" doll: 14" - $465.00, $145.00. "American Child" doll: 21" - $1,200.00 up, $600.00.

Honey: 1949–1955. All hard plastic, closed mouth. Must have excellent face color. (Add more for unusual, original clothes.) 14" - $225.00, $80.00; 18" - $325.00, $135.00; 21" - $425.00, $150.00. **Walker:** 14" - $265.00, 19" - $365.00. **Jointed knees:** 18" - $375.00.

Honey: 1947–1948. Composition, flirty eyes: 14" - $250.00, $100.00; 21" - $400.00, $150.00; 27" - $600.00, $250.00.

Howdy Doody: 1949: Composition/cloth. String operated mouth. 19" - $250.00. **Puppet on string:** Composition head/limbs. 17" - $200.00; 20" - $265.00. **1947–1949:** Composition/cloth, puppet mouth formed but not moveable. 18" - $300.00. **1950s:** Hard plastic/cloth doll. 18" - $225.00.

Humpty Dumpty: 1985. $70.00 up.

Ice Queen: 1937. Skater outfit. Composition with open mouth. 17" - $850.00 up, $225.00.

Lamkins: 1930. Composition/cloth. (See photo in Series 9, pg. 226.) 16" - $450.00 up; 19" - $600.00 up; 23" - $725.00.

Legend Series and Personalities: 1980: W.C. Fields - $250.00. **1981:** John Wayne as soldier. $300.00. **1982:** John Wayne as cowboy. $350.00. **1982:** Mae West - $100.00. 1983: Groucho Marx - $95.00. **1984:** Judy Garland dressed as "Dorothy" from *Wizard of Oz*. $90.00. **1985:** Lucille Ball. $85.00. **1986:** Liberace - $95.00. **1987:** James Cagney - $70.00.

Lil Sweetie: 1967. Nurser with no lashes or brow. 16" - $40.00, $20.00.

18" all hard plastic "Honey" with brunette wig, sleep eyes, and closed mouth. Mint condition with original box and tags. This example - $500.00 up. *Courtesy Susan Girardot.*

16" "Lamkins" made of composition and cloth. Fingers curled with molded painted ring on middle finger. Shown with 13" tall billy goat by Steiff. Doll - $450.00. Goat - $275.00. *Courtesy Turn of Century Antiques.*

15" "Groucho Marx" from the Legend Series of 1983. Made of plastic and vinyl with painted features. Has molded-on glasses, mustache, and cigar. All original. $95.00. *Courtesy Kathy Tvrdik.*

Limited Edition Club: Limited editions are noted by (number of issues). **1975:** (872) Precious Baby - $350.00. **1976:** (1,200) Patsy - $285.00. **1977:** (3,166) DeeWeese Cochran - $135.00. **1978:** (2,200) Crowning Glory - $100.00. **1979:** (3,485) Skippy - $250.00. **1980:** (3,485) Susan B. Anthony - $100.00. **1981:** (3,835) Girl with watering can - $85.00. **1982:** (4,220) Princess Diana - $95.00. **1983:** (4,470) Sherlock Holmes - $100.00. **1984:** (4,470) Bubbles - $100.00. **1985:** (4,470) Red Boy - $85.00. **1986:** (4,470) China head - $60.00. **1987/1988:** (2,500) porcelain Grumpy - $125.00; (5,000) vinyl Grumpy - $50.00.

Little Lady: 1939–1947. All composition. (Add more for original clothes.)

15" - $250.00, $85.00; 17" - $325.00, $115.00; 21" - $375.00, $125.00; 27" - $500.00, $200.00.

Little Lady: 1943. **Cloth body:** Yarn hair. 21" - $325.00 up. **Pink cloth body:** Wig. 17" - $225.00 up. **Magnets** in hands: 15" (doll only) - $325.00 up. Doll/accessories - $400.00 up.

Lovums: 1928. Composition/cloth. Open smiling mouth. Marked with name. 16" - $235.00, $95.00. 21" - $350.00, $125.00; 24" - $400.00, $150.00. **Vinyl:** 1979. $35.00 up.

Mae Starr: Record player in torso. Composition/cloth. Marked with name. 30" - $450.00, $185.00.

Marionettes: Composition/wood. 14" - $135.00 up.

Martha and George Washington: 1976. 11", pair - $150.00.

16½" "DeeWeese Cochran" from Effanbee Limited Edition Doll Club of 1977. There were 3,166 produced. Original and in mint condition. $135.00. *Courtesy Pat Graff.*

Mary Ann or Lee: 1928–1937. Open smile mouth. Composition and cloth or all composition. Marked with name. 16" - $275.00, $100.00; 18" - $300.00, $125.00; 20" - $350.00, $150.00; 24" - $450.00, $175.00.

Marilee: 1920s. Composition/cloth. Open mouth. Marked with name. 14" - $235.00, $90.00; 17" - $285.00, $115.00; 25" - $435.00, $165.00; 29" - $500.00; $225.00.

Mary Jane: 1917–1920. Composition. Jointed body or cloth. "Mama" type. 20" - $250.00, $145.00. 24" - $300.00, $175.00.

Mary Jane: 1960. Plastic/vinyl walker with freckles. 31" - $175.00, $85.00. Flirty eye walker: 30" - $225.00, $100.00. **Nurse:** 32" - $250.00, $125.00.

Mickey: 1946. Composition/cloth with flirty eyes. (Also Tommy Tucker and Bright Eyes.) 16" - $285.00; 18" - $325.00, $100.00; 22–23" - $425.00, $135.00.

Mickey: 1956. All vinyl. (Some have molded-on hats.) 11" - $70.00, $20.00.

Miss Chips: 1965 on. Plastic/vinyl. White: 18" - $30.00. **Black:** 18" - $40.00.

Pat-O-Pat: Composition/cloth with painted eyes. Press stomach and hands pats together. 13–14" - $150.00, $75.00.

Patricia: 1932–1936. All composition. 14" - $445.00, $170.00. Original: $500.00 up.

Patricia-kin: 1929–1930s. 11" - $350.00, $130.00.

Patsy: 1927–1930s. All composition: 14" - $385.00, $165.00. **Composition/ cloth:** 14" - $400.00, $185.00. Original: $425.00 up.

Patsy look-alike: Composition arm bent at elbow. Excellent quality, original: $275.00. Medium quality: $165.00. Poor quality: $95.00.

Patsy Baby: Cloth body. Can have straight legs. 11" - $250.00, $95.00. Black/brown: $450.00, $150.00.

Patsy Babyette: 1930s, 1940s. 9" - $250.00, $90.00. Original: $325.00 up.

"Lovums" is made of vinyl with cloth body, sleep eyes, and rooted hair. From 1979. $35.00 up. *Courtesy Kathy Tvrdik.*

30" "Mae Starr" has composition head and limbs with cloth body. Has open mouth with two teeth and human hair wig. Sleep eyes are celluloid over tin. She has a record player in torso. $450.00 up. *Courtesy Jeannie Mauldin.*

Patsyette: 1930s. 9" - $265.00, $100.00. Original: $300.00 up. Black: $325.00, $125.00.

Patsy Ann: 1930s. 19" - $475.00, $175.00. Original: $550.00 up. Vinyl: 1959. 15" - $175.00, $65.00. Original: $225.00 up. Vinyl with jointed wasit: 15" - $200.00.

Patsy Joan: 1927–1930. Reissued 1946–1949. 16" - $465.00, $165.00. Original: $500.00 up. **Black:** 16" - $600.00 up, $200.00.

Patsy Junior: 11" - $325.00, $95.00. Original: $375.00 up.

Patsy Lou: 1929–1930s. 22" - $500.00, $185.00. Original: $600.00 up.

Patsy Mae: 1932. 30" - $750.00, $300.00. Original: $825.00 up.

Patsy Ruth: 1935. 26–27" - $775.00, $300.00. Original: $825.00 up.

Patsy, Wee: 1930s. 5–6" - $325.00, $100.00. Original: $350.00 up.

Polka Dottie: 1953. 21" - $150.00, $50.00.

Portrait Dolls: 1940. All composition. "Bo Peep," "Ballerina," "Bride," "Groom," "Gibson Girl," "Colonial," etc. 11" - $265.00, $100.00.

Presidents: 1984. Lincoln: 18" - $75.00. Washington: 16" - $65.00. Teddy Roosevelt: 17" - $75.00. F.D. Roosevelt: 1985. $75.00.

Prince Charming or Cinderella (Honey): All hard plastic. 16" - $400.00 up, $150.00.

Pum'kin: 1966 on. All vinyl with freckles. 10½" - $25.00, $10.00.

Quints: Used "Babyette" doll. All five dressed alike in box with extra clothes. Mint - $875.00 up.

Rootie Kazootie: 1953. 21" - $150.00, $50.00.

Roosevelt, Eleanor: 1985. 14½" - $70.00.

Rosemary: 1925 on. Composition/cloth. Marked with name. 14" - $235.00, $80.00; 17" - $285.00, $125.00; 25" - $435.00, $165.00; 29" - $500.00, $225.00.

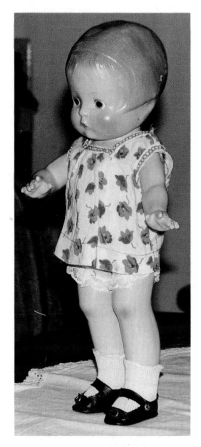

14" "Mi-Mi" is an all composition "Patsy" wearing all original clothes. She dates from the early 1930s. Doll was obtained from the original owner. Marked "EFF AN BEE/MI-MI-/pat. pend./Doll" on back. Dress tagged "EFFanBEE/DOLL/Finest-Best" in oval, then "Made in U.S.A." $465.00 up. *Courtesy Ellie Bustos.*

Santa Claus: 19" composition with molded beard and hat. (See photo in Series 8, pg. 223.) $1,000.00 up.

Skippy: 1929, 1940s. All composition. 14" - $465.00, $175.00. **Soldier:** $500.00. **Sailor:** $565.00. **Aviator:** $565.00. **Safari, cowboy, or farmer:** $450.00.

Suzanne: 1940. All composition. Marked with name. 14" - $285.00, $115.00.

Suzie Sunshine: 1961 on. Has freckles. 17–18" - $40.00, 10.00. **Black:** 17–18" - $60.00, $30.00.

Suzette: 1939. Marked with name. All composition. 12" - $245.00, $90.00.

Sweetie Pie: 1938–1940s. (See photo in Series 10, pg. 229.) Composition/cloth. 14" - $165.00, $50.00; 18" - $275.00, $90.00; 24" - $375.00, $165.00.

Tommy Tucker: 1946. Composition/cloth with flirty eyes. (Also "Mickey" and "Bright Eyes.") 16" - $285.00, 18" - $325.00, 22–23" - $425.00.

Twain, Mark: 1984. 16" - $65.00.

Witch: Designed by Faith Wick. 18" - $50.00 up.

10" "Florence Nightingale" of 1977. Plastic with vinyl head and arms. All original and in mint condition. $35.00. *Courtesy Sally Bethschieder.*

GALOOB

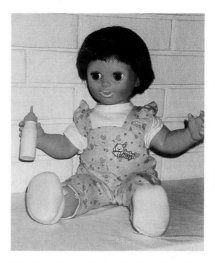

17½" "So Funny Natalie" from the Baby Face Collection. Made of plastic and vinyl with inset eyes. Knees and elbows are jointed. Marked "Galoob/1990." Original. $55.00 up. *Courtesy Jeannie Mauldin.*

19" all original "Baby Talk" with sleep eyes/lashes. Made of vinyl with cloth body. This doll speaks Spanish. Made by Galoob in 1990. $45.00. *Courtesy Pat Graff.*

1936: 8" all printed cloth doll. Holds can of baby food and toy dog. Rare. $350.00.

1954: 12" rubber doll made by Sun Rubber Co. Mint - $85.00 up; Mint in box - $175.00 up.

1966: 14" soft vinyl doll made by Arrow Industries. Has lopsided smile. $75.00 up.

1972: 10" plastic/vinyl doll made by Uneeda Doll Co. $40.00 up.

GIBBS, RUTH

Ruth Gibbs of Flemington, New Jersey, made dolls with and without china glaze heads and limbs. They had pink cloth bodies and were between 7" and 13" tall. Dolls are marked "R.G." on back shoulder plate. Boxes state "Godey Little Lady Dolls" but not all dolls represent Godey ladies. Dolls were designed by Herbert Johnson.

7-8": In box - $200.00. Doll only: $90.00.

10-12": In box - $250.00. Doll only: $125.00.

10" wigged: $165.00.

11" hard plastic: Must be in box and be identified. $200.00.

#1105 "Miss Moppet" in red and white striped box, ca. 1956. Ruth Gibbs purchased 11" nude dolls from another company and then outfitted them. The doll has sleep eyes, glued-on saran wig, and painted-on shoes with bow. Jointed at neck, shoulders, and hips. $200.00. *Courtesy Ciny Young*

7" Ruth Gibbs "Godey's Little Lady Doll" came with heart locket. Has cloth body and china glazed head and limbs. Doll is all original and shown in original box. This example - $225.00. *Courtesy Susan Girardot.*

HARTLAND INDUSTRIES

Hartland Industries made many figures with horses during the mid to late 1950s. These are extremely collectible as they are rare, especially when the horses have saddles. Most came from the Warner Brothers television productions. The figures included:

James Arness as "Matt Dillon" on *Gunsmoke.* (Sept. 1955–Sept. 1975)

James Garner as "Bret Maverick" on *Maverick.* (See photo Series 8, pg. 228.)

John Lupton as "Tom Jeffords" on *Broken Arrow.* (Sept. 1956–Sept. 1960)

Gail Davis as "Annie Oakley" on *Annie Oakley* (April 1953–Dec. 1956)

Hugh O'Brien as "Wyatt Earp" on *Life and Legend of Wyatt Earp* (Sept. 1955–Sept. 1961)

Dale Robertson as "Jim Hardie" on *Tales of Wells Fargo.* (March 1957–Sept. 1962)

Pat Conway as "Clay Hollister" on *Tombstone Territory.* (Oct. 1957–Oct. 1959)

Wayde Preston as "Capt. Chris Colt" on *Colt .45.* (Oct. 1957–Sept. 1960)

Richard Boone as "Paladin" on *Have Gun Will Travel.* (Sept. 1957–Sept. 1963)

John Payne as "Vint Bonner" on *The Restless Gun.* (Sept. 1957–Sept. 1959)

Clint Walker as "Cheyenne Bodie" on *Cheyenne.* (Sept. 1955–Sept. 1963)

Ward Bond as "Major Seth Adams" on *Wagon Train.* (Sept. 1957–Sept. 1965)

Chief Thunderbird with his horse "Northwind."

Robert E. Lee with his horse "Traveler."

General George Custer and his horse "Bugler."

Brave Eagle with his horse "White Cloud."

General George Washington with his horse "Ajax."

"Lone Ranger" with his horse "Silver."

"Tonto" with his horse "Scout."

Jim Bowie with his horse "Blaze."

"Sgt. Preston of the Yukon" with his horse.

Roy Rogers with his horse "Trigger."

Dale Evans with her horse "Buttermilk."

Cochise with pinto horse.

Buffalo Bill with horse.

Other figures made by the company include baseball notables Mickey Mantle, Ted Williams, Stan Musial, Henry Aaron, Ed Mathews, and George "Babe" Ruth.

Figure and horse: Mint condition. $300.00 up.

Figure in box with horse and accessories: $500.00 up.

Figure alone: $125.00.

Horse alone: $175.00.

Baseball figure: $325.00 up.

"Jim Hardie" (Dale Robertson) from TV show, *Tales of Wells Fargo,* that ran from March 1957 to September 1962. Ears on horse are laid back. $300.00. *Courtesy Steve Humphries.*

All prices are for mint condition dolls.

Adam: 1971. Boy for World of Love series. 9" - $15.00.

Aimee: 1972. Plastic/vinyl. 18" - $45.00.

Charlie's Angels: 1977. Jill, Kelly or Sabrina. (Allow more for mint in box) 8½" - $15.00 each.

Defender: 1974. One-piece arms and legs. 11½" - $95.00 up.

Dolly Darling: 1965. 4½" - $8.00.

Flying Nun: Plastic/vinyl, 1967. 5" - $35.00.

G.I. JOE:

(Add $50.00 more in mint in box on G.I. Joe.)

G.I. Joe Action figures: 12" figure. 1964: Marked on right lower back: "G.I. Joe™/Copyright 1964/By Hasbro ®/Patent Pending/Made in U.S.A." 1965: Slight change in marking. G.I. Joe®/Copyright 1964/By Hasbro ®/Patent Pending/Made in U.S.A." (This mark appears on all four armed service branches, excluding the Black action figures.) Hard plastic head with facial scar, painted hair, and no beard. **Soldier:** Flocked hair. $400.00. Painted hair: $225.00. Black painted hair: $950.00. **Marine:** $325.00. **Sailor:** $325.00. **Pilot:** $550.00. **Figures only:** $45.00–100.00. With factory painted black hair: $300.00.

G.I. Joe Action Soldiers of the World (1966): Figures in this set may have any hair and eye color combination. Hard plastic heads. No scar on face. Same markings as 1965. **Russian infantry:** In box: $650.00. Figure only: $225.00. **German soldier:** In box: $650.00. Figure only: $225.00. **Japanese Imperial soldier:** In box: $900.00. Figure only: $450.00. **British commando:** In box: $225.00. Figure only: $175.00. **Australian jungle fighter:** In box: $550.00. Figure only: $250.00.

French resistance: In box: $550.00. Figure only: $225.00.

G.I. Joe, Talking (1967–1969): Marked "G.I. Joe ®/Copyright 1964/By Hasbro ®/Pat. No. 3,277,602/Made In U.S.A. Talking mechanism added, excluding Black figure. Semi-hard vinyl head. **Talking action soldier:** No scar, blonde, brown eyes. $165.00 up. **Sailor:** $475.00. **Marine:** $385.00. **Pilot:** $750.00.

G.I. Joe Nurse (1967): The only female in this action series. Hard plastic jointed body, vinyl head. Rooted short blonde hair. Blue/green painted eyes. Marked across back waist: "Patent Pending ®/1967Hasbro/Made in Hong Kong. In box: $1,400.00. Dressed doll: $650.00. Nude doll: $200.00.

G.I. Joe, Man of Action (1970–1975): Marked "G.I. Joe ®/Copyright 1964/By Hasbro ®/Pat. no. 3,277,602/Made in U.S.A." Flocked hair, scar on face. Dressed in fatigues with Adventure Team emblem on shirt. Plastic cap. $70.00 up. Talking: $185.00.

G.I. Joe Adventure Team (1975–1976): Marked in small of back "© 1975 Hasbro ®/Pat. Pend., Pawt. R.I." Six team members. Flocked hair and beard. **Team Commander (talking):** Olive fatigues. $425.00 up. **Land Adventurer (Black):** Tan fatigues. No beard. $325.00 up. **Land Adventurer (talking):** Camouflage fatigues. $325.00 up. **Sea Adventurer:** Light blue shirt, navy pants. $300.00 up. **Air Adventurer:** Orange flight suit. $300.00 up. **Astronaut (talking):** White flight suit. $475.00 up.

G.I. Joe with kung fu grip: Adventure Team: $185.00 up. Black talking: $245.00.

G.I. Joe, "Mike Powers, Atomic Man": $85.00 up.

"Eagle Eye" G.I. Joe: $145.00.

G.I. Joe Secret Agent: Unusual face, mustache. $500.00 up.

Boxed G.I. Joe with uniform: Mint condition. Fighter pilot: $650.00. Tank G.I. Joe: $600.00. Action Soldier Sabotage: $500.00. Air Force dress uniform: $400.00.

These are the six foreign G.I. Joes with weapons and full gear. No scars on faces. Top: Australian. Left to right: Japanese, American, English (with headphones), German, and Russian. Each $225.00–300.00. *Courtesy Renie Culp. Photo courtesy of LeRoy Seeley of Foshaug Studios.*

Airborne military police: Green or tan outfits. $1,200.00.

Adventures of G.I. Joe sets: No figures included. Deep sea diver: **"Eight Ropes of Danger."** $285.00 up. Scuba diver: **"Jaws of Death."** $285.00 up. Safari: **"White Tiger Hunt."** $325.00 up. **Test pilot:** $550.00 up. Jungle explorer: **"Mouth of Doom."** $325.00 up. Secret agent: **"Secret Mission To Spy Island."** $275.00 up. Astronaut: **"Space Walk Mystery."** $500.00 up. **"The Hidden Missile."** $425.00 up. Polar explorer: **"Fight For Survival."** $500.00 up. **"Shark's Surprise":** $325.00 up. Pilot: **"Fantastic Free Fall":** $300.00.

Packs or boxed uniforms and accessories: Green Beret: $300.00. Secret Agent: $165.00. Marine mine detector: $285.00. Marine jungle fighter: $775.00. Action sailor: $325.00. Frogman demolition set: $325.00. Military police: $400.00. Landing signal officer: $275.00. Rescue diver: $325.00. Crash crew fire fighter: $300.00. Deep sea diver: $225.00. Annapolis, West Point, Air Force Academy cadet: Figure - $500.00; in box - $700.00. Astronaut: $275.00. Marine dress parade: $300.00. Pilot scramble set: $250.00. Shore patrol: $250.00. Ski patrol: $375.00. Deep Freeze with sled: $300.00.

G.I. Joe accessories: Armored car: 20" - $175.00 up. **Motorcycle and side car:** By Irwin. $225.00 up. **Desert jeep:** Tan. $200.00 up. **Turbo swamp craft:** $200.00 up. **Space capsule:** $175.00 up. **Footlocker:** $25.00 up. **Sea sled:** $80.00 up. **Tank:** $185.00 up. **Jeep:** Olive green. $165.00 up. **Helicopter:** $250.00 up. **All terrain vehicle:** $175.00 up. **Aircraft carrier:** 1982. $500.00.

Jem and others: Must be original. **Jem:** $35.00 up. **Kimber:** $40.00. **Shana:** $45.00. **Roxy:** $45.00. **Aja:** $40.00. **Pizazz:** $40.00. **Stormer:** $45.00. **Banee:** $40.00.

Leggie: 1972. (See photo in Series 9, pg. 236.) 10" - $25.00. Black: $35.00.

12½" "Rock 'n Curl Jem" with open/closed smiling mouth and painted features. Hair goes from blonde to light pink. Made by Hasbro in 1986. $55.00.

Little Miss No Name: 1965. 15" - $90.00.

Mamas and Papas: 1967. (See photo in Series 8, pg. 230.) $40.00 each. **Show Biz Babies:** 1967. $50.00 each. Mama Cass: $50.00.

Monkees: Set of four. 4" - $100.00 up.

Storybooks: 1967. 3" dolls. Complete set: Sleeping Beauty: $45.00. Rumplestilskin: $50.00. Goldilocks: $45.00. Snow White and Dwarfs: $100.00. Prince Charming: $55.00. Doll only: $10.00–20.00.

Sweet Cookie: 1972. 18" - $30.00.

That Kid: 1967. 21" - $90.00.

World of Love Dolls: 1971. (See photo in Series 10, pg. 236.) White: 9" - $15.00. Black: 9" - $15.00.

15" "Little Miss No Name" with sad and lonely look. Has teardrop molded to cheek. Original box has illusion of rain on front plastic. Made by Hasbro in 1965. Doll only - $90.00 up. In box (rare) - $200.00. *Courtesy Cynthia Matus.*

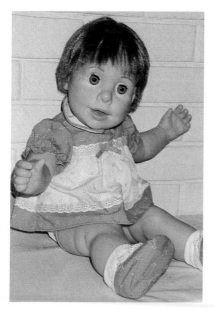

12½" vinyl "Banee" with swivel waist, bendable knees, and painted features. She is one of the "Starlight Girls" from the "Jem" series. Original and mint. From 1987. $40.00. *Courtesy Pat Graff.*

19" "Real Baby" designed by Judith Turner. Vinyl with cloth body, inset eyes, and open/closed mouth. Also came with eyes modeled closed. Made by Hasbro from 1984 to 1986. $40.00. *Courtesy Pat Graff.*

Hollywood Doll purchased between 1949 and 1952. Made of all hard plastic with sleep eyes. This one is called "Little Girl Where Have You Been?" from the "Toyland Series." Original in original box which has blue stars all over it. Original doll only - $30.00 up. In box - $45.00 up. *Courtesy Sharon Hamilton.*

HORSMAN DOLL COMPANY

Center: 16" all original "Baby Dimples" with composition swivel head, sleep eyes, molded hair, dimples, and open mouth. Has cloth body with composition limbs. Ca. 1928. Marked "E.I.H. Co. Inc." Left: 15" bisque head "Hilda." Right: 16½" bisque head "Hilda." Baby - $225.00. 15" - $2,600.00. 16½" - $3,400.00. *Courtesy Frasher Doll Auctions.*

HORSMAN DOLL COMPANY

First prices are for mint condition dolls; second prices for ones that have been played with, are dirty and soiled or not original. Marked "Horsman" or "E.I.H."

Angelove: 1974. Plastic/vinyl. Made for Hallmark. 12" - $20.00.

Answer Doll: 1966. Button in back moves head. 10" - $18.00, $9.00.

Billiken: 1909. Composition head, slant eyes, plush or velvet body. 12" - $365.00, $130.00; 16" - $450.00.

Baby Bumps: 1910. Composition/cloth. 12" - $225.00, $75.00; 14" - $275.00, $100.00. **Black:** 11" - $275.00, $95.00; 15" - $325.00, $130.00.

Baby Butterfly: Oriental: 12" - $250.00. Black: 12" - $350.00.

Baby First Tooth: 1966. Cloth/vinyl. Cry mouth with one tooth. Tears on cheeks. 16" - $25.00, $16.00.

Baby Tweaks: 1967. Cloth/vinyl, inset eyes. 20" - $25.00, $14.00.

Ballerina: 1957. One-piece vinyl body and legs with jointed elbows. 18" - $35.00.

Betty: All composition. 16" - $245.00, $95.00. All vinyl: 1951. One-piece body and limbs: 14" - $45.00. **Plastic/vinyl:** 16" - $20.00, $10.00.

Betty Jo: All composition. 16" - $250.00, $100.00. **Plastic/vinyl:** 1962. 16" - $20.00, $10.00.

Betty Ann: Add more for original clothes. All composition: 19" - $350.00, $150.00. **Plastic/vinyl:** 19" - $75.00, $30.00.

Betty Jane: All composition. 25" - $400.00, $165.00. **Plastic/vinyl:** 25" - $85.00, $45.00.

Blink (Also called **"Happy"**) **and Skinney:** 1916 Gene Carr designed character. Cloth body, composition head and limbs. Painted eyes are almost closed. Watermelon-style open/closed mouth with one lower tooth. Very prominent ears, painted hair. 14–15" - $365.00 up.

Bye-Lo Baby: 1972. Made for 100th anniversary for Wards. Cloth/vinyl. 14" - $45.00. Reissued: 1980–1990s. 14" - $20.00.

22" "Brother and Sister" with cloth bodies and composition heads and limbs. Both have sleep eyes, molded hair, and tiny closed mouths. Marked on head "Horsman 1937." Each - $275.00. *Courtesy Jeannie Mauldin.*

36" "Buffy" from TV series, *Family Affair.* Uses the plastic and vinyl body and limbs from the 1963 "Princess Peggy" dolls. Head is vinyl with sleep eyes, freckles, and rooted hair. Nicely redressed. $600.00. *Courtesy Jeannie Nespoli.*

Body Twist: 1929–1930. All composition. Top of body fits down into torso. 11" - $245.00, $90.00.

Bright Star: 1937–1946. (See photo in Series 8, pg. 233.) All composition: 18–19" - $325.00, $150.00. **All hard plastic:** 1952. 15" - $300.00, $125.00.

Brother: Composition/cloth. 22" - $275.00 up, $100.00. Vinyl: 13" - $50.00, $25.00.

Campbell Kids: Circa 1911. Cloth/composition with painted features. Marked "E.I.H." 12" - $250.00 up; 15" - $350.00 up. "Dolly Dingle" style face: 1930–1940s. All composition. Painted-on black slippers and white socks. 13" - $350.00 up.

Celeste portrait doll: In frame. Eyes painted to side. 12" - $30.00, $12.00.

Christopher Robin: 11" - $30.00, $10.00.

Child dolls: 1930–1940s. **All composition:** 14" - $195.00, $90.00; 16" - $275.00, $100.00; 18" - $345.00, $100.00. **All hard plastic:** 14" - $175.00, $65.00; 18" - $300.00 up, $125.00. **Toddler:** All composition, very chubby. 14" - $145.00, $60.00; 17" - $250.00, $95.00. **Mama style babies:** Cloth bodies. 13" - $175.00, $55.00. 17" - $265.00, $100.00.

Cindy: 1950s. Marked "170." All hard plastic: 15" - $185.00 up, $65.00; 17" - $225.00 up, $125.00. All early vinyl: 1953. 18" - $70.00, $20.00. **Lady** type with jointed waist: 1959. 19" - $85.00, $35.00. **Walker:** 16" - $245.00.

Cindy Kay: 1950–on. All vinyl child with long legs. (See photo in Series 9, pg. 239.) 15" - $90.00, $35.00; 20" - $135.00; 27" - $250.00.

Cinderella: 1965. Plastic/vinyl with painted eyes to side. 11½" - $25.00, $10.00.

Composition dolls: 1910s–1920s. "Can't Break 'Em" composition/cloth body. Marked "E.I.H." 12" - $165.00, $50.00; 16" - $225.00, $125.00. 1930s: 16" - $165.00, $85.00; 18" - $200.00, $85.00; 22" - $275.00, $125.00.

Composition type reissued dolls: **1985:** 1928 Baby. **1986:** Tynie Baby. **1987:** Heebee-Shebee. **1988:** Billiken, Ella Cinders. **1989:** Sister, Baby Bright Eyes. **1990:** Dimples. **1991:** Brother, Dolly Record. **1992:** Buttercup. **1993:** Baby Rosebud.

Crawling Baby: 1967. Vinyl. 14" - $30.00, $15.00.

Dimples: 1928–1933. Composition/cloth. (See photo in Series 9, pg. 238.) 16" - $225.00, $80.00; 20" - $300.00, $135.00; 24" - $375.00, $150.00. **Toddler:** 20" - $400.00, $175.00; 24" - $475.00, $185.00. **Laughing:** Painted teeth. 22" - $500.00, $200.00.

8" tiny "Little Miss Betty" from 1954. Has one-piece stuffed vinyl body and limbs. Vinyl head has rooted hair, sleep eyes, and molded lashes. Wearing original dress. $20.00. *Courtesy Kathy Tvrdik.*

Disney exclusives: "Cinderella," "Snow White," "Mary Poppins," "Alice in Wonderland." 1981. 8" - $35.00 each.

Gold Medal doll: 1930s: Composition/cloth with upper & lower teeth. 21" - $250.00, $100.00. 1953: Vinyl with molded hair. 26" - $200.00, $90.00. 1954: Vinyl boy. 15" - $85.00, $35.00.

Ella Cinders: 1925. Comic character. Composition/cloth. Marked "1925 MNS." 14" - $375.00; 18" - $600.00.

Elizabeth Taylor: 1976. In box: 11½" - $50.00, $30.00.

Floppy: 1965. Foam body and legs, rest is vinyl. 18" - $20.00.

Flying Nun: (Sally Field) 1965. (See photo in Series 9, pg. 240.) Original: 12" - $45.00, $12.00. MIB.: $100.00.

6" all vinyl "Twistie" with rooted hair and painted eyes. Wind-up key in back makes her twist. Re-dressed. Original dress is cut in one piece and has a guitar imprinted on front. Marked " Horsman Dolls Inc. 1967." on back. $10.00. *Courtesy Kathy Tvrdik.*

Hansel & Gretel: 1963. Sleep eyes, unusual faces. (See photo in Series 7, pg. 238.) Each - $225.00.

Hebee-Shebee: 1925. All composition. 10½" - $525.00, $250.00

Jackie Coogan: 1921. Composition/cloth, painted eyes. (See photo in Series 11, pg. 221.) 14" - $450.00, $135.00.

Jackie Kennedy: 1961. Marked "Horsman J.K." Plastic/vinyl adult body. 25" - $150.00, $70.00.

Jeanie Horsman: 1937. All composition: 14" - $245.00, $85.00. Composition/cloth: 16" - $200.00, $75.00.

Jojo: 1937. All composition. 12" - $225.00, $90.00. 16" - $285.00, $135.00.

Life-size baby: Plastic/vinyl. 26" - $200.00, $100.00.

Lullabye baby: 1964, 1967. Cloth/vinyl. Music box in body. 12" - $18.00, $6.00. All vinyl: 12" - $10.00, $5.00.

Mary Poppins: 1964: 12" - $25.00, $10.00; 16" - $60.00, $25.00; 26" (1966) - $185.00, $100.00; 36" - $300.00, $165.00. In box with "Michael" and "Wendy": 12" and 8" - $125.00.

Mama style babies: 1920s– 1930s. Composition/cloth. Marked "E.I.H" or "Horsman." 14" - $175.00, $75.00; 18" - $265.00, $90.00. **Girl dolls:** 14" - $225.00, $85.00; 18" - $300.00, $115.00; 24" - $350.00, $150.00. Hard plastic/cloth: 16" - $65.00; $30.00; 22" - $85.00, $40.00. Vinyl/cloth: 16" - $20.00, $8.00; 22" - $30.00, $18.00.

Michael: (Mary Poppins) 1965. 8" - $20.00, $10.00.

Mousketeer: 1971. Boy or girl. 8" - $20.00, $10.00.

Patty Duke: 1965. Posable arms. 12" - $35.00, $15.00.

Peek-A-Boo: Designed by Grace Drayton. Cloth and composition. 7½–8" - $165.00 up.

Peggy: 1957. All vinyl child with one-piece body and legs. 25" - $135.00, $60.00.

Peggy Ann: 1930. Composition/cloth. (See photo in Series 9, pg. 240.) Mint condition. 28" - $200.00 up.

Peggy Pen Pal: 1970. Multi-jointed arms. Plastic/vinyl. 18" - $30.00, $15.00.

Peterkin: 1915–1930. All composition. Painted googly-style eyes. 10" - $275.00, $100.00; 14" - $400.00 up.

Pippi Longstocking: 1972. Vinyl/cloth. 1972. 18" - $25.00, $15.00.

Polly & Pete: 1957. All vinyl Black dolls with molded hair. 13" - $175.00, $50.00.

Poor Pitiful Pearl: 1963, 1976. 12" - $45.00, $20.00; 17" - $85.00, $45.00.

Pudgie Baby: Plastic/vinyl. 1978: 12" - $25.00, $10.00. 1980: 24" - $35.00, $15.00.

Pudgy: 1974. All vinyl, very large painted eyes. 12½" - $25.00, $8.00.

Roberta: 1928: All composition. 1937: Molded hair or wigs. 14" - $225.00,

$80.00; 20" - $300.00, $100.00. 24" - $350.00, $150.00.

Rosebud: 1928. Composition/cloth. Dimples and smile. Sleep eyes and wig. Marked with name. 14" - $225.00, $80.00; 18" - $275.00, $100.00. 24" - $350.00, $140.00.

Ruthie: 1958–1966. All vinyl or plastic/vinyl. 14" - $25.00, $10.00; 20" - $35.00, $15.00.

Sleepy Baby: 1965. Vinyl/cloth. Eyes molded closed. 24" - $45.00, $28.00.

Tuffie: 1966. All vinyl. Upper lip molded over lower. 16" - $30.00, $18.00.

Tynie Baby: See that section for bisque. **Vinyl with crying face:** 1950. Oil cloth or cloth body. 16" - $100.00 up. **Composition head:** 15" - $285.00.

HOYER, MARY

The Mary Hoyer Doll Mfg. Co. operated in Reading, Pennsylvania, from 1925. The dolls were made in all composition, all hard plastic, and last ones produced were in plastic and vinyl. Older dolls are marked in a circle on back "Original Mary Hoyer Doll" or "The Mary Hoyer Doll" embossed on lower back.

First price is for perfect doll in tagged factory clothes. Second price for perfect doll in outfits made from Mary Hoyer patterns and third price is for redressed doll in good condition with only light craze to composition or slight soil to others.

Composition: Early dolls have left arm bent at elbow and can have extra joints just below breast line or at waist. ("Blanks" purchased from Knickerbocker Toy Co.) 14" - $450.00, $400.00 up, $185.00.

Hard plastic: 14" - $450.00 up, $400.00, $175.00; 18" - $550.00 up, $475.00, $225.00. Boy: 14" - $500.00–425.00.

Plastic/vinyl (Margie): 14–15" marked "AE23." 12" - $125.00, $60.00, $10.00; 14" - $175.00, $90.00; $20.00.

18" "Gigi" by Mary Hoyer. Made of all hard plastic with sleep eyes and platinum mohair wig. Original calf length gown. This example - $800.00. *Courtesy Susan Girardot.*

14" all composition "Mary Hoyer" doll that has sleep eyes and is dressed in original costume crocheted from a Mary Hoyer pattern. Includes tam and purse. $450.00. *Courtesy Jeannie Nespoli.*

IDEAL NOVELTY AND TOY COMPANY

First prices are for mint condition dolls. Second prices are for cracked, crazed, dirty, soiled or not original dolls.

April Showers: 1968. Battery operated. Splashes with hands and head turns. (See photo in Series 7, pg. 242.) 14" - $20.00, $10.00.

Belly Button Babies: 1970. Plastic/vinyl. White: 9½" - $15.00, $6.00. Black: 9½" - $20.00, $8.00.

Baby Crissy: 1973–1975. Pull string to make hair grow. White: 24" - $65.00, $25.00. Black: 24" - $80.00, $30.00. Reissued in 1981: No grow hair. 24" - $35.00, $10.00.

Baby Snooks: See Flexies.

Bam-Bam: 1963. Plastic/vinyl or all vinyl. 12" - $15.00, $8.00; 16" - $25.00, $10.00.

Batgirl and other female super heroes: Vinyl. Must be original. (See photo in Series 7, pg. 243.) 12" - $175.00 up.

Betsy McCall: See that section.

Betsy Wetsy: 1937 on. **Composition head:** Excellent rubber body. 14" - $125.00, $25.00; 16" - $165.00, $40.00. **Hard plastic/vinyl:** 12" - $80.00, $25.00; 14" - $145.00, $50.00. **All vinyl:** (See photo in Series 9, pg. 243.) 12" - $30.00, $10.00; 18" - $60.00, $22.00.

Betty Big Girl: 1968. Plastic/vinyl. (See photo in Series 10, pg. 243.) 32" - $250.00, $100.00.

Betty Jane: 1930s–1944. Shirley Temple type. All composition, sleep eyes, open mouth. 14" - $250.00, $95.00; 16" - $275.00, $100.00; 24" - $300.00, $135.00.

Blessed Event: 1951. Also called "Kiss Me." Cloth body with plunger in back to make doll cry or pout. Vinyl head with eyes almost squinted closed. (See photo in Series 9, pg. 246.) 21" - $145.00, $60.00.

Bonny Braids: 1951. Hard plastic/vinyl head. (See photo in Series 7, pg. 245.) **Mint:** 13½" - $165.00, $50.00. **Baby:** 13" - $140.00; $30.00.

Bonnie Walker: 1956. Hard plastic. Pin-jointed hips. Open mouth, flirty eyes. Marked "Ideal W-25." 23" - $95.00, $45.00.

Brandi: 1972. Of Crissy family. 17½" - $45.00, $15.00.

Brother/Baby Coos: 1951. Cloth/composition with hard plastic head. 25" - $150.00, $75.00. Composition head/latex: 24" - $90.00, $20.00. Hard plastic head/vinyl: 24" - $85.00, $25.00.

Bizzie Lizzie: 1971. 18" - $35.00, $12.00.

Bud: Tammy's boyfriend, 1964. 12½" - $65.00.

Bye-Bye Baby: 1960. Lifelike modeling. 12" - $185.00, $60.00; 25" - $375.00, $165.00.

Captain Action: 1966. Extra joints. (Add $50.00 if mint in box.) Complete, no box: 12" - $300.00 up. As Batman, etc.: $350.00 up.

Cinnamon: 1971. Of Crissy family. 13½" - $40.00, $15.00. **Black:** $50.00, $25.00. Hair Doodler: $30.00. Curly Ribbons: $35.00.

Comic heroines: Batgirl, Mera, Queen of Atlantis, Super Girl, Wonder Woman. Vinyl. (See photo in Series 7, pg. 243.) 11½" - $175.00, $65.00 up.

Composition baby: 1930s–1940s. (Also see "Mama Dolls.") Composition head and limbs with cloth body. Closed mouth. Sleep eyes, allow more for flirty eyes. Original. In excellent condition. 16" - $200.00, $80.00; 18" - $250.00, $90.00; 22" - $300.00, $115.00; 25" - $345.00, $160.00. **Flirty eyes:** 16" - $250.00, $90.00; 18" - $345.00, $135.00.

Composition child: All composition girl with sleep eyes, some flirty. Open mouth. Original clothes. Excellent condition. Marked "Ideal" and a number or "Ideal" in a diamond. 14" - $185.00, $75.00; 18" - $285.00, $95.00; 22" - $350.00, $125.00. **Cloth body:** With straight composition legs. 14" - $145.00, $55.00; 18" - $225.00, $80.00; 22" - $225.00, $85.00.

Composition/wood segmented characters: 1940s. Composition head and wooden segmented body. **King Little:** 9" - $265.00; 13" - $365.00. **Jiminy Cricket:** 9" - $365.00, $150.00. **Pinnochio:** 10" - $275.00; 12" - $325.00.

7" all vinyl "Evil Knievel" is completely bendable. One of three original outfits. Marked "1972 Ideal" in oval "Hong Kong." $22.00. *Courtesy Kathy Tvrdik.*

Cricket: 1970–1971. Of Crissy family. 15½" - $45.00, $15.00. **Black:** $55.00, $20.00. Look-a-round: $40.00, $15.00.

Crissy: 1968–1971. 17½" - $40.00, $15.00. **Black:** $55.00, $30.00. Look-a-round: 1972. $35.00, $15.00. Talking: 1971. $45.00, $20.00. **Floor length hair:** First issue in 1968. $150.00, $65.00. Moving: $35.00, $15.00. Swirls Curler: 1973. $35.00, $15.00. Twirly Beads: 1974. $30.00, $12.00. Hair Magic: 1977. No ponytail. $25.00, $10.00.

Daddy's Girl: 1961–1962. 29" - $675.00 up, $225.00. 42" - $875.00 up, $325.00 up.

Deanna Durbin: 1939. All composition. (See photo in Series 10, pg. 245.) 14" - $450.00, $175.00; 17" - $625.00, $185.00; 21" - $700.00, $265.00; 24" - $875.00, $300.00; 27" - $1,000.00 up, $350.00. "Gulliver's Travels": Tight pants, boots, full sleeves, black wig. 21" - $1,200.00, $500.00.

Diana Ross: Plastic/vinyl. 17½" - $185.00, $90.00.

Dina: 1972. Of Crissy family. 15" - $45.00, $20.00.

Doctor Evil: 1965. Multi-jointed. Came with face masks. 11" - $75.00 up, $30.00.

Dodi: 1964. Of Tammy family. Marked "1964-Ideal-D0-9E." 9" - $30.00, $9.00.

Dorothy Hamil: 1977. 11½" - $20.00, $9.00.

Electro-Man: 1977. Switch sets off alarm. Activated by beam of light. 16" - $265.00 up.

15" "Jackie," also called "Carol Brent," is made of plastic and vinyl with eyes painted to side, upswept rooted hair, and high heel feet. Her detailed hands are very beautiful. Clothes are original. Marked "Ideal Toy Corp./M-15-L" on head and "Ideal Toy Corp./M-15" on body. $125.00 up. *Courtesy Jeannie Nespoli.*

21" all composition "Judy Garland" is in mint condition and all original. Marked with backward "21" on back and "Ideal Doll." $700.00. *Courtesy Jeannie Nespoli.*

Eric: 1976. Tuesday Taylor's boyfriend. 12" - $20.00, $10.00.

Flatsy: 1968–1970. Set of nine in frames. (See photo in Series 9, pg. 244.) 5" - $15.00 each, $5.00 each. With train, bicycle, etc.: $20.00 each, $7.00 each. 8" on own stand: $22.00. Fashion: 1969. 8" - $18.00 each, $8.00 each.

Flexies: Wire and composition dolls that include a Black figure (1938–1942), soldier (1938), clown (1938), and **Sunny Sue or Sam** (1938). **Soldier, children:** 12" - $200.00, $100.00. **Baby Snooks (Fannie Brice), Mortimer Snerd:** 1938. 12" - $285.00 up, $125.00.

Flossie Flirt: 1938–1945. Cloth/composition. Flirty eyes: 20" - $285.00, $100.00; 24" - $375.00, $135.00. **Black:** $375.00, $135.00. Boy: 17" - $285.00, $125.00.

Giggles: Plastic/vinyl. 16" - $45.00, $18.00; 18" - $40.00, $20.00. **Black:** 18" - $75.00, $35.00. Baby: 15" - $25.00, $10.00.

Goody Two Shoes: 1965. 19" - $125.00, $40.00. **Walking/talking:** 19" - $150.00, $50.00; 27" - $250.00, $75.00.

Harmony: 1971. Battery operated. (See photo in Series 10, pg. 246.) 21" - $35.00, $20.00.

Harriet Hubbard Ayer: 1953. Hard plastic/vinyl. 15" - $185.00 up, $65.00; 17" - $285.00 up, $115.00.

Honey Moon: 1965. From "Dick Tracy." White yarn hair, Magic Skin body. (See photo in Series 9, pg. 245.) 15" - $40.00, $8.00. With helmet: $50.00. Cloth/vinyl: $50.00, $20.00.

Howdy Doody: 1940s. Composition head/cloth body. Floating disc eyes. Mouth moves by string in back of head. Original cowboy clothes. (See photo in Series 8, pg. 240.) 20" - $245.00 up.

Joan Palooka: 1952. 14" - $90.00, $40.00.

Joey Stivic (baby): 1976. One-piece body and limbs. Sexed boy. 15" - $25.00, $10.00.

Jiminy Cricket: 1939–1940. Composition/wood. 9" - $365.00, $150.00.

Judy Garland: 1939. All composition. Original: 14" - $1,100.00, $475.00; 18" - $1,500.00 up, $600.00. Replaced clothes: 14" - $800.00. **Marked with backward "21":** From 1941. 14" - $450.00, $150.00; 21" - $700.00, $185.00.

"Little Miss Marker" as played by Sara Stimson in remake of a Shirley Temple movie. Made of vinyl and plastic with large, round head on smaller body. Doll was marketed in 1980 only, but head will be marked "1979." Marked "UFI Studios - Ideal" in oval, "H-3-30/Hong Kong." $20.00.
Courtesy Kathy Tvrdik.

Judy Splinters: 1951. Cloth/vinyl/latex. Yarn hair, painted eyes. Must be in good condition. 18" - $150.00, $35.00; 22" - $185.00, $70.00; 36" - $425.00, $135.00.

Katie Kachoo: 1968. Raise arm and she sneezes. 17" - $25.00; $10.00.

Kerry: 1971. Of Crissy family. 17½" - $40.00, $15.00.

King Little: 1940. Composition/wood. 14" - $265.00, $100.00.

Kiss Me: 1951. See "Blessed Event."

Kissy: 22" - $40.00, $25.00. **Black:** $75.00, $40.00. Cuddly: 1964. Cloth/vinyl. 17" - $25.00, $10.00.

21" composition "Miss Curity" is a difficult doll to find in any outfit. Uses the "Sara Ann" composition doll of mid-1940s. $850.00 up. *Courtesy Peggy Millhouse.*

Kissy, Tiny: 1962. 16" - $25.00, $10.00. **Black:** $55.00, $25.00. Baby: 1966. Kisses when stomach is pressed. 12" - $20.00, $8.00.

Liberty Boy: 1918. 12" - $300.00, $100.00.

Little Lost Baby: 1968. Three-faced doll. (See photo in Series 7, pg. 249.) 22" - $50.00, $25.00.

Little Princess: Shirley Temple type from 1930s–1940s. All composition with open mouth. Marked "Ideal." 14" - $265.00; 18" - $325.00.

Magic Lips: 1955. Vinyl coated cloth/vinyl. Lower teeth. 24" - $45.00, $20.00.

Magic Skin Baby: 1940s. Composition or hard plastic head. Stuffed latex rubber body and limbs. Good condition. 14" - $80.00; 17" - $95.00.

Mama style dolls: 1920–1930s. Composition/cloth: 14" - $225.00, $75.00; 16" - $265.00, $100.00; 18" - $325.00, $125.00; 24" - $365.00, $135.00. **Hard plastic/cloth:** 18" - $125.00, $65.00; 23" - $165.00, $75.00.

Mary Hartline: 1952 on. **All hard plastic:** (See photo in Series 8, pg. 241.) 14" - $325.00, $95.00; 22": $550.00 up, $185.00. **White dress:** 14" - $425.00, $125.00. **8" in box:** $100.00. Doll only: $60.00. **Vinyl head:** 16" - $475.00.

Mary Jane or Betty Jane: All composition, sleep eyes, open mouth. (Allow more for flirty eyes.) Marked "Ideal 18": 18" - $285.00 up, $125.00. 21" - $365.00, $165.00.

Mia: 1970. Of Crissy family. 15" - $40.00, $15.00.

Mini Monsters: (Dracky, Franky, etc.) 8½" - $10.00, $6.00.

Miss Clairol (Glamour Misty): 1965. Marked "W-12-3." 12" - $30.00, $12.00.

Miss Curity: 1952 on. Hard plastic: 8" - $90.00; 14" - $285.00 up, $95.00. Composition: 21" - $465.00, $135.00.

Miss Ideal: 1961. Multi-jointed. (See photo in Series 10, pg. 247.) 25" - $365.00 up, $95.00; 28" - $400.00, $145.00.

Miss Revlon, Little Miss Revlon: 1956–on. Mint. 10½" - $90.00, $40.00; 17" - $175.00 up, $60.00. 20" - $225.00, $80.00. In box/trunk: (See photo in Series 9, pg. 247.) 20" - $465.00 up.

Mitzi: 1960. Teen. 12" - $185.00 up, $50.00.

Patti Playpal: 1960–on. 18" - $265.00 up, $70.00; 30" - $275.00, $90.00; 36" - $375.00, $125.00. **Black:** 30" - $325.00, $150.00; 36" - $400.00, $200.00. **1979–1982:** (See photo in Series 10, pg. 247.) 32" - $80.00. **Black:** 32" - $95.00. **Petite Patti Playpal:** 15" - $250.00 up.

Pebbles: 1963. Plastic/vinyl and all vinyl. 8" - $10.00, $6.00; 12" - $18.00, $7.00; 16" - $30.00, $10.00.

Penny Playpal: 1959. 32" - $145.00, $60.00.

Pepper: 1964. Freckles. Marked "Ideal - P9-3." 9" - $20.00, $10.00.

Pete: 1964. Freckles. Marked "Ideal - P8." 7½" - $25.00, $12.00.

Peter Playpal: 1961. 36-38" - $385.00, $165.00.

Pinocchio: 1938–1941. Composition/ wood. (See photo in Series 8, pg. 243.) Mint condition: 10" - $275.00; 12" - $325.00. Near mint: 10" - $175.00; 12" - $265.00, $95.00; 21" - $550.00, $225.00.

Pixie: 1967. Foam body. 16" - $15.00, $8.00.

Plassie: 1942. Composition and cloth body. 14" - $165.00, 22" - $300.00. **Magic Skin (latex) body:** 1950s. 14" - $90.00; 22" - $175.00.

Posie Walker: 1953–1956. Hard plastic with vinyl head. Jointed knees. Marked "Ideal VP-17." 17" - $75.00, $30.00.

Real Live Baby: 1965. Head bobs. 20" - $20.00, $10.00.

Sally-Sallykins: 1934. Composition/ cloth. Flirty eyes, two upper and lower teeth. 14" - $145.00, $65.00; 19" - $225.00, $85.00; 25" - $285.00, $125.00.

Samantha The Witch: 1965. Green eyes. Marked "M-12-E-2." (See photo in Series 9, pg. 248.) 12" - $125.00, $40.00.

Sandy McCall: See Betsy McCall section.

Sara Ann: 1952 on. Hard plastic. Marked "P-90." (See photo in Series 7, pg. 248.) Saran wig: 14" - $265.00 up, $90.00. Marked "P-93": 21" - $365.00 up, $115.00.

Saralee: 1950. Cloth/vinyl. **Black:** 18" - $275.00, $135.00.

Sara Stimson: (Little Miss Marker) 1980. Marked "1979." $18.00, $6.00.

Saucy Walker: 1951 on. 16" - $100.00, $40.00; 17" - $135.00, $60.00; 22" - $185.00, $80.00. **Black:** 18" - $225.00, $95.00.

17" "Posey" ("Posie") is a walker with jointed knees from 1954. Has vinyl head with sleep eyes and rooted hair. Hard plastic body is pin-jointed at hips. Marked "VP-17/Ideal Doll." $75.00 up. *Courtesy Kathy Tvrdik.*

This elusive 15" "Miss Revlon" is a perfect, mint in box, and never played with doll. Doll is a rare size and is wearing a rare dress. Color of rooted saran hair is also hard to find. This example would be above book value. *Courtesy Cris Johnson.*

This "Pattite Playpal" by Ideal is in mint condition and has original box (not shown). This is an unusual example. $650.00. *Courtesy Cris Johnson.*

Seven Dwarfs: Composition: 12" - $375.00 each; 16" - $465.00 each. Cloth body, composition head: 16" - $565.00 each; 18–20" - $650.00 each. Puppet: Cloth/composition. Pull string operates mouth. 20" - $375.00.

Shirley Temple: See that section.

Snoozie: 1933. Composition/cloth. Molded hair, sleep eyes, open yawning mouth. Marked "B Lipfert." 13" - $150.00, $50.00; 16" - $265.00, $125.00; 20" - $350.00, $135.00.

Snow White: 1937 on. All composition with black wig. Has sleep and/or flirty eyes. On marked Shirley Temple body. (See photo in Series 10, pg. 248.) 12" - $465.00, $185.00; 18" - $600.00, $250.00. **Molded hair:** 1939. Eyes painted to side. 14" - $185.00, $75.00; 18" - $365.00,

$115.00. **All cloth:** Oil cloth with mask face. (See photo in Series 10, pg. 248.) Clean: 16" - $325.00. Mint in box: $475.00.

Sparkle Plenty: 1947. Hard plastic and vinyl. 15" - $100.00, $30.00. **Magic Skin (latex):** 15" - $95.00, $30.00.

Suzy Playpal: 1960–1961. Chubby vinyl body and limbs. Marked "Ideal O.E.B. 24-3." 24" - $85.00, $30.00.

Tabitha: 1966. Cloth/vinyl. Eyes painted to side. Marked "Tat-14-H-62" or "82." 15" - $35.00, $18.00.

Tara: 1976. Black doll with growing hair. 16" - $42.00, $18.00.

Tammy: 1962. 12" - $45.00, $18.00. **Black:** Rare. Marked "BS-12-Ideal." $250.00. Grown-up: 1965. 12" - $40.00, $18.00. Black: $65.00. Sun Tan: $20.00, $10.00.

22" all hard plastic "Saucy Walker" with sleep, flirty eyes and open mouth. In mint condition and all original with box. A beautiful example of this doll. Usually $185.00, but due to condition, this example is $275.00 up. *Courtesy Chris McWilliams.*

Very cute 16" "Saucy Walker" with sleep eyes and open mouth. She is a pin-hipped walker. Completely original. In mint condition and never played with. Usually $100.00, but due to condition, this example is $185.00. *Courtesy Ciny Young.*

Tammy's mom: 1963. Eyes to side. Marked: "Ideal W-18-L." 12" - $45.00, $22.00.

Ted: 1963. Tammy's brother. Molded hair. Marked "Ideal B-12-U-2." (See photo in Series 9, pg. 249.) 12½" - $45.00, $25.00.

Thumbelina: 1962 on. **Kissing:** 10½" - $15.00, $6.00. **Tearful:** 15" - $20.00, $10.00. **Wake Up:** 17" - $40.00, $15.00. **Black:** 10½" - $40.00, $15.00.

Tickletoes: 1930s. Composition/cloth. 15" - $165.00, $90.00; 21" - $250.00, $125.00. **Magic Skin:** 1948. Hard plastic head. 15" - $50.00, $10.00.

Tiffany Taylor: 1973. Top of head swivels to change hair color. 19" - $28.00, $10.00. **Black:** 19" - $35.00, $18.00.

Tippy or Timmy Tumbles: 16" - $15.00, $10.00. **Black:** $20.00, $12.00.

Toni: 1949–on. (Allow more for mint in box.) 14" P-90: 14" - $275.00 up, $75.00. P-91: 15" - $300.00 up, $100.00. P-92: 17–18" - $385.00 up, $125.00. P-93: 21" - $465.00 up, $135.00. P-94: 23" - $550.00 up, $225.00. Walker: $325.00 up, $85.00.

Tressy: Of Crissy family. 17½" - $40.00, $15.00. Black: $50.00, $20.00.

Trilby: 1940s. (See photo in Series 9, pg. 251.) Composition: Mint and original. 15" - $235.00. **Three-faced baby:** 1951. Cloth/vinyl. 20" - $50.00, $20.00.

Tubsy: 1966. Plastic/vinyl. Battery operated. 18" - $20.00, $8.00.

Tuesday Taylor: 1977. 11½" - $20.00, $10.00.

A very beautiful 20" all hard plastic "Toni" with nylon wig and original outfit. Marked "P-93." This example - $565.00.
Courtesy Jeannie Nespoli.

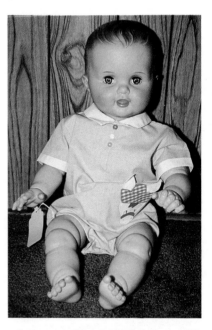

14" all vinyl "Wonder Baby" from 1960–1961 with chubby modeling, deeply molded hair, sleep eyes, open/closed smiling mouth, and molded tongue. During these same years, this doll was made with jointed knees and called "Wonderkins." Marked "Ideal Doll 2B-24-3." Original - $40.00; redressed - $20.00. *Courtesy Jeannie Mauldin.*

Uneeda Kid: 1914–1919. Looks like Schoenhut doll. Cloth body, composition head/limbs. Bent right arm. Painted eyes and hair. Yellow rain slicker and hat. Molded-on black boots. (See photo in Series 9, pg. 251.) 16" - $465.00, $165.00; 24" - $700.00, $250.00.

Upsy Dazy: 1972. Foam body. Stands on head. 15" - $15.00, $6.00.

Velvet: 1970–1971. Of Crissy family. 15" - $40.00, $15.00. **Black:** $60.00, $25.00. Look-a-round: $45.00, $15.00. Talking: $40.00, $15.00. Moving: $35.00, $10.00. Beauty Braider: 1973. $35.00, $10.00. Swirly Daisies: 1974. $35.00, $10.00.

Wingy: Hard plastic body, vinyl head. From Dick Tracy comics. (See photo in Series 8, pg. 247.) 14" - $165.00 up, $60.00.

JOLLY TOYS INC.

14" "Dixie-Pixie" is a cute character doll made of all vinyl with sleep eyes/lashes, impish smile, and rooted hair in original set. Marked "Jolly Toys 1966" on head. $15.00.

14½" "Christy" is made of all heavy vinyl with sleep eyes and lashes. Dress may be original. Marked "Jolly Toys Inc./1965" on head. $15.00. *Courtesy Phyllis Kates.*

38" all original "Dance Me, Hilda Doll" from 1955 was made by Juro to represent Arthur Murray Dance Studios. All cloth doll has plastic mask face with yarn hair and painted features. Has wide straps on bottom of feet for child to slip onto their own feet to dance with doll. In mint and unplayed with condition. This condition - $185.00. *Courtesy Jeannie Nespoli.*

30" "Mortimer Snerd" ventriloquist doll made of plastic and cloth. Mouth movable by pull strings in back of head. Made by Juro Novelty Co. and was first on the market in this suit in 1968. $60.00. *Courtesy Kathy Tvrdik.*

K & H

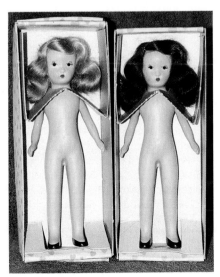

7½" Kerr & Heniz painted bisque dolls that are jointed at shoulders only. The doll came either nude or in child's dress and was called "Peg of My Heart." Original boxes have pink hearts printed on them. Nude in box - $40.00 each. *Courtesy Gloria Anderson.*

These 4" painted bisque dolls are marked with the initials of Kerr & Heinz. They were made at the Santa Clara Tile Company during the 1940s. Each doll has a one-piece body and head with painted features. These are mint in box with high chair. Baby in box - $45.00 each. *Courtesy Glorya Woods.*

All original Kerr & Heinz nun made of painted bisque with painted features. Jointed at shoulders only. Marked "K&H." $30.00. *Courtesy Kathy Tvrdik.*

KENNER

First prices are for mint condition dolls; second prices are for played with, dirty or missing clothing and accessories.

Baby Bundles: 16" - $18.00, $8.00. Black: $20.00, $10.00.

Baby Yawnie: 1974. Cloth/vinyl. 15" - $15.00, $6.00.

Big Foot: All rigid vinyl. (See photo in Series 7, pg. 253.) 13" - $12.00, $5.00.

Bionic Woman: 12" - $20.00, $8.00.

Butch Cassidy or Sundance Kid: 4" - $30.00, $10.00 each.

Blythe: 1972. Pull string to change the color of eyes. (See photo in Series 9, pg. 254.) 11½" - $35.00, $12.00.

Charlie Chaplin: 1973. All cloth with walking mechanism. 14" - $85.00, $30.00.

Cover Girls: 1978. 12½" dolls with bendable elbows and knees. **Dana: Black** doll. $55.00, $15.00. **Darci:** Blonde hair. $45.00, $15.00. **Erica:** Auburn hair. A few also had brunette or red hair. Add $10.00 extra for these colors. (See photo in Series 10, pg. 252.) $85.00, $15.00.

Crumpet: 1970. Plastic/vinyl. 18" - $27.00, $9.00.

Dusty: 12" - $15.00, $6.00.

Gabbigale: 1972. 18" - $30.00, $10.00. **Black**: $40.00, $15.00.

Garden Gals: 1972. Hand bent to hold watering can. 6½" - $8.00, $3.00.

Hardy Boys: 1978. Shaun Cassidy and Parker Stevenson. 12" - $25.00, $10.00.

International Velvet: 1976. Tatum O'Neill. 11½" - $20.00, $12.00.

Jenny Jones and Baby: 1973. All vinyl. 9" Jenny and 2½" baby. $10.00, $3.00. Set - $20.00, $9.00.

Oscar Goldman: 13" - $30.00, $10.00.

Six Million Dollar Man: Lee Majors. 13" - $25.00, $10.00.

Skye: Black doll. 12" - $20.00, $8.00.

Star Wars: 1974–1978. Large size figures. **R2-D2:** 7½" - $175.00 up, $50.00. **C-3PO:** 12" - $175.00 up, $50.00. **Darth Vader:** 15" - $185.00 up, $25.00. **Boba Fett:** 13" - $275.00 up, $50.00. **Jawa:** 8½" - $80.00, $20.00. **IG-88:** 15" - $400.00 up, $70.00. **Stormtrooper:** 12" - $225.00 up, $50.00. Leia: 11½" - $165.00 up, $30.00. **Han Solo:** 12" - $165.00, $30.00. **Luke Skywalker:** 13½" - $200.00, $22.00. **Chewbacca:** 15" - $145.00 up, $35.00. **Obi Wan Kenobi:** 12" - $200.00, $50.00. **Yoda:** 9" - $85.00 up. **Star Wars characters, MIB:** Sealed box. Any of above - $550.00 up.

Strawberry Shortcake: 1980s. 4½–5". Each - $10.00 up. **Sleep eyes:** Each - $35.00. **Sour Grapes, etc.:** 9" characters. $16.00. Mint in box: 4½–5". Each - $22.00. **Purple Pie Man:** $16.00.

Steve Scout: 1974. 9" - $18.00, $7.00. **Bob Scout: Black.** $20.00, $9.00.

Sweet Cookie: 1972. 18" - $28.00, $10.00.

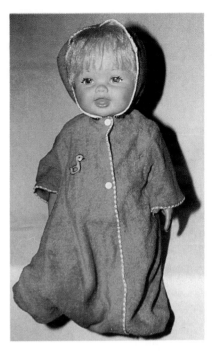

17" "Baby Won't Let Go" is made of plastic and vinyl with painted features and rooted hair. Doll's hands will curl when arms are lifted. Marked "4046 Taiwan K002 G.M.F.I. 1977-93" on head and "G.M.F.I. 1977 Kenner Prod." on back. $18.00. *Courtesy Kathy Tvrdik.*

12" "Dr. Hugo" vinyl and cloth hand puppet came with disguise kit. This puppet is being sold as Yul Brenner figure and collectors should be aware that this is not a personality item. Marked " M.F.G.I./1975" on head and on front "1975 General Mills Fun Group by its division Kenner Products. Made in Hong Kong." $25.00. *Courtesy Jeannie Mauldin.*

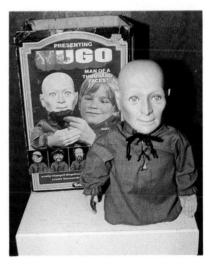

First prices are for mint condition dolls; second prices are for dolls played with, crazed or cracked, dirty, soiled or not original.

Bisque Kewpies: See Antique Kewpie section.

All composition: Jointed shoulder only. 9" - $150.00, $65.00; 12" - $245.00, $90.00; 14" - $295.00, $95.00. Jointed hips, neck and shoulder: 9" - $200.00, $85.00; 14" - $350.00, $125.00. **Black:** 12" - $425.00.

Talcum powder container: 7–8" - $185.00.

Celluloid: (See photo in Series 8, pg. 253.) 2½" - $40.00; 5" - $80.00; 9" - $135.00; 12" - $225.00, 20" - $465.00. **Black:** 5" - $165.00.

Chalk or plaster Kewpies: See Antique section.

Bean bag body: Must be clean. 10" - $40.00, $12.00.

All cloth: See Antique section.

Cloth body: Vinyl head and limbs. 16" - $165.00, $90.00. Composition head: 12" - $200.00; 16" - $345.00.

Kewpie Gal: With molded hair and ribbon. 8" - $30.00, $15.00.

Hard plastic: 1950s. One-piece body and head. 8" - $115.00, $25.00; 12" - $175.00, $80.00; 16" - $250.00, $100.00. Fully jointed at shoulder, neck and hips: 12–13" - $425.00, $180.00; 16" - $525.00, $250.00.

Ragsy: 1964. Vinyl with one-piece molded-on clothes with heart on chest. 8" - $35.00, $15.00. Without heart: 1971. 8" - $15.00, $8.00.

Thinker: 1971. One-piece vinyl. Sitting down. 4" - $15.00, $6.00.

Kewpie, vinyl: Hinge jointed: (Miss Peep body) 16" - $200.00, $85.00. **Jointed at shoulder only:** 9" - $35.00, $8.00; 12" - $55.00, $15.00; 14" - $65.00, $25.00. **Jointed at neck, shoulders and hips:** 9" - $70.00, $20.00; 12" - $125.00, $40.00; 14" - $165.00,

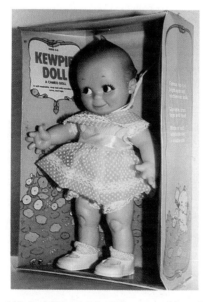

11" vinyl "Kewpie" from Cameo molds and made by Amsco. Clothing on the Amsco dolls as very good. $25.00. *Courtesy Glorya Woods.*

13" "Kewpie Baby" is made in one piece with all vinyl stuffed body and limbs and set glass eyes. Doll has been re-dressed. From the 1950s. Marked "Cameo." $135.00. *Courtesy Glorya Woods.*

$40.00; 27" - $250.00, $150.00. **No joints:** 9" - $20.00, $8.00; 12" - $35.00, $10.00; 14" - $50.00, $15.00. **Black:** 9" - $45.00, $10.00; 12" - $65.00, $20.00; 14" - $110.00, $35.00. **Bean bag type body:** 1970s. Vinyl head. 10" - $30.00, $10.00.

Ward's Anniversary: 1972. 8" - $50.00, $15.00.

All cloth: Made by Kreuger. All one-piece: Including clothing. 12" - $200.00, $85.00; 16" - $285.00, $90.00; 20" - $385.00, $165.00. Removable dress and bonnet:

12" - $250.00, $80.00; 16" - $365.00, $125.00; 20" - $525.00, $175.00; 25" - $950.00, $300.00.

Kewpie Baby: 1960s. With hinged joints. 15" - $200.00, $85.00; 18" - $245.00, $90.00.

Kewpie Baby: One-piece stuffed body and limbs. 15" - $200.00, $80.00; 18" - $275.00, $65.00.

Plush: 1960s. Usually red body with vinyl face mask. Made by Knickerbocker. 6" - $35.00, $15.00; 10" - $50.00, $20.00.

This looks exactly like a Klumpe and is a copy made in Japan. The quality of the clothing and accessories are not as good as the Klumpes made in Spain. The majority of the Japanese heads are made of a painted composition type material. Paper sticker tag marked "Made in Japan." This same style doll can also be made in Spain and will be tagged "Spain." $50.00.

First prices are for mint condition dolls; second prices are for dolls played with, crazed or cracked, dirty, soiled or not original.

Alexander: Comic character from "Blondie." All composition, painted hair and features. 9" - $400.00 up, $185.00.

Bozo Clown: 14" - $20.00; 24" - $55.00.

Cinderella: With two heads – one is sad; the other with tiara. 16" - $18.00.

Cloth: All early cloth dolls look like Madame Alexander or Averill dolls.

Stitched fingers, free-standing thumb, seam down middle of leg, long lashes, mohair wig. 23" - $450.00 up.

Clown: Cloth. 17" - $22.00.

Composition child: 1938–on. Bent right arm at elbow. 15" - $250.00 up; 20" - $350.00 up.

Daddy Warbucks: 1982. 7" - $15.00, $8.00.

Dagwood: Composition, painted hair and features. 14" - $625.00, $250.00.

Disney: 1930s. Donald Duck, Mickey Mouse, etc. All cloth. $400.00 up, $150.00.

20" all composition doll made for Knickerbacker by Horsman Doll Co. Has sleep glassene eyes with dark eyeshadow, open mouth, and human hair wig. Right arm bent at elbow is a typical Knickerbacker design. Wearing Juliet style dress. Ca. 1944–1946. $350.00 up. *Courtesy Pat Graff.*

15" "Sleeping Beauty" by Knickerbocker. Made of all composition with human hair wig and sleep eyes. Original. $500.00. *Courtesy June Schultz.*

Flintstones: 6" - $9.00 each; 17" - $40.00 each.

Jiminy Cricket: All composition. 10" - $385.00, $185.00.

Kewpie: See Kewpie section.

Little House on the Prairie: 1978. 12" - $20.00 each.

Little Orphan Annie: 1982. 6" - $15.00, $6.00.

Mickey and Minnie Mouse: 1930–1940s. Composition and cloth: 18" - $1,000.00 up. All composition: 16" - $550.00 up.

Miss Hannigan: 7" - $18.00, $8.00.

Molly: 5½" - $10.00, $6.00.

Pinocchio: All plush and cloth: 13" - $225.00 up. All composition: 13" - $275.00 up.

Punjab: 7" - $18.00, $7.00.

Scarecrow: Made of cloth. 23½" - $375.00 up.

Seven Dwarfs: 10" all composition. Each - $265.00 up. All cloth: 14" - $250.00 each.

Sleeping Beauty: 1939. All composition. Bent right arm. 15" - $425.00 up; 18" - $485.00.

Snow White: 1937. All composition. Bent right arm. Black wig. (See photo in Series 10, pg. 257.) 15" - $425.00 up; 20" - $485.00 up. Molded hair and ribbon: 13" - $350.00. All cloth: 16" - $400.00.

Soupy Sales: 1966. Vinyl and cloth. Non-removeable clothes. 13" - $135.00.

Two-headed dolls: 1960s. Vinyl face masks – one crying, one smiling. 12" - $16.00.

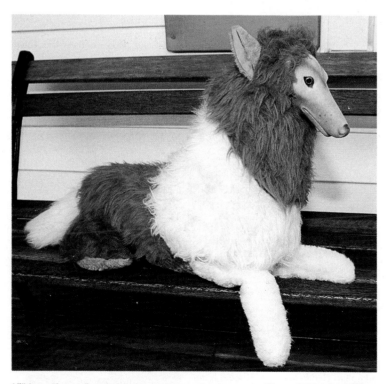

15" long "Lassie" with felt face and mouth, glass eyes. Tagged "Knickerbocker. Lassie. 1965." $85.00 up. *Courtesy Jeannie Mauldin.*

New versions of Lenci dolls were introduced in 1978 and used the old molds and styling for faces and clothings. The quality of these new Lenci dolls equals the older versions. The new doll is numbered on the back of its heads and comes with a certificate. Each were limited to 999 editions worldwide. The two middle fingers are sewn together until 1982 when Lenci began sewing all the fingers together on most models.

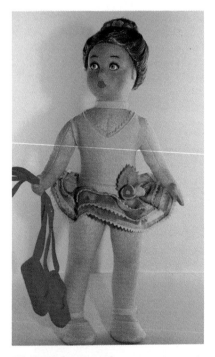

20" Lenci boy named "Bubi" from 1983 shown with 17" "Bienchila" made by Anili in the 1980s. Anili is a member of the Lenci family but makes dolls without using the Lenci name. Like Lenci, her dolls are all felt, but eyes are painted differently and they have individual fingers. Clothes are made of organdy and felt. 20" - $400.00; 17" - $465.00. *Courtesy of Glorya Woods.*

13" "Moira" was made to commemorate the International Convention of Original Doll Artists and Antique Collectors in 1984. The theme of the convention was "The Red Ballet Slippers." Marked on head "AZ-610." Tagged "Lenci Torino/New York Paris London." $385.00.

18" pouty "Glenda" from 1980s. Has crimp pleated collar. Hands are sewn to hold jump rope. Marked "B1250" and tagged "905582." $425.00. *Courtesy Glorya Woods.*

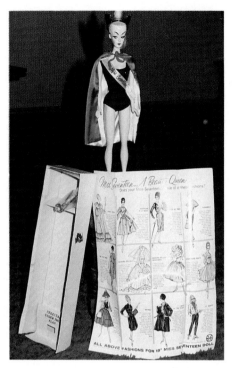

17" all plastic "Miss Seventeen" with inset skull cap and painted features. Original with original stand. Doll marked "US Patent 2925784/British Patent 804566/Made in Hong Kong." Box marked "Louis Marx & Co. 1961." $300.00 up. *Courtesy Margaret Mandel.*

16" "First Love" made of all vinyl with swivel waist, rooted hair, and sleep eyes/lashes. Original. Marked "Made in USA & Italy/1979 Louis Marx & Co." $45.00. *Courtesy Kathy Tvrdik.*

First prices are for mint condition dolls; second prices are for dolls that have been played with, are dirty, soiled, not original and/or do not have accessories. Except for Barbie family dolls, these prices are for mint dolls.

Allan: Bendable legs: 12" - $200.00. Straight legs: $125.00. Dressed boxed doll: $600.00 up.

Baby First Step: 1964. 18" - $20.00, $10.00. Talking: $25.00, $10.00.

Baby Go Bye Bye: 1968. 12" - $10.00, $6.00.

Baby's Hungry: 1966. 17" - $20.00, $10.00.

Baby Love Light: 1970. Battery operated. 16" - $15.00, $8.00.

Baby Pataburp: 13" - $20.00, $10.00.

Baby Play-A-Lot: 1971. 16" - $15.00, $8.00.

Baby Say 'n See: 1965. 17" - $15.00, $8.00.

Baby Secret: 1965. 18" - $25.00, $10.00.

Baby Small Talk: 1967. 11" - $10.00, $7.00. **Cinderella:** $15.00, $8.00. **Black:** $20.00, $8.00.

Baby Tenderlove: 1969. **Newborn:** 13" - $10.00, $4.00. **Talking:** 1969. 16" - $15.00, $8.00. **Living:** 1970. 20" - $20.00. **Molded hair piece:** 1972. (See photo in Series 10, pg. 258.) 11½" - $30.00. **Brother:** 1972. Sexed. 13" - $35.00.

Baby Teenie Talk: 1965. 17" - $20.00, $9.00.

Baby Walk 'n Play: 1968. 11" - $10.00, $6.00.

Baby Walk 'n See: 18" - $15.00, $10.00.

Barbie: See that section.

Bozo: 18" - $25.00, $12.00.

Brad: 1971. Bend knees. $150.00. Talking: 1970. $150.00.

Bucky Love Notes: 1974. Press body parts for tunes. 12" - $15.00.

Buffy with Mrs. Beasley: 1967. Character from TV show "Family Affair." 6" - $65.00, $30.00; 10" - $165.00, $35.00.

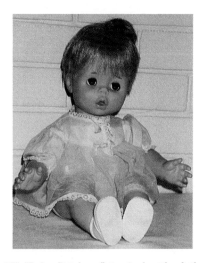

17" "Baby Pataburp" is vinyl with cloth body. Has rooted hair and open/closed mouth. When placed over shoulder and patted on back, she will burp. Original - $20.00 up. *Courtesy Pat Graff.*

18" "Baby Secret" is a pull string talker that whispers as her mouth moves. Made of cloth over foam body with vinyl head, gauntlet hands, painted features, and rooted hair. In mint condition and unplayed with. $25.00 up, but in this condition - $125.00 up. *Courtesy Susan Girardot.*

Capt. Lazer: 1967. (See photo in Series 9, pg. 259.) 12½" - $300.00 up, $75.00.

Cara: 1975. Black doll. **Free Movin':** $20.00. **Ballerina:** $28.00. **Quick Curl:** $20.00.

Casey: 1975. Packaged in baggie: 11½" - $50.00. **Twist 'n Turn:** $225.00 up.

Casper The Ghost: 1964: 16" - $25.00, $8.00. 1971: 5" - $10.00, $5.00.

Charlie's Angels: 1978. Marked "1966." 11½" - $15.00, $6.00.

Charmin' Chatty: 1961. 25" - $125.00, $45.00.

Chatty Brother, Tiny: 1963. 15" - $25.00, $8.00. **Baby:** 1962. $20.00, $8.00. **Black:** $135.00, $70.00.

Chatty Cathy: 1962 on. 20" - $95.00 up, $45.00. **Brunette:** Brown eyes. $125.00 up, $50.00. **Black:** $600.00 up, $300.00.

Cheerleader: 1965. 13" - $15.00, $8.00.

Cheerful Tearful: 1965. (See photo in Series 10, pg. 259.) 13" - $15.00, $6.00. **Tiny:** 1966. 6½" - $15.00, $6.00.

Chris: 1967–1968. 6" - $150.00.

Christie: 1968. Black doll. 11½" - $95.00 up. **Talking:** 1969. $185.00 up.

6½" "Buffy & Mrs. Beasley" dolls made by Mattel. "Buffy" is all vinyl with body made in one piece with limbs. Uses same body as "Tutti" and "Todd." Has painted features. "Mrs. Beasley" has a vinyl head with cloth body and limbs. Both dolls have rooted hair, and both are all original. $85.00 up. *Courtesy Pat Graff.*

10" "Buffy and Mrs. Beasley" from 1967. "Buffy" is vinyl with painted features and freckles. Wearing original dress. "Mrs. Beasley" is cloth and missing her little glasses. (The televsion show, *Family Affair,* ran from 1966 to 1971. Anissa Jones played the character "Buffy.") $165.00 up. *Courtesy Kathy Tvrdik.*

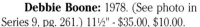

Super Star: 1976. $70.00 up. **Kissing:** 1979. $40.00. **Golden Dream:** 1980. $40.00. **Live Action:** $160.00. **Beauty Secrets:** $30.00. **Fashion Photo:** $60.00. **Pink & Pretty:** $60.00. **Supersize:** $100.00. **Twist 'n Turn:** $200.00.

Curtis: Free Movin': 1976. $55.00.

Cynthia: 1971. 20" - $40.00, $15.00.

Dancerina: 1968. (See photo in Series 11, pg. 245.) 24" - $45.00, $15.00. **Black:** $65.00, $25.00. **Tiny:** Not battery operated. 16" - $30.00, $10.00. **Black:** $45.00, $20.00. **Teeny:** 12" - $25.00.

Debbie Boone: 1978. (See photo in Series 9, pg. 261.) 11½" - $35.00, $10.00.

Dick Van Dyke: 25" - $85.00, $40.00.

Donny Osmond: 1978. Marked "1968." 12" - $30.00, $10.00.

Drowsy: 1966. Pull string talker. 15" - $15.00, $5.00.

Dr. Doolittle: 1967. Talker. Cloth/vinyl: 22½" - $50.00, $20.00. All vinyl: 6" - $20.00, $5.00.

Fluff: 9" - $145.00.

Francie: 1966. (See photo in Series 8, pg. 265.) 11½" - $150.00 up. No bangs:

7½" "Gorgeous Creatures" doll with Mae West style body with molded-on underclothes. Had different animal heads. Made in 1979 only. Marked "Mattel Inc. 1979 Phillipines." $18.00. *Courtesy Kathy Tvrdik.*

10" "Jimmy Osmond," the younger brother of Donnie and Marie Osmond, with molded hair and painted features. Right elbow bent and hand cupped to hold microphone. Made in 1979. $40.00 *Courtesy Kathy Tvrdik.*

$900.00 up. **Black:** 1967. $950.00 up. **Twist n' Turn:** 1967. $350.00. **Quick Curl:** 1973. $75.00. **Malibu:** 1978. $40.00. **Grow Pretty Hair:** $165.00. **Hair Happening:** $250.00. **Packed in baggie:** $125.00. **Bendable legs:** $265.00. **Straight legs:** $165.00. **Busy:** $300.00.

Grandma Beans: 11" - $10.00, $3.00.

Gorgeous Creatures: 1979. Mae West style body with animal heads. Each - $18.00, $7.00.

Grizzly Adams: 1971. (See photo in Series 10, pg. 260.) 10" - $35.00, $10.00.

Guardian Goddesses: 1979. 11½", mint condition. Each - $165.00 up, $50.00.

Herman Munster: 16" - $25.00, $12.00.

Heros In Action: 1975. Set of 14. Marked "Mattel Hong Kong. Pat Pending." 3" - $65.00 each.

Hi Dottie: 1969. 17" - $25.00, $10.00.

Honey Hill Bunch: 1975. Set of six. 6" - $8.00, $2.00.

How West Was Won: 1971. 10" - $50.00. Indians: 10" - $60.00.

Hush Lil Baby: 15" - $15.00, $7.00.

Jamie, Walking: 1969. With dog. (See photo in Series 8, pg. 265.) 11½" - $325.00 up.

Jimmy Osmond: 1979. 10" - $40.00, $10.00.

Julia: 1969. 11½" nurse from TV show by same name. One-piece uniform: $125.00 up. Two-piece uniform: $150.00. Talking: $150.00 up.

Kelley: 11½". **Quick Curl:** $80.00. **Yellowstone:** $185.00.

Ken: Bendable legs: $350.00. **Busy:** $175.00. **Busy Talking:** $150.00. **Crystal:** $30.00. **Day To Night:** $30.00. **Dream Date:** $40.00. **Dressed boxed doll:** $250.00 up. **Fashion Jeans:** $25.00. **Flocked hair:** $165.00. **Free Movin':** $45.00. **Gold Metal Skier:** $90.00. **Horse Lovin':** $40.00. **Live Action:** $125.00. **Live Action On Stage:** $150.00. **Mod Hair:** $165.00. **Now Look:** $65.00. **Paint-**ed hair, straight legs: $125.00. **Super Star:** $85.00. **Talking:** $150.00. **Walk Lively:** $85.00. **Prince:** $350.00. **King Arthur:** $300.00. **Arabian Nights:** $350.00.

Kiddles: 1966–on. Doll only: Mint condition. (Add $10.00 more for Black dolls.) $20.00 up. **With cars:** $40.00 up. **With planes:** $50.00 up. **In ice cream cones:** $20.00 up. **In jewelry:** $30.00 up. **In perfume bottles:** (See photo in Series 10, pg. 260.) $15.00 up. **In bottles:** $25.00 up. **With lollipops:** $25.00. **With cup and saucer:** $125.00 up. **Storybooks:** With accessories. $150.00. **Mint in box -** $225.00 up. **Baby Beddle:** In carriage. $150.00 up. **Peter Paniddle:** Made one year. With accessories. $165.00. Mint in box - $265.00. **Santa:** Complete - $145.00 up. **Tinkerbelle:** Mint - $90.00. Fair condition - $25.00. **Animals:** $30.00 up. **Circus necklace:** 1968. $75.00 each.

Kitty O'Neill: 1978. (See photo in Series 9, pg. 261.) 11½" - $20.00, $8.00.

17" "Hi Dottie" with phones. She is a pull string talker made of all rigid vinyl with painted features. Made by Mattel. $30.00.
Courtesy Shirley's Doll House.

Lazer Fire: From Brave Starr set, 1986. (See photo in Series 10, pg. 261.) $18.00.

Lil Big Guy: 13" - $18.00, $9.00.

Midge: 1963. Has freckles. 11½" - $135.00 up. 1965: **Bendable legs:** $500.00 up. **Dressed boxed doll:** $500.00 up. **Wig wardrobe:** $275.00.

21" "Scooby Doo" made by Mattel in 1964. Has cloth body, vinyl head with long rooted hair, and almond-shaped eyes. The eye makeup is typical of the early 1960s styles, including the very light lip color. She is important because she exhibits a part of history from the 1960s. Original - $55.00.

11½" "Midge," Barbie's best friend, shown in an original outfit, minus shoes. Has red rooted hair and painted features including freckles. Dolls from 1963 to 1964 have straight legs. After 1965, they had bendable knees. In played with condition - $135.00 up. *Courtesy Kathy Tvrdik.*

Miss America: Walk Lively: White gown. 1972. $185.00. **Quick Curl:** 1974. $160.00.

Mother Goose: 20" - $20.00, $8.00.

Mrs. Beasley: Talking. 16" - $50.00, $20.00.

Peachy & Puppets: 1972. 17" - $15.00, $7.00.

P.J.: 11½" - $65.00 up. **Talking:** $145.00 up. **Live Action:** 1971. $100.00. **Gold Medal:** 1975. $85.00. **Deluxe Quick Curl:** 1976. $75.00. **Free Movin':** $50.00. **Twist 'N Turn:** $250.00. **Fashion Photo:** $40.00. **Sweet Roses:** $40.00.

Randy Reader: 1967. 19" - $35.00, $16.00.

Real Sister: 14" - $15.00, $8.00.

Ricky: 1965. Has red hair and freckles. (See photo in Series 9, pg. 262.) $145.00 up.

Rockers: 1986–1987. Dana, Dee-Dee, Derek, Diva. 11½" - $40.00 each.

Rockflowers: 1970. 6½" - $20.00, $8.00.

Rose Bud Babies: 6½" - $10.00 up, $6.00.

Saucy: 1972. (See photo in Series 11, pg. 247.) 15" - $40.00. Black: $55.00.

Scooby Doo: 1964. Vinyl and cloth girl. Mint: 21" - $55.00, $30.00.

Shaun: 1979. 12" - $30.00, $12.00.

Shogun Warrior: 23½". All plastic. Battery operated. Each - $275.00 up.

Shrinking Violet: 1962. Pull string talker, features move. Cloth, yarn hair. (See photo in Series 7, pg. 265.) 15" - $35.00 up, $10.00.

Singing Chatty: 1964. Pull string. 17" - $25.00, $8.00.

Sister Belle: 1961. 17" - $25.00, $10.00.

Skediddles: 1966–on. (See photo in Series 9, pg. 264.) 4" - $40.00 up. Disney: $80.00 up. Cherry Blossom: 1967. $80.00. Cartoon: $55.00.

Skipper: 1963. (See photo in Series 9, pg. 263.) $125.00 up. **Growing up:** 1976. $75.00 up. **Living:** $60.00. **Funtime:** 1967. Bend knees. $80.00. **Pose 'N Play:** 1970. $60.00; **Super Teen:** 1979. $40.00. **Western:** 1981. $40.00. **Malibu:** $25.00. **Bendable legs:** $250.00. **Dressed boxed doll:** $325.00 up. **Quick Curl:** $70.00. **Twist 'N Turn:** $185.00.

Skooter: 1964. Freckles. (See photo in Series 9, pg. 263.) $135.00 up. **Bendable legs:** $300.00.

Small Talk: 1967. Pull string. 11" - $15.00, $6.00. **Sister:** 1967. 10" - $15.00, $6.00. **Cinderella:** 1968. $20.00, $8.00.

Small Walk, Sister: 1967. 11½" - $20.00, $8.00.

Spectra and friends: 1986. Vinyl and see-through plastic. $45.00 each.

Stacey: Talking: $285.00. **Twist 'N Turn:** 1968. $285.00. **Short turned-up hair:** $300.00.

Star Spangled Dolls: 1976. Uses Sunshine Family adults. Marked "1973." Regina & Richard Stanton, Southern Belle, New England Girl, Pioneer Daughter, etc. Each - $40.00.

Steffie: 1972. Busy or Talking: $195.00 up. Walk Lively: $175.00.

Swingy: 20" - $25.00, $10.00.

Tatters: 10" - $35.00, $10.00.

Teachy Keen: 1966. 17" - $30.00, $10.00.

Teeners: 4" - $35.00, $12.00.

Tiff: Pose 'N Play: $265.00.

Timey Tell: (Chatty Tell) 1964, watch attached to wrist. 17" - $25.00, $8.00.

Tinkerbelle: 19" - $20.00, $8.00.

16" battery-operated "Tippy Toes" is made of plastic and vinyl and shown here riding her original tricycle. She also had a horse to ride. Made in 1967. Doll - $15.00; tricycle - $15.00. *Courtesy Kathy Tvrdik.*

Tippy Toes: 1967. 16" - $15.00, $8.00. Tricycle or horse: $15.00, $4.00.

Truly Scrumptious: 11½", original. $250.00 up. **Straight legs:** $400.00 up. **Talking:** 1968. $350.00 up.

Tutti: 1965. 6" - $165.00 up. Packaged sets: **Cookin' Goodies:** $325.00. **Me and My Dog:** $425.00. **Melody in Pink:** $375.00. **Night, Night:** $225.00. **Sundae Treat:** $475.00. **Swing-A-Ling:** $365.00. **Walkin' My Dolly:** $300.00.

Todd: 1965. 6" - $165.00 up. Sundae Treat: $475.00.

Twiggy: 1967. 11½" - $265.00 up.

Upsy-Downsy: 1969. 3" - $25.00, $6.00.

Welcome Back Kotter: 1973. 9" figures. Each - $10.00–30.00.

Zython: 1977. Has glow-in-dark head. Enemy in "Space 1999" series. $95.00, $30.00.

Figures from the TV series *Welcome Back Kotter* that ran from 1975 to 1979. Left to right: "Freddie 'Boom Boom' Washington" (Lawrence Hilton Jacobs), "Arnold Horshack" (Ron Palillo), and "Gabe Kotter" (Gabriel Kaplan.) All are original. Washington - $15.00; Horshack - $20.00; Kotter - $30.00. *Courtesy Don Tvrdik.*

MEGO

First prices are for mint condition dolls; second prices are for ones that are dirty or not original. For full Mego listing, see *Modern Collector Dolls, Volume 4,* page 172–177.

Action Jackson: 1971–1972. Beard and no beard. 8" - $35.00 up. Outfits: $15.00 up.

Batman: 1974. Action figure. 8" - $15.00, $7.00. Arch enemy set: Four figures in series. 8" - $15.00, $7.00.

Camelot: 1974. Five figures in series. 8" - $70.00, $12.00.

Captain & Tenille: 1977. Designer accidently left Toni Tenille's ears off when making mold sculpture. She is the only 12½" doll without ears. 12½" - $20.00, $12.00.

Cher: 12" - $40.00 up, $8.00. Dressed in Indian outfit: $60.00, $20.00.

CHiPs: Ponch and Jon, 1977. 8" - $10.00, $5.00.

Diana Ross: 12½" - $40.00 up, $10.00.

Dinah Mite: 1973. 7½" - $10.00, $5.00. Black: $15.00, $7.00.

Farrah Fawcett: 12½" - $35.00.

Haddie Mod: 1971. Teen type. 11½" - $15.00, $6.00.

Happy Days Set: 1974. (See photo in Series 9, pg. 267.) **Fonzie:** $20.00, $8.00. Others: $15.00, $6.00.

Jaclyn Smith: 1975. 12½" - $30.00, $12.00.

Joe Namath: 1971. 12" - $50.00, $18.00.

KISS: 1978. Four figures in series. 12½" - $75.00, $25.00.

Kojack: 1977–1978. (See photo in Series 9, pg. 267.) 9" - $20.00, $8.00.

Lainie: 1973. Jointed waist. Battery operated. 19" - $35.00, $18.00.

Laverne & Shirley: 1977. 11½" - $20.00, $8.00. **Lenny & Squiggy:** 12" - $25.00, $9.00.

One Million BC: 1974–1975. Five figures in series. 8" - $20.00, $8.00.

Our Gang set: 1975. Six figures in series. Mickey: 5" - $18.00, $9.00. Others: 5" - $14.00, $7.00.

Planet of Apes: 1974–1975. Five figures in series. 8" - $25.00, $10.00.

Pirates: 1971. Four figures in series. 8" - $60.00, $35.00.

Robin Hood set: 1971. Four figures in series) 8" - $30.00–65.00.

Soldiers: 8" - $18.00 up, $9.00.

Sonny: Smiling in 1977; not smiling in 1976. 12" - $45.00 up, $12.00.

Starsky or Hutch: 1975. 8" - $20.00, $10.00. **Captain or Huggy Bear:** $25.00,

12½" "Captain & Tenille" dolls from 1977. Marked "Moonlight & Magnolias, Inc./Made in Hong Kong." Of all the 12½" Mego dolls, "Tenille" is the only one without ears. The sculpturer accidentally left them off. Each - $20.00. *Courtesy David Spurgeon.*

$10.00. **Chopper:** $30.00, $15.00. **Car:** Red and white. $95.00 up.

Star Trek set: 1974–1975. Six figures in series. (See photo in Series 8, pg. 269, Series 10, pg. 263.) 8" - $20.00–30.00.

Star Trek aliens: 1974–1977. Mugatu, Romulan, Talos, Andorian, Cheron, The Gorn, The Keeper, and Neptunian. 8" - $45.00–85.00.

Super Women: 1973. Four action figures in series. 8" - $20.00, $8.00.

Suzanne Somers: 1975. 12½" - $25.00, $10.00.

Waltons: 1975. Six figures in series. 8" - $18.00, $7.00.

Wild West set: 1974. **Cochise:** $45.00. **Sitting Bull:** $35.00. **Wild Bill Hickok:** $35.00. **Buffalo Bill:** $35.00. **Wyatt Earp:** $40.00. **Davy Crockett:** $50.00.

Wonder Woman: (Lynda Carter) 1975. 12½" - $20.00, $9.00.

World's Greatest Super Heros: 1974–1975. Eight figures in series. (See photo in Series 9, pg. 267.) 8" - $15.00, $7.00. **Arch Enemy set:** Eight figures in series. 8" - $22.00, $9.00.

World's Greatest Super Heros: 1975–1976. Second set with six figures in series.) **Isis:** 1977. 8" - $14.00. **Teen Titans:** 6" "Aqua Lad," "Kid Flash," "Wonder Girl," or "Speedy." Each - $10.00, $5.00.

Wizard of Oz: 1974. (See photo in Series 5, pg. 224.) Dorothy: $20.00, $10.00. Munchkins: $20.00, $10.00. Wizard: $30.00, $15.00. Others: $10.00–7.00. 15" size: Cloth/vinyl. Each - $165.00, $50.00.

12½" "Decker" from *Star Trek: The Motion Picture.* One of the rarest large size figures. Marked "PPC" on neck and "Mego Corp. 1975/Made in Hong Kong" on back. $195.00. *Courtesy Phyllis Kates.*

9" "Talosian" from the first TV pilot for *Star Trek.* Made of vinyl and jointed at shoulders only. Has excellent modeling. Marked "Paramount Pictures 1991." $45.00. *Courtesy Phyllis Kates.*

Left: 12½" "Diana Ross" from 1977. Marked "Motown Record Corp./ Made in Hong Kong." Right: 12½" "Suzanne Sommers" who played "Chrissy" on TV's Three's Company in 1978. Marked "Three's Company/ Made in Hong Kong." Both were made by Mego Corp. Diana - $40.00; Suzanne - $25.00. *Courtesy David Spurgeon.*

14" "Michelle" from TV series *Full House* is a pull string talker. Has cloth body with vinyl head and limbs, painted eyes, open/closed mouth, and upper and lower teeth. Marked "1991 Meritus, Ind., Inc." $45.00. *Courtesy Jeannie Mauldin.*

Mollye Goldman of International Doll Company and Hollywood Cinema Fashions of Philadephia, PA made dolls from cloth, composition, hard plastic, and plastic/vinyl. Only the vinyl dolls will be marked with her name. The rest usually have paper wrist tag. Mollye purchased unmarked dolls from many other firms and dressed them to be sold under her name. She designed clothes for many other makers, including Eegee (Goldberger), Horsman, and Ideal.

First prices are for mint condition dolls; second prices are for crazed, cracked, dirty dolls or ones without original clothes.

Airline doll: Hard plastic. 14" - $250.00 up, $95.00; 18" - $325.00 up, $125.00; 23" - $400.00 up, $125.00.

Babies, composition: 15" - $165.00, $70.00; 21" - $245.00, $100.00. Composition/ cloth: 18" - $95.00 up, $40.00. **Toddler:** All composition. 15" - $225.00, $70.00; 21" - $285.00, $85.00.

Babies, hard plastic: 14" - $90.00, $45.00; 20" - $145.00, $70.00. Hard plastic/ cloth: 17" - $85.00, $35.00; 23" - $135.00, $65.00.

Babies, vinyl: 8½" - $20.00, $9.00; 12" - $25.00, $10.00; 15" - $40.00, $15.00.

Cloth children: 15" - $145.00, $40.00; 18" - $160.00, $50.00; 24" - $225.00, $75.00; 29" - $300.00, $100.00.

Cloth young ladies: In dresses or gowns. 16" - $175.00, $70.00; 21" - $250.00, $90.00.

Cloth: Princess, Thief of Bagdad. Blue painted eyes with Oriental look. In harem outfit. $300.00 up.

Cloth: Internationals. 13" - $90.00, $35.00; 15" - $135.00 up, $60.00; 27" - $300.00 up, $90.00.

18" all hard plastic bride from the early 1950s. Has floss wig, sleep eyes/lashes, and fully painted mouth. Doll is strung and was made by American Character using "Sweet Sue" doll with full lips. Dressed and marketed by Mollye International. $375.00 up. *Courtesy Kris Lundquist.*

Composition children: 15" - $175.00, $65.00; 18" - $250.00, $95.00.

Composition young ladies: In dress: 16" - $350.00, $95.00; 21" - $500.00, $125.00. Gowns: 16" - $450.00; 21" - $575.00.

Jeanette McDonald: Composition. (See photo in Series 1, pg. 225.) 27" - $950.00 up, $300.00.

Thief of Bagdad dolls: Composition. (See entire set in Series 1, pg. 223.) 14" - $500.00, $145.00; 19" - $600.00, $125.00. **Sultan:** 19" - $700.00, $250.00. **Sabu:** 15" - $650.00, $250.00. **Princess:** Head covered by cloth veil, no wig. Long gown. Mint condition. $625.00.

Vinyl children: 8" - $20.00, $8.00; 11" - $35.00, $10.00; 16" - $60.00, $15.00.

Hard plastic young ladies: 17" - $300.00 up, $100.00; 20" - $400.00 up, $125.00; 25" - $450.00, $135.00.

Little Women: Vinyl. 9" - $40.00, $18.00.

Lone Ranger or Tonto: Hard plastic/ latex. 22" - $150.00, $60.00.

Raggedy Ann or Andy, Beloved Belindy: See Raggedy Ann section.

20" all hard plastic character faced child dressed and marketed by Mollye. Has mohair wig, sleep eyes, and original wrist tag. A cute example that is in mint condition and unplayed with. $400.00. *Courtesy Kris Lundquist.*

This beautiful 18" bride was dressed by Mollye International. She was made of all hard plastic with sleep eyes and open mouth. Mollye did not make dolls but purchased them nude from other companies, then dressed and marketed them. This doll was most likely made by Roberta Dolls or Horsman. $325.00 up. *Courtesy Jeannie Nespoli.*

Monica Dolls were made from late 1930s and early 1940s. They were all composition with painted eyes. Human hair rooted into composition heads made these doll very unique.

11" dolls: Mint condition: $285.00. Played with: $150.00.

15" dolls: Mint condition: $500.00. Played with: $325.00.

18" dolls: Mint condition: $750.00. Played with: $400.00.

21" dolls: Mint condition: $975.00. Played with: $475.00.

17" all composition "Monica" with human hair embedded into the composition head. Features are painted. Original - $750.00. *Courtesy Pat Graff.*

NABER KIDS

Three things stand out in a Naber Kid – humor, happiness, and a smile of tolerance. Even if that Naber Kid disagrees or looks different than his or her Naber, the smile shows that no intolerant words are spoken.

Harold Naber began carving wooden figures of Eskimos while living and working mainly as a bush pilot for 22 years in Alaska. The early works of this very talented man are highly prized by those who own them. (See photo in Series 9, pg. 271.) Many of his early carvings were done for his Native American friends and some were sold in Naber's own store

called Fur Traders in Anchorage. This was during the 1970s. "Jake," "Molli," and "Max" were his first production dolls to be introduced in 1984.

In 1988, Prescott, Arizona, became the site of a new doll factory. The "Arizona finish" was perfected and used mostly for "Peter" and "Darina." This finish shows very little wood grain and has a satin surface. On January 1, 1994, production of Naber Kids ended, but he has continued to make his Wild Wood Babies.

There is a newspaper called Naber Kids News Report put out by the company that can be ordered from Naber Kids

News Report Subscription Service, 8915 S. Suncoast Blvd., Homosassa, FL 32646. Included in the newspaper are dolls for sale or trade, plus new information, list of dealers, and list of places Mr. Naber will be visiting.

Retirement dates:

See text concerning Arizona Finish.

06-21-87: Molli - $3,500.00 up.
01-16-88: Jake - $1,100.00 up.
05-04-88: Max - $950.00 up.
03-04-89: Ashley - $700.00 up.
(See photo in Series 9, pg. 271.)
07-15-89: Milli - $500.00.
09-28-90: Maurice - $650.00 up.
03-04-90: Maxine - $375.00 up.
19-28-90: Sissi, regular issue - $750.00.
Arizona finish, 39 made - $800.00.
11-30-90: Frieda, regular issue - $625.00.
Arizona finish, 28 made - $700.00.
12-17-90: Walter, regular issue - $500.00 up.
Arizona finish, 67 made - $650.00.
05-03-91: Peter , regular issue - $425.00.
Arizona finish, 325 made - $550.00.

05-03-91: Pam, regular issue - $425.00.
Arizona finish, 289 made - $500.00.
07-28-91: Darina, regular issue - $425.00.
Arizona finish, 224 made - $500.00.
03-09-92: Henry * - $650.00 up.
*as Pirate - $750.00 up.
*as Diver (yellow) - $1,200.00 up.
*as Diver (green) - $1,200.00 up.
*as Diver (beige) - $1,350.00 up.
(See photo in Series 10, pg. 269.)
*as Farmer - $700.00 up.
*as Carpenter - $700.00 up.
(See photo in Series 9, pg. 271.)
04-13-92: Sami and Samantha,
each - $325.00.
04-20-92: Freddi - $325.00.
06-28-92: Amy - $300.00.
12-08-92: Heide ** - $425.00.
** Without braces - $625.00 up.
05-27-93: Mishi - $265.00.
05-27-93: Hoey - $265.00.
07-25-93: Paula - $275.00.
(See photo in Series 10, pg. 268.)
11-07-93: Willi - $265.00.
11-13-93: Eric - $275.00.
(See photo in Series 10, pg. 268.)

This group of Wild Wood Babies all look natural with brich canoe and paddle. All have extra joints at the elbows and knees. Left to right: Erwin, Clarence, Gisela, Dolli, Felix, and Herbert. Each limited to 1,001. Each - $135.00 up. *Courtesy Naber Gestalt Corp.*

11-21-93: Denise - $265.00.
12-31-93: Elsi - $275.00.
12-31-93: Benni - $275.00.
(See photo in Series 10, pg. 269.)
12-31-93: Posi - $225.00.
12-31-94: Sarah, Joseph, Josi, Tony,
Juanita, Christina, Rita Witch,
Richie & Flink, Marcie.
$265.00 each.

Early handcarved figures: Marked on head or foot. $900.00 up.

Later 1980s figures: Marked, plus tag. $300.00 up.

Specialty dressed: Alpine, Baker, Cheerleader, Detective, Doctor, Eskimo, Farmer, Gangster, Golfer, Indian, Nurse, Pilot, Waitress. Each - $250.00 up.

Specials: Phil Racer - $650.00. Sarah and Benni Indians (20 sets made) - $700.00 up.

Micki and Iko: Produced in 1993. Only 101 made of each. 38" - $1,900.00 up.

Wildwood Babies: Horace: 1994. 339 made. $135.00. Ivan: 1994. 653 made. $145.00. Kilo: 1994. Sleeping Eskimo baby. 669 made. $135.00.

14" "Rufus" is a Naber Baby made of wooden resin with painted features and red burlap hair. Pulls his uncle's wood wagon. Less than 600 made. $128.00 up. *Photo courtesy of Harold Naber.*

The painted bisque Nancy Ann dolls will be marked "Storybook Doll U.S.A." and the hard plastic dolls marked "Storybook Doll U.S.A. Trademark Reg." The only identity as to who the doll represents is a paper tag around the wrist with the doll's name on it. The boxes are marked with the name, but many of these dolls are found in the wrong box. Dolls were made 1937–1948.

First prices are for mint condition dolls; second prices are for played with, dirty dolls.

Bisque: 1937–1948. Marked "Made in Japan 1146 or 1148," "Japan," or "America." 5" - $100.00 up, $40.00; 7½–8" - $150.00 up, $40.00. Black: 5" - $165.00 up, $50.00; 7½–8" - $200.00 up, $70.00. With white painted socks: $250.00 up.

Bisque with jointed hips (slim): 5" - $150.00 up, $45.00; 7½–8" - $200.00 up, $60.00. **With pudgy tummy:** Molded bangs. $225.00 up.

Bisque with swivel neck: 5" - $150.00 up, $40.00; 7½–8" - $175.00 up, $50.00. Swivel neck, jointed hips: 5" - $150.00, $40.00; 7½–8" - $185.00, $50.00.

Bisque bent leg baby: 1936–1948. Marked "88 or 87 Made in Japan" on gold sticker. (See photo in Series 8, pg. 275.) 3½–4½" - $165.00 up, $45.00. In sunburst box - $400.00.

Plastic: (1948–1953) 5" - $50.00 up, $18.00; 7½–8" - $55.00, $18.00. Black: $75.00, $25.00.

Plastic bent leg baby: 1948–1953. 3½–4½" - $65.00 up, $18.00.

Judy Ann: Name incised on back. Molded socks and bangs. 5" - $350.00 up, $125.00.

Audrey Ann: Heavy doll with toddler legs. Marked "Nancy Ann Storybook 12." 6" - $950.00 up, $250.00.

Lori Ann or Little Miss Nancy Ann: All vinyl. (See photo in Series 4, pg. 17.) 7½" - $175.00.

Margie Ann: Bisque. In school dress. 6" - $165.00 up, $40.00.

5" "Cinderella" with jointed legs, pudgy tummy, and molded bangs. All original including silver slippers. $250.00. *Courtesy Susan Girardot.*

"Muffie" in unidentified outfit. She is a walker and has painted eyebrows. $185.00 up. *Courtesy Peggy Millhouse.*

Debbie: Hard plastic in school dress. Name on wrist tag/box. 10" - $165.00 up, $45.00.

Debbie: Hard plastic, vinyl head. 10" - $100.00, $40.00.

Debbie: 1950s. All hard plastic walker in dressy Sunday dress. 10½" - $150.00, $45.00. Same, vinyl head: $85.00, $25.00.

Teen type (Margie Ann): All vinyl. Also called "Miss Nancy Ann." Marked "Nancy Ann." 10½" - $165.00 up, $45.00.

Muffie: All hard plastic. (If strung, add $50.00.) **Walker:** $185.00 up. Dress: 8" - $185.00 up, $80.00. Ballgown: $250.00 up, $90.00. Riding Habit: $200.00 up, $85.00. **Poodle:** Made by Steiff. (See photo in Series 9, pg. 273.) $85.00. In box - $125.00 up.

Muffie: Hard plastic. Reintroduced doll. 8" - $75.00 up, $15.00.

Nancy Ann Fairytale Dolls: All vinyl. From 1960s. In box: 5½" - $45.00. Doll only: $25.00.

Nancy Ann Style Show Doll: All hard plastic. All dressed in ballgowns. Unmarked. (See photo in Series 8, pg. 273.) 17–18" - $600.00 up, $225.00.

18" Nancy Ann Style Show Doll as "Demure Miss." She is a strung hard plastic doll. Stock #1903 is on silver wrist booklet. Original retail price was $19.95. Has original polka dot box. $600.00 up. *Courtesy Susan Girardot.*

Left: 8" all vinyl "Little Miss Nancy Ann" with sleep eyes, molded lashes, and high heel feet. Clothes tagged "Styled by Nancy Ann." Center: 10½" all vinyl "Miss Nancy Ann" with sleep eyes, molded lashes, and high heel feet. Marked "Nancy Ann" on head. Clothes tagged "Styled by Nancy Ann." Right: 8" all hard plastic "Muffie." All dolls are original. 8" dolls - $185.00 each; 10½" - $165.00 up. *Courtesy Maureen Fukushima.*

12" "Hello, Dolly! Doll" (Carol Channing) is mint in box. Fully jointed doll is vinyl with rooted hair and painted features. Dressed in original costume. Made by Nasco Dolls, N.Y. in 1961. In box - $100.00 up. *Courtesy Ann Wencel.*

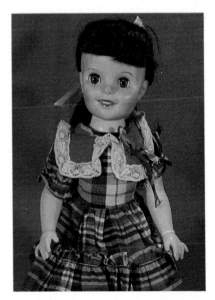

20" "Linda Williams" doll that is all original. She was marketed in 12 different outfits. Made by Natural Doll Company in 1963. Also came in 14" and 30" sizes. 14" - $35.00; 20" - $50.00; 30" - $125.00.

14" "Dolly Ann" using the "Linda Williams" mold, and it can be seen where the mold marks were marked out. Has red rooted hair, freckles, and green sleep eyes. Made by Natural Dolls in 1963. $48.00. *Courtesy Lani Pettit.*

OLD COTTAGE DOLLS

Dollmaker Mrs. M.E. Fleischmann registered the name "Old Cottage Dolls" in 1948. Early dolls have heads made of a material similar to composition. Heads changed to hard plastic in the 1950s. The faces are hand painted. Bodies and limbs are made of stuffed flesh-colored cloth. They are jointed with armiture wires to allow the the necks and limbs to move. A quick way to identity them is by the unusual formation of large feet which allow the doll to stand. Both dolls and clothes are of excellent quality.

Child: 5" - $140.00–165.00; 9" - $175.00–185.00; 12" - $200.00–300.00.

Baby: 5" - $85.00 up.

Child with animal: 9" - $195.00.

Internationals: Such as Wales and Scotland. 9" - $90.00.

9" all felt "Court Man and Woman" with composition heads, mohair wigs, painted features, and removable clothes. Jointed at shoulders and hips. Marked "Old Cottage/Doll/Hand made in Great Britain." Each - $175.00. *Courtesy Marge Meisinger.*

9" "Victorian Girl in Party Dress" was made in the late 1940s. Has composition type head with painted features and felt body with mitt-style hands. Doll alone - $175.00. In box - $200.00. *Courtesy Pat Graff.*

9" "Girl With Hoop" is an Old Cottage Doll from the late 1980s. Has hand-painted features. Mint condition and still tied to her box. Doll only - $175.00. In box - $200.00. *Courtesy Peggy Millhouse.*

P.M. SALES

19" "Robin Hood" is made of lightweight plastic with vinyl head, rooted hair, and heavy face make-up. Shirt is snapped at neck, but the rest of the clothes are stapled onto doll. Head marked "AE7/P.M. Sales Inc./1966." Original - $35.00. *Courtesy Marie Ernst.*

PARIS DOLL CO.

25" "Rita Walking Doll" is made of all hard plastic with sleep eyes, open mouth, and saran wig. Wearing original clothes. Her original price of $19.95 was considered expensive at the time. Made by the Paris Doll Co. in the 1940s to 1991. This doll was also called "Peggy." Played with - $145.00. *Courtesy Kathy Tvrdik.*

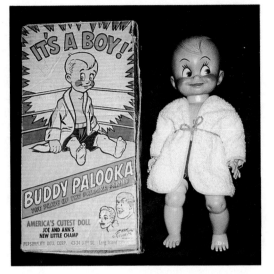

16" original "Buddy Palooka" with vinyl head, large painted eyes, and molded hair. Has one-piece body and limbs. Marked "H. Fisher. Made by Personality Doll Corp. 1953" or can be unmarked. Mint in box - $600.00. Played with - $200.00. *Courtesy Chris McWilliams.*

PLATED MOULDS

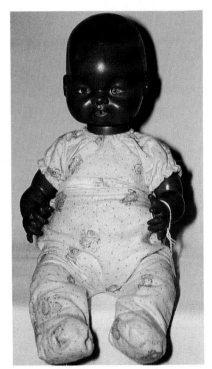

19" "Just Born Baby" marked "Plated Moulds Co." Was reintroduced in 1984 at the cost of $16.99 by unknown maker. The original mold was made by Plated Moulds in 1961 and will be marked with the year. Old models have cloth body and vinyl arms and legs. This one has plastic body. Marked "1961" - $35.00. Plastic body - $18.00. *Courtesy Kathy Tvrdik.*

Designed by Johnny B. Gruelle in 1915, these dolls are still being made. Early dolls will be marked "Patented Sept. 7, 1915." All cloth, brown yarn hair, tin or wooden button eyes, thin nose, painted lashes far below eyes and no white outline around eyes. Some are jointed by having knees or elbows sewn. Features of early dolls are painted on cloth.

Gruelle had three children. Marcella, the only girl, suffered a long illness caused by a contaminated smallpox vaccine. During her illness, Marcella found a rag doll with worn off features, and her father painted a face on it. The doll was named by combining two James Whitcomb Riley poem titles, "The Raggedy Man" and "Orphan Annie." Gruelle made up stories about the doll's adventures to entertain his sick child. Marcella died at the age of 12.

First prices are for mint condition dolls; second prices are for played with, dirty, missing clothes or redressed dolls.

Marked with patent date: 15–16" - $1,300.00 up; 23–24" - $2,000.00 up; 30" - $2,800.00. Worn and dirty: 15–16" - $650.00; 23–24" - $850.00; 30" - $950.00. Pair in mint condition: 16" - $3,400.00 up. **Camel with the Wrinkled Knees:** See Volland Co. at end of this section. $1,300.00.

Applause dolls: 1981. Will have tag sewn in seam. 12" - $28.00; 17" - $45.00; 25" - $65.00; 36" - $150.00 up.

Averill, Georgene: Red yarn hair, painted features. Sewn cloth label in side seam of body. (See photo in Series 9, pg. 275.) **Mid-1930s:** 15" - $325.00, $150.00 up; 19" - $525.00; 22" - $675.00. With black outlined nose: 18" - $475.00. Worn - $300.00. **1940s:** 18" - $265.00. **1950s:** 18" - $185.00. **1960–1963:** 15" - $100.00; 18" - $145.00. **Asleep/Awake:** Early doll. 13–14" - $625.00 up. Worn and dirty: $175.00 up.

Black outlined nose: Any early maker. Pair - $800.00.

Beloved Belindy: Knickerbocker. 1965. Black doll. (See photo in Series 7,

18" "Raggedy Ann & Andy" made by Volland. She has patent number and wooden heart. Both may be wearing original clothes. $1,700.00 each. *Courtesy Ellen Dodge.*

23" "Raggedy Ann & Andy" by Georgene Averill that are in mint condition with paper heart tags. "Raggedy Ann" has maroon and gold legs and "Raggedy Andy" has blue and white. From 1940s. $325.00 each. *Courtesy Ellen Dodge.*

pg. 276.) 15" - $775.00 up, $400.00. **Volland Co.:** Smile mouth, two rows of teeth, button eyes. Red/white legs, red feet. (See photo in Series 8, pg. 278.) 13" - $1,900.00, $700.00; 15" - $2,200.00, $900.00. **Averill:** (See photo in Series 8, pg. 276; Series 9, pg. 277.) 15" - $1,300.00 up. **Mollye:** 15" - $1,400.00; 17" - $1,600.00. **Hallmark:** Black yarn hair, brown legs, printed features, red button nose. She looks more like a little girl doll than a "Beloved Belindy." Tagged "Hallmark Cards, Inc. by Bobbs-Merrill Co." $600.00 up.

Hasbro: 1983 to date. Under Playskool label. Still available.

Knickerbocker Toy Co.: 1963–1982. Printed features, red yarn hair. Tag sewn to seam. **1960s:** 8" - $65.00; 12" - $100.00; 16" - $150.00; 23–24" - $275.00; 30–36" - $350.00–525.00. **1970s:** 12" - $35.00; 16" - $75.00; 23–24" - $125.00; 30–36" - $200.00–300.00. **1980s:** 16" - $20.00; 23–25" - $50.00; 30–36" - $70.00–100.00. **Talking:** 1974. 12" - $40.00; 19" - $175.00. **Camel with the Wrinkled Knees:**

$165.00. **Asleep-Awake:** 18" - $300.00. Played with - $125.00. **Teaching:** One-piece undies with lacing. Dress and pinafore have buttons, zipper, and snaps to teach dressing skills. 1960s - $125.00; 1970s - $75.00; 1980s - $50.00.

Mollye Dolls: Red yarn hair, printed features, and heavy outlined nose. Lower lashes closer to eyes. Most will have multicolored socks and blue shoes. Will be marked in printed writing on front of torso "Raggedy Ann and Andy Doll/Manufactured by Mollye Doll Outfitters." First company to imprint solid red heart on chest. (See photo in Series 8, pg. 278; Series 9, pg. 275.) 15" - $650.00 up, $225.00; 22" - $950.00 up, $325.00. "Baby": 16" - $850.00.

Nasco/Hobbs-Merrill: 1973. Plastic/vinyl with rooted yarn hair. 24" - $145.00, $50.00.

Vinyl dolls: 8½" - $15.00, $4.00; 12" - $20.00, $8.00; 16" - $25.00, $10.00; 20" - $30.00, $15.00.

Volland Co.: 1920–1934. Lashes low on cheeks. Feet turn outward. Can have brown yarn hair. Some have oversized hands with free-standing thumbs. Long thin nose, lines low under eyes. Different mouth appearances are:

Body tagged "Johnny Gruelle's Own Raggedy Ann & Andy. Volland. 1918, 1920, 1925, 1926." (See photo in Series 8, pg. 277–278; Series 9, pg. 276.) 15" - $1,500.00 up; 18" - $1,700.00 up; 22" - $1,900.00 up; 24" - $2,200.00 up; 29" - $2,700.00 up.

Percy or Uncle Clem: Has center face seam, prominent nose. Red yarn hair and mustache. Red/white stripe socks and black shoes. Scots costume. 16–17" - $1,800.00 each.

8" and 24" "Raggedy Ann & Andy" made by Knickerbocker in 1970s. The little one has been well played with and most of the hair is gone. All are original. 8" - $65.00; 24" - $125.00 each.

18" "Asleep-Awake Raggedy Ann" made by Knickerbocker. In mint condition. $300.00.
Courtesy Ellen Dodge.

12" "Raggedy Ann" marionette with line controls made by Knickerbocker from 1963 to 1982. In mint condition and has never been played with. $85.00. *Courtesy Ellen Dodge.*

REMCO

First prices are for mint condition dolls; second prices are for played with, dirty or not original dolls.

Addams Family: 5½" - $18.00, $7.00.

Baby Crawlalong: 1967. 20" - $18.00, $9.00.

Baby Grow A Tooth: 1969. 14" - $20.00, $8.00. Black: $25.00, $10.00.

Baby Know It All: 1969. 17" - $18.00, $9.00.

Baby Laugh A Lot: 1970. (See photo in Series 7, pg. 277.) 16" - $15.00, $8.00. Black: $20.00, $12.00.

Baby Sad or Glad: 1966. 14" - $15.00, $9.00.

Baby Stroll-A-Long: 1966. 15" - $10.00, $7.00.

Dave Clark 5: 1964. 4½", each - $40.00, $15.00.

Heidi: 1965. (See photo in Series 9, pg. 279.) 5½" - $10.00, $4.00. **Herby:** 4½" - $14.00, $6.00. **Spunky:** Has glasses. 5½" - $16.00, $6.00. **Jan:** Oriental. 5½" - $15.00, $6.00.

Winking Heidi: 1968. $12.00, $6.00.

Jeannie, I Dream Of: 6" - $15.00, $6.00.

Jumpsy: 1970. (See photo in Series 7, pg. 277.) 14" - $15.00, $7.00. Black: $18.00, $9.00.

Laurie Partridge: 1973. 19" - $80.00, $35.00.

Lindalee: 1970. Cloth/vinyl. 10" - $20.00, $8.00.

19" "Laurie" doll from the TV show *The Partridge Family*. Based on character played by actress Susan Dey. Marked "1973/Remco Ind. Inc./Harrison N.J. Item No. 3461." $80.00. *Courtesy David Spurgeon.*

L.B.J.: 1964. Portrait. 5½" - $45.00, $16.00.

Littlechap Family: 1963. Set of four. Mint condition, no box. $350.00, $125.00. **Dr. John:** 14½" - $95.00, $35.00. **Lisa:** 13½" - $55.00, $20.00. **Libby:** 10½" - $45.00, $12.00. **Judy:** 12" - $55.00, $20.00. **Dr. John's office:** $300.00. **Family room:** $100.00 up. **Bedroom:** $100.00 up. **Clothes:** All clothes are tagged. **Dr. John's clothes:** Medical outfit - $60.00. Business suit - $45.00. Tuxedo - $65.00. Golf outfit - $30.00. **Lisa's clothes:** Evening ensemble - $85.00. Fur/suede coat - $45.00. **Libby's clothes:** 3-piece blazer set - $30.00. Jeans & sweater - $25.00. **Judy's clothes:** Football outfit - $45.00. Dance dress - $40.00.

Mimi: 1972–1973. Battery-operated singer. (See photo in Series 9, pg. 279.) 19" - $45.00, $18.00. Black: $50.00, $22.00.

Orphan Annie: 1967. Plastic/vinyl with disc eyes. 15" - $40.00, $15.00.

Sweet April: 1971. All vinyl baby. 5½" - $8.00, $2.00. Black: 5½" - $10.00, $4.00.

Tippy Tumbles: 1966. 16" - $15.00, $6.00.

Tumbling Tomboy: 1969. 16" - $15.00, $6.00.

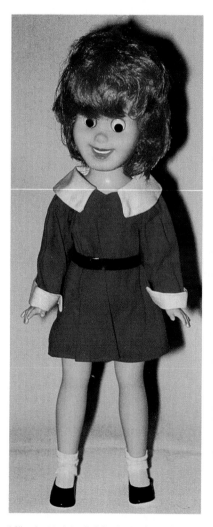

16" plastic/vinyl "Orphan Annie" with painted teeth and plastic disc eyes. Marked "Remco, Inc./Copyright 1967" on head. Original and in mint condition. $40.00. *Courtesy Kathy Tvrdik.*

The 8" "Sandra Sue" doll has a slim body and limbs. She is a walker, but the head does not turn as she walks. The doll and her clothes are of excellent quality and she was first made in the late 1940s and into the 1950s. A large wardrobe of clothing was available for the doll along with accessories and scaled furniture of the finest quality. She is unmarked except for a number under an arm or leg.

Prices are for excellent condition dolls.

Nude: Flat feet: $55.00. High heel feet: $65.00.

School/street dress: $95.00 up.

Dress, coat & hat: $135.00 up.

Ballgown: $165.00 up.

Sports clothes: Cheerleader, baseball, etc. $165.00 up. (Add $40.00 if in box.)

8" "Sandra Sue" is made of all hard plastic with neck, shoulder, and hip joints. Has slender limbs, sleep eyes, and flat feet with molded shoes. All original. $100.00 up. *Courtesy Peggy Pergande.*

A beautiful close-up of "Sandra Sue." Note molded eyelashes over eyes and painted eyelashes below. *Courtesy Peggy Millhouse.*

Flat footed "Sandra Sue" shown with original box and insert. All original and in mint condition. Doll only - $100.00 up. In box - $145.00 up. *Courtesy Maureen Fukushima.*

Three sets of tagged Russian cloth dolls that are all original. Large dolls have stockinette faces and the smaller ones have composition heads. Prices range from $65.00 to $185.00.
Courtesy Patricia Wood.

SASHA

Sasha dolls were manufactured by Trenton Toys, Ltd., Reddish, Stockport, England from 1965 to 1986, when they went out of business. The original designer of these dolls was Sasha Morgenthaler of Switzerland. All dolls are 16" tall and are made of all rigid vinyl with painted features. The only marks will be a wrist tag.

From 1963 to 1964 only, Sasha dolls were made by Gotz of Germany and marked on head "Sasha Serie" inside a circle along with three concentric circles.

Gotz girl or boy: 1960s. Marked inside circle. $1,000.00 up. Reintroduced by Gotz in 1995 - $300.00.

Boy or girl in box: $275.00. No box: $175.00 up.

Boy or girl in cylinder: $325.00 up.
Boy: "Gregor" - $185.00 up.
Girl: $175.00 up.
Black boy: "Caleb" - $275.00 up.

Black baby: $265.00 up.
Cora: #119 (Black) - $275.00 up; #111 (White) - $225.00 up.
White baby: $165.00 up.
Sexed baby: Pre-1979. $275.00 up.
Early dolls: Tube/sack packaging. Girl or boy. $325.00 each.
Limited edition dolls: Limited to 5,000. Incised #763. Dressed in navy velvet. 1981: $300.00. 1982: Pintucks dress. $325.00. 1983: Kiltie plaid. $350.00. 1985: "Prince Gregor." $375.00. 1986: "Princess." $1,250.00. 1986: Dressed in sari from India. $1,300.00 up.
Made by Morgenthaler: 1950s. Mint: 20" - $6,000.00 up. Fair: $2,900.00 up.

An original Sasha girl that came packaged in a round tube. The lid for the tube turns into stand for doll. Made in 1975. In mint condition - $325.00 up. *Courtesy Susan Girardot.*

All original Sasha boy who came packaged in window box. Made in 1975. In mint condition. $300.00 up. *Courtesy Susan Girardot.*

SHINDANA

12" "Baby Zuri" made of all vinyl with molded hair and painted features. (*Zuri* means "beautiful" in Swahili.) Marked "Shindana Toy/1972/Div. Operation Bootstraps, Inc." Original - $35.00. *Courtesy Gloria Anderson.*

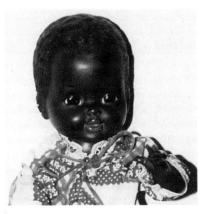

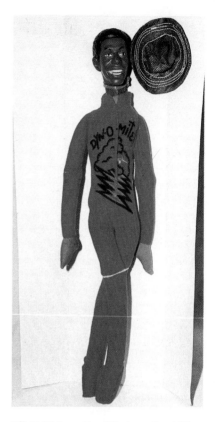

9½" "O.J. Simpson" full-action figure made by Shindana in 1976. This doll was made when he played for the Buffalo Bills football team, 1969–1977. He also played for the San Francisco 49ers from 1978 to 1979. $400.00–800.00. *Courtesy Phyllis Kates.*

15" "J.J." from the TV show *Good Times* and made by Shindana. Has vinyl head and cloth body. Hat is all that is removable. Character was played by Jimmy Walker. The show ran from 1974 to 1979. $40.00. *Courtesy Kathy Tvrdik.*

SHIRLEY TEMPLE

First prices are for *mint condition* dolls; second prices are for played with, dirty, cracked or crazed or not original dolls. Allow extra for special outfits such as "Little Colonel," "Cowgirl," "Bluebird," etc. (Allow 25% to 50% more for mint in box dolls. Price depends upon clothes.)

Marks:

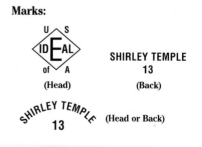

IDEAL
U S
of A
(Head)

SHIRLEY TEMPLE
13
(Back)

SHIRLEY TEMPLE
13
(Head or Back)

All **composition:** All composition child made from 1934 to late 1930s. Marked head and body or can be marked only on head or the body. **11"** - $850.00, $425.00. **11" cowgirl:** $800.00, $450.00. **13"** - $725.00, $425.00. **15–16"** - $825.00, $475.00. **17–18"** - $950.00, $400.00. **20"** - $1,000.00, $600.00. **22"** - $1,100.00, $800.00. **25"** - $1,300.00, $850.00. **25" cowgirl:** $1,500.00, $700.00. **27"** - $1,500.00, $700.00. **27" cowgirl:** $1,600.00, $700.00.

Vinyl of 1950s: Allow more for flirty eyes in 17" and 19" sizes. **12"** in box - $225.00. Mint, not in box - $175.00. Played with, dirty - $50.00. **15"** in box - $350.00. Mint, not in box - $285.00. Played with, dirty - $90.00. **17"** in box - $425.00. Mint, not in box - $350.00. Played with, dirty - $100.00. **19"** in box - $475.00. Mint, not in box - $425.00. Played with, dirty - $135.00. **36"** in box. (See photo in Series 9, pg. 283.) $1,900.00. Mint, not in box - $1,500.00. Played with, dirty - $750.00.

1972: Reissue from Montgomery Ward. Came in plain unmarked box. 17" in box: $225.00. Mint, not in box - $150.00; Dirty - $50.00.

1973: Has box with many pictures of Shirley on it. Doll in red polka dot dress. 16" in box - $175.00. Mint, no box - $135.00. Played with, dirty - $50.00.

1982–1983: Plastic/vinyl. Made by Ideal. (See photo in Series 9, pg. 284.) 8" - $35.00, 12" - $40.00.

1984: Marked "Dolls, Dreams & Love." Henry Garfinkle Co. 36" - $275.00.

Shirley display stand: Mechanical doll. $3,000.00 up. At organ: $3,800.00.

Left: 11" all composition "Shirley Temple" with hair in original set. Has celluloid over tin sleep eyes that are beginning to craze. $850.00 *Courtesy Kathy Riddick.* Right: 15" all composition "Shirley Temple" from 1935. Outfit is from the movie Curly Top. This is what a mint condition "Shirley Temple" should look like. $800.00 *Courtesy Glorya Woods.*

"Hawaiian": Marked Shirley Temple, but not meant to be a Shirley Temple. (See photo in Series 6, pg. 291.) 18" - $975.00, $425.00.

Japan: All painted bisque: Molded hair. 6" - $185.00. **Composition:** 7–8" - $250.00. **All celluloid:** 5" - $145.00; 8" - $225.00.

German: 1936. All composition, sleep eyes, open mouth smile. Marked "GB42." 16" - $650.00 up.

Mold #480, 510X: German. Sleep, flirty eyes. Open mouth. 13" - $600.00 up.

15" "Shirley Temple" baby with flirty eyes, open mouth, and two upper and lower teeth. Composition head with cloth body. Clothes are tagged. 18" "Mirama" from the movie *Hurricane* uses the "Shirley Temple" mold with mouth left uncut and eyes painted to the side. She is original. Baby - $1,100.00. "Mirama" - $975.00. *Courtesy Turn of Century Antiques.*

Composition babies: Open mouth with upper and lower teeth. Flirty, sleep eyes. Marked on head. 16" - $1,100.00, $650.00; 18" - $1,200.00, $700.00; 22" - $1,400.00, $800.00; 25" - $1,600.00, $900.00; 27" - $1,900.00, $1,000.00.

Look-alike dolls: Composition, with dimples. 16" - $200.00; 20" - $350.00; 27" - $600.00. Vinyl: 36" - $800.00.

Shirley Temple accessories: Script name pin: $25.00–35.00. Pin button: Old 1930s doll pin. $150.00; others - $15.00. Charm bracelet: 1930s. $265.00.

Boxed outfits: 1950s: $50.00 up. 1970s: $40.00 up.

Tagged 1930s dress: $150.00 up. **Purse with name:** $20.00–30.00.

Buggy: Made of wood. (See photo in Series 7, pg. 283.) 20" - $500.00 up; 26" - $425.00 up; 32" - $475.00 up; 34" - $525.00 up. Wicker: 26" - $550.00 up.

19" "Shirley Temple" is a very pretty example of all vinyl dolls from 1950s. Some have flirty eyes. This doll is in mint condtion and has never been played with. Marked "Ideal Doll/ST-19-1." $285.00 up. *Courtesy Carmen Holshoe.*

Trunk: No doll: $150.00 up. Gift set: 1950s. Doll and clothes. $475.00 up.

Statuette: Chalk in dancing dress. 7–8" - $200.00; 4½" - $145.00.

8" Japanese painted bisque "Shirley Temple" with painted-on shoes and socks. All original. Marked "Made in Japan/S 1224." $250.00. *Courtesy Jo Keelen.*

Four "Shirley Temple" style chalk carnival figures. Usually given to winner for throwing hoops or baseballs at stacked bottles. Each - $225.00. *Courtesy Pat Sparks.*

13" "Dinosaur Babyee" from the 1991 TV show *Dinosaurs*. He has cloth body with vinyl head and limbs. Made by Street Kids Corp. $35.00. *Courtesy Jeannie Mauldin.*

SUN RUBBER

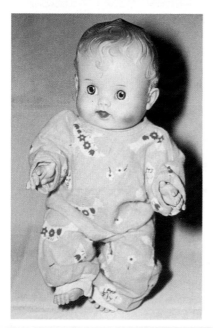

10" all vinyl "So Wee" with molded hair, inset eyes, and one-piece body and head. Ruth Newton was the designer of the doll. Marked "Sunbabe/So Wee/Ruth Newton/New York" on head and "Sun Rubber 1957" on back. Played with - $45.00. *Courtesy Kathy Tvrdik.*

First prices are for mint condition dolls, which could be higher due to the outfit on the doll. Second prices are for soiled, poor wig or not original.

Terri Lee: Composition: $365.00 up, $125.00. **Hard plastic:** Marked "Pat. Pend." $300.00 up, $125.00. **Majorette, cowgirl, etc:** $425.00 up. **In original box:** $450.00 up. Others: $265.00 up, $125.00. **Vinyl:** $225.00, $85.00. **Talking:** $425.00, $195.00. Mint in box: $600.00 up.

Extremely rare "Masquerade" costume for "Terri Lee." Mask replaced but of correct style. Mint condition - $450.00 up. *Courtesy Cyndie Matus.*

Jerri Lee: Hard plastic. Caracul wig. 16" - $300.00, $195.00. Mint in box: $550.00 up.

Tiny Terri Lee: 10" - $165.00, $65.00.

Tiny Jerri Lee: 10" - $185.00, $75.00.

Patti Jo, Bonnie Lou: Black dolls. (See photo in Series 8, pg. 285.) $600.00 up, $250.00.

Benjie: Black doll. (See photo in Series 8, pg. 285.) $600.00, $275.00.

Connie Lynn: 19" - $365.00 up, $150.00.

Gene Autry: 16" - $1,600.00 up, $700.00.

Very pretty "Bonnie Lou" using the "Terri Lee" doll. Her pleated skirt and jackets are a pale yellow color. Original - $600.00 up. *Courtesy Cyndie Matus.*

Linda Baby (Linda Lee): 10–12" - $165.00 up, $80.00.

So Sleepy: 9½" - $250.00 up, $80.00.

Clothes: Ballgown: $95.00 up. Riding habit: $95.00 up. Skater: $95.00 up. School dresses: $40.00 up. Coats: $30.00 up. Brownie uniform: $50.00 up.

Clothes for Jerri Lee: Two-piece pants suit: $125.00 up. Short pants suits: $125.00 up. Western shirt and jeans: $85.00 up.

Mary Jane: Plastic walker. Terri Lee look-alike with long molded eyelids. (See photo in Series 9, pg. 285.) 16" - $300.00 up.

Ginger Girl Scout: 8" - $145.00–165.00.

Monkey: Tony and Penelope. Made by Steiff. 8" - $145.00 each.

Poodle with Terri Lee blanket: Made by Steiff. 5½" long, 3" tall. $145.00.

16" "Gene Autry" is a very rare member of the "Terri Lee" family. Rodeo outfit tagged "Terri Lee" and made for "Jerri Lee" with pants having the Gene Autry signature stamp. $1,600.00 up. *Courtesy Cyndie Matus.*

16" all hard plastic "Terri and Jerri Lee" in wonderful mint condition. Both have painted features. He has pale blonde caracul wig. Dutch outfits include wooden shoes. These dolls have never been played with. Each - $425.00 up. *Courtesy Cyndie Matus.*

19" all hard plastic "Connie Lynn" with sleep eyes, hair lashes, and caracul wig. 10" all vinyl "Linda Baby" with painted eyes and molded hair. Both are all original and in mint condition. 19" - $365.00; 10" - $165.00. *Courtesy Susan Girardot.*

TROLLS

Trolls: 2½–3" - $12.00 up; 5" - $15.00–28.00; 7" - $32.00–45.00; 10" - $55.00; 12" - $65.00; 15" - $85.00 up.

Troll animals: Large size: cow - $75.00; donkey - $85.00; ape - $85.00; turtle - $60.00; giraffe - $80.00. Small size: cow - $25.00; donkey - $55.00; ape - $40.00; turtle - $40.00.

4½" Norfin angel troll made in 1986 and marked "Dam" on foot. $15.00. *Courtesy Gloria Anderson.*

UNEEDA

First prices are for mint condition dolls; second prices are for soiled, dirty or not original dolls.

Baby Dollikins: 1958. 21" - $40.00, $15.00.

Baby Trix: 1964. 16" - $25.00, $10.00.

Ballerina: Vinyl. 14" - $20.00, $8.00.

Blabby: 1962. $25.00, $10.00.

Bare Bottom Baby: (See photo in Series 7, pg. 289.) 12" - $15.00, $10.00.

Bob: 1963. 10½" - $20.00, $8.00.

Coquette: 1963. 16" - $25.00, $10.00. Black: 16" - $28.00.

Original "Blabby" is vinyl with oil cloth body and sleep eyes. Upper lip is over lower one. Mouth moves and talks baby talk when stomach is pressed. Marked "Uneeda Doll Co. Inc." in circle/"1962." Mint - $40.00 up. *Courtesy Jeannie Mauldin.*

Dollikins: 1957. (See photo in Series 9, pg. 288.) 8" - $25.00, $8.00; 11" - $30.00, $9.00; 19" - $45.00, $20.00.

Fairy Princess: 32" - $100.00, $35.00.

Freckles: 1960. 32" - $95.00, $30.00.

Freckles Marionette: 30" - $70.00, $35.00.

Grannykins: 1974. Painted-on half-glasses. 6" - $9.00, $3.00.

Lucky Lindy: (Charles Lindbergh) Composition. 14" - $425.00, $250.00.

Magic Meg, Miss Deb: 1971. Grow hair. 16" - $20.00, $10.00.

Pollyanna: 1960. 10½" - $25.00, $8.00; 17" - $45.00, $18.00; 31" - $100.00, $45.00.

Pri-Thilla: 1958. 12" - $15.00, $8.00.

Purty: 1961. Press stomach to make eyes squint. (See photo in Series 7, pg. 289.) 15" - $20.00, $12.00.

Rita Hayworth: 1948. Composition. 14" - $550.00, $200.00.

Serenade: 1962. Battery-operated singer. 21" - $45.00, $15.00.

15½" vinyl doll with high heels, green sleep eyes/lashes, and long rooted hair. Could possible be "Scarlett." Has unusual face. Marked on back "1968" in Roman numerals and "Made by Uneeda." All original and in mint condition. $22.00. *Courtesy Pat Graff.*

22" "Dew Drop" is made of good quality vinyl and is fully jointed. Head has rooted saran hair and is marked "Uneeda." Wears fleece snowsuit with bells. In mint condition and has never been played with. $45.00 up. *Courtesy Ciny Young.*

Suzette: 1959–1960, 1962. 10½" - $55.00, $30.00; 11½" - $60.00, $35.00. Sleep eyes: 11½" - $95.00, $45.00. **Blue Fairy:** (See photo in Series 9, pg. 288.) $70.00, $30.00.

Tiny Teens: 1957. 5" - $8.00.

Set of "Wee Three" dolls made of plastic and vinyl. The mother is a Madame Alexander "Cissy" look-alike and has high heel feet. Made by Uneeda and shown in original box. (See *Doll Values #10,* pg. 239 for another set accidently shown under Horsman, who owned original molds.) In mint condition - $95.00 up for set. *Courtesy Ciny Young.*

VOGUE

The last year Ginny dolls were made in America was 1969. Tonka purchased the Vogue name in 1973 and continued to make dolls. The dolls and clothes did not sell well though, due greatly to inferior designs and materials and poor manufacturing. In 1977, Tonka sold the Vogue rights to Lesney of England which made a tall slender Sasson Ginny for three years. During the first two production years, the Sasson Ginny had sleep eyes. The last issue had painted eyes. Although the Sasson Ginny did not look like the earlier Ginny versions, she was dressed and made better.

In 1983, Lesney sold its rights to the Meritus Corporation. With much work, Walter Reiling, owner of Meritus, made a public impact once more with Ginny. In 1986, Dakin purchased the Vogue rights and are the current manufacturer of Ginnys. Dolls manufactured now closely resemble the original 1950s rigid vinyl dolls. One person responsible for the "Ginny Renewal" through her wonderful clothes designs and calendars is Sue Nettlingham Roberts.

First prices are for mint condition dolls. Second prices are for dirty, crazed, or played with dolls, those with messed up wigs, or doll that are not original.

Baby Dear: 1960–1961. 12" - $55.00, $25.00; 17" - $90.00, $45.00. 1964: 12" - $35.00, $15.00. **Newborn:** 1960. Sleep eyes. $85.00.

Baby Dear One: 25" - $165.00, $80.00. **Baby Dear Two:** 27" - $200.00, $80.00.

Baby Wide Eyes: 1976. Very large brown sleep eyes. All vinyl. 16" - $35.00, $10.00.

Composition doll (Betty Ann, Mary Jane): Clothes tagged "Vogue." 12" - $265.00 up; 15" - $365.00 up.

Brickette: 1960. 22" - $60.00, $20.00. Reissued: 1979–1980. 18" - $35.00.

Ginny (Toodles): 1948–1949. **Composition** 7½–8" - $275.00–325.00, $80.00.

Ginny: 1950–1953. Hard plastic, strung, painted eyes. 8"- $285.00–350.00, $125.00. Outfits: $90.00 up.

Ginny: Hard plastic, sleep eyes, painted lashes and strung. 8" - $350.00 up, $95.00.

Ginny: Caracul (lamb's wool) wig. Child, not baby. $400.00 up, $145.00. Outfits: $60.00 up.

Ginny: 1954. Painted lashes, sleep eyes, hard plastic walker. $265.00 up, $85.00. Outfits: $30.00 up.

Ginny: 1955–1957. Hard plastic molded lash walker. $200.00 up, $80.00. Outfits: $40.00 up.

Ginny: 1957–1962. Hard plastic, jointed knee, molded lash walker. $165.00 up, $65.00. Outfits: $35.00 up.

Ginny Hawaiian: Brown/black doll. 8" - $650.00 up, $350.00.

Ginny Queen: $950.00 up, $350.00.

Ginny Crib Crowd: Bent leg baby with caracul (lamb's wool) wig. $675.00 up, $325.00.

Crib Crowd Easter Bunny: $1,400.00 up, $600.00.

Ginny: 1977. All vinyl with round face. Internationals: $50.00 up. Other: $55.00 up.

Sasson Ginny: 1978–1979. Thin bodied doll with thin limbs. Sleep eyes: 8" - $35.00 up. Painted eyes: 8" - $30.00.

Ginny Exclusives: 1986–1991. **Shirley's Doll House:** Ginny Goes Country (1985) - $85.00. Ginny Goes To Country Fair (1986) - $85.00; Black Ginny in swimsuit (1987) - $90.00; Santa/Mrs. Claus (1988) - $75.00; Babysitter: $60.00; Sunday Best (1989). Black boy or girl - $55.00.

Meyers Collectables: All birthday specials designed by Anne Cottrell. Gigi's Favorite (1985) - $75.00. Fairy Godmother (1986) - $150.00. Cinderella and Prince Charming (1987) - $185.00. Clown (1988) - $90.00. Cowgirl (1989) - $85.00. Storytime

Super mint in box "Ginny Crib Crowd" with bent limb baby body, caracul wig, and wrist tag. This is a strung doll that also came with romper suit and coat in box. Box is marked "#46 Judy." This example - $1,000.00. *Courtesy Ellen Dodge.*

Wonderful "Ginny Cowgirl" is an early strung doll. It is rare to find hat with doll. All original and in mint condition. This example - $425.00. *Courtesy Ellen Dodge.*

8" "Sasson Ginny" dolls that are all vinyl and original. Made between 1973–1977. Doll on far left has painted eyes; the rest have sleep eyes. Each - $45.00 up. *Courtesy Kris Lundquist.*

Ginny (1992), limited - $95.00. Sweet Violet Ginny (1993), limited - $125.00. Remember Jackie (1994) - $100.00.

Little Friends: Alaska (1991) - $65.00.

Toy Village: Lansing, Michigan. Ashley Rose - $65.00.

Enchanted Doll House: Enchanted Ginny (1988) - $125.00.

Modern Doll Conventions: Rose Queen (1986) - $265.00. Ginny At Seashore (1987) - $95.00. Ginny's Claim (1988) - $85.00. Ginny in Nashville (1989) - $130.00. Ginny in Orlando (1990) - $85.00.

U.F.D.C.: Miss Unity (1987) - $150.00. Luncheon Ginny (1988) - $135.00.

Vogue Review Luncheon: 1989 - $165.00. 1990 - $95.00. 1991 - $80.00.

Vogue Doll Club: Member Special, 1990 - $100.00.

Ginny Accessories: Ginny gym: $250.00 up. Ginny pup: Steiff. $185.00 up. Luggage Set: $85.00 up. Shoes/shoe bag: $35.00 up. Furniture: Chair, bed, dresser, wardrobe, rocking chair. $50.00 each. Name pin: $45.00. Book: *Ginny's First Secret* - $100.00. Parasol: $10.00. School bag: $50.00.

Hug A Bye Baby: 1975. 16" - $15.00, $8.00. Black: $20.00, $10.00.

Jan: 1957. Rigid vinyl body and limbs with vinyl head and swivel waist. 12" - $145.00, $60.00.

Jeff: 1957. 10" - $95.00 up, $45.00.

Jill: 1957–1960: All hard plastic. 10" - $185.00, $60.00. In box with ballgown: $350.00 up. 1962–1965: All vinyl with rooted hair, sleep eyes, pale pink lips. $135.00.

Lil Imp: 11" - $60.00, $30.00.

Love Me Linda: 15" - $20.00, $8.00.

Miss Ginny: 1967–1970s. Young lady type. 11–12" - $30.00, $10.00; 15" - $40.00, $20.00.

Star Bright: 1966. 18" - $85.00, $25.00. Baby: 18" - $55.00, $20.00.

Welcome Home or Welcome Home Baby Turns Two: 20–24" - $65.00, $30.00.

Wee Imp: Has red wig. 8" - $365.00 up, $100.00.

This very special "Ginny" was made for the annual Ginny Luncheon held at Meyer's Collectables in June 1994. Wears sheath dress, coat, and pill box hat. She is very limited and collectible. The doll designer is Anne Cottrell and the owner of *Life* magazine is Pat & John Riggs. Doll - $100.00. *Courtesy Arline Shapiro of Meyer's.*

8" "Wee Imp" with hard plastic body and bend knees. Has vinyl head with green sleep eyes and red-orange rooted hair. Original and in unplayed with condition. This condition - $365.00. *Courtesy Kris Lundquist.*

"Jill" dressed in hard-to-find outfit #3160-1958. Hat made of pleated ribbon. Should have clutch purse and has replaced shoes. In this mint condition - $265.00 up. Played with condition - $125.00 up. *Courtesy Peggy Millhouse.*

20" "Betsy Walker," made by the Walkalon Mfg. Co., is a key wind walker with rollers on the bottom of her feet. Head turns from side to side as she walks. Made of all hard plastic with molded brown hair, sleep eyes, and non-removable boots. All original. This example - $450.00. Played with - $185.00 up.
Courtesy Janet & Bob Slivka.

WOODS, ROBIN

The dolls designed and made by the Robin Woods Company over the years have been some of the finest quality dolls available in their price range. These dolls stand out in a crowd because Robin Woods used imagination and creative talent that bears her signature. The dolls are beginning to show up on the secondary market and more will appear as time goes on. The last "pure" Robin Woods doll appeared on the market during 1991. In 1992, Robin Woods became the creative designer for the Alexander Doll Company and was designing dolls under the name of "Alice Darling."

The following are dolls that can be found on the secondary market.

1986: Associated Dollmakers: Adults sculpted by Avigail Brahms. "Dancers In Action," "Great Women In The Arts." Children sculpted by Yolanda Bello. "Little Miss Deb" series. All are rare. Sets limted to 1,200 pieces. **Sleep eyes:** Three different dolls made. 17" - original price in 1986 was $130.00; now - $425.00.

1987: Cathryn: 15" - $450.00 up. Christmas dolls: 14" - $350.00 each. Callie: Toddler doll. $450.00.

1988: Merry Carol: 14" - $350.00 up. Scarlett Christmas: 14" - $300.00 up.

17" "Elizabeth Barrett Browning" by Robin Woods in 1986. She was first in a series of three dolls with sleep eyes. The eyeholes of this doll are cut a little larger than the other two in the series. All original. $425.00. *Courtesy Pat Graff.*

1989: Hope: $300.00. Lorna Doone: $250.00. Heidi: $265.00. William Noel: $250.00. Elizabeth St. John: $250.00. Dickens Boy: $250.00 up. Mary of Secret Garden: 14" - $265.00 up.

1990: "Camelot Series." Kyliegh Christmas: $245.00; Melanie Phebe: $225.00; Tess Circus: $225.00; Bobbi: $250.00; Marjorie: $250.00; Meaghan: $300.00; Tess of the D'urbervilles: $300.00.

1991: "Shades of Day" collection. 5,000 pieces each. Dawn, Glory, Stormy, Joy, Sunny Veil, Star, Serenity. 14" - $300.00 each.

1991: Laurel, Lily, Bouquet, Rosemary, Rose, Violet: 14" - $200.00 each. Delores: $225.00. Victoria: $185.00. Miss Muffet: $160.00. Sleeping Beauty: Set - $385.00. Pumpkin Eaters: 8" - $100.00. Eliza Doolittle: $200.00. Mistress Mary: 8" -

$125.00. Bette Jack: $300.00. Alena: $275.00. Tennison: $300.00.

Robin Woods Limited Editions: Merri: 1991 Doll Convention, **Disney World.** Limited edition. 14" - $450.00 up. **Mindy:** Made for **Disney's "Robin Woods Day."** Limited to 300. 14" - $300.00 up. **Rainey:** 1991 **Robin Woods Club** doll. Limited to 300. 14" - $250.00 up.

J.C. Penney: Angelina: 1990 Christmas angel. Limited edition. 14" - $550.00. Noelle: Limited edition Christmas angel. 14" - $250.00 up. Julianna: 1991. Little girl holiday shopping. Limited edition. 14" - $300.00.

Robin Woods exclusives: Gina, The Earthquake Doll: For Ann's of Burlingame, CA. $650.00. Camelot Castle collection: 1989–1990. 14" - $250.00 each. 1991: 8" - $100.00–130.00 each. Christmas Tree Doll: Doll becomes the tree. For Disney. $675.00.

21" "Callie" is made of cloth and vinyl with sleep eyes/lashes and wig. Made in 1988. All original. $450.00 up. *Courtesy Pat Graff.*

These all original dolls use the "sweetheart face" produced by Robin Woods in 1989 for one year only. Both have pointed chins and painted eyes. On the left is "Pippa's Song" and on the right is "Marjorie Reagan Bedsloe" dressed as Argentine gaucho. Left - $400.00; right - $485.00. *Courtesy Katie & Melissa Levitt.*

14" "Scarlett Sweetheart" is all vinyl with painted features and rooted hair. Made by Robin Woods in 1989. $325.00. *Courtesy Pat Graff.*

Both of these are all vinyl "Little Women" dolls made by Robin Woods in 1986. "Meg" is on the left and "Jo" is on the right. They are all original. Each - $185.00. *Courtesy Pat Graff.*

14" all vinyl "Laurie" from the "Little Women" set was made in 1987. He has sleep eyes and is all original. $200.00. *Courtesy Pat Graff.*

INDEX

312

NUMBERS

LETTERS AND SYMBOLS

ABOUT THE AUTHOR

Patricia R. Smith was born and raised in Santa Barbara, California. She attended Nevada State University in Reno, Nevada, and St. Theresa in Kansas City, Missouri, receiving degrees in pedogogy and adult and child psychology. She claims her studies for a degree in "apologetics" is a work-in-progress.

Smith has authored over 50 books on collectible antique and modern dolls, with over one million in print. She has also published numerous articles and short stories, including a monthly doll column for *Antique Trader.* Adding to her writing credits is a novel, *Tuesday Island,* that was published in 1986. Her past employment includes her work as a psychiatric occupational therapist, a social worker/counselor for the welfare system, and an assistant advertising director for a large mail-order firm.

Smith is associated with many organizations, including Women's Ad Club, United Federation of Doll Clubs, Madame Alexander Doll Club, American Appraiser Association, International Kewpie Club, and the Annalee Society. She is also a voting member of the Doll of the Year Award. In 1989, she received the Service Award from the Madame Alexander Doll Club. Her name is listed in *Contemporary Authors,* a reference book for libraries, editors, publishers, schools, and the public.

Because of her doll expertise, Smith has appeared on several television and radio shows and has been a judge at competitive doll shows across the country. Along with conducting doll appraisal clinics, she has been the keynote speaker at conventions, organizations, and clubs.

Pat Smith resides in Independence, Missouri, with her husband, Dwight, and co-exists with two cats, Harley and Elvis.

Schroeder's
ANTIQUES
Price Guide

... is the #1 best-selling antiques & collectibles value guide on the market today, and here's why . . .

Schroeder's ANTIQUES Price Guide

OUR #1 BEST SELLER!

Identification & Values Of Over 50,000 Antiques & Collectibles

8½ x 11 • 608 Pgs. • PB • $14.95

• *More than 300 advisors, well-known dealers, and top-notch collectors work together with our editors to bring you accurate information regarding pricing and identification.*

• *More than 45,000 items in almost 500 categories are listed along with hundreds of sharp original photos that illustrate not only the rare and unusual, but the common, popular collectibles as well.*

• *Each large close-up shot shows important details clearly. Every subject is represented with histories and background information, a feature not found in any of our competitors' publications.*

• *Our editors keep abreast of newly developing trends, often adding several new categories a year as the need arises.*

If it merits the interest of today's collector, you'll find it in *Schroeder's*. And you can feel confident that the information we publish is up to date and accurate. Our advisors thoroughly check each category to spot inconsistencies, listings that may not be entirely reflective of market dealings, and lines too vague to be of merit. Only the best of the lot remains for publication.

Without doubt, you'll find
SCHROEDER'S ANTIQUES PRICE GUIDE
the only one to buy for
reliable information and values.

COLLECTOR BOOKS
A Division of Schroeder Publishing Co., Inc.